CW00550757

The Letters of —
JOHN BERRIDGE OF EVERTON

Here lay the earthly Remains of JOHN BERRIDGE
late Vicar of Everton and an itinerant Servant
of JESUS CHRIST who loved his Master and his Work
and after running on his Errands many Years was called
up to wait on him above Reader art thou born again
No Salvation without a new Birth.
 I was born in Sin Feb. 1716
 Remained ignorant of my fallen State till 1730
 Lived proudly on Faith & Works for Salvation till 1754
 Admitted to Everton Vicarage 1755.
 Fled to JESUS alone for Refuge 1756.
 Fell asleep in Christ Jany 22d 1793.

The epitaph on John Berridge's grave, Everton

— *The Letters of* —

JOHN BERRIDGE
OF EVERTON

A Singular Spirituality

Edited and annotated by
Nigel R. Pibworth

press

www.joshuapress.com

Published by
Joshua Press Inc., Kitchener, Ontario, Canada
Distributed by
Sola Scriptura Ministries International
www.sola-scriptura.ca

Cover design: Janice Van Eck
Book design: Clare Baalham

Library and Archives Canada Cataloguing in Publication

Berridge, John, 1716-1793
[Correspondence. Selections]
    The letters of John Berridge of Everton : a singular spirituality / edited and annotated by Nigel R. Pibworth.

Includes bibliographical references and indexes.
ISBN 978-1-894400-61-9 (bound).—ISBN 978-1-894400-62-6 (pbk.)

    1. Berridge, John, 1716-1793—Correspondence. 2. Evangelists—Great Britain—Correspondence. 3. Spirituality. I. Pibworth, Nigel R., editor II. Title.

BV3785.B44A3 2015   269'.2092   C2014-905467-X

Contents

Foreword

Michael A.G. Haykin

I still remember the first time that I saw the name of Nigel Pibworth. It was on the cover of his then recently published biography of John Berridge of Everton: *The Gospel Pedlar: The Story of John Berridge and the Eighteenth-Century Revival* (1987). At the time, I was increasingly being drawn to the study of the revivals of Berridge's day, though I knew very little about Berridge, most of my reading to that point having focused on George Whitefield, the Wesleys, Jonathan Edwards, and the Edwardsean Baptist Andrew Fuller. I had soon devoured the book, discovered a point of contact between Berridge and Fuller—a meeting of the two men during the winter of 1790–1791 that signaled a major change in the way that Baptists like Fuller and his friends viewed Anglican preachers of the Gospel such as Berridge (it was an extremely positive change)— and made initial contact with the book's author. I was impressed by the remarkable ministry that Berridge had had in Everton, but I was also impressed with Nigel's skill as an author and historian.

Little did I know that the reading of this biography of Berridge would lead to what is now a friendship of nearly twenty-five years. I count Nigel one of my dearest friends and highly esteem his scholarship, of which the present volume of Berridge's letters is a superb example. In some ways even more than works prepared for publication, letters reveal the soul of their writer, and these letters of the Bedfordshire Evangelical are no exception. Nigel has spent the best part of three decades searching through library catalogues to assemble this collection, which contains all of the known letters of Berridge and provides students of eighteenth-century Evangelicalism with another fabulous tool for understanding a truly remarkable period of church history. But these letters are of more than simply historical interest; they are bearers of a rich strain of Evangelical piety that has the power still to nourish the soul. Soli Deo Gloria.

Dundas, Ontario
August, 2014

Preface and acknowledgements

This work was initially completed several years ago but was providentially withdrawn as the publisher downsized. When I returned to the manuscript after a break of many years, thinking it only needed to be tidied up, I found there was a need for a thorough revision. More work had to be done on tracing references and, more significantly, I discovered further letters, such as those held in the Countess of Huntingdon Connexion Archives, the Henry Martyn Centre, Westminster College, Cambridge, and the John Wesley Family Papers, 1734–1864, in the Manuscript, Archives and Rare Book Library, Emory University, Atlanta, and the National Archives of Scotland, Edinburgh, sources of which I had been ignorant.

Most information has been gained through searching biographies, letters, journals, magazines, etc. of the period, but since I have returned to the project I have been most grateful for the *Blackwell Dictionary of Evangelical Biography, 1730–1860* (ed. Donald M. Lewis) and the online resources of the Clergy Database and the Surman Index, which have often provided the clues for more detailed searching. I have provided a guide for further study with the place of publication being London unless otherwise stated. A short title is normally used after the initial reference, and a list of full titles of the books referenced has been provided for additional ease. A full reference to a person has not always been placed in the first occurrence as the important connection may come later in the text. There has been some limited repetition where appropriate.

There are several letters of Berridge in manuscript. As some of these were published in Berridge's *Works* and religious journals, it enables us to understand the approach taken by nineteenth-century editors. Besides the normal practice of altering punctuation and providing paragraphs sometimes letters were shortened or just an extract was given. At times controversial statements or personal details were omitted, although the *Congregational Magazine* was more free with its red pen in this respect than others. I have dealt with particular examples of previous editing in the notes to the letters themselves. Generally, the letters have been minimally edited by me, unless there was a particular reason to do so: abbreviations have been spelled out; spelling, punctuation, and capitalization have only occasionally been modernized, or made consistent with Berridge's preferences where we can be pretty sure what they would have been. The letters are cross-referenced by date and a list of sources is provided at the back of the book.

I have not attempted to explain in any detail Berridge's figurative language, which would have meant that the notes would have taken on the character of exposition and expanded far beyond the size of the original letters. The problem of understanding Berridge's highly original figures and imagery can only be solved by grasping the context of the letters themselves. I remain convinced that most of Berridge's language is understandable, although, of course, those sharing the same Christian perspective as Berridge should grasp his thought more fully. Where Berridge's language remains obscure, it is at times due to the lack of background information on the matter under discussion and at other times to Berridge's own singularity.

I am grateful for the use of Cambridge University Library; the John Rylands University Library, Manchester; the Gospel Standard Baptist Library, Hove, and the British Library. The staff at the Evangelical Library, London, have always provided an excellent service and have been most helpful. My local library at Biggleswade has nearly always met my requests for library loans. Mrs. Staplehurst, the archivist for the Countess of Huntingdon Connexion Archives, has been most helpful. Brian W. Smith supplied details of Berridge's family through his local history study on Kingston-on-Soar.

I wish to thank the many readers over the years who have helped prepare the manuscript by reading and correcting. In the first production of the manuscript in the 1990s these include my father, before he died; daughter Clare; David Kingdon, when he was director of the Evangelical Press of Wales; David Gay, and Terry and Sue Clarke. I would also like to thank David T. Wood, Jonathan Rodell, and Raymond Brown for their willingness to review the final manuscript. Of course all mistakes are mine. I am grateful to Michael Haykin for writing a foreword. My thanks to my daughter Clare, who has kindly acted as the final editor and set the work for publication.

I would like to thank Lady Balgonie, for letters held in the National Archives of Scotland, Edinburgh; the Bodleian Library,

Oxford; the Bridwell Library Special Collections, Perkins School of Theology, Southern Methodist University, Dallas, Texas; the Centre for Buckinghamshire Studies, Aylesbury; the Countess of Huntingdon Connexion Archives, Cottenham; the Cowper Museum, Olney; the Henry Martyn Centre, Westminster College, Cambridge; the Frank Baker Collection of Wesleyana and British Methodism in the David M. Rubenstein Rare Book and Manuscript Library, Duke University; the Historical Society of Pennsylvania, Philadelphia; the Methodist Archives and Research Centre, John Rylands University Library, Manchester; Lambeth Palace Library, London; the John Wesley Family Papers, Manuscript, Archives and Rare Book Library, Emory University, Atlanta, Georgia; the Church Missionary Society Archives, Special Collections, University of Birmingham; the Wesley Historical Society Library, Oxford, and the Dr. Williams's Trust, London, for the use of Berridge manuscript letters in this work.

Most of all I thank my wife, Janice, without whom the many years of work on this project would not have been possible. May God bless these letters and through them point people to his own Son.

Abbreviations

AM	*Arminian Magazine*
Beds Mag	*Bedfordshire Magazine*
BHRS	Bedfordshire Historical Record Society
BL	Bodleian Library, Oxford
BLSC	Bridwell Library Special Collections, Perkins School of Theology, Southern Methodist University, Dallas, Texas
BM	*Baptist Magazine*
BoT	*Banner of Truth* (magazine)
BR	*Boston Recorder*
CBS	Centre for Buckinghamshire Studies, Aylesbury
CCA	Cheshunt College Archive, Westminster College, Cambridge
CCM	*Christian Cottagers' Magazine*
CHCA	Countess of Huntingdon Connexion Archives, Cottenham, Cambridge
CM	*Congregational Magazine*
CMR	*Christian Monthly Record*
CMus	Cowper Museum, Olney
CO	*Christian Observer*
CS	*Christian Secretary*
CUL	Cambridge University Library
CW	*Christian Watchman*
EM	*Evangelical Magazine*
EMMC	*Evangelical Magazine and Missionary Chronicle*
EpRec	*Episcopal Recorder*

ER	*Evangelical Register, or Magazine for the Connexion of the Late Countess of Huntingdon*
ex.	extract
FBC	Frank Baker Collection of Wesleyana and British Methodism, David M. Rubenstein Rare Book and Manuscript Library, Duke University, Durham, North Carolina
FCEM	*Free Church of England Magazine and Harbinger of the Countess of Huntingdon Connexion*
GB	*Gospel Banner*
Gent Mag	*Gentleman's Magazine*
GH	*Gospel Herald*
GM	*Gospel Magazine*
GS	*Gospel Standard*
GTOP	*Gospel Truths, or Old Paths*
HEC	Howard Edwards Collection, Historical Society of Pennsylvania, Philadelphia
HMC	Henry Martyn Centre, Westminster College, Cambridge
HRS	Hertfordshire Record Society
In	*Investigator*
JWFP MARBL	The John Wesley Family Papers, Manuscript, Archives, and Rare Book Library, Emory University, Atlanta, Georgia
LPL	Lambeth Palace Library, London
MARC	Methodist Archives and Research Centre, University of Manchester
MissM	*Missionary Magazine*
MNCM	*Methodist New Connexion Magazine*
NYMM	*New York Missionary Magazine and Repository of Religious Intelligence*
PLFELM	Papers of the Leslie family, Earls of Leven and Melville, National Archives of Scotland, Edinburgh
UCL	University College London
S	*Sower*
SGC	Simon Gratz Autograph Collection, the Historical Society of Pennsylvania, Philadelphia
SPCK	Society for Promoting Christian Knowledge

ST	*Sword and Trowel*
TM	*Theological Magazine, or Synopsis of Modern Religious Sentiment*
VM	Venn Manuscripts, Church Missionary Society Archives, Cadbury Research Library, University of Birmingham
WB (1838)	*The Works of the Rev. John Berridge, AM, late Fellow of Clare Hall, Cambridge, vicar of Everton, Bedfordshire, and Chaplain to the Right Honourable Earl of Buchan, with an enlarged memoir of his life: numerous letters, anecdotes, outlines of sermons, and observations on passages of Scripture; and his original Sion's songs*, ed. Rev. Richard Whittingham (1838)
WB (1864)	*The Works of the Rev. John Berridge, AM, late Fellow of Clare Hall, Cambridge, Vicar of Everton, Bedfordshire, and Chaplain to the Earl of Buchan, with an memoir of his life, by the Rev. Richard Whittingham, late vicar of Potton, Bedfordshire, and previously curate to the author at Everton*, 2nd ed. with additions (Ebenezer Palmer, 1864)
WHS	*Proceedings of the Wesley Historical Society*
WHSLMB	Wesley Historical Society Library Manuscript Book
WW	John Wesley, *The Works of John Wesley, Vol. 21, Journal and Diaries IV (1755–1765)*, ed. W. Reginald Ward and Richard P. Heitzenrater (Nashville: Abingdon Press, 1992, 1993)
ZC	*Zion's Casket or the Penny Spiritual Treasury*
ZT	*Zion's Trumpet or the Penny Spiritual Magazine*

Introduction

Approaching Berridge

John Berridge has been a neglected figure in both academic[1] and Christian circles.[2] No critical study of his life has been attempted,[3] as has been with many of the other leaders of the eighteenth-century revival,

---

[1] Charles Smyth's study *Simeon and Church Order: A Study of the Origins of the Evangelical Revival in Cambridge in the Eighteenth Century* (Cambridge: Cambridge University Press, 1940) is still the best academic study of Berridge, although Smyth examines Berridge as a foil to Simeon rather than as a figure in his own right. Recently David T. Wood has produced "The Eccentric Vicar of Everton: John Berridge, the Cambridgeshire Revival, and the Life of Pastoral Ministry," D.Min. thesis, Gordon-Cowell Theological Seminary (2012), with the aim of reintroducing Berridge to contemporary readership as well as of using Berridge to reflect on key pastoral issues today. Jonathan Rodell covers Berridge in his study of the variety of religious communities with Methodistic character-istics in the eighteenth and nineteenth centuries: "The Appeal of Methodism in Bedfordshire, 1736–1851," Ph.D. thesis, Cambridge University (2010). See also Rodell, *The Rise of Methodism: A Study of Bedfordshire, 1736–1851* (BHRS, 2014).

[2] One exception is the small group of Strict and Particular Baptists known as Gospel Standard Strict Baptists. They have an interest in Berridge due to the inclusion of Berridge's experiential hymns in their hymn book. William Gadsby, speaking about a new supplement to his hymn book, remarked that the hymns "have been principally selected from Hart and Berridge, these two men, I believe the sweetest and greatest experimental writers that have left any hymns on record" (*A Selection of Hymns for Public Worship* [Manchester: 1838; repr., Gospel Standard Societies, 1977], vi). Daniel Webber, "John Berridge: An Eighteenth Century Boanerges," *The Trials of Puritanism: Papers Read at the 1993 Westminster Conference* (Westminster Conference, 1993), 136–156, exam-ined Berridge primarily as a preacher.

[3] One of my reasons for writing *The Gospel Pedlar: The Story of John Berridge and the Eighteenth-Century Revival* (Welwyn: Evangelical Press, 1987) was the hope that it would stimulate scholars to provide a more serious study.

and Christians on the whole are ignorant of the great blessing Berridge experienced as a preacher of the gospel. This neglect of Berridge may stem from Berridge's own focus on preaching rather than writing, the fact that he did not leave followers to promote his name,[4] his lack of churchmanship (felt particularly by the following generation of Evangelicals) both in terms of irregularity—i.e., his preaching in other parishes—and his bleak view of the national Church, discomfort and embarrassment over the strange accompaniments of the initial revival at Everton, and his own highly colourful and unusual personality that formed the basis of a singular spirituality.

His curate and biographer, Richard Whittingham (1758–1845),[5] allowed some forty-five years to pass after Berridge's death before he published *The Works of the Rev. John Berridge, AM, late Fellow of Clare Hall, Cambridge, vicar of Everton, Bedfordshire, and chaplain to the Right Honourable Earl of Buchan with an enlarged memoir of his life: numerous letters, anecdotes, outlines of sermons, and observations on passages of Scripture; and his original Sion's Songs* (Simpkin, Marshall, and Co., 1838).[6] Whittingham apologizes for the delay, saying: "Desirous of availing myself of every letter he wrote, I have made application to everyone, who, I had any reason to conclude, could subserve my wishes. This step has occasioned the loss of much time; but it has been the means of obtaining what could not otherwise have been realized."[7] Berridge did not keep a journal nor did he hold on to his letters. His only literary productions were *Justification by Faith Alone: being the substance of a letter from the Rev. Mr. Berridge in Cambridge to a clergyman in Nottinghamshire, giving an account of a great work of God wrought in his own heart* (1760); *A Collection of Divine Songs, designed chiefly for the religious societies of Churchmen, in the neighbourhood of Everton, Bedfordshire* (1760), which he later withdrew; a small book on the Calvinistic controversy of his day called *The Christian World Unmasked: pray come and peep* (Edward and

---

4   Many of his "shops"—his preaching stations—developed into independent churches.

5   See October 3, 1783.

6   A recent reprint in two volumes has been published by Gospel Press, Montana. Samuel Whittingham, DD (1783–1874), Richard Whittingham's son, fellow of Corpus Christi College, Oxford (*WB* [1864]) and rector of Childrey, Berkshire, gave his permission for a new and expanded edition of *WB* in 1864, although he does not seem to have contributed any new letters.

7   *WB* (1864), vi. He in fact missed many letters, even some published in religious magazines.

Charles Dilly, 1773); and two collections of his own hymns called *Sion's Songs, or Hymns: composed for the use of them that love and follow the Lord Jesus Christ in sincerity* (Vallance and Conder, 1785) and *Cheerful Piety: or religion without gloom: exemplified in selected letters on the most important truths of Christianity* (J. S. Jordan, J. Matthews, H. Trapp, and G. Terry, 1792).[8] After his death in January 1793 there was published *The Last Farewell Sermon, preached at the Tabernacle, near Moorfields, April 1, 1792. By the Rev. John Berridge, MA, late vicar of Everton, Bedfordshire* (J. Chalmers, 1793), which Whittingham includes in his works. In 1882, William Wileman (1848–1944) published *Gospel Gems: a collection of notes from the margins of the Bible of John Berridge, Vicar of Everton, 1755–1793*, and in 1891 Charles P. Phinn edited *Bogatsky's Golden Treasury: a reprint of Mr. John Thornton's edition of 1775 together with critical notes hitherto unpublished, by John Berridge, vicar of Everton, and important corrections by the same hand.*

Berridge may have produced far more than his literary remains suggest. Ronald Knox (1888–1957) notes: "Is not this a man who, if his life had been devoted to amusing the public instead of saving souls, might have taken a place side by side with Sterne?"[9] The simple fact is that much of Berridge's life as a Christian, after his conversion in his early forties, was devoted to preaching the gospel; and itinerate preaching left little leisure or emotional reserves for writing, even if he had so wished. His memorials were people who had been helped by his preaching, rather than books, for as J.C. Ryle (1816–1900) reminds us: "Few preachers, perhaps, at this period were more honoured by God and more useful to souls than the eccentric John Berridge."[10]

A further reason for the neglect of Berridge was Victorian embarrassment at his openness, frankness, and unconventionality. Whittingham opens his account of Berridge by challenging his reader to evaluate the life from a spiritual viewpoint and not just a natural one:

> Whatever opinion may be entertained of his proceedings, it appears that they were attended, with great success, and blessed to thousands. Will those who condemn him for acting as he did, find in the

---

8   It seems unlikely that Berridge gave permission for this publication.

9   *Enthusiasm: A Chapter in the History of Religion* (Oxford: Clarendon Press, 1950), 489. Laurence Sterne (1713–1768) was an Anglican clergyman and novelist — and a contemporary of Berridge. Sterne's most famous work was *The Life and Opinions of Tristram Shandy, Gentleman.*

10   *The Christian Leaders of the Last Century* (T. Nelson, 1876), 217.

great day, when every work will be fully developed, that they were equally useful in bringing sinners to the knowledge of the truth? Will not in *that day* his crown of rejoicing appear far more brilliant than the crowns of numerous ministers of religion? Whatever therefore appeared disorderly in the manner of performing his ministry on earth, the Judge will forgive, and assign him a place in the firmament of heaven amongst the stars of the first magnitude.[11]

A.C.H. Seymour (1789–1870), biographer of Lady Huntingdon who used many of Berridge's letters, felt the need to warn others not to emulate Berridge in the serious matter of religion:

The Christian cannot take offence at the exhibition of Christian weakness. If any such weak brother be offended by the quaint strength of Mr. Berridge's epistolary language, let him remember how the apostles speak of their own weakness and that of each other, and let self-examination lead to better thoughts and milder judgments. The exuberant humour of Berridge, and his very figurative and even whimsical mode of illustration, should act as a warning on all who feel any tendency to singularity in this way. Let them remember, whether in writing or in speaking, this sacred injunction—in doctrine show incorruptness, *gravity*, and sincerity.[12]

Ryle also felt the necessity to excuse Berridge by reminding his readers that a rural standard of taste is not that of Oxford and Cambridge and that any coarseness and vulgarity must be understood in terms of Berridge's successful attempt to reach the more uncultured. However, Ryle, asserts:

I do not defend Berridge's escapades and transgressions of good taste. I do not recommend him as a model to young preachers. I only say that those who run him down and depreciate him because of his quaintness would do well to remember that he did what many do not—he awakened and converted souls. Thousands of correct, and smooth, and prim, and proper clergyman are creeping through this world, who never broke a canon of taste in

---

[11] *WB* (1838), iv.
[12] *The Life and Times of Selina, Countess of Huntingdon*, 2 vols. (William Painter, 1839–1840), 1:370.

the pulpit, never told an anecdote, never used a vulgar illustration, and never raised a smile. They have their reward.[13]

Those who did not share Berridge's convictions or aims were offended with Berridge. For example, Robert F. Housman, whose father, Robert Housman, had married the daughter of a convert of Berridge's, sees in Berridge "the uncouth extravagances of a fermentitious faith."[14]

An overemphasis on the sensational and physical paroxysms of the initial revival, particularly in 1759, which were reported in John Wesley's *Journal*, has produced a distorted picture of Berridge taken as a whole.[15] In this light, Berridge is seen as a modern American tele-evangelist, not the subject of serious enquiry. Visions, convulsions, people falling to the floor and breaking benches, howling, weeping and crying, swooning, trances, roarings, hideous laughter, being filled with unspeakable joy, and dropping down unconscious as they were walking away from the meeting, as well as men being unable to work later through extreme physical weakness, are some of the reported events. Berridge himself initially had a positive view of such things but he quickly came to re-evaluate them.[16] Wesley writes on Sunday, January 3, 1762:

I read prayers and preached, morning and evening, to a numerous and lively congregation. I found the people in general were more settled than when I was here before, but they were in danger of running from east to west. Instead of thinking, as many then did, that none can possibly have true faith but those that have trances or visions, they were now ready to think that whoever had anything of this kind had no faith.[17]

Charles Smyth points out that it was these extraordinary physical manifestations of the early revival which were "so scandalous alike to the sober piety of Southey in 1820 and to the fastidious rationalism of

---

13 *Christian Leaders*, 239.
14 Robert F. Housman, *The Life and Remains of the Rev. Robert Housman* (Simpkin, Marshall and Co., 1841), xxv.
15 See Pibworth, *Gospel Pedlar*, chapters 7 and 8, for a description and evaluation of these "signs."
16 See July 16, 1759.
17 *The Works of John Wesley, Vol. 21, Journal and Diaries IV (1755–1765)*, ed. W. Reginald Ward and Richard P. Heitzenrater (Nashville: Abingdon Press, 1992), 347.

Lecky in 1878."[18] It was the evaluations of such men that influenced the historians who followed. For example, Leslie Stephen (1832–1904) asserts: "When a man like Berridge could throw a congregation into fits, and bring on all the phenomena of epidemic excitement, he took it for a plain proof that God was with him."[19] C.E. Vulliamy (1886–1971) suggests that a stranger going to Everton "and knowing nothing about the 'spiritual influenza,' would have thought he had come to a place where every other man was a lunatic or a drunkard."[20] Charles Abbey (1833–1919) and John Overton (1835–1903),[21] as well as G.M. Trevelyan (1838–1928),[22] give the impression that paroxysms were a constant feature of Berridge's preaching rather than being confined to the initial period and occurring with a variety of preachers. Eric Walker's reconstruction of Berridge's preaching in highly sensationalistic tones owes more to literary imagination than historical research.[23] The initial revival at Everton prompted the controversial psychiatrist William Sargant (1907–1988) to declare that Berridge had inadvertently discovered the "basic mechanics of the sudden conversion process."[24] However we interpret the events associated with the Everton revival of 1758–1761, the sensational reporting and the lack of serious evaluation, together with false generalizations applied to Berridge's life, have caused a serious stumbling block to investigating Berridge.

There is little doubt that Berridge was an uncomfortable figure for the following generation of Evangelicals in the national Church. The *Evangelical Magazine* in 1839, reviewing Seymour's work on Lady

---

[18] *Simeon and Church Order*, 166. Robert Southey (1774–1843), quoting large sections from Wesley's *Journal*, describes Berridge as "the insane vicar" and a "buffoon as well as fanatic" (*The Life of Wesley, and the Rise and Progress of Methodism*, 2nd ed., 2 vols. [Longman, 1820], 2:321, 374). He describes the Everton revival as a case of "spiritual influenza" (331) and regrets "that there should be no authority capable of restraining extravagances and indecencies like these" (326). William Lecky (1838–1903) says that Berridge was "eccentric almost to insanity" (*A History of England in the Eighteenth Century*, 6 vols. [New York: Appleton, 1888], 2:582).

[19] *History of English Thought in the Eighteenth Century*, 2 vols. (Smith, Elder, and Co., 1876; repr., New York: Peter Smith, 1949), 2:429.

[20] *John Wesley* (Geoffrey Bles, 1933), 278.

[21] *The English Church in the Eighteenth Century*, 2 vols. (Longmans, Green, and Co., 1878), 2:178

[22] *Illustrated English Social History*, 4 vols. (Longmans, 1951), 3:64.

[23] "John Berridge of Everton," *Bedfordshire Magazine*, 4:30 (1954), 247.

[24] *Battle for the Mind: A Physiology of Conversion and Brain-Washing* (Heinemann, 1957), 83.

Huntingdon, comments: "We know that the doctrine of Churchmen now is, 'we do not want the irregularities of the Methodists now.'"[25] In the same year the reviewer of Berridge's *Works* in the *Christian Observer* shows his caution, although he recognizes and appreciates the character and success of Berridge. He writes:

> Be it recollected also, that some, who at first were hurried into irregularities, were led, by more mature reflection and experience, to discern the importance of conformity and order, and their own duty as clergymen of the Church of England; and have left upon record, both in their writings and by their example, a far stronger protest against irregularity, than if they had never fallen into it.... To take the extreme case of Berridge himself, it is no more necessary to applaud or imitate his breaches of church discipline, than his eccentricity of conduct, or his frequently coarse humour.[26]

Abner Brown (1800–1872) records Charles Simeon's (1759–1836) comments on Berridge's irregularity:

> He was, perhaps, right in preaching from place to place as he did. But I, who knew him well, was hardly satisfied that he was doing right. He was a clever man: once a moderator in the University; a wag, a man quite *sui generis*. He lived when few Ministers cared about the gospel, and when disorder was almost needful. I don't think he would do now as he did then; for there are so many means of hearing the gospel, and a much greater spread of it; a much greater call for order, and much less need of disorder. To do now as he did then would do much harm.[27]

Another editor, when reviewing Berridge's *Works* published in 1838, takes the same approach, affirming that "few persons in the present day are prepared entirely to justify, and still less to imitate, Mr. Berridge in these labours," but points to the state of religion at the time as an extenuating circumstance as well as the great success of his activities: "Under such extraordinary circumstances, extraordinary efforts were

---

25 *EM* (1839), 277.

26 "Review of the Rev. John Berridge's Works," *CO* (1839), 122–123.

27 *Recollections of the Conversation Parties of the Rev. Charles Simeon, MA: Senior Fellow of King's College, and Perpetual Curate of Trinity Church, Cambridge* (Hamilton, Adams, and Co., 1863), 200.

necessary, and even those who are not prepared to defend, in all respects, the measures which were adopted, must yet feel that they have eventually been productive of incalculable benefit to our land."[28]

When an old friend reminded Simeon that Simeon himself had preached in a barn, his reaction, as recorded by his biographer, was as follows: "After a most significant look, instantly turning his face aside, and then with both hands uplifted to hide it, he exclaimed—*O spare me! spare me! I was a young man then*."[29] Berridge's irregularity was excused because of the special conditions of Berridge's time and the weakness of the Evangelical cause, but Evangelicals had become a significant and growing party in the national Church and must act accordingly.[30] Charles Simeon with his attempt to infiltrate the national Church for the gospel by being an exemplary churchman and thus rejecting completely any ideas of "irregularity" and being "evangelically scandalous,"[31] had won the day. The battle that Henry Venn (1725–1797) had fought with Berridge over Simeon's irregularity at Bluntisham as a young man had vital implications for the future of Evangelicalism in the national Church.[32] Michael Webster, commenting on Smyth, says that he "traces the fascinating battle between Henry Venn and John Berridge showing how Venn was determined to dissuade Simeon from continuing the ecclesiastical irregularities practised by Berridge and how, through a successful outcome of this policy, the Evangelicals were in all probability

---

[28] *The Christian Guardian and Church of England Magazine* (March 1839), 87, 89.

[29] William Carus, *Memoirs of the Life of the Rev. Charles Simeon, MA* (Hatchard, 1848), 200.

[30] John Walsh and Stephen Taylor remind us of the great change in the Evangelical cause that occurred during Berridge's life: "The numbers of such 'Gospel clergy' were at first tiny, but grew rapidly after the 1780s. The first-generation London Evangelical William Romaine, who annually set aside a day on which to pray for each of them by name, began his list with only twenty names; by the time of his death in 1795 he prayed for 500. Estimates of Evangelical clerical numbers for the early nineteenth century vary considerably, but by 1830 they were clearly a formidable phalanx" ("Introduction: The Church and Anglicanism in the 'Long' Eighteenth Century" in *The Church of England c.1689–c.1833: From Toleration to Tractarianism*, ed. John Walsh, Colin Haydon and Stephen Taylor [Cambridge: Cambridge University Press, 1993], 44).

[31] Rowland Hill's adoption of itinerancy was a great encouragement to Berridge, who writes: "The more scandalous you grow I mean evangelically scandalous—the more I must love you" (June 17, 1776).

[32] See July 2, 1785.

prevented from leaving the Church of England for dissent or to form a sect of their own."[33] The history of Evangelicalism in the Church of England might have been different if Simeon had followed Berridge and not Venn. The tension over this debate was still being felt in the 1830s and 1840s. In a memoir of his father published in 1835, John Venn stated that Henry Venn did not advocate irregularity in others and regretted his own involvement.[34] Seymour, in his 1839 work on Lady Huntingdon, challenged this view, saying that Venn continued his irregular practice of preaching in barns and other unconsecrated places until inability stopped him in 1790.[35] Seymour suggested that John Venn wished to draw a veil over the issue of irregularity. Henry Venn, John Venn's son, who edited and published his grandfather's letters, which included the John Venn memoir, took issue with Seymour's account and published a letter in the *Christian Observer* (May 1840), entitled "The Rev. H. Venn on Certain Strictures on the Life of his Grandfather," in which he responded to Seymour's charges of his giving a false account of Henry Venn's "mature and final opinion on the subject of ecclesiastical irregularities" and that he had as editor of the letters "endeavoured unfairly to separate my grandfather's name from the reproach of Methodism."[36]

To understand Berridge's own churchmanship,[37] or lack of it, one must see his pragmatism in taking advantage of the freedom afforded him by his position as a clergyman for spreading truth. He says:

> …though I do think the best Christianity was found before estab-
> lishments began; and that usually there are more true ministers out
> of an establishment than in it; and that establishments are com-
> monly of an intolerant spirit, and draw in shoals of hirelings by
> their loaves and fishes; yet I am very thankful for an establishment
> which afford me a preaching-house and an eating-house, without
> clapping a padlock on my lips, or a fetter on my foot. However, I
> am not indebted to the mercy of church canons or church gover-
> nors for itinerant liberty, but to the secret overruling providence

---

[33] "Simeon's Doctrine of the Church." In *Charles Simeon (1759–1836)*, ed. Arthur Pollard and Michael Hennell (SPCK, 1959), 125. See Smyth, *Simeon and Church Order*, 270–281.

[34] Henry Venn, *The Life and a Selection from the Letters of the Late Rev. Henry Venn, MA … with a memoir by John Venn* (Hatchard, 1836, 1993), 177.

[35] Seymour, *Life of Huntingdon*, 1:292.

[36] *CO* (1840), 261.

[37] See chapter 23, "Berridge: The Churchman" in Pibworth, *Gospel Pedlar*.

of Jesus, which rescued me at various times from the claws of a church commissary, an archdeacon, and a bishop....[38]

Everything was to be understood in the light of the need to preach the gospel. His lack of conscience in breaking the rules of the national Church;[39] his lack of confidence in the national Church, believing that if God did not intervene she would suffer the same fate as the African and Asiatic churches;[40] his pessimistic views about the problem of Evangelical succession;[41] his founding congregations that naturally developed into Nonconformist bodies; his ambiguous views about infant baptism and the value of the Prayer Book;[42] his opinion that most real Christians were forced to leave their local parish church in order to survive spiritually; his clear distinction between converted and unconverted clergy; his close relationship with Nonconformity; and the opposition and difficulty he experienced from most of his fellow clergy were factors unlikely to endear him to the next generation of Evangelicals in the national Church. There is little doubt that Berridge has suffered neglect because of his churchmanship, or should we say lack of it.

Probably the most fundamental reason for Berridge's neglect is the individuality of the man himself. It is not merely a matter of the peculiar and individual features of his own personality, rather the way in which his natural gifts and predilections were blended with his Christian faith and witness. As D. Bruce Hindmarsh says in non-pejorative language: "John Berridge was one of the most colourful clergyman of the Evangelical Revival."[43] Gaius Davies, a Christian psychiatrist, says that he has "found it helpful to think of saving grace as light, and the human personality as a prism through which it shines and is diffracted into all the colours of the spectrum."[44] Certainly Berridge's prism was

---

[38] Letter to John Thornton, November 17, 1784.

[39] "Must salvation give place to a fanciful decency, and sinners go flocking to hell through our dread of irregularity?" (Letter to John Thornton, August 10, 1774).

[40] *The Christian World Unmasked*, 3rd ed., revised and corrected (Edward and Charles Dilly, 1774), 209.

[41] See April 26, 1777.

[42] See *Christian World*, 222–223, and his letter to John Thornton, October 27, 1787.

[43] *The Evangelical Conversion Narrative: Spiritual Autobiography in Early Modern England* (Oxford: Oxford University Press, 2005), 89–90.

[44] *Genius and Grace* (London: Hodder and Stoughton, 1992), 14. I do hope that Dr. Davies will include a chapter on Berridge in his next exploration of the

most unusual. In terms of the eighteenth-century revivals, if George Whitefield (1714–1770) was the unrivalled revival preacher; John Wesley the theological synthesiser and organizer; William Cowper (1731–1800) the poet; John Thornton (1720–1790) the philanthropist; Jonathan Edwards (1703–1758) the philosopher and thinker; Thomas Scott (1747–1821) the theologian; John Newton (1725–1807) the middleman; William Grimshaw (1707–1763) the knight-errant riding forth to battle; Charles Wesley (1707–1788) the hymn writer; Lady Huntingdon (1707–1791) the patron; John Fletcher (1729–1785) the saint; Berridge was the *personality*. After his conversion his unusual personality expressed itself in an unconventional spirituality as seen in the contrast to the normal standards of his day but more particularly in contrast to the generation that followed him.

Berridge has been described as quaint, singular, peculiar, odd, idiosyncratic, brash, passionate, original, extraordinary and facetious. However, most historians have followed Berridge's curate and biographer and described him as eccentric, referring not to peculiar personal habits, but to the fact that Berridge said and did his own thing in his own way.[45] He was prepared to move out of the normal pattern of behaviour associated with a vicar holding a living. Whittingham confesses that some "may not approve of his eccentricity: for he did not move in a regular orbit; but like a planet; steered his course with great irregularity."[46] Some have put more emphasis on his unusual language. John Overton speaks of him being "eccentric, in his words at least if not in his deeds,"[47] and Thomas Wright (1859–1836) sees Berridge as the "'Rabelais of evangelicalism' whose language was at times as homely as to be almost coarse."[48] Marcus Loane (1911–2009) effectively sum-

---

interplay between a believer's personality and faith, as seen through medical eyes.

[45] We must recognize the danger of historians strengthening and intensifying characteristics over time, rather than re-evaluating them with original research. Frederick E. Maser reminds us that once an image has been put forward "the picture will often be deepened and fixed, rather than obliterated by future historians ("The Task of the Methodist Historian Today," *A.M.E. Zion Quarterly Review, Methodist History and New Bulletin* [July 1974], 6).

[46] *WB* (1838), iii.

[47] John H. Overton and Frederic Relton, *History of the English Church, 1714–1800* (Macmillan, 1906), 149.

[48] *Augustus M. Toplady and Contemporary Hymn-Writers* (Farncombe, 1911), 257.

marizes: "he was naturally mercurial in mind and thought, a man *sui generis*, one who had to stand in a class by himself, one who said and did things which no one else could do or say."[49] Berridge's personality, with its unusual combinations of humour and seriousness, bluntness and compassion, scholarship and simplicity, honesty and pragmatism, thought and feeling, has proved an insurmountable barrier to many and a distraction to others. P.E. Sangster (1927–2010) recognizes the difficulties when describing Berridge as

> One of the greatest of the Evangelicals, the very eccentricity of the man has helped to obscure his greatness. To his contemporaries he was a joke, and has remained so to succeeding generations. Author of one of the most unconsciously funny pieces of writing in our language, one of the most brilliant letter-writers of his time, as odd out of the pulpit as in it, Berridge was doomed to be remembered for the irrelevancies of his nature: his essential greatness is forgotten....[50]

We must be careful not to evaluate Berridge through the lens of early Victorian respectability. Things that shocked a reviewer of Berridge's *Works* in 1839 do not shock us today. The reviewer comments: "we have considerable dislike to the levity of humorous religious anecdotes and smart sayings." He gives an example of Berridge mocking a preacher who thought that he would be carried up to heaven in a chariot of fire and asking him: "When you are carried up to heaven in a chariot of fire I request that you will grant me the honour of being your postilion." The reviewer does not like the story about Berridge putting down a lady who arrived at Everton from London explaining that God had revealed to her that she was to marry Berridge or the fact that Berridge's father, seeing that nothing could make Berridge a farmer, sent him to college in order to make him "a light to lighten the Gentiles." Berridge's quoting the contemporary stage while preaching in London adds to the weight of evidence against Berridge and demonstrates his lack of respect for sacred subjects like heaven, marriage and the office of minister. He concludes, "Such speeches are unhallowed and inexcusable."[51] Another Victorian editor, in response to a letter where Berridge seeks to encourage his

---

[49] *Cambridge and the Evangelical Succession* (Lutterworth, 1952), 102.
[50] "The Life of the Rev. Rowland Hill (1744–1833) and His Position in the Evangelical Revival," D.Phil. thesis, Oxford University (1964), 23–24.
[51] *CO* (1839), 312–313. See also June 7, 1776.

young friend Rowland Hill in the "old trade of devil-hunting, which is neither profitable nor an honourable business, as the world goes, yet a more suitable employment for Gospel ministers than fox hunting or card-hunting," expresses his caution in publishing the letter. "We insert the above with some scruple. It is no doubt eminently characteristic, and contains sound truth; but we feel there is a lightness about it inconsistent with the solemnity of the subject, and that it is rather amusing than edifying."[52] John Henry Newman's (1801–1890) critique follows a similar path: "This gentleman…amid many good points of character, was totally destitute of reverence…."[53]

Berridge's own contemporaries, even though they lived to some extent in an age of order, reason and decorum, did not focus their critique on Berridge's personality. It was his message, his preaching, his itinerating throughout the area irrespective of the wishes of the local squires and parsons that drew opposition. He, a senior Fellow of Clare College, had become an "enthusiast" and had lost his reason. This was the joke. As Berridge confessed: "all that wear the gospel cloak of faith, full and deep, are thought enthusiasts or impostors; men who have lost their wits, or lost their honesty, and only fit for Bedlam or for Newgate."[54] It was not his personality that caused him to lose his friends and his reputation; it was his personality expressing his new faith. Two years after his conversion Berridge was crystal clear about this matter:

I want nothing in this World and through God's Grace I covet nothing. The concern I have for lost sinners makes me willing to undergo painful Labours for their sake, Labours which make me accounted vile, and suffer the loss of what was once most dear unto me, my reputation. If any think otherwise, and imagine that my Field-Preaching is occasioned by a desire of Popularity, or a thirst after filthy lucre, I must refer them to the last day; that will reveal it.[55]

Again the same lack of interest in Berridge's peculiarities is evidenced in his peers. It is his Christian life expressed in benevolence, fellowship, earnestness, and witness that draws their unstinted praise. John Newton recommends Berridge to a friend in 1772: "I am

---

52 *Gospel Standard* (1856), 121.
53 *Essays Critical and Historical*, 2 vols. (Longmans, Green, and Co., 1914), 1:419.
54 *Christian World*, 161.
55 *Divine Songs*, xxiii–xxiv.

persuaded that as he gets opportunity to know you, he will love you dearly, and though he has some singularities, I know no person whose converse is more spiritual and edifying."[56] A close friend, Henry Venn, speaking in the context of Berridge preaching beyond his natural strength in London for three months in 1776 to the largest congregations that had been seen, writes: "He is often telling me that he is sick of all he does, and loathes himself for the inexpressible corruption he feels within: yet his life is a pattern to us all, and an incitement to love and serve the Lord with all our strength."[57] John Fletcher of Madeley, with whom Berridge had fundamental theological disagreements, warmly acknowledged: "Few, very few, of our elders equal him in devotedness to Christ, zeal, diligence and ministerial success. His indefatigable labours in the Word and Doctrine entitle him to a double share of honour."[58] William Bull (1738–1874) reported to his wife the death of the "venerable and holy Mr Berridge."[59] To Cornelius Winter (1742–1808) Berridge was that "truly apostolic man."[60] There are many such quotations from his fellow preachers. Although Whittingham freely recognized Berridge's eccentricity, including many funny illustrations of Berridge's wit, this is not the theme of his memoir. His testimony to Berridge is one of a deeply spiritual man. He testifies:

> During all the years of my acquaintance with him, notwithstanding his unabated popularity, I never saw him betray the least symptom of vanity on any occasion. And so happily did this most desirable grace emancipate him from the shackles of religious bigotry that it rendered him equally easy in the company of the poor and the peasant, and alike familiar with the dignified clergy, and the unpolished lay-preacher. He never spoke of himself, but in language the most depreciating; and when he related any interfering providence, or display of studious grace on his behalf, it would generally be with streaming eyes, and the sweetest expression of

---

56 Letter to Symonds; January 1772; in H.G. Tibbutt, *Bunyan Meeting Bedford, 1650–1950* (Bedford: Trustees of Bunyan Meeting, 1950), 39.
57 *The Life and Letters of Venn*, 233.
58 *The Works of the Reverend John Fletcher, late vicar of Madeley*, 7 vols. (John Kershaw, 1826), 2:268.
59 *Memorials of the Rev. William Bull* (Nisbet, 1864), 217.
60 William Jay, *Memoirs of the Life and Character of the late Reverend Cornelius Winter* (Bath: M. Gye, 1808), 86.

praise upon his lips. I can scarcely recollect a man so conscientious, so uniformly, and yet so pleasantly spiritual. None who intimately knew him will consider this as an exaggerated history....[61]

Berridge knew himself to be unusual and during his many years at university he had no doubt employed the whimsical side of his nature in order to make himself popular. Whittingham says: "Being of a witty turn of mind, he cultivated an acquaintance with works of wit. *Hudibras* was so familiar to him, that he was at no loss in using any part of it on any occasion. While he was at college, if it was known that he would be present at any public dinner, the table was crowded with company, who were highly delighted with the singularity of his conversation and witty sayings."[62] And just as he used his natural gift at Cambridge so he seems to have seasoned his conversation and preaching with his wit. He gives the impression that this was something that he could not help. "Odd things break from me as abruptly as croaking from a raven."[63] But it is just as likely that Berridge used his natural propensity to say unusual things to gain the attention of his hearers. This is at least what John Thornton supposed.[64] Gordon Rupp (1910–1986) concludes: "His wit was the trait which endured through the unregenerate and evangelical phases of his life."[65] Balleine comments on the fact that Berridge's sermon notes have nothing remarkable about them, and they are a trifle dull if one is looking for the unusual. He suggests that it was the interpolations that made Berridge a pithy and homely preacher.[66] Berridge's great success as a preacher, not only at Everton, where many flocked on Sunday, but in his itinerate work throughout Bedfordshire, Cambridgeshire, Essex, Huntingdonshire, and Hertfordshire, and his

---

[61] *WB* (1838), 38.

[62] *WB* (1838), 4.

[63] October 22, 1775.

[64] Letter from John Thornton to Berridge, October 17, 1775. See *WB* (1864), 522.

[65] *Religion in England, 1688–1791* (Oxford: Clarendon Press, 1986), 479.

[66] *A History of the Evangelical Party in the Church of England* (Longman, Green and Co., 1908), 99. In the two sermons we possess there is no evidence of such asides. They are examples of sober, serious experimental expository preaching. Were the asides taken out or has this side of Berridge been exaggerated? The farewell sermon preached at the Tabernacle on April 1, 1792, was taken down in shorthand at the time whereas the sermon preached at Tottenham Court Road Chapel on February 18, 1787, printed in *GS* (February 1985), 34–39, is definitely a summary and probably not by Berridge.

regular winter preaching at the Moorfields Tabernacle and Tottenham Court Road Chapel for over thirty years to two of the largest congregations in London must be in some degree related to his personality. Whittingham notes that:

> The mode of his *public ministrations* was emphatically original. He evidently observed method in all his sermons, but it was unhacknied [sic]. It was not his custom to range his subject under general heads of discourse; but when he made the attempt his divisions would be peculiarly natural, and rigidly adhered to. As he rarely allegorized, or accommodated the scriptures, he was less liable to mistake their meaning. He seldom referred to the original text; but when he did, his remarks were pertinent. In his discussion of general topics, his figures were new, his illustrations apposite, and his arguments conclusive. His stature was tall, but not awkward; his make was lusty, but not corpulent; his voice was deep, but not hoarse; strong, but not noisy; his pronunciation was distinct, but not broad. In his countenance there was gravity, without grimace; his address was solemn, but not sour; easy, but not careless; deliberate, but not drawling; pointed but not personal; affectionate, but not fawning. He would often weep, but never whine. His sentences were short, but not ambiguous. His ideas were collected, but not crowded. Upon the whole his manner and person were agreeable and majestic. But what transcended all the above excellencies, and gave him such an ascendancy in the consciences of his numerous hearers, were the *doctrines* he taught, together with their unbounded influence upon all the powers of his mind, and transactions of his life. Deep necessity compelled him to embrace and preach Jesus Christ; and the same necessity led him into more enlarged discoveries of his grace.[67]

Directness, freshness, simplicity, earnestness, illustrations, passion, and emotion all joined with originality to make Berridge a very effective communicator. More importantly Berridge was not a man of style with little content, the great danger for preachers with personality. He had content, theology and substance, a message of forgiveness through Christ that had burned into his own heart, although he sought to present his message in a way that all could understand.

---

67 *WB* (1838), 20–21.

The extraordinary things Berridge sometimes writes in his private correspondence would suggest that he often opened his mouth before he engaged his brain. He confesses to Lady Huntingdon: "I am a strange, blunt fellow, and have always been thought a blundering fool...."[68] Berridge was aware of the dangers of this side of his personality. He writes:

O thou unruly tongue
The sinner's pride and shame!
A member small, yet far too strong
For mortal men to tame!

Who shall deliver me
From all its deadly woe?
No man has might to set me free
None, but the Lord, I know.

Lord Jesus, shew thy pow'r
And make this tiger calm;
Bar up his passage, bolt the door,
And screen the mouth from harm.

My tongue is apt to start,
And hasty words let slip;
Oh, bid thy love command my heart,
And that will guard my lip.[69]

Many of Berridge's hymns reveal his struggles and perplexity about himself[70] and the resolution that he found in Christ.[71] He confesses:

---

68 July 16, 1763.

69 *Sion's Songs*, 60–61, Hymn 37, verses 1,4,5, and 6. See *WB* (1838), 13–14.

70 Gordon Mursell calls this "strong interior dynamic" a feature of Evangelical spirituality (*English Spirituality: From 1700 to the Present Day* [Louisville: Westminster John Knox Press, 2001], 31).

71 For an appreciation of subjective truth shown in Berridge's hymns, see J.C. Philpot's preface to *Zion's Songs, or Hymns: Composed for the Use of Them That Love and Follow the Lord Jesus Christ With Sincerity* (London: Simpkin, Marshall and Co., 1842) and "Review of the *Christian World Unmasked*," *GS* (1851), 318–422.

What a motley wretch am I,
Full of inconsistency,
Sure the plague is in my heart,
Else I could not act this part.

Let me come unto my Lord
Self-condemned and aborr'd
Take the sinner's safe retreat,
Lay and blush at Jesu's feet.[72]

Berridge's personality was not so distinct and his experiences were not so foreign as to be inaccessible in the twenty-first century to a wide range of people, although the Christian will find most to stimulate and encourage his own heart as he considers this most unusual man.

Short account of Berridge's life

John Berridge was born on February 29, 1716, at Kingston-on-Soar near Nottingham.[73] His father, John Berridge (1689–1740), was a prosperous farmer, and Berridge was the eldest of four sons.[74] His early life was spent with an aunt in Nottingham, and at fourteen he returned home to learn the family business. At this time he became aware of his sinful state and found help in visiting a local tailor to discuss religious subjects and pray.[75] Because of his failure to make progress in learning the farming business at home and because of his religious interest, he was sent to Cambridge in 1734, where he "pursued his studies with uncommon avidity, and made such progress in every branch of literature, as rendered him in no respect inferior to any of his contemporaries."[76] Berridge recounts:

---

[72] *Sion's Songs*, 153–4, Hymn 112, verses 5 and 6. See *WB* (1838), 33.

[73] See Brian W. Smith, *A History of Kingston-on-Soar up to the 19th Century* (Nottingham: Brickyard Publishing, 1988), which includes a short account of Berridge. Smith in a letter says: "No baptism recorded for John Berridge, preacher, only birthdate on leap year!" This explains the confusion over whether March or February was his birth month.

[74] See June 9, 1770.

[75] See Whittingham's "Memoirs" in *WB* (1838), 1–44, for early details.

[76] "The Late Rev. John Berridge," *EM* (1793), 9. *EM* was started in July 1793 and was planned on interdenominational lines. Whittingham's article, which he used as the basis for his memoir forty-five years later, was one of the first articles in the new magazine. Berridge's portrait, aged seventy-seven, was opposite the title page.

When I first came to the university, I applied myself diligently to my studies, thinking human learning to be a necessary qualification for the divine, and that no one ought to preach unless he had taken a degree in the university. Accordingly I studied the classics, mathematics, philosophy, logic, metaphysics and read the works of our most eminent divines; and this I did for twenty years.[77]

Berridge enjoyed success at Cambridge,[78] rising to be a senior fellow at Clare College, and for at least one year he acted as one of the two moderators who controlled and evaluated the examinations, which, as Symth notes, was a very real honour.[79] During his early years at Cambridge, Berridge lost his spiritual interest, being influenced by the latitudinarian atmosphere, where all views, except those considered extreme, were acceptable. John Gascoigne says that there was "a very wide spectrum of religious opinion provided that at least the external forms of Christianity were preserved."[80] Whittingham recounts that Berridge was so influenced by the Socinian scheme (where Christ is viewed as a creature rather than God) that he discontinued private prayer for ten years. However, Berridge did regain more orthodox views on the person of Christ, and after being ordained in 1745[81] by John Thomas, the Bishop of Lincoln, he obtained in 1751 a curacy at Stapleford, just outside Cambridge.[82] The seriousness with which he approached his new role made people suspect that he had Methodist leanings, but Berridge, in common with most of his academic and ecclesiastical contemporaries, dismissed the revivalism associated with Wesley, Whitefield and others as a doctrinal aberration. Yet during his time at Stapleford, Berridge became more and more dissatisfied with the failure of his own preaching, and his epitaph—"Lived proudly on

---

[77] July 3, 1758.
[78] Matriculated 1735, BA 1748–1749, MA 1742, Exeter Fellow 1740, Diggons Fellow 1742, Clare Fellow 1748–1764, Taxor 1746.
[79] *Simeon and Church Order*, 158. For the work of the moderator, see D.A. Winstanley, *Unreformed Cambridge: A Study of Certain Aspects of the University in the Eighteenth Century* (Cambridge: Cambridge University Press, 1935), 43–46.
[80] *Cambridge in the Age of the Enlightenment* (Cambridge: Cambridge University Press, 1989), 140.
[81] As a deacon March 10, 1745, and as a priest June 9, 1745, both at Buckden Prebendal Church (Clergy Database).
[82] Appointed by Thomas Gooch, bishop of Ely, November 29, 1751 (Clergy Database).

Faith and Works of Salvation till 1754"—suggests that his failure was related to his own inadequate view of the gospel.[83]

Berridge was admitted by Bishop John Thomas (1691–1766),[84] on July 7, 1755, to the living of Everton-cum-Tetworth, which was under the patronage of his college.[85] Everton was a small village on the Bedfordshire, Huntingdonshire and Cambridgeshire border (Everton was in Bedfordshire, Tetworth was in Huntingdonshire). Berridge did not immediately move to Everton. He employed John Jones (1700–1770),[86] Rector of Bolnhurst (1749–1767) as resident curate, Berridge himself agreeing to preach on the first Sunday of every month, thus freeing Jones to attend Bolnhurst. The arrangement only lasted until April 1756, with Jones complaining strongly of Berridge staying too long at the vicarage and thus putting strain on his domestic arrange-ments, his difficult and moody character, his unwillingness to take advice in parish affairs, and his ill will toward himself. After leav-ing, Jones penned a withering critique of Berridge's character, which included hypochondria, inconsistency, meddling and slander.[87]

---

[83] Wesley records meeting Berridge at Stapleford on July 18, 1759, during the initial revival period: "His heart was particularly set on this people, because he was curate here five or six years, but never preached a gospel sermon among them till this evening. About 1500 persons met in a close to hear him, great part of whom were laughers and mockers" (*WW*, 21:216).

[84] John Thomas was bishop of Lincoln from 1744 to 1761 before he moved to Salisbury. He had ordained Berridge a few months after becoming the bishop of Lincoln. We can assume that it was at the bishop's residence at Buckden that Berridge later had his famous encounter with his bishop.

[85] At the dissolution of the monasteries, Clare Hall paid £144 for the rectory of Everton, which had belonged to the monastery at St. Neots. See Mansfield D. Forbes, ed., *Clare College, 1326–1926*, 2 vols. (Cambridge: Cambridge University Press, 1928, 1930), 1:75

[86] John Jones would be classified as a liberal churchman who wished for a broader national Church. In 1749 he published anonymously *Free and Candid Disquisitions Relating to the Church of England, and the Means of Advancing Religion Therein*, in which he called for modifications of the liturgy, queried the use of the sign of the cross and sponsors in baptism, argued against the use of the Athanasian Creed, questioned the need for subscription to the Thirty-Nine Articles and challenged the status of the Book of Homilies. In 1757 he became curate for the poet Edward Young at Welwyn. In 1767 he became vicar of Shaphall, Hertfordshire, where he died after falling from his horse. See *Oxford Dictionary of National Biography* (Oxford: Oxford University Press, 2004; online ed., January 2008). See August 25, 1755.

[87] See "A Collection of Papers in a Folder Inscribed on the Spine 'Grievances:

It was at Everton, in December 1757,[88] that Berridge experienced his conversion or, as he expressed it so succinctly on his epitaph, "Fled to Jesus alone for refuge." Berridge's conversion is the story of a mature, educated and earnest vicar in the Church of England rejecting the combination of a "good life" and orthodox theology as the way to God and coming to see the need of "a spiritual renovation of nature, a real but secret work of the Holy Spirit on the souls of men, producing a new and spiritual service."[89] After much inner turmoil and prayer for enlightenment if he was wrong, the words "cease from thine own works, only believe" came powerfully into his mind as he was meditating on a text of Scripture.[90] He saw the primacy of faith in the person and work of Christ, and recognized that his secret reliance on his own morality and good works had in practice negated the work of Christ.

Berridge started preaching his new message. After a few converts, Berridge was convinced he was now in the right way, and not only did he start attracting hearers from other villages, but he began to experience opposition from his squire and fellow clergy.[91] John Walsh (1745–1799) walked over to Everton on June 2, 1758, and reported to Wesley: "He had many great friends and admirers before, who now turned enemies and persecutors. They attempted to deprive him of his living, but failed. They have nick-named him the Apostle of Clare-Hall, of which he is Fellow. He meets little companies of his converts from several towns and villages, at his own house. He was once ashamed of the word Methodist, but takes it to himself now as freely as I do. The country seems to kindle round him."[92] He discovered that he could preach without the aid of a manuscript, and by June he had started preaching outside his parish. On the fly-leaf at the end of his Bible he wrote: "I Chron. 17:1, 2. June 22, 1758, when I began to itinerate, and when my Squire and Potton Vicar complained of me to the

---

Enthusiasm: etc.'; Chiefly Written by John Jones and Concerning His Period as Assistant Curate to John Berridge at Everton, 1755–56, with Numerous Later Notes and Reflections," held at Dr. Williams's Library (Jones 39.B.24). See also Bernard O'Connor, *Rev. John Berridge, Vicar of Everton, Bedfordshire, 1716–1793* (2001), where he quotes extensively from these papers.

[88] Berridge's date on the epitaph—1756—is wrong. See Pibworth, *Gospel Pedlar*, 26, for evidence.

[89] *Christian World*, 219.

[90] *WB* (1838), 10. See July 3, 1758.

[91] See April 1758.

[92] From a letter dated August 25, 1758, in *Arminian Magazine* (1780), 105.

Bishop."[93] Berridge was indeed called before his bishop, John Thomas, but was saved by the intervention on Berridge's behalf of the Bishop's own patron.[94] During 1758, a local clergyman from Wrestlingworth, Samuel Hicks (c.1721–1796),[95] who at first actively opposed Berridge, was converted and then supported him. Famous evangelists John Wesley (1703–1791) and George Whitefield (1714–1770) came and preached at Everton. During the growing revival, Berridge was visited, in his first year of gospel preaching, by over a thousand persons under "serious impressions."[96]

In May 1759, Berridge started preaching in the open air, and thus greatly expanded his sphere of service. The physical symptoms associated with some of the hearers, which had begun on a small scale in the

---

[93] *Gospel Gems*, iv. This was the verse that Berridge used in a conference with Samuel Walker and George Whitefield about his irregularity. "Mr. Berridge, probably pressed closely by Mr. Walker as to his authority for the course he pursued, stated what he conceived to be the Scriptural grounds for it. He laid much stress upon Nathan's reply to David concerning his design to build the temple, 'do all that is in thine heart, for the Lord is with thee,' and declared it to have greatly moved him in the line of conduct he had adopted. 'This' said Mr Walker in his account of that remarkable interview, 'appeared to poor Berridge a strong warrant to go on with his object, though the context showed that it was the contrary in the case of King David'" (Edwin Sidney, *The Life and Ministry of the Rev. Samuel Walker, BA, formerly of Truro* [Seeley, 1838], 150).

[94] See J. Sutcliff, "An Interview with the Late Mr. Berridge," *Evangelical Magazine* (1794), 73–6, and Michael A.G. Haykin, "John Sutcliff's testimony to John Berridge," *BoT* (June 1989), 13–18.

[95] Admitted as a sizar at Clare College on January 5, 1738, matriculated in 1739 and graduated in 1742. If he was about seventeen when he went to Cambridge he was probably born around 1721. He was inducted into the living at Wrestlingworth in 1744 by John Thomas, bishop of Lincoln, and remained there until his death in 1796. His father Robert (d.1745) held the living at Potton (1720–1745) and that of Wrestlingworth (1730–1744).

[96] *WB* (1838), 32. From a human perspective religious revivals are not easy to explain. It is true that "the specific human and material factors at work remain difficult to identify with confidence" (Mark Hutchinson and John Wolffe, *A Short History of Global Evangelicalism* [Cambridge: Cambridge University Press, 2012], 46). The best brief examination of the various approaches to explaining revivals is David Bebbington's chapter, "The Interpretation of Revival: Religious Awakenings and Modern Historiography," in his *Victorian Religious Revivals: Culture and Piety in Local and Global Contexts* (Oxford: Oxford University Press, 2012), 21–52. For accounts of the Evangelical Revival in the eighteenth century, see G.M. Ditchfield, *The Evangelical Revival* (UCL, 1998) and Mark A. Noll, *The Rise of Evangelicalism: The Age of Edwards, Whitefield and the Wesleys* (Leicester: InterVarsity Press, 2004).

previous year, were to rise to a peak in the summer of 1759. Opposition continued, but the work drew widespread attention, with Berridge preaching before the university and Evangelical leaders coming from London to investigate the authenticity of the work. The following year Berridge received substantive criticism from John Green (1706–1779),[97] Master of Corpus Christi and dean of Lincoln in *The Principles and Practices of the Methodists Considered: in some letters to the leaders of that sect. The first addressed to the Reverend Mr. Berridge. Wherein are some remarks in his two letters to a clergyman in Nottinghamshire, lately published* (London: W. Bristow, 1760). Green presented three areas of criticism. He argued that Berridge's method at arriving at truth was based on the supernatural and thus beyond the test of reason, and that there was abundant evidence that such pretensions had brought ridicule from sensible people; he evaluated what he considered to be the real reasons for Berridge's success "in that such preaching on the doctrines of free grace, election and reprobation would be popular with the poor as it gave the vulgar too high notions of their favour and interest in heaven."[98] He thought that Berridge's message was an easier gospel that encouraged antinomianism. Finally, he attacked Berridge's main doctrinal thrust of justification by faith alone seeing justification as a conditional and, therefore, weaker concept. God's compassion he argued "is never exercised in a capricious manner, without any regard to the moral qualifications of the object…."[99] Green finishes by saying he is delaying any further discussion because he has heard that Berridge was in the process of publishing his sermons preached on this subject before the university in November 1759 and that he expected Berridge to have more cogent reasons and learning than those expressed in a private letter.

During the same year as Green's criticisms, Samuel Hallifax (1733–1790), later professor of Arabic and also Regius Professor of Civil Law as well as a bishop, preached three sermons before the university on Romans 3:28—"Therefore we conclude that a man is justified by faith without the deeds of the Law"—in response to Berridge's understanding of the apostle Paul's teaching. He begins his preface:

---

[97] See July 3, 1758. Green was a leading academic and churchman. His second letter "On the Principles and Practices of the Methodists" was addressed to Whitefield. From 1761 he was Berridge's bishop and so highly thought of was he that when Archbishop Secker was indisposed in 1762 he "visited" the diocese of Canterbury as his proxy.

[98] *Principles*, 14.

[99] *Principles*, 39.

The following Discourses owe their birth not so much to choice as chance. A certain teacher among the METHODISTS [footnote: "The Reverend Mr. B____e, Fellow of *Clare-Hall*"] was led to try the success of his preaching before the University of *Cambridge*. His subject, the reader need hardly be told, was *Justification by Faith* alone, without works; which he appeared, in the opinion of many of his hearers, to treat in a manner so contrary to the true meaning of the Scriptures, and so unbecoming the character, which he was under a double obligation to support, as a Member of the University, and a Minister of the Gospel; as to urge or rather provoke the Author to enter the lists himself against this formidable advocate of modern *Methodism*, and, to endeavour, in the following three discourses, to rescue the subject of Justification by Faith from the dishonour, which he conceived were put upon it by this unfair and uncandid adversary.[100]

Hallifax's sermons are serious, weighty and learned, but they fundamentally fail to engage with Berridge as they are based on a crucial error of seeing the Methodist understanding of faith in terms of a bare profession of belief in Christ removed from fruits displayed in the life of a believer.[101]

William Law (1686–1761), from his home in Kings Cliffe, Northamptonshire, where he presumably saw Berridge's letter, joined in the condemnation of Berridge, which was to prove one of his last works. He starts his discussion between a "Methodist" and a "Churchman" with a quotation from the unofficial publication of Berridge's letter and ends with an explicit challenge to Berridge in the character of "Methodist": "But if you come forth with the new-fangled Ungospel Doctrines of a *Calvin*, a *Zinzendorf*, etc. be your zeal as great as it will, it only unites you with the Brick and Mortar-Builders of that Anti-Christian Babel, which the Prince of the Power of the Air has set up, in full opposition to that Rock, on which Christ has built his one, Catholic, universal Salvation-Church."[102] Such a critical reaction from

---

[100] *Saint Paul's Doctrine of Justification by Faith, explained in three discourses, preached before the University of Cambridge, in the year 1760*, 2nd ed., corrected and enlarged (Cambridge: 1762), iii–iv.

[101] *Saint Paul's doctrine*, v.

[102] "A Dialogue between a Methodist and a Churchman" in *The Works of Reverend William Law, M.A.*, 9 vols. (Richardson, 1762; repr., Canterbury: Morton, 1893), 8:251.

such an impressive group of churchmen in a short time shows something of the effect that Berridge's message had.[103]

In 1760, Berridge was visited at Everton by Lady Huntingdon (1707–
1791), who was accompanied by Henry Venn (1724–1797) and Martin
Madan (1726–1790). Berridge returned with Lady Huntingdon to preach
at her house in London. This was the start of a life-long relationship.

In the winter of 1761, he started preaching in London for Whitefield,
who was ill. Preaching in London from January to March became his
normal pattern, since it was difficult to sustain circuit preaching in winter
months, and it was also the time in which London congregations were
at their peak. During the 1760s Berridge's circuit was to extend into the
neighbouring counties, to include forty preaching stations, with Berridge
employing helpers in the work. It took Berridge six weeks to visit the
congregations connected with him.[104] He would go out on Monday
and return Friday night or Saturday morning, preaching evenings and
mornings.[105] "He hired barns, he paid preachers, and on these and works
of charity, he expended the whole proceeds of his vicarage and Fellowship,
the price of his family plate, and the whole of a large patrimonial
fortune. He kept nothing back—he did nothing by halves—although
sometimes indeed he brought himself thereby into difficulties…."[106]

During the early 1760s Berridge's relationship with Wesley
cooled, probably as a result of Berridge wishing to maintain his own
independence and his moving away from perfectionist teaching.
Berridge's later adoption of more explicit Calvinistic views, and his
writing about that issue in the controversy of the 1770s, cemented

---

[103] The Regius Professor of Divinity at Cambridge, Thomas Rutherforth (1712–
1771), a senior colleague of Berridge at the university, accused Berridge and
other Methodists of "adopting the language and opinions of the conventicle in
maintaining anyone with the gift can preach" (*Four Charges to the Clergy of the
Archdeaconry of Essex*, 8 vols. [Cambridge: 1763], 2). He quotes directly from
the unofficial publication of Berridge's letter. One can appreciate the response
to Berridge and the revival in the separate sermon titles. For Rutherford's death
and the sermon titles, see October 20, 1771.

[104] *WB* (1838), 38.

[105] May 18, 1763. See Spring 1785 for advice to Simeon on preaching times.

[106] Thomas Guthrie, "Life of the Author," in the 1853 edition of *The Christian
World Unmasked* (Edinburgh: Adam and Charles Black, 1853), xii. See the auto-
biographical section, where Berridge describes the man who spends his income
yearly and has to pray to God when in difficulties. "Such prayers, he said, never
failed to bring supplies—some from those who cared for him and some from such
as did avoid his company" (*Christian World*, 61).

the division. Berridge does not seem to have had much effect on the university, but he was a succour and help to some students, particularly Rowland Hill, whom he first contacted in 1764.[107] From 1768 to 1773 chronic asthma, and probably nervous exhaustion, confined the once energetic and enthusiastic field preacher to his own home for long periods. He usually succeeded in taking the service on Sunday, but sometimes even that was beyond his powers. Although he fretted and suffered depression at first,[108] he came to bless God for these years of difficulty and trial.[109] Enforced rest led to a serious evaluation of himself and his theology. During these years he composed over 300 hymns and wrote *The Christian World Unmasked*. Although Berridge had a hatred of sectarianism and was aware of the detrimental effects of controversy, he felt compelled to enter the Calvinistic controversy of the time for several reasons. Evangelistically, he wished to arouse the dead professor; pastorally, he felt the need to testify to the experimental nature of the subject, particularly in the light of his own troubles; and theologically he wished to challenge the liberalizing and watering down of the main Revival doctrine of justification by faith alone that he saw occurring in the Methodism associated with Wesley. During these difficult years the work among Berridge's preaching stations carried on because of the lay preachers whom he supported.[110] One such "shop" was at Waterbeach, which he first visited in 1759 and preached on the green. A contemporary shows the lay character of the work associated with Berridge when he speaks of Waterbeach having a "numerous seminary of the disciples of Mr. Berridge of Clare Hall, called from him 'Berridges' and who to this day send out preachers, gardeners, collar-makers, shop-keepers, etc., into many of the adjacent villages."[111]

When Berridge resumed his local itinerating in 1774, he found a warmer reception than before his illness. He reports in a letter to John

---

[107] See December 18, 1764.
[108] Whittingham says: "To be laid aside in the plenitude of his success was so irritating to his nature, that like Jonah, *his heart fretted against the Lord*, and he wished he had never been employed in the work of the ministry. To such a pitch of criminal exasperation was he carried against the government of God, for checking his ministerial career, that he could not even endure the sight of his Bible, nor bear the people sing in his adjoining church" (*WB* [1838], 14–15).
[109] See September 29, 1772.
[110] See May 3, 1773 and June 9, 1773.
[111] Thomas Baker, *History of the College of St. John the Evangelist*, ed. John E. Mayor, 2 vols. (Cambridge: Cambridge University Press, 1869), 1:1046.

Thornton that in most places there were large crowds who were attentive and silent in comparison with the common mockings and outrages that had once occurred.[112] Nevertheless, some summers proved too difficult, and his health collapsed. In 1776 he was able to make a start but had to return home.[113] In June 1778 his spring fever kept him at home, and he found even writing a letter an exhausting task.[114] The summers of 1782 and 1783 were a struggle for Berridge, and he just managed to preach once each Sunday at Everton.[115] In the summer of 1786 he was only able to walk the two hundred yards from the vicarage to the church building.[116] Even so there were periods of intense activity, and in any case the wider work carried on, helped with financial aid from friends in London.[117] After a decline in the early 1780s, Berridge writes that the church was very full in the afternoon and that the congregation was almost a new one. Many of the old hearers had died or supported local meetings and only occasionally visited Everton.[118] During this decade he continued to enjoy the fellowship of Henry Venn and his family at Yelling, although they had a significant disagreement over whether Charles Simeon should go down the same irregular path as themselves. And while Berridge at first found it difficult to obtain suitable help because of the job description,[119] he was able to employ curates at Everton.[120] He did compromise his own convictions in order to obtain help.[121] During these latter years he was still a fruitful preacher. John A. Clark, rector of St. Andrew's Church, Philadelphia, recounts a testimony from an Englishman of his conversion from these years:

> It was nearly at the end of his course, that he came into my native parish, and preached one evening. I had always attended the parish church. I had been baptized and confirmed, and had also taken

---

112 August 10, 1774.
113 June 7, 1776.
114 June 12, 1778.
115 October 3, 1783.
116 November 7, 1786.
117 See the yearly thank-you letters to Benjamin Mills and the letters to the generous John Thornton.
118 July 13, 1785.
119 See December 12, 1780.
120 Richard Whittingham from 1782, John Elard (c.1757–1798) from 1789.
121 See March 7, 1789.

the sacrament, and thought I was a good Christian. Though I was not openly immoral, I had no more idea of heartfelt religion than a heathen. Drawn out by curiosity to hear one preach, of whom so much was said, I heard words from the lips of Mr. Berridge that evening that I could not forget. He tore up all my old foundation. Though I resisted the convictions of my own mind a long time, I was obliged at last to flee to Christ as my only refuge. Then I saw everything in a new light. Old things had passed away, and all things had become new. And now, sir, I hope your course, as I said, will be like that of good Mr. Berridge.[122]

Berridge seems to have kept mentally alert during his final years although he was suffering the usual problems of old age, such as deafness and lameness. The first-hand evidence—including letters, the crowds that still attended Everton on Sunday, reports of the preaching, comments of friends and associates, and the last sermon preached in London—all witness to the clarity of his mind even though his memory and eyesight were weakening fast. Abner Brown's second-hand comments when in his sixties, seventy years after Berridge's death, that Berridge suffered delusions in his old age (for example, that he was made of glass and that his body would swell up and burst),[123] are not supported by any material from the period. Of course, such things could have happened, but it is difficult to believe that a mentally ill man could have sustained a large congregation both at Everton and in London, and even more difficult to believe that his many opponents did not remark on this fact.

Henry Venn alludes in several letters written in the autumn of 1791 to a visit that he paid to Berridge, whom he calls "the venerable pastor of Everton":

I lately visited my dear brother Berridge. His sight is very dim, his ears can scarcely hear, and his faculties are fast decaying; so that, if he continues any time, he may outlive the use of them. But in this ruin of his earthly tabernacle, it is surprising to see the joy in his countenance, and the lively hope with which he looks for the day of his dissolution. In his prayer with me and my children

---

[122] *Gathered Fragments* (Philadelphia: Marshall, 1836), 392.
[123] *Conversation Parties*, 200–202. Brown was an undergraduate divinity student at Cambridge between 1827 and 1830 and attended meetings in Simeon's rooms taking detailed notes of what Simeon said during the "conversation parties."

(for two of them accompanied me) we were much affected by his commending himself to the Lord as quite alone, not able to read, or hear, or do anything; 'but if I have, Lord,' said he, 'Thy presence and love, *that* sufficeth.'[124]

His health did improve. In the following April he went to London and preached the sermon that was published as *The Last Farewell Sermon*. John Warner gives a report of his preaching at Everton in the summer of 1792.[125]

Sometime during 1792, John Sutcliff (1752–1814) and Andrew Fuller (1754–1815) spent some time with Berridge at Everton, which made a deep impression on them both, as Berridge, weak as he was, shared the story of his life with them. Fuller gave an account to his friend John Ryland Jr. (1753–1825) of Northampton.

I greatly admired that divine savour that all along mingled with his facetiousness, and sufficiently chastised it—His conversation tended to produce a frequent, but guiltless smile, a smile accompanied with a tear of pleasure—His love to Christ appears to be intense. I requested him to give us a few of the outlines of his life and ministry. These were interesting, but too long to write—they will enrich an evening's conversation if I should some time come to Northampton—When he had gone through I asked him to pray for us—he was so faint, he said he could not yet—he requested me to pray—I prayed, and concluded as usual by asking all in Christ's name—He, without getting off his knees took up the prayer where I had left it, in some such manner as this "O Lord God! This prayer has been offered up in the name of Jesus, accept it I beseech thee and so on, for five or six minutes in a most solemn and savory manner. We then took leave with solemn prayer for blessings on each other as if we had been acquainted for 40 years, and were never to see each other again in this world—The visit left a strong and lasting impression on my heart of the beauty of holiness, of holiness almost matured...."[126]

---

124 Venn, *Life and Letters of Venn*, 500–501.
125 John Warner's visit to Everton is recorded in "Diary of the Rev. B. Gilpin," ex. in *Bedfordshire Magazine*, 18:138 (1981), 25.
126 Timothy D. Whelan, *Baptist Autographs in the John Rylands University Library, 1741–1845, transcribed and edited by Timothy D. Whelan* (Mercer: Mercer University Press, 2009), 53.

Berridge died on Tuesday, January 22, 1793, after contracting a violent attack of asthma on January 12, the very morning he was due to set out for London. The following Sunday, Charles Simeon preached at the funeral from 2 Timothy 4:7, 8. Berridge, ever the preacher, had prepared his own testimony, recorded on his tombstone, which has continued to challenge people to this day:

Here lay the earthly Remains of JOHN BERRIDGE
late Vicar of Everton and an itinerant Servant
of JESUS CHRIST who loved his Master and his Work
and after running on his Errands many years was called
up to wait on Him above. Reader art thou born again?
No Salvation without a new Birth.
I was born in Sin Feb. 1716
Remained ignorant of my fallen State till 1730
Lived proudly on Faith & Works for Salvation till 1754
Admitted to Everton Vicarage 1755
Fled to JESUS alone for Refuge 1756
Fell asleep in Christ Jan.ʸ 22ⁿᵈ 1793.

Kenneth Hylson-Smith sums up his life: "He was a gifted man of real humility, constant self-denial and self-discipline, abundantly kind and utterly devoted to his calling."[127]

The letters

Charles Smyth (1903–1987) declared seventy years ago that "there is room for a new edition of Berridge's letters, many of which are scattered through the files of defunct religious periodicals."[128] The number of letters available for such a work is comparatively small, but perhaps their interest and significance compensate for their scarceness. There are sixty-five letters in *The Works of the Rev. John Berridge*, edited by Berridge's curate Richard Whittingham and published in 1838, forty-five years after the death of Berridge. When the second edition of *Works* was published in 1864 the number had increased to ninety. This present collection, after much searching, includes one hundred

---

[127] *Evangelicals in the Church of England, 1734–1984* (Edinburgh: T. and T. Clark, 1988), 44.
[128] *Simeon and Church Order*, xvi.

and sixty letters and extracts as well as added material to some previously published letters and extracts.

The eighteenth century was a period of great letter-writing. This was made possible by the development of the postal service, which, although it was not what it was to become in the nineteenth century, was effective. Post was carried on horseback, and the roads were bad, with the added danger of robberies (mail coaches with armed guards were introduced in 1783). The journey between London and Edinburgh took a week. Government officials could open and examine correspondence if they suspected sedition. Nevertheless, the educated used the postal system freely and corresponded on all sorts of subjects, serious and trivial, similar to today. However, there was a vital difference:

> ...many of them spent more thought and care on their letters than we are apt to spend on ours. They did not write so often perhaps, but when they did they deemed it worth while to bestow more attention on style and expression. They did so as much out of compliment to those whom they addressed as for their own repute. This gave their epistles an air of formality which we would avoid in these days.[129]

The fact that the recipient of the letter paid for the postage may also have ensured that the content was worth sending. Private letters were also written with the thought that they might be read to others in a more public setting. An eighteenth-century letter might appear spontaneous but it was often the result of considerable art and based on distinct ideas of correctness, formality, and social ease between members of the same group. In comparison with previous times, "the eighteenth-century writer liked to compare his letters with polite conversation."[130]

In some ways, perhaps, Berridge's epistolary tone is more in the style of the eighteenth century than many have credited. He might have paid more attention and spent more care on his "quaint mixture of wit, sense and bluntness"[131] than some have supposed. He mentions that letter

---

[129] James Aitken, ed., *English Letters of the XVIII Century* (Pelican, 1946), 8.

[130] Howard Anderson and Irvin Ehrenpreis, "The Familiar Letter in the Eighteenth Century: Some Generalizations." In Howard Anderson, Philip B. Daghlian, and Irvin Ehrenpreis, eds., *The Familiar Letter in the Eighteenth Century* (Kansas: University Press of Kansas, 1996), 274.

[131] Helen C. Knight, *Lady Huntingdon and Her Friends* (New York: American Tract Society, 1853), 123.

writers as well as preachers "often study to say smart things" that yield pleasure rather than profit.[132] It is normally felt that Berridge's openness and bluntness not only offend our sensibilities but certainly went against the normal standards of his own day. C.E. Vulliamy, speaking of Berridge's letters to Lady Huntingdon, says they "are often full of a jocular sanctimonious extravagance, a shocking warmth and vulgarity of metaphor which are probably without a parallel in any other correspondence."[133] In an age when an air of formality pervades most letters, Berridge's certainly appear different. "In the correspondence of the time, so heavily weighed with solemn, stereotyped language, his letters stand out in their spontaneity and raciness, and call forth a smile even when they deal with the most serious subjects."[134] Berridge did indeed have a singular style.[135] C.H. Spurgeon noted that "his style was very remarkable, and entirely his own."[136]

Patricia Spacks, in discussing the question of the literary nature of published letters, points out that they pose particular problems for the reader. She argues that

> since letters belong to social as well as personal history, adequate understanding of them demands knowledge of the conventions on which they draw: social conventions governing relationships as well as literary conventions controlling expression. Reading letters, in short, amounts to a particularly challenging literary exercise. Its challenges call attention to important critical issues: the assumptions we bring to texts, the meaning of audience, the real sense in which reading constitutes an act of violation, the ambiguities of context and of intentionality.[137]

In evaluating Berridge's writings, some have not risen to the challenge. Edmund Gosse (1849–1928) dismissed Berridge's style because of Berridge's spiritual objectives: "With such a writer all the charms of intellectual expression were so many narcotics provided

---

[132] November 17, 1784.

[133] *John Wesley*, 284.

[134] Sarah Tytler, *The Countess of Huntingdon and Her Circle* (Pitman, 1907), 110.

[135] Whittingham, his editor, notes that his letters were "written in a style of singular originality" (*WB* [1838], vi).

[136] *Eccentric Preachers* (Passmore and Alabaster, 1879), 129.

[137] "Forgotten Genres," *Modern Language Studies*, 18 (1988), 52.

to dull the soul's sense of its awful condition."[138] William Lecky's own rationalist philosophy prevented any appreciation, and he claimed that it was "impossible to find among his scanty remains a single page of real eloquence or a single thought of real originality."[139] Even some from the same theological stable give a very limited appreciation. "His letters also are full of queer conceits which give them a certain piquance, though they often offend against good taste."[140] P.E. Sangster, however, gives another view and recognizes the uniqueness of Berridge's letters, full as they are of "vivid phrases, startling analogies, and caustic wit." He concludes: "Had Berridge not chosen to be an Evangelical, or rather been called to be, as he would have phrased it, he could have been a great writer."[141]

Berridge himself was "not very fond of letter writing,"[142] particularly in the busyness of his preaching life. He says, when resting; "through mercy I have been able to itinerate thirteen weeks this summer, and am now resting my old bones during harvest, and sitting down to pay my epistolary debts, which have risen to a large amount. Indeed they have lain too long unnoticed, but writing does not suit when I ramble....."[143] He apologizes to a London friend: "What with itinerant preaching and feebleness of body when I come home, I have long delayed writing to my London friends. At length being quite ashamed of this neglect I stayed at home this week, and set it apart for this purpose."[144] He says that "when I ramble about to preach I have neither leisure nor inclination to write."[145] Sometimes he did not answer correspondents. He confesses to Lady Huntingdon: "My good Lady, though I use you very ill, in omitting at sometimes, and in delaying [at?] all times the payment of my epistolary debts, yet you are much upon my heart, and I believe upon the heart of every well wisher to our Sion."[146] But Berridge's struggle with answering friends also occurred during periods of inactivity due to illness. He excuses

---

138 *A History of Eighteenth Century Literature, 1660–1780* (Macmillan, 1891), 396.
139 *England in the Eighteenth Century*, 126.
140 L.E. Elliott-Binns, *The Early Evangelicals: A Religious and Social Study* (Lutterworth, 1853), 282.
141 "Life of the Rev. Rowland Hill," 232.
142 Whittingham's comment in *WB* (1838), vi.
143 August 10, 1774.
144 June 29, 1781.
145 August 16, 1774.
146 March 6, 1766.

himself from answering a letter by saying he was kept at home for twelve weeks during the summer through illness, which "forbade me all literary correspondence."[147] He admits to his London friend Samuel Wilks (d.1803),[148] "my spirits have been so weak and shattered since my late long illness, that writing of letters is a real burden to me, and makes me a very tardy correspondent. At times, when I am very low, a letter that demands a speedy answer will vapour[149] me as much as a large bill requiring prompt payment would a sinking tradesman."[150] He says to John Newton that for a month he had not looked at his letter for fear he might see the date. He confesses: "During my latter years I have been continually making apologies for slack returns to my corresponding friends, and am not one jot better yet."[151] Berridge was indeed a slack correspondent.

Berridge did not keep copies of letters. He seems never to have considered publication in the future. The only exception to this is the letter published describing his conversion and five letters published toward the end of his life. But even here we do not know whether Berridge had given his permission. The only reason that we have some of Berridge's letters is because friends chose to keep them, and that some of these found their way to the collection of his works, the biographies of others or religious journals.

There are some remaining manuscripts of letters that show the editors employing the normal procedure of the nineteenth century of missing out personal details and controversial statements. They also tidy up some letters by including the odd word to make up the sense, break up long sentences and lengthen short sentences, put the text into paragraphs, translate the odd Latin phrase, and elucidate abbreviations. Editorial changes, when known, are commented on in the text. I include the record of the various publications of the same letter so that letters can be examined for changes. Manuscripts were still circulating in the late nineteenth century, and there is evidence that some of these latter publications were not just copying previous publications but were working from originals. Those cited in the *Sower* are particularly valuable in this regard, as the magazine originated in

---

[147] October 23, 1779.
[148] See April 8, 1774.
[149] Worry.
[150] August 16, 1774.
[151] September 17, 1782.

the same area as Berridge and was founded by people who had an interest in his life. In 1893, the *Sower* published several letters to his family, stating: "The letters are in a plain, bold, round hand, and still in excellent preservation."[152]

There are various kinds of letters in this collection. There are short notes scribbled in haste and longer letters arguing a case. Some letters are to family while others convey news of events at Everton. There are requests for help and thank-you notes for gifts received. Some are to people seeking help and advice, while others give encouragement to fellow Christian workers. There are letters to the aristocracy and rich and letters to the poor. Most were written at Everton, but some were written during his winter preaching in London. In many, he opens his own heart and writes with passionate feeling. Berridge's unusual letters are capable of reaching across two centuries and touching our hearts today.

---

[152] *S* (1893), 31.

PART 1

1755–1767

The revival years

To John Jones[1]

Nottingham, August 25, 1755

Dear Sir,

I am sorry you undertook so long a journey to no purpose. I should have been glad to see you at Henfield,[2] not only for the pleasure of conversing with you, but also to settle the business of Everton, which might have been better done in person than by letter. I shall not be able to reside at Everton till midsummer next, when Mr. Welby[3] leaves me; and afterward but six months in the year unless my health compels me to be away from college longer, in which case the master will dispense with my absence. I purpose therefore to look out for an elderly woman about fifty, who can make a pudding, and boil or roast a bit of mutton—to let her live in the house constantly, and mind her own business in my absence; but when I am there to wait a little upon me, and eat with me. In respect to my horse; I purpose to get my clerk or some other neighbouring person to

---

[1]   This is a pre-conversion letter to John Jones, the rector of Bolnhurst, whom Berridge was seeking to employ as curate at Everton. See Introduction, p.20. The letter is in the papers of John Jones at Dr. Williams's Library, 39.B.24 f.3. Although he says his friendship with Berridge was of "long standing" (39.B.24 f.13), he soon fell out with Berridge, their common friend William Talbot, and his bishop, who refused his resignation at Bolnhurst, as well as with the patron of Bolnhurst, Fleetwood Churchill. See "A series of papers relating to John Jones' period as rector of Bolnhurst, Bedfordshire, and his troubles there" (39.B.13). He was very critical of Berridge's preaching after Berridge was converted, seeing Berridge as deeply affected by the spirit delusion and Enthusiasm. See Jones' comments on a letter from James Pointer (January 3, 1760; 39.B.24 f.22), where he described Berridge as "An opinionated, self-willed, headstrong animal; frantic with zeal, extremely vapoured, abounding with spleen, and too often in baseness as well as fickleness of temper, etc."
[2]   Henfield is some seventy miles south of Everton, eleven miles north-west of Brighton.
[3]   William Earle Welby (c.1724–1815) of Denton Hall, Lincolnshire. Welby had been a student at Clare College, and as he entered Middle Temple to study Law in 1756, he was probably being tutored by Berridge at this time. In 1802 he was elected MP for Grantham.

look after him. This is my present intention, but perhaps I may see reason hereafter to alter it; I design to furnish two bed chambers, a parlour, hall and kitchen; then beds and furniture will come from London at new Micmas.[4] There is already in the house a bed for a servant. I have a good stable for two horses, four or five loads of hay, a very convenient close of four acres behind the house, a pretty large churchyard near the house. Now, dear friend, if you have a mind to serve my church from the beginning or middle of November to the beginning or middle of April, you are very welcome, and I will make you as good an allowance as the vicarage will afford. When my house is furnished you may come to it immediately, and bring your servant and your cattle along with you, or not, as you please. If you bring Mrs. Hall along with you (and indeed I think you cannot do well without her) then I shall have no occasion to look out for an house-keeper; and when I come to reside (after this summer) I will bear my share of house-keeping if you desire to continue with me; which you are welcome to do.

If you choose to come to Everton yourself, and leave your family at Bolnhurst,[5] then the only difficulty will be to get a house-keeper to our minds, which must be sought after, when I am upon the spot, and we meet together. I intend to be at Everton at new Micmas, and to wait upon you soon after my arrival there, in order to settle this business. In the meantime, let me hear from you, and be as explicit in this matter as you can; but before you write, take a ride over to Everton, and view the premises. Direct to—John Berridge at William Welby's esq., at Denton near Grantham, Lincolnshire—received your letter at Denton, and went to Nottingham the next day to see my friends, where I now am, and purpose to return to Denton in a day or two. Give my hearty respect to Mr. Talbot[6] when you see him and believe me your affectionate friend and servant,

John Berridge

---

[4] Michaelmas—the Festival of St. Michael and All Angels—had been moved in the calendar revision of 1752 from September 29 to October 10.

[5] Bolnhurst, about twelve miles north-west of Everton.

[6] William Talbot was a co-fellow at Clare College. He later became rector of Elmseth, Suffolk, and prebendary at Salisbury. In May 1761, the Duke of Newcastle, who was a member of Clare and chancellor of the university, appointed him as his secretary for university business. See William T. Gibson, "Patronage and Connection: The Career of the Rev. William Talbot (1720–1811), Chancellor of Salisbury," British Library Journal (1999), 77–84.

To Mr. Daw[1]

[April] 1758

...God has been pleased to bless and prosper my labours, in a very extraordinary manner, for these last three months. Since I preached the real gospel of Christ, seven people in my own parish have now received the gospel in the appointed way of repentance towards God, and faith towards our Lord Jesus Christ.[2] Nine or ten from Potton are

---

[1] This extract is included in a letter from Martin Madan to Wesley written on April 29, 1758. It is found in *AM* (1797), 612–613, and *EM* (1797), 460–462. The quoted section, Berridge to a Mr. Daw, is included to show how another gospel minister had been raised up. Madan says: "Thus far are Mr. Berridge's own words; he adds a desire of being remembered at the Throne of Grace by all our Christian friends: and I trust, dear Sir, that you amongst the rest won't forget him...." This was probably the first that Wesley heard of Berridge.

[2] Berridge's conversion had occurred during the Christmas period of 1757. His faith alone in Christ for salvation produced new sermons with different results from his previous preaching of Christ and works. See ch. 4, "Conversion," in Pibworth, *Gospel Pedlar*. Whittingham recounts how after Berridge came to his new convictions he "began to think upon the words, *Faith* and *Believe*, and looking into his concordance, found them inserted in many successive columns. This surprised him to a great degree, and he instantly formed the resolution to preach Jesus Christ, and salvation by faith. He therefore composed several sermons of this description, and addressed his hearers in a manner very unusual, and far more pointed than before. Now God began to bless his ministry; after he had preached in this strain two or three sabbaths, and was ruminating whether he was yet right, as he had perceived no better effects from these than from his former discourses, one of his parishioners came to inquire for him. Being introduced, 'Well, Sarah', said he. She replied, 'Well, not so well I fear'. 'Why, what is the matter, Sarah?'—'Matter, why I don't know what's the matter. These *new Sermons*. I find we are all to be lost now. I can neither eat, drink, nor sleep. I don't know what's to become of me'. The same week came two or three more on a like errand. It is easy to conceive what relief these visits must have afforded his mind in a state of such anxiety and suspense. So confirmed was he thereby, in the persuasion that his late impressions were from God, that he determined in future *to know nothing but Jesus Christ, and him crucified*. Now he was deeply humbled, that he should have spent so many years of his life to no better purpose, than to confirm his hearers in their ignorance. Thereupon, immediately, he burnt all his old sermons, and shed a flood of tears of joy in their destruction.

in a very hopeful way, two at Gamlingay, and two at Eaton.[3] There is now such a storm arising that I know not how it will end, or when. I bless God, my mind is easy and quiet. Thou, O God, will keep him in perfect peace, whose mind is stayed on thee![4] The tempest is now whistling about my ears, but it does not ruffle or discompose my heart. Some time ago, I was told by several hands, that twelve clergymen had combined together, in order to oppose and prosecute me, if they could. My Squire[5] swears he will do my business; and last Lord's-day evening, when I came from church, he stopped me, and called me the usual names of Enthusiast,[6] etc., etc. Today, I hear the Squire has sent

---

These circumstances alarmed the neighbourhood; the church quickly became crowded, and God gave testimony to the word of his grace, in the frequent conviction and conversion of sinners" (*WB* [1838], 10–11).

[3] Potton, a small market town a mile and a half away from Everton, where Berridge would later have a "cathedral" (a barn); Gamlingay, a village two miles north-east; and Eaton, five miles to the north-west. People had started travelling to Everton. Berridge would start itinerating to such places on June 22. As an old man Berridge remembered his bishop complaining: "Well Berridge, they tell me you go about preaching out of your own parish. Did I institute you to the livings of Abbotsley, or Eaton, or Potton" (Sutcliff, "An Interview with Berridge," 74).

[4] Isaiah 26:3.

[5] Richard Astell (1717–1777), the son and heir of William Astell (1672–1741), who had acquired considerable property in the area. He became Lieutenant-Colonel of the Huntingdonshire militia and JP for Bedford and Huntingdon. His first wife, Sarah Bagnall, died in 1767, and he then married Hannah Kennett, daughter of the vicar of Bradford, in 1770. He died without an heir and the property passed by entail to his nephew William Thornton (1733–1801), grandson of William Astell.

[6] The term "Enthusiast," with its connotations of inspiration, certainty, and personal revelation (literally, "God within you"), shows both the theological and social fear of revivalism. John Walsh speaks of Anglican Evangelicals having to overcome the "deeply ingrained eighteenth century dread of 'enthusiasm', the imaginary belief of fanatics in private revelations from God. This fear had social as well as religious grounds. After the Commonwealth, men feared that ideas of personal inspiration by the Spirit would again dissolve the bonds of civil authority. Dr. Johnson spoke for his age when he pronounced the 'inner-light' principle to be 'utterly incompatible with social or civil security'. *Boswell's Life of Johnson*, ed. G.B. Hill, 6 vols. (Oxford: Clarendon Press, 1934–1964), 2:126. It was widely feared that 'Methodism' led crazy plough-boys to defy their magistrates, or inspired cobblers to argue with the parson. Theologians feared that the illuminism of the Evangelical Revival encouraged the growth of Deism by bringing rational Christianity into disrepute" ("The Anglican

for such of his tenants as are disposed to hear the word of God, and has given them warning to leave their farms directly. He tells all what things he will do, against me; and to show he is in earnest, swears by his Maker, *he will do it....*

Evangelicals in the Eighteenth Century," in *Aspects de l'Anglicanisme*, Marcel Simon, ed. [Paris: Presses universitaries de France, 1974], 95). John Kent in his analysis of Archbishop Secker's response to Berridge's account of his conversion (July 3, 1758) gives the intellectual and theological underpinning of the fear of the subjective claims of "Enthusiasm." He argues that since the Reformation in England the religious imagination had been naturalized, with the supernatural ceasing to be a vital part of Protestantism because of the distinction drawn with Catholicism. See John Kent, *Wesley and the Wesleyans: Religion in Eighteenth-Century Britain* (Cambridge: Cambridge University Press, 2002), 159–167.

TO A NOTTINGHAMSHIRE CLERGYMAN[1]

Everton, July 3, 1758

Rev. and Dear Sir,

My desire and intention, in this letter, is to inform you what the Lord has lately done for my soul; in order to do this, it may be needful to give a little previous information of my manner of life, from my youth up to the present time.

When I was about the age of fourteen, God was pleased to show me that I was a sinner, and that I must be born again before I could enter into his kingdom. Accordingly I betook myself to reading, praying and watching; and was enabled hereby to make some progress in

---

[1] This letter was first published without Berridge's permission from the many handwritten copies that were being circulated by someone who was obviously not sympathetic to Berridge's account of his conversion and his extensive witness to the need and priority of faith in Christ alone. It was published on February 2, 1760, from Grantham some sixty miles north of Everton and entitled *A Fragment of the True Religion, being the substance of two letters from a Methodist-Preacher in Cambridgeshire, to a clergyman in Nottinghamshire* (J. Williams, 1760). Less than a year later the letter was published with Berridge's permission as *Justification by Faith Alone: being the substance of a letter from the Rev. Mr. Berridge in Cambridge to a clergyman in Nottinghamshire, giving an account of a great work of God wrought in his own heart.* It was the circulating manuscripts and the unauthorized publication that produced the serious criticism of a colleague at Cambridge, John Green, DD, Master of Corpus Christi, dean of Lincoln and earlier Regius Professor of Divinity. Green explains: "This epistle, which I had preserved as an invaluable treasure in manuscript and had made a few remarks upon at the request of some country friends, where it was much handed about, is lately published; and on that account I write to you in this public manner" (*Principles and Practices of Methodists*, 2). The text above is from the third edition of the letter (1762) and is included in *WB* (1864), 345–357—an earlier edition is also included in *WB* (1838), 349–364. Berridge's conversion experience had occurred a few months earlier in December 1757. The original recipient was Dr. Thomas Poynton (d.1765), vicar of Bunny and Bradmore (1714–1765), a parish that is just a few miles from Berridge's birthplace. There are manuscript annotations to Thomas Secker's (1693–1768) copy of the letter; Lambeth Palace Library, MS 2595 ff.80–83.

sanctification.[2] In this manner I went on, though not always with the same diligence, till about half a year ago. I thought myself in the right way to heaven, though as yet I was wholly out of the way; and imagining I was travelling towards Zion, though I had never yet set my face thitherwards. Indeed God would have shown me that I was wrong, by not owning my ministry; but I paid no regard to this for a long time, imputing my want of success to the naughty hearts of my hearers, and not to my own naughty doctrine.

You may ask, perhaps, what was my doctrine? Why, dear Sir, it was the doctrine that every man will naturally hold whilst he continues in an unregenerate state, viz., that we are to be justified partly by our faith, and partly by our works. This doctrine I preached for six years, at a curacy, which I served from college;[3] and though I took some extraordinary pains, and pressed sanctification upon them very earnestly, yet they continued as unsanctified as before, and not one soul was brought to Christ. There was indeed a little more of the form of religion in the parish, but not a whit more of the power. At length I removed to Everton,[4] where I have lived altogether. Here again I pressed sanctification and regeneration as vigorously as I could; but finding no success,

---

[2] "In this letter there are some expressions, which he himself, when his knowledge and experience were more matured, would not have used. This is one instance, where he speaks of making progress in sanctification, before, as he himself acknowledges, he has taken one step in the right road to heaven" (*WB* [1838], 349). For Berridge's mature view on this letter—where he protests against its republication and calls it "the chirping of a chicken newly hatched." See August 30, 1774.

[3] Berridge, while a fellow at Clare College, was a curate at Stapleford, a small village about five miles south of Cambridge, from 1749 to 1755. Wesley met Berridge preaching there on July 18, 1759. For a description of his sermon that evening, see Introduction, p.20.

[4] According to the notes on the fly-leaf in his Bible, Berridge was admitted to the vicarage of Everton on July 7, 1755, but he did not take up residence until March 25, 1756. Everton was a small village in Bedfordshire on the border of Huntingdonshire (as was) and Cambridgeshire. It stands on the highest ground in the district and commands a picturesque view of the Ouse valley. Although Bedfordshire parishes were at that time in the diocese of Lincoln, the actual church building at Everton-cum-Tetworth stood in a detached portion of Huntingdonshire and was in the diocese of Ely. For a description of the parish and its history, see Chris Pickford, *Bedfordshire Churches in the Nineteenth Century* (Bedford: BHRS, 2001), 80:887–991, and Bernard O'Connor, *The History of St. Mary's Church, Everton-cum-Tetworth* (O'Connor, 2002).

after two years preaching in this manner, I began to be discouraged, and now some secret misgivings arose in my mind, that I was not right myself. This happened about Christmas last. Those misgivings grew stronger, and at last very painful. Being then under great doubts, I cried unto the Lord very earnestly. The constant language of my heart was this, "Lord, if I am right, keep me so; if I am not right, make me so. Lead me to the knowledge of the truth as it is in Jesus." After about ten days crying unto the Lord, he was pleased to return an answer to my prayers, and in the following wonderful manner. As I was sitting in my house one morning, and musing upon a text of Scripture, the following words were darted into my mind with wonderful power, and seemed like a voice from heaven, viz., "Cease from thine own works." Before I heard these words, my mind was in a very unusual calm; but as soon as I heard them, my soul was in a tempest directly, and the tears flowed from my eyes like a torrent. The scales fell from mine eyes immediately, and I now clearly saw the rock I had been splitting on for near thirty years.

Do you ask what this rock was? Why, it was some secret reliance on my own works for salvation. I had hoped to be saved partly in my own name, and partly in Christ's name; though I am told there is salvation in no other name, except in the name of Jesus Christ (Acts 4:12). I had hoped to be saved partly through my own works, and partly through Christ's mercies; though I am told we are saved by grace through faith, and not of works (Eph. 2:7,8). I had hoped to make myself acceptable to God partly through my own good works, though we are told that we are accepted through the Beloved (Eph. 1:6). I had hoped to make my peace with God partly through my own obedience to the law, though I am told that peace is only to be had by faith (Rom. 5:1). I had hoped to make myself a child of God by sanctification, though we are told that we are made children of God by faith in Christ Jesus (Gal. 3:26). I had thought that regeneration, the new birth or new creature, consisted in sanctification, but now I know it consists in faith (1 John 5:1). Compare also these two passages together, Gal. 6:15 and Gal. 5:6, where you will find that the new creature is faith working by love; the apostle adds these words, *working by love*, in order to distinguish a living faith from a dead one. I had thought that sanctification was the way to justification, but now I am assured that sanctification follows after justification; or in other words, that we must first be justified by faith, before we can have any true sanctification by the Spirit. When we are justified, it is done freely, i.e., graciously, without any the least merits of ours, and solely by the grace of God, through Jesus Christ (Rom. 3:24–28).

All that is previously needful to justification is this, that we are convinced, by the Spirit of God, of our own utter sinfulness (Isa. 64:6), convinced that we are children of wrath by nature, on account of our birth-sin (Eph. 2:3), and that we are under the curse of God, on account of actual sin (Gal. 3:10). And under these convictions come to the Lord Jesus Christ, renouncing all righteousness of our own, and relying solely on him, who is appointed to be the Lord our righteousness (Jer. 23:6). Again, Christ says, "Come unto me, all ye that labour and are heavy laden" with the burden of sin, "and I will give you rest,"[5] i.e., I will take the burden away; I will release you from the guilt of sin. Where you may observe that the only thing required of us when we come to Christ is to come burdened, and sensible that none can remove this burden but Christ. Again, Christ did not come to call the righteous, but sinners to repentance. See also Luke 4:18. Hear how he cries out in Isaiah 55:1. "Ho, everyone that thirsteth, come ye to the waters," and drink; "come buy wine and milk," i.e., the blessings of the gospel, "without money and without price." Where we are ordered to bring no money, i.e., no merits of our own; we must not think to make a purchase of these blessings any deserts of ours. They are offered freely, i.e., graciously, and must be received freely. Nothing more is required from us, but to thirst after them. Why was the Pharisee rejected? (Luke 18:10, etc.), because he came pleading his own works before God. He was devout, just, chaste, and abstemious; and thanked God for enabling him to be so. Very well; so far all was right. But then he had some reliance on these works, and therefore pleads the merits of them before God. Which showed that he did not know what a sinner he was, and that he could only be saved by grace, through faith. He opens his mouth before God, and pleads his own cause; though God declares that every mouth shall be stopped before him, and the whole world brought in guilty before God (Rom. 3:19). And why was the publican justified? Not on account of his own good works, but because he was sensible of his evil ones; and accordingly came self-accused, self-condemned, and crying out only for mercy. And now, dear Sir, hear what is the rise and progress of true religion in the soul of man. When the Spirit of God has convinced any person that he is a child of wrath, and under the curse of God (in which state everyone continues to be till he has received Jesus Christ into his heart by faith), then the heart of such an one becomes broken for

---

5   Matthew 11:28.

sin; then, too, he feels that he never knew before, that he has no faith, and accordingly laments his evil heart of unbelief. In this state men continue, some a longer, some a less time, till God is pleased to work faith in them. Then they are justified, and are at peace with God (Rom. 5:1), i.e., have their sins forgiven them, for that is the meaning of the word *Peace*. See Luke 7:48–50. When we have received faith from God (for it is his gift, Eph. 2:8), to justify our persons, then we afterwards receive the Spirit to sanctify our natures (Eph. 1:14; Gal. 3:14). And now the work of sanctification goes forward; now his fruit is more and more unto holiness; now the love of God is shed abroad in his heart by the Holy Spirit (Rom. 5:5). Now he is filled with joy and peace in believing (Rom. 15:13). Now he rejoiceth with joy unspeakable, and full of glory (1 Pet. 1:8). And now he hath the Spirit of God bearing witness with his own spirit that he is a child of God (Rom. 8:16; 1 John 5:10). These are things that I was an utter stranger to before, not withstanding all my reading, watching, and praying; and these are things that everyone must be a stranger to, until he is made a child of God by faith in Christ Jesus.

But to proceed; though a believer is continually more and more sanctified in body, soul, and spirit, yet his hopes of heaven are not built on his sanctification, but on his faith in Christ; he knows that he is only complete in Christ (Col. 2:10). And that the moment he seeks to be justified by his own obedience to God's law, that moment he falls from Christ, and ceases to have an interest in Christ (Gal. 5:4). Accordingly, though he labours to abound in all the fruits of righteousness; yet, like St. Paul, he desires to be found only in Christ, not having, i.e., not relying on his own righteousness, but on the righteousness of God by faith (Phil. 3:8,9). And now let me point out to you the grand delusion which had liked to have ruined my soul. I saw very early something of the unholiness of my nature, and the necessity of being born again. Accordingly I watched, prayed, and fasted too, thinking to purify my heart by these means, whereas it can only be purified by faith (Acts 15:9). Watching, praying, and fasting, are necessary duties, but I, like many others, placed some secret reliances on them, thinking they were to do that for me, in part at least, which Christ only could. The truth is, though I saw myself to be a sinner, and a great sinner, yet I did not see myself an utter lost sinner, and therefore I could not come to Jesus Christ alone to save me; despised the doctrine of justification by faith alone, looking on it as a foolish and a dangerous doctrine; I was not yet stripped of all my righteousness, could not consider it all as filthy rags, and therefore I went about to establish a righteousness of my own, and did not submit to the righteousness of God by faith (Rom. 10:3). I did not seek after righteousness through faith, but as it were by the works of the law. Thus I stumbled and fell (Rom. 9:31,32). In short, to use a homely similitude, I put the justice of God into one scale, and as many good works of my own as I could into the other and when I found, as I always did, my own good works not to be a balance to the divine justice, I then threw in Christ as a makeweight. And this every one really does, who hopes for salvation partly by doing what he can for himself, and then relying on Christ for the rest.

But, dear Sir, Christ will either be a whole Saviour or none at all. And if you think you have any good service of your own to recommend you unto God, you are certainly without any interest in Christ: be you ever so sober, serious, just, and devout, you are still under the curse of God, as I was, and know it not, provided you have any allowed reliance on your own works, and think they are to do something for you, and Christ to do the rest.

I now proceed to acquaint you with the success I have lately had in my ministry. As soon as God had opened my own eyes, and showed me the true way to salvation, I began immediately to preach it. And now I dealt with my hearers in a very different way from what I had used to do. I told them very plainly, that they were children of wrath, and under the curse of God, though they knew it not; and that none but Jesus Christ could deliver them from that curse. I asked them, if they had ever broken the law of God once in thought, word, or deed? If they had, they were then under the curse: for it is written, "Cursed is everyone that continueth not in all things that are written in the book of the law to do them."[6] And again: "He that keepeth the whole law, and yet offendeth in one point, is guilty of all."[7] If indeed, we could keep the whole law, without offending in one point; if we had done, and could continue to do, all the things in God's law, then, indeed, we might lay claim to eternal life on the score of our own works. But who is sufficient for these things? If we break God's law we immediately fall under the curse of it; and none can deliver us from this curse but Jesus Christ. There is an end, forever after, of any justification from our own works. No future good behaviour can make any atonement for past miscarriages. If I keep all God's laws to-day this is no amends

---

6   Galatians 3:10.
7   James 2:10.

for breaking them yesterday. If I behave peaceably to my neighbour this day, it is no satisfaction for having broken his head yesterday.

If therefore, I am once under the curse of God, for having broken God's law, I can never after do anything, of myself, to deliver me from this curse. I may then cry out, O wretched man that I am! Who shall deliver me from this body of sin?[8] And find none able to deliver, but Jesus Christ can cleanse me from sin. All my hopes are then in him; and I must fly to him as the only refuge set before me. In this manner, dear Sir, I preached, and do preach, to my flock, labouring to beat down self-righteousness; labouring to show them that they were all in a lost and perishing state, and that nothing could recover them out of this state, and make them children of God, but faith in the Lord Jesus Christ. And now see the consequence. This was strange doctrine to my hearers. They were surprised, alarmed, and vexed. The old man, the carnal nature, was stirred up, and railed, and opposed the truth. However, the minds of most were seized with some convictions, and the hearts of some were truly broken for sin, so that they came to me as those mentioned in the Acts, thoroughly pricked to the heart, and crying out with strong and bitter cries, What must I do to be saved? I then laid the promises before them, and told them, if they found themselves under the curse, Christ was ready to deliver them from it; if they were really weary and heavy laden, Christ would give them rest; if their hearts were broken for sin, and they would look up unto Christ, he would heal them. I exhorted them also to thank God for these convictions, assuring them it was a token for good to their souls. For God must first smite the heart, before he can heal it (Isa. 19:22). I generally found that they received comfort from the promises; and though they complained much of the burden of sin, and of an evil heart of unbelief, yet they always went away refreshed and comforted. Many have come to me in this manner, and more are continually coming; and though some fall off from their first convictions, yet others cleave steadfastly unto the Lord. They begin to rejoice in him, and to love him; they exercise themselves in prayer, and adorn their profession by a suitable life and conversation.

And now let me make one reflection. I preached up sanctification[9] very earnestly for six years in a former parish, and never brought one soul to Christ. I did the same at this parish for two years, without any

---

8   Romans 7:24.
9   Editor notes: "By the works of the law he means."

success at all, but as soon as ever I preached Jesus Christ, and faith in his blood, then believers were added to the church continually, then people flocked from all parts to hear the glorious sound of the gospel, some coming six miles, others eight, and others ten, and that constantly.

Let me now apply myself to your own heart, and may God dispose you to receive my words in the spirit of meekness. Indeed, Sir, I love and respect you,[10] else I could not have written to you so freely. Are you then in the same error that I was in for near forty years, viz., that you must be saved partly by faith and partly by works? And have you constantly preached this doctrine? Then you may be certainly assured of these two things: first, that you never yet brought one soul to Christ by your ministry. And, secondly, that you are not yet in the way to salvation yourself. Oh! be not displeased with me for telling you the truth.

But you will say, perhaps, that you have not only been sincere, but ever zealous in preaching the word of God. So was I; but there is a zeal which is not according to knowledge; and that zeal I had, though I knew it not. You may say farther, that you have read and prayed much; so have I; but still I knew nothing, as I ought to know, until God was pleased to show me that I was blind, and then I cried heartily to him for light and direction, and he opened mine eyes (John 9:39).

Dear Sir, will you attend to the following advice, it is very safe advice, be the state of your soul what it will. Pray to God to lead you into the knowledge of the truth as it is in Jesus. Beseech God to keep you in the truth, if you have received it; or if you are in error, to reveal it unto you. If you will do this heartily and constantly, God will not suffer you to abide long in darkness, if, indeed, you are in darkness (James 1:5).

I now proceed to give you some further account of myself, and of the impediments which kept me from the truth. When I first came to the University,[11] I applied myself diligently to my studies, thinking human learning to be a necessary qualification for a divine, and that no one ought to preach unless he had taken a degree in the University. Accordingly I studied the classics, mathematics, philosophy, logic, metaphysics, and read the works of our most eminent divines; and

---

10 On the back of the title page the editor records: "This letter was written by Mr. Berridge, to an intimate acquaintance, in order to give an account of himself, and what God had done for his soul." Berridge himself came from Kingston-on-Soar, near Kegworth, six miles south of Nottingham.

11 Berridge records in the fly-leaf of his Bible that he entered Clare Hall on October 24, 1734. His college records him matriculating on June 12, 1735.

this I did for twenty years; and all the while was departing more and more from the truth as it is in Jesus; vainly hoping to receive that light and instruction from human wisdom, which could only be had from the word of God and prayer.

During this time I was thought a Methodist[12] by some people, only because I was a little more grave, and took a little more pains in my ministry than some others of my brethren; but, in truth, I was no Methodist at all, for I had no sort of acquaintance with them, and could not abide their fundamental doctrine of justification by faith, and thought it high presumption in any to preach, unless they had taken holy orders. But when God was pleased to open mine eyes, about half a year ago, he showed and taught me other things. Now I saw that nothing had kept me so much from the truth as a desire of human wisdom. Now I perceived, that it was as difficult for a wise or learned man to be saved, as it was for a rich man or a nobleman (1 Cor. 1:26). Now I saw that God chose the foolish things of the world to confound the wise, and the weak things to confound the mighty, for two plain reasons; first, that no flesh should glory in his presence (1 Cor. 1:29), and, secondly, to show that faith did not stand, or was not produced, by the wisdom of man, but in the power of God (1 Cor. 2:5). Now I discerned that no one could understand the word of God, but by the Spirit of God (1 Cor. 2:12). Now I say, that every believer was anointed by the Holy Spirit, and thereby led to the knowledge of all needful truths (1 John 2:20); and, of course, that every true believer was qualified to preach the gospel, provided he had the gift of utterance. Now I saw that the Methodists' doctrine of justification by faith, was the very doctrine of the gospel; and I did no longer wonder at the success which those preachers met with, whether they were clergymen or laymen. They preached Christ's doctrine, and Christ owned it; so that many were added to the faith daily.

---

[12] The term "Methodist" was first applied to the Holy Club associated with John and Charles Wesley at Oxford in 1729 because of the disciplined and methodical lives of the members. It became a general term of abuse for those who were overly enthusiastic about their religion and attached importance to some kind of experiential basis for faith. Edwin Welch explains: "For many years in the eighteenth century the term Methodist was in common use as a term of denigration for any enthusiast from Anglican to Unitarian. Like so many of these terms of abuse it was eventually adopted by the supporters of the movement. In the eighteenth century, however, Methodism remained a movement rather than a church or congregation" (*The Bedford Moravian Church in the Eighteenth Century* [Bedford: BHRS, 1989], 68:4).

But you will say, perhaps, that these Methodists are schismatics. Let us therefore examine the matter. A schismatic is one that dissents from and divides an established church; at least this is the general notion of a schismatic. Now, I ask, what do you mean by a church? Or, what is it that makes one church differ from another? It is the doctrine. The Church of England differs from the Church of Rome, not by its steeples, bells, or vestments, but by its doctrines. Schism, therefore, consists in departing from the doctrines of a church, and not from the walls of a church. In the time of Stirbitch fair,[13] one sermon is always preached in the open fields to the people at the fair, and preached by some Fellow of a College, or Clergyman at Cambridge. Now, I ask, would you call this Clergyman a schismatic? No, surely, and yet he preaches in the open fields, and upon unconsecrated ground. It is plain, then, that schism doth not consist in preaching out of the walls of a church, but in preaching contrary to the doctrines of the church.

And now, dear Sir, let me lay open my sin and my shame unto you. I solemnly subscribed to the articles of our church; and gave my hearty assent and consent to them. Amongst the rest, I declared that "we are accounted righteous before God, only for the merits of our Lord and Saviour Jesus Christ by faith, and not for our own works and deservings, and that we are justified by faith only," as it is expressed in the eleventh article. But though I solemnly subscribed this article, I neither believed nor preached it; but preached salvation partly by faith and partly by works. And oh, what dreadful hypocrisy, what shameful prevarication was this! I called and thought myself a Churchman, though I was really a Dissenter and a schismatic; for I was undermining the fundamental doctrine of our church, and the fundamental doctrine of the gospel, namely justification by faith only, and yet, dreadful as my case was, I fear it is the case of most of the clergy in England. Scarce anything is preached but justification by faith and works. And what is the consequence? Why, there is scarce any true religion amongst us, the gospel of Christ is not

---

13 Stourbridge Fair was held annually on the common of that name on the north-east outskirts of Cambridge. It had been the largest fair in Europe, with merchants coming from all over the Continent, but by the eighteenth century it was declining in importance, finally ceasing in 1923. It was the inspiration for Bunyan's Vanity Fair. See Margaret Baker, *Discovering English Fairs* (Tring: Shire, n.d.) and Honor Ridout, *Cambridge and Stourbridge Fair* (Cambridge: Blue Ocean Publishing, 2011) for an account of the importance and working of the fair.

truly preached by us, and Christ will not own our ministry. Look around the parishes which are near you and see whether you can find anything besides the form of religion, and not much of that. Nay, amongst those who are thought religious people; who are sober, serious, just and devout; who read, and fast, and pray, and give alms, amongst those you will scarce find one who knows anything of the power of religion, and has experimental knowledge of it. For if you ask such people, in the very words of Scripture: Whether they know that Jesus Christ is in them, otherwise they are reprobates (2 Cor. 13:5). Whether Christ dwells in their hearts by faith (Eph. 3:17). Whether their sins are forgiven for Christ's name sake (1 John 2:12). Whether they have received an unction from the Holy One (1 John 2:20). Whether the love of God has been shed abroad in their hearts by the Holy Ghost (Rom. 5:5). Whether they are filled with joy and peace in believing (Rom. 15:13). Whether they walk in the comfort of the Holy Ghost, and do ever rejoice, with joy unspeakable and full of glory (Acts 9:31; 1 Peter 1:8), and lastly, whether the Holy Spirit bears witness with their own spirits that they are the children of God (Rom. 8:14–16). If, I say, you ask the better sort amongst us, whether they have any experience of these matters, they would stare at you with the utmost amazement, and would think you an enthusiast,[14] if they did not call you so.

Now such people who have all the form, but none of the power of religion; who are outwardly reformed, but not inwardly renewed by the Holy Ghost; these are what our Saviour called whited sepulchres, beautiful without, but full of rottenness within.[15] They are striving to enter into the kingdom of heaven but are not able; because they do not strive lawfully. For they do not seek to enter in through Jesus Christ, but partly through Christ, and partly through themselves; partly by faith and partly by works. These are the almost but not altogether Christians. And if at any time it happens, that some amongst us are seized with deep convictions, and are made sensible of their utter need of Christ, and that they can only be justified by faith in his blood; these people, not finding proper food for their souls in our churches, are obliged to go elsewhere, and seek it where they can find it. It is no wonder, therefore, that there are so few real Christians amongst us.

---

14 See April 1758.
15 Matthew 23:27.

If you read over the homilies[16] of the Church, if you read over the Fathers of the church, if you read the works of the good old Bishops that were published a hundred years ago, you will there find the gospel of Christ preached, and the true doctrine of our own church. But since that time, I mean in the last century, our Clergy have been gradually departing more and more from our doctrines, articles, and homilies; so that at length there was scarce a Clergyman to be found, but who preached contrary to the articles he subscribed. And almost all the sermons that have been published in the last century both by bishops and curates, are full of that soul-destroying doctrine, that we are to be justified partly by our own works, and partly by Christ's merits.

Do you ask how all the clergy came to fall into this pernicious doctrine? I answer, very easily. Every man, whilst he continues under the power of the carnal mind, and is not awakened to see his utter lost condition, is naturally disposed to embrace this doctrine. For not being yet convinced by the Spirit of God, that all his righteousness is as filthy rags (Isa. 64:6), and that he is without help and strength in himself (Rom. 5:6), I say, not being convinced of this, he naturally goes about to establish some righteousness of his own, and cannot submit to the righteousness of God by faith. Not being yet sensible of his utter lost and helpless state, he must have some reliance on himself; and thus, instead of looking wholly to Jesus Christ for salvation, he looks partly to Christ, and partly to himself; instead of seeking for righteousness and strength from the Lord Jesus Christ, he seeks for it partly from Christ, and partly from himself; instead of seeking to be justified in the Lord, he seeks after justification partly through the Lord, and partly through himself. But see what Christ saith of this matter (Isa. 45:22–25).

And now let me ask how the whole Church of Rome happened to depart from the simplicity of the gospel, and to fall into this doctrine of works and faith which we now preach? It was owing to the depraved nature of man, which makes him think himself to be something, and that he can do something, though he is nothing, and can do nothing to justify himself in God's sight.

At the reformation, our Church returned again to Jesus Christ, and placed justification on the gospel footing of faith only. And so it

---

16 Two volumes of set sermons (1547 and 1571) composed in the sixteenth century for the clergy. From that time they acquired status along with the Thirty-Nine Articles as being a repository of Anglican doctrine.

continues to this day; but though our articles and homilies continue sound and evangelic, yet our clergy have departed once more from both, and are advancing to Rome again with hasty strides; preaching, in spite of articles and subscription, that most pernicious, papistical, and damnable doctrine of justification by faith and works. Which doctrine, I am verily assured, no one can hold, and be in a state of salvation. But I trust God is once more visiting, in mercy, our poor distressed church. He raised up Mr. Whitefield[17] and Mr. Wesley[18] about twenty years ago, who have courageously and successfully preached up the doctrines of our church. And he is now daily raising up more and more clergymen. At Christmas last, I was informed, there were forty clergymen who were brought to the acknowledgement of the truth; and three more have been added to the faith within the last six weeks. And oh, for ever adored be the mercy of God in opening mine eyes and leading me to the knowledge of the truth as it is in Jesus!

I have sent you a couple of books,[19] and a pamphlet, and I make you a present of them. Read them over carefully; and before you begin to read at any time, always look up to the fountain of wisdom for light and direction. For if you rely on your own abilities, or other men's labours, God may keep you ignorant of his glorious gospel, as a punishment for your presumption and neglect of him.

When I sat down to write, I did not intend to have filled more than half a sheet, but when I took my pen in hand, I knew not how to lay it

---

[17] George Whitefield (1714–1770), an ordained clergyman of the Church of England, was the foremost Methodist preacher. Awakened in 1735, he began preaching in the open air in 1739 and quickly became a celebrity on both sides of the Atlantic. He paid his first visit to Everton later in the month, and subsequently Berridge was to preach regularly during the winter months at Whitefield's London chapels. For the only surviving letter from Berridge to Whitefield, see May 22, 1769.

[18] John Wesley (1703–1791) originally worked closely with Whitefield but quickly established a rival connexion espousing an Arminian theology. Although at first very much in the minority, the greater discipline of Wesley's connexion meant it would eventually become the predominant Methodist grouping. He was to make his first visit to Everton in November 1758. See July 16, 1759; November 22, 1760; and January 1, 1768.

[19] In *Fragment*, 23, there is a short postscript: "Let me advise you to read over Rawlin's book in the first place." This probably referred to a publication by the Independent minister Richard Rawlin (1687–1757), *Christ the Righteousness of His People, or the doctrine of justification by faith in him, represented by several sermons at Pinner Hall* (1741).

aside. I have written my sentiments with great freedom, and, I hope, without offence. May God give a blessing to what I have written; may he enlighten your eyes, as he hath done mine, adored be his mercy; may he lead you by his Spirit to the knowledge of the truth as it is in Jesus; and make you instrumental in bringing souls from darkness into light, and translating them out of the kingdom of Satan into the glorious kingdom of his dear Son. Amen, Amen.

John Berridge

SECOND LETTER TO A
NOTTINGHAMSHIRE CLERGYMAN[1]

Everton [July–August 1758]

Rev. and dear Sir,

...This I do, not through any pain for the contents of the letter, nor yet through the fear of paper war (which is almost as terrible a thing as a paper kite with a flaming Lanthorn[2] at the tail of it in a dark night) but out of civility to you. The letter was designed for your perusal: copies were taken of it, without my leave, or even my knowledge and I was as much displeased as yourself could be when first I heard it had been copied. But enough of this matter. You charge me with being a Moravian. Credulous mortal! Why do you not charge me with being a murderer? You have just as much reason to call me one as the other. If you had lived in this neighbourhood, you would have known that I am utterly detested and continually reviled by the Moravians.[3] And

---

[1] This is Berridge's response to the reply he received to his previous letter. It is taken from *Fragment*, 24–25, which was published without Berridge's permission. The publisher states: "The Reader may be assured, that these excellent letters are the Genuine productions of the Author, to whom they are ascribed. But though Copies of them are now in a thousand Hands, and the more Hands they are in, of the more extensive use they will be; yet the Writer refused to consent to the Publication of them, which one of my female Acquaintance here much wished for, and offered to undertake" (vi). In his introduction the publisher mocks Berridge as an antinomian and signs himself "Faith Workless." It is only part of the letter.

[2] Lantern.

[3] The Moravians played a leading part in the early years of the Evangelical Revival, both in their influence on Evangelical leaders and in their missionary and evangelistic work throughout the country. The church, originally from Moravia, had experienced revival as a community on the estate of Count Zinzendorf in Germany and had spread throughout the world. It is difficult to understand Berridge's extreme antagonism except in the normal prejudices because of their strict discipline, quietistic emphasis, use of strange theological terms, foreignness, community living, and accusations of antinomianism. Their financial collapse in 1753 after they incurred massive debts, as well as the

no wonder; for I warn all my hearers against them both in public and private. Nay, I have been to Bedford,[4] where there is a nest of them, to bear a preaching testimony against their corrupt principles and practices. However, since you are determined to call me a Moravian, and Mr. Wheler[5] is pleased to call me a mad man, I think myself obliged to come down into the country as soon as I can, and I hope it will be next summer, to convince my friends and your neighbourhood, and, with God's help, preach twice a day. Twice a day, you will say! Why then I am certainly mad, yea, and a Moravian too, and a murderer into the bargain. Well, be it so. I am much accustomed to hard names; and by

---

departure of Zinzendorf from England in 1755 after his failure to establish the centre of the whole movement in London, may also have underpinned Berridge's negative evaluations. During the 1750s there was a whole series of attacks on the theology and practice of the Moravians, ranging from the bishop of Exeter and Evangelicals such as Wesley and Whitefield to the unscrupulous propaganda of Henry Rimius and tabloid confessions of Andrew Frey. In Berridge's 1760 hymn book, which he later withdrew, he gives a caution "concerning some foreigners, who have entered our land under the Name of Moravians." He accuses them of ruining souls, getting money by flattery, financial improbity, and hypocrisy. He calls them "wolves in sheeps clothings" and finishes: "Deliver us, O Lord, from these locusts! And let them not lay waste thine heritage" (*Divine Songs,* xix-xxi). As some of Berridge's close friends (Venn, Thornton, Haweis) supported Moravian missions (see J.C.S. Mason, *The Moravian Church and the Missionary Awakening in England, 1760-1800* [Woodbridge, Boydell, and Brewer, 2001], 54–55), he may well have been embarrassed by these early views. Whitefield's *An Expostulatory Letter, Addressed to Nicholas Lewis, Count Zinzendorf* (G. Keith, 1753) may have influenced him. For an account of how the Moravians were viewed at this time, see ch. 13, "The Battle of the Books," in J. Hutton, *A History of the Moravian Church* (Moravian Publication Office, 1909), and Colin Podmore, *The Moravian Church in England, 1728-1760* (Oxford: Oxford University Press, 1998).

4   The Bedford group was founded in the early 1740s. Two of its leaders, Jacob Rogers (1715-1779) and Francis Okely (1719-1794), were contemporaries of Berridge at Cambridge. See Edwin Welch, ed., *The Bedford Moravian Church* and J.D. Walsh, "The Cambridge Methodists." In *Christian Spirituality: Essays in Honour of Gordon Rupp,* ed. Peter Brooks (Student Christian Movement, 1975), 251–283.

5   Granville Wheler (1701-1770), rector of West Leake (1737-1770), two miles north of Berridge's birthplace. It seems that his curate, Theophilus Henry Hastings, had been keeping his rector, who spent his time at his estate in Kent, informed of Berridge's preaching and his letters. Wheler was a scientist well known for his experiments in electricity. He had been elected to the Royal Society in 1728.

God's grace, am pretty well enabled to bear them. If your brethren will allow me the use of their pulpits they shall have my thanks; if they will not, the fields are open, and I shall take a mountain for my pulpit, and the heavens for my sounding board. My blessed Master has set me the example; and I trust I shall neither be ashamed nor afraid to tread in his steps. I send you this letter sealed, as indeed the other would have been could I have suspected what has happened....[6]

---

[6] The previous letter was read and copied without Berridge's permission.

To Mr. Pilkington[1]

November 28, 1758

He insists, that faith is the only thing necessary to justification; and proves it chiefly from Rom. and Gal. For he saith, St. Paul knew not how the first had been evangelised, and therefore writes as he would have preached to them at first, and accurately delineates the whole scheme of redemption, beginning with the ruin, and proceeding to the recovery, of mankind. The latter had been well taught; but seduced to rely partly on faith, partly on works, which he tells them was falling from grace, and reproves them more severely, than the immoral persons of other churches; and will not call them saints or churches of God, as he doth all others but simply churches of Galatia. In the other epistles we must not so much expect him to teach the rudiments of Christianity, to which however occasionally he points. When St. Paul saith, Rom. 3:20, that by the deeds of the law no man shall be justified,

---

[1] This is a summary by Archbishop Secker, with quotations, of a letter from Berridge to Mr. Pilkington. The Rev. Matthew Pilkington (1705–1765) was the vicar of Stanton by Dale (1734–1765), just eight miles north of Berridge's birthplace of Kingston-on-Soar. He also held the appointments of prebend of Ryton at Lichfield Cathedral (1748–1765) and rector of Fenny Bentley (1747–1765). He had graduated from Jesus College, Cambridge, in 1728 and was ordained the following year. He was well known as an author, producing *The Evangelical History and Harmony* (Bowyer, 1747) and *A Rational Concordance, or an Index to the Bible* (Ayscough, 1749). Secker tells us that on seeing the letter to Poynton, Pilkington wrote to Berridge on November 20, 1758, expressing his "sorrow that they differ so much in opinion, and referring him to his printed index to the Bible for proof, that Faith, though necessary, and the Foundation on which good works must be built, will be ineffectual without them." Secker gives a summary of Berridge's reply, saying that he repeated much of what he had said in his previous letter, as well as seemingly quoting from the letter directly. As in the July 3 letter Secker makes his own comments, showing his fundamental disagreement, on the opposite page of his manuscript book. This reported letter is important as it shows Berridge's theological thinking at this early stage of his preaching. He would later come to modify many of his early convictions. The letter is found in Thomas Secker's Cabinet papers, Lambeth Palace Library, MS 2595 ff. 83–90.

the preceding verses shows he means the moral law. So the curse Gal. 3:10 refers to Deut. 27:26 which relates to the moral law. Advising a sinner to repent and do better, is sending him to that law to save him, which must condemn him. Law, of God or man, as Law, can show no mercy. Dispensing with itself would be destroying itself. Besides, we can never do more than we ought: therefore we can never make amends for what we have done amiss. The Law like a harsh schoolmaster scourges us to Christ. And after faith is come, we are no longer under the schoolmaster.

"The world is apt to imagine, that Baptism brings us directly into a covenant of grace. Nothing like it. We must believe, as well as be baptised. I speak now in respect to adults, and such as are capable of faith. Where the Law is revealed, it binds; and when broken, denounces a curse; and nothing can remove it, but faith; which is not born with us, nor received at baptism, nor acquired by human learning, but communicated by God's Spirit to all, who having felt their lost estate, seek earnestly after it."

"[2]Faith is not in the head, but the heart, Rom. 10:9,10. It doth not consist in believing, that Christ came from heaven, and died for sinners, and rose again, and nor that he alone can save us. This the devils believe, yet have no faith. How [?] are to have it? Not from ourselves by any means. It is the gift of God. It is such a reliance on Christ, wrought on us by the Spirit, as assures our hearts, that God is reconciled to us. It is knowing that Christ loveth me, and hath died for me, Gal. 2:20. In short, it is receiving the forgiveness of our sins. Being justified by faith we have, not may have, peace with God, Rom. 5:1. To receive a pardon and not know it, is a flat contradiction. He that believeth hath, not shall have, eternal life, John 3:36. Believing ye rejoice with joy unspeakable, 1 Pet. 1:8, a joy, which many souls in my parish and neighbourhood happily experience. This is spoken in general of all that are Christians indeed. Some may say, this faith then is a very mysterious thing; so it is and so St. Paul saith, holding the mystery of the faith in a pure conscience, 1 Tim. 3:9. There is nothing more mysterious in believing the Scripture to be the word of God, than the *Iliad* to be Homer's.[3] There is moral proof for each.

---

[2]   The quotation marks open here but there are no closing quotation marks.
[3]   Ancient Greek epic poem set during the Trojan War and attributed to Homer (seventh or eighth century). With its sequel, the *Odyssey*, it is one of the oldest works in Western literature.

When we know, that God hath forgiven us, then and not before we begin to love him; though we may before have something, which seems like love and thankfulness which he saith was his case. Love will show itself in obedience, John 14:22. But both spring from faith and if the root die, the branches wither. But neither justifies, in whole or in part: but only faith which worketh by love. This is different from, partly faith, partly love producing works. And he speaks thus, to keep us from taking up with a notional dead belief, mentioned by James: mentioning the fruit, to make us distinguish the tree the better.

Our hearts are purified by faith, Acts 15:9: therefore not sanctified before we are justified; faith is our victory over the world. Thus we are justified before we overcome it. Christ doth not say, come unto me ye that are sanctified, and I will justify you: but come to me ye that are laden. And when he hath relieved them from the burden of guilt, they seek that of rest from the power of sin; Christ's mission is to heal the broken hearted. These are not yet sanctified. We are justified freely without the deeds of the law, Rom. 3:28, of that law, by which none can be justified, v.20, v.9, of the moral Law. Compare v.9 etc. and 4:5 saith, we are justified while we are ungodly. Thus Christ is to us first wisdom by showing us our state, then righteousness, then sanctification and lastly redemption from the power of the grave.

These things being so, in how deplorable a state is the Christian World! Most have little or no regard to their salvation. Yet methinks their case is still more pitiable, who aiming to be sanctified before they are justified, seek to enter into the kingdom of God, but shall not be able. Some again, who are truly enlightened by God's Spirit, and so have received Christ as wisdom, never receive him as righteousness: neglect to improve the grace given, so God withdraws it; and they become as insensible again, as if they had never been awakened. Others, when they have received Christ as Righteousness, after a while neglect to stir up the gift of faith: and so that and their love and obedience languish. Of these, some recover; others grow more remiss, and at length make shipwreck of their faith. Thus very few are truly enlightened: many of these, never justified: some of the justified, never sanctified.

All that believe are, not shall be, justified from what they could not by the Law of Moses, i.e., their own obedience.

Objection: If we are justified wholly by faith, how doth God reward every man according to his works? Answer: All are children of wrath by nature, and for actual sin. And if the regular and serious say, are not we better than others? God saith no in no wise: all are under Sin, Rom. 3:9. Now neither original nor actual sin damneth sinners. For there is a fountain set open, etc. But it is unbelief, Mark 16:16; John 3:18,36; Luke 12:46. But still the degree of punishment shall be in proportion to sins and so we are saved by faith: but our reward shall be in proportion to our good deeds.

Christians are said to be adopted. Adoption, which makes men children and heirs of God, is, as in men a gratuitory act. But each may declare an intention to portion out the inheritance according to the degree of good behaviour.

Whoever lives in the allowed practice of any one sin, hath no saving faith, but is a child of the devil, 1 John 3:8,9. But supposing a person forgiven could live wholly free from sin, and abound in all righteousness, he is justified only by faith; and if he seeks for any justification from his own works, he falls from grace and becomes a debtor to the whole Law. If a man lives exemplarily 80 years, and then commits a capital crime, the law will condemn him; and only an act of grace in the Lawgiver can reprieve him; and that may be procured by the mediation of the King's Son.

To an Unknown Recipient[1]

Everton, [May?] 1759

...On Sunday sennight[2] a man of Wyboston,[3] a Nathaniel[4] indeed, was so filled with the love of God during morning prayer that he dropped down, and lay as one dead for two hours. He had been so filled with love all the week before that he was often for a time unable to work.

On Sunday night last, as I was speaking in my house, there was a violent outcry. One soul was set at liberty. We sung near an hour, and the Lord released three more out of captivity.

On Monday sennight Mr. Hicks[5] accompanied me to Meldreth.[6] On the way we called at a farmer's house. After dinner I went into his yard, and, seeing near a hundred and fifty people, I called for a table, and preached, for the first time, in the open air.[7] Two persons were

---

1   This letter appears in the course of a report to John Wesley on events at Everton in May 1759, which Wesley subsequently published in his *Journal*. The author of the report, and recipient of the letter, has often been assumed to be Elizabeth Blackwell, wife of the banker Ebenezer Blackwell. In *Rise of Methodism*, however, Jonathan Rodell argues that the correspondent was John Walsh, a London Methodist, and that his companion, Mr. B__ll, was George Bell. See September 2, 1763. The extract is from *WW*, 21:199–200; *WB* (1838), 50–51; and *WB* (1864), xv.

2   A week.

3   A village about six miles north-west of Everton.

4   John 1:37: "Behold, an Israelite indeed in whom there is no deceit."

5   Samuel Hicks was rector of Wrestlingworth (1744–1796), a village about four miles due east of Everton. After initial hostility to Berridge—he forbade his parishioners to hear him—he was himself converted and itinerated with Berridge in the early days of revival. Walsh in Wesley's *Journal* reports Hicks as saying: "he was first convinced of sin August 1, 1758 and finding peace in about six weeks, first preached the gospel on September 17. From that time he was accounted a fool and a madman" (*WW*, 21:213). In 1766 he published six sermons entitled *Six Discourses on the Following Subjects: The Use of the Law —The Insufficiency of the Creature—The All-Sufficiency of Christ—The Effect of the Grace of God upon the Hearts and Lives of Professors—The Parable of the Sower* (J. and W. Oliver, 1766).

6   About ten miles south of Cambridge and twelve miles from Everton.

7   Whittingham says this was May 14, 1759. See *WB* (1864), xvi.

65

seized with strong convictions, fell down, and cried out most bitterly. We then went to Meldreth, where I preached in a field to about four thousand people. In the morning, at five, Mr. Hicks preached in the same field to about a thousand. And now the presence of the Lord was wonderfully among us. There was abundance of weeping and strong crying, and, I trust, beside many that were slightly wounded, near thirty received true heart-felt conviction.[8]

At ten we returned and called again at the farmer's house. Seeing about a dozen people in the brewhouse, I spoke a few words. Immediately the farmer's daughter dropped down in strong convictions. Another also was miserably torn by Satan, but set at liberty before I had done prayer. At four I preached in my own house, and God gave the Spirit of adoption to another mourner.

On Monday last I went to Shelford,[9] four miles from Cambridge, near twenty from Everton. The journey made me quite ill, being so weary with riding that I was obliged to walk part of the way. When I came thither a table was set for me on the common, and, to my great surprise, I found near ten thousand people round it, among whom were many gownsmen from Cambridge. I was hardly able to stand on my feet, and extremely hoarse with a cold. When I lifted up my foot to get on the table, a horrible dread overwhelmed me; but the moment I was fixed thereon I seemed as unconcerned as a statue. I gave out my text (Gal. 3:10,11) and made a pause, to think of something pretty to set off with; but the Lord so confounded me (as indeed it was meet, for I was seeking not his glory, but my own), that I was in a perfect labyrinth and found, if I did not begin immediately, I must go down without speaking. So I broke out with the first word that occurred, not knowing whether I should be able to add any more. Then the Lord opened my mouth, enabling me to speak near an hour, without any kind of perplexity; and so loud that everyone might hear. The audience behaved with great decency. When sermon was over, I found myself so cool and easy, so cheerful in spirit, and wonderfully strengthened in body, I went into a house, and spoke again near an hour to about two hundred people. In the morning I preached again to about a thousand. Mr. Hicks [is] engaged to preach in Orwell Field[10] on Tuesday

---

8 This charismatic account was cut in the first edition of *WB*. See *WB* (1838), 50–51.
9 Great Shelford is four miles south of Cambridge.
10 Orwell is ten miles east of Everton.

evening. I gave notice that I designed to preach on Monday sennight at Grantchester,[11] a mile from Cambridge.

Mr. Hicks and I have agreed to go into Hertfordshire; afterwards to separate, and go round the neighbourhood, preaching in the fields wherever a door is opened, three or four days in every week....

Believe me, your affectionate servant,

John Berridge

---

[11] Grantchester became a popular preaching station for Berridge since it was a convenient location for students and scholars to walk out to if they wished to hear him. It was from Grantchester that Berridge made contact with Rowland Hill. See December 18, 1764.

To James Berridge[1]

Everton, July 9, 1759

Dear Brother,

I am well in health, much better than I have been for many years; so well that I am now enabled to preach thirteen times in a week, and feel less inconvenience from this than I formerly did from preaching once a week. I was very low spirited for many years, and had cause to be so, and so have you now. Oh, dear brother, when will you begin to think? Death is coming apace, and you are not in a proper state to meet your Judge. As yet you are a stranger to your own wretchedness, and if you continue so you must certainly perish, and perish everlastingly. You have no interest in Christ, no pardon of your sins, no living faith in your Redeemer, nor at present any desire to partake of these blessings. Give my love to my sister.[2] May God raise both your affections up to things above, and make you wise unto salvation. I am, your affectionate brother,

John Berridge

---

[1] Written to his brother James. See also June 9, 1770. The letter is taken from *S* (1893), 28–29, a magazine that was started in 1862 by Septimus Sears (1819–1877), Strict Baptist minister at Clifton, only a few miles from Everton. This may be just the concluding section of the letter but because of Berridge's busy life at this time he may equally have had only a brief amount of time to keep up with his family. John Berridge (1683–1740) and Sarah Huthwaite (1681–1749) had five sons: John (1716–1793), James (1718–1772), Matthew (b.1720), Thomas (b.&d.1723) and Thomas (b.1725). James had presumably inherited some of his father's land as Berridge had. See May 3, 1773. At the time of Berridge's death only Thomas was alive, living at Chatteris and planning a book on his famous brother. See "Biography: The Late Rev. JOHN BERRIDGE…," *EM* (1793), 7.

[2] James's wife Theodosia Sheppard.

To John Wesley[1]

Everton, July 16, 1759

Dear Sir,

Mr. Hicks[2] and myself have been preaching in the fields for this month past, and the power of the Lord is wonderfully present with the word. We have been casting the gospel-net in the neighbourhood; but success at present only, or chiefly attends us in the eastern parts: and there we now direct the whole of our endeavours. Near twenty towns have received the gospel in a greater or less degree; and we continually receive fresh invitations, whenever we go out. The word is everywhere like a hammer, breaking the rock in pieces. People fall down, cry out most bitterly, and struggle so vehemently, that five or six men can scarcely hold them. It is wonderful to see how the fear of the Lord falls even upon unawakened

---

[1] The letter is taken from Wesley's own magazine, *AM* (1780), 611, and was presumably published at that time to reveal Berridge's "charismatic" past. The letter is a report on some of the sensational accompaniments of the religious revival, which later Berridge was to re-evaluate. At first, Berridge's relationship with Wesley had been close, but it later cooled due to Berridge's rejection of Wesley's teaching on sanctification—although he was initially influenced by it—his change in theology in adopting a more Calvinistic stance, and his independence of character, wishing to be his own man. Wesley's earliest evaluations of Berridge were positive. He described him to Lady Huntingdon as "one of the most simple as well as most sensible men of all whom it has pleased God to employ in reviving primitive Christianity" (John Wesley, *The Letters of the Rev. John Wesley, AM*, ed. John Telford, 8 vols. [Epworth Press, 1931], 4:58). He would later describe those who led the work at Everton in unfavourable terms: "None of them were more than 'babes in Christ', if any of them so much" (*WW*, 22:336). For an examination of their relationship, see ch. 12, "Relationship with Wesley and Changing Theology," in Pibworth, *Gospel Pedlar*. To explore the literature on Wesley, see Henry D. Rack, *Reasonable Enthusiast: John Wesley and the Rise of Methodism* (Epworth Press, 1989); Randy L. Maddox and Jason E. Vickers, *The Cambridge Companion to John Wesley* (Cambridge: Cambridge University Press, 2010); and Richard Heitzenrater, *The Elusive Mr. Wesley* (Nashville: Abingdon, 2003). See November 22, 1760 and January 1, 1768.

[2] Berridge's early preaching companion. See note May 1759.

sinners. When we enter a new village, the people stare, and laugh, and rail abundantly; but when we have preached night and morning, and they have heard the outcries of wounded sinners, they seem as much alarmed and terrified, as if the French were at their doors.[3] As soon as three or four receive convictions in a village, they are desired to meet together two or three nights in a week, which they readily comply with. At first they only sing; afterwards they join reading and prayer to singing: and the presence of the Lord is greatly with them. Let me mention two instances. At Orwell ten people were broken down in one night, only by hearing a few people sing hymns. At Grandchester,[4] a mile from Cambridge, seventeen people were seized with strong convictions last week, only by hearing hymns sung. When societies[5] get a little strength and courage, they begin to read and pray, and then the Lord magnifies his love as well as power amongst them by releasing souls out of bondage.

Of late, there has been a wonderful out-pouring of the spirit of love amongst believers. Insomuch that they have fainted under it, fallen down, and lain upon the ground, as dead, for some hours. And their bodies have been so weakened by these transports of joy, that they were not able to endure hard labour for some days afterwards. Before Mr. Hicks and myself preached abroad,[6] the enemy was menacing us much for going into houses and barns.[7]

I would not have you publish the account of A.T.[8] which Mr. W.[9]

---

3   Britain declared war on France in 1756; a treaty was signed in 1763 in Paris.

4   Grantchester.

5   Converts were joined together but not with strict rules and regulations as with some other Methodist leaders. For the importance of societies, see John Walsh, "Religious Societies: Methodist and Evangelical, 1738–1800," in W.J. Sheils and D. Wood, eds., *Voluntary Religion* (Studies in Church History 23), (Oxford: Blackwell, 1986), 279–302.

6   It was only recently that they had started preaching in the open air. See May 1759.

7   Berridge had started itinerating the previous summer and immediately his local squire and the Potton vicar (Rev. William Woodhouse) complained to the bishop and tried to have him removed. Local vicars and squires obviously opposed Berridge preaching within their parishes inside buildings let alone in the open air.

8   Ann Thorn, an early convert who experienced trances and visions. John Walsh reports to Wesley after a visit to Everton: "I discoursed also with Ann Thorn, who told me of much heaviness following the visions with which she had been favoured; but said she was at intervals visited still with such overpowering love and joy, especially at the Lord's Supper, that she often lay in a trance for many hours. She is twenty-one years old" (*WW*, 21:211).

9   John Walsh, a converted deist and correspondent of Wesley. His report about

has sent you. It might only prejudice people against the Lord's work in this place: and I find our friends in town begin to be in great pain about the work. They are very slow of heart to believe what they do not see with their own eyes. Indeed these things seem only designed for the spot on which they are wrought. What men see or hear they will be brought to credit. Men's attention is raised, and their prejudices against what is called a new doctrine removed by them. And thus the design of God is answered. But where people lie out of the reach of the doctrine, you will find them lie out of the reach of conviction. These signs are not for them, and so are disregarded by them. Give my love to Mr. Grimshaw,[10] and John Nelson,[11] and believe me your affectionate servant for Christ's sake,

John Berridge

---

the visit to Everton on June 2 is included in a letter to Wesley on June 21, 1758. See *AM* (1780), 103–105. He was also the writer of another account of the sensational events at Everton, which was included in Wesley's *Journal* for July 29, 1759. See *WW*, 21:211–221. See July 16, 1761.

[10] William Grimshaw (1708–1763), vicar of Haworth in Yorkshire. Famous for his passionate and racy preaching, his itineration as a gospel preacher and his pastoral care in his parish. See December 26, 1767.

[11] John Nelson (1707–1774), converted stonemason of Birstall who worked with both Ingham (see January 22, 1766) and Wesley and helped to establish Methodism in many places in West Yorkshire. See Thomas Jackson, *The Lives of Early Methodist Preachers, chiefly written by themselves* (Wesleyan Conference Office, 1871).

To John Wesley[1]

Everton, November 22, 1760

Dear Sir,

I received your letter from Ireland, and purposely delayed my answer till your return to England, that I might not write in a spirit unbecoming the gospel. I wish all that love the Lord Jesus Christ were perfectly agreed in their religious sentiments; but this, I find, is a matter rather to be wished than expected. And perhaps a little disagreement, in nonessentials, may be designed as one part of our trial, for the exercise of our candour and patience. I discourage the reading of any books, except the Bible and the Homilies,[2] not because of the jealousy mentioned by you, but because I find they who read many books usually neglect the Bible, and soon become eager disputants, and in the end

---

[1] Wesley had written a very critical letter to Berridge from Dublin on April 18, 1760. Twenty years later Wesley published his letter with the criticisms in italics. See *AM* (1780), 499. Berridge's reply was not published until after Wesley's death. See *AM* (1797), 305–306. Wesley complains that Berridge is stubborn, proud, hard to convince, critical of others, independent by wishing to remain unconnected and that he changes hymns and discourages new converts from reading anything except the Bible. He finishes his strong letter by saying: "I can hardly imagine that you discourage reading even our little tracts, out of jealousy, lest we should undermine you or steal away the affections of the people. I think you cannot easily suspect this. I myself did not desire to come among them; but you desired me to come. I should not have obtruded myself either upon them or you; for I have really work enough, full as much as either my body or mind is able to go through; and I have, blessed be God, friends enough—I mean, as many as I have time to converse with. Nevertheless, I never repented of that I spent at Everton; and I trust it was not spent in vain" (*Letters of John Wesley*, 4:93).

[2] Berridge moderated his position and later distributed large quantities of literature in his area, much of it supplied by his rich friend, John Thornton. His fear of neglecting the Scriptures can be understood against the background of his many years of study at Cambridge, when he considered he made little spiritual progress. See July 3, 1758, for how he viewed academic study in the light of his conversion and his letter to Miss L__ on May 6, 1792, where he calls such learning "useless lumber, that wisdom of the world which is foolishness with God."

turn out Predestinarians.[3] At least, this has so happened with me. If my sentiments do not yet altogether harmonise with yours, they differ the least from yours of any others'. And as there is nothing catching or cankering[4] in those sentiments of yours which are contrary to mine, I am not only willing but desirous you should preach at Everton, as often as you can favour us with your company.[5] Last week, I was at Bedford, and preached to your society; from whom I heard you were returned from the west, and purposed to come amongst us soon. Will you call at Everton, as you go to, or return from Bedford? You will be welcome. My invitation is sincere and friendly; accept of it.

I send my love to your brother,[6] and to all that labour among you. May grace, mercy, and peace be multiplied on you, and your affectionate servant,

John Berridge

---

3   Those who believe in predestination, that individual salvation is solely due to God's sovereign grace and election. Berridge himself was later to become a convinced predestinarian or Calvinist.

4   Ensnaring and corrupting.

5   Wesley took up the invitation and was at Everton next on February 4, 1761.

6   Charles Wesley (1707–1788), the youngest son of Samuel and Susanna Wesley. He was actively involved with his brother John in evangelical activities in his early days. Although famous for his hymns, he has been overshadowed by his brother in scholars' works in terms of his influence on Methodism and the eighteenth-century revival. More recent books reappraise Charles's position and impact. See Gareth Lloyd, *Charles Wesley and the Struggle for Methodist Identity* (Oxford: Oxford University Press, 2007) and Kenneth G.C. Newport and Ted A. Campbell, eds., *Charles Wesley: Life, Literature and Legacy* (Peterborough: Epworth Press, 2007). For an overview of his life from his own works, see John R. Tyson, *Charles Wesley: A Reader* (Oxford: Oxford University Press, 1989).

To the Rev. Alexander Coats[1]

Everton, April 22, 1761

Dear Sir,

I received your letter, and dare not say I am sorry for your fall, nor indeed for any afflictions that God layeth upon his children; they are all[2] tokens of his fatherly love, and needful physic for us; rather would I pray that whilst God keepeth you in the furnace, you may be still, and feel your dross and tin purged[3] away. The Lord Jesus gives me a dose of physic frequently;[4] and I am never so well as when I am taking it, although I frequently make wry faces thereat: and if your heart be anything like mine it will need many a bitter potion to cleanse and strengthen it.

Why do you write to me with so much reverence, and make so many apologies for writing? Is this becoming language from one sinner to another? Ought the dust of the earth to elevate itself above its kindred ashes? Or should a frog croak out a compliment to a toad? It will make me swell the more, and spit out the more poison.[5] And need I this? Nay if you love me, do not hurt me. I do not want to be taught to think too highly[6] of myself; the devil and my own corrupt heart

---

[1] This is probably Alexander Coats, a Scotsman who, Wesley says, when noting his death in 1765, was the "oldest preacher in our connexion" (*WW*, 22:23), meaning the longest-serving itinerant. Coats is obviously having problems with Wesley's doctrine of sanctification-perfection at this time, as Wesley, in a letter of July 21, 1761, answers a letter on the same subject by him (*Letters of John Wesley*, 4:157–159). *The Missionary Magazine: A Periodical Monthly Publication* (1801), 162–163, which has this letter as 1769, seems the earlier text. It is also in *WB* (1838), 364–366, and *WB* (1864), 361–362, where it was considerably edited, with several minor differences. I have noted the more significant changes adopted by the editor of Berridge's *Works*, changes made presumably in the light of Berridge being influenced by Wesley's doctrine of sanctification during his early years at Everton.

[2] *WB* omits "all."

[3] *WB* has "purging."

[4] *WB* has "most days."

[5] Sentence is omitted in *WB*.

[6] *WB* has "taught well of myself."

teach this daily, and he is so skilful a doctor in this[7] business, that he needeth not a helping hand from God's own children. Before you write to me again look into yourself, and if you find anything there that causeth loathing,[8] then sit down and write to John Berridge, as you would write to another A.C.[9] I find you have got to your crutches; well, thank God for a crutch to help a lame leg: this both sheweth and helpeth your weakness. And truly, friend, my case[10] is just the same as your own: I am not able to walk one step without a crutch, so lame I am. The wood comes from Calvary. And my crutch is Christ my Saviour;[11] and a blessed one he is. And oh, let me lean my whole weight here;[12] whilst I am walking through this wilderness-world![13]

Last Candlemas[14] I betook myself wholly to crutches; till then I was not sensible of my own utter[15] lameness, and did not know that Christ was to be my whole strength, as well as my[16] righteousness. I saw then[17] his blood alone[18] could purge away the guilt of sin. Thinking I had some native strength against the power of sin[19] I accordingly laboured to tear out[20] my own corruptions, and force away my own perverse will.[21] Labouring in the fire[22] at length God hath shewn me that John Berridge can never drive the devil out of himself; but Jesus Christ, blessed be his name, says to a legion,[23] "Come out." I see that faith alone can purify the heart and pacify[24]

---

7   *WB* has "his own."

8   *WB* has "something."

9   *WB* has "Alexander Coats."

10 *WB* has "cross."

11 *WB* omits "my Saviour."

12 *WB* has "upon him."

13 *WB* omits "world."

14 February 2. The feast of the purification of the Virgin Mary or presentation of Christ in the Temple. *WB* adds "day."

15 *WB* omits "utter."

16 *WB* omits "my."

17 *WB* omits "then."

18 *WB* omits "alone."

19 "Thinking I had…sin" is omitted in *WB*.

20 *WB* changes to "cut out."

21 *WB* has "and fray away my own will."

22 *WB* has "but laboured in the fire."

23 Legion was the man possessed with many demons living in the tombs whom Jesus cured. Luke 8:26–39.

24 *WB* has "purify."

the conscience; and Christ is become my all in everything,[25] my all in wisdom, in justification, sanctification and complete[26] redemption.[27] Prayer and faith, two handmaids never to be separated—are to carry me through the wilderness; and whilst I am diligent in the use of God's appointed blessed ordinances, I am then to sit still, and quietly wait for the salvation of God. And since God has shown me that he alone is to work all this work in me,[28] I see very clearly that he can as fully remove all the corruption of my heart, as all the guilt of my sins; that he can as perfectly restore me to his image, as to his favour;[29] that[30] Jesus Christ is called the second Adam, because he is to restore to us the whole of what we lost in the first.[31] This, I know, is God's good will, because I

---

[25] *WB* has "Christ is worthy to be my all in everything."

[26] *WB* omits "complete."

[27] 1 Corinthians 1:30.

[28] *WB* misses out "And since God has shown me that he alone is to work all this work in me."

[29] Wesley, writing later in the year (November 29), recounts the experience: "We had a comfortable lovefeast, at which several declared the blessings they had found lately. We need not be careful by what *name* to call them, while *the thing* is beyond dispute. Many have, and many do daily experience an unspeakable change. After being deeply convinced of inbred sin, particularly of pride, anger, self-will, and unbelief, in a moment they *feel* all faith and love—no pride, no self-will, or anger; and from that moment they have continual fellowship with God, always rejoicing, praying, and giving thanks. Whoever ascribes such a change to the devil, I ascribe it to the Spirit of God. And I say, let whoever feels it wrought, cry to God that it may continue; which it will, if he walks closely with God—otherwise it will not" (*WW*, 21:344). See John Wesley, *A Plain Account of Christian Perfection*. It seems that Berridge is waiting for some experience of sanctification while he puts his full confidence in Christ in this matter (he will rest on Christ fully as his crutch) as he did for his justification. John Walsh reports in a letter to Charles Wesley concerning the doctrine of perfection that he heard that Berridge was persuaded to believe the doctrine on January 14, 1761, in a love feast, although this seems to be contradicted by this letter. See John Walsh to Charles Wesley, August 11–15, 1762, MARC, EMV-134 3, in which Walsh comments that Berridge finally opposed the doctrine of perfection after receiving a letter sent by himself on May 28, 1761, outlining his own experiences and the experiences of others. For the background of the controversy in the early 1760s, see Robert Webster, *Methodism and the Miraculous: John Wesley's Idea of the Supernatural and the Identification of Methodists in the Eighteenth Century* (Lexington: Emeth Press, 2014), 134–144. See September 2, 1763.

[30] *WB* has "favour. And."

[31] *WB* has "the whole of what he died for."

have his blessed word for the truth thereof, that we should be "renewed in the spirit of our minds."[32] For this my spirit waiteth, for this my soul longeth and hungreth,[33] for this my flesh and heart cry out unto the Lord. Come, Lord, and fill me, take me, and make me wholly thine. Great persecutions, and vile proceedings await us. Satan is indeed let loose, but his time is short.[34] Lord, increase my faith and patience.

Give my kind love to all your fellow labourers.[35] May the Lord water your soul and vineyard, and teach you to know and teach[36] nothing but Jesus Christ and him crucified,[37] for whose sake, I am your servant,

John Berridge

---

[32] Ephesians 4:23.

[33] *WB* omits "hungreth."

[34] See Revelation 20:7. See September 25, 1773, for Berridge's views on the millennium still to come.

[35] *WB* adds "Great persecutions…your fellow labourers."

[36] *WB* has "preach" instead of "teach."

[37] *WB* omits "and him crucified."

To John Walsh[1]

Received July 16, 1762

Dear Sir,

I received your letter of July 1 and a former of March[2] which I returned no answer, because I know not how to speak or write to perfect people, and therefore avoid correspondence with them. Many things I saw in them, when at London, which grieved me much; and many things here in the country which have grieved me more. Such pride! Such boasting! Such censoriousness! Such contempt of others! But what is mighty strange, these perfect people still talk of growing. If they are really perfect, what can be lacking, except to continue in that state? As far as I can discern, they are unwillingly growing or grown out of Christ. They apply to the Lord for grace by prayer and faith, and grace is obtained: with this stock they set up, and trade against the Redeemer, not seeking, as Paul says, to be presented perfect in Christ, Col. 1:28, but to be presented perfect in themselves.

---

[1] John Walsh had met Berridge when investigating the initial revival at Everton. He sent reports of Berridge and the revival to Wesley. See *WW*, 21:211–221, and *AM* (1780), 103–105. This extract is contained in a long letter to Charles Wesley by Walsh in which he gives an account of his life and outlines his own experiences of the doctrine of perfection, particularly as it affected some of the London societies in the early 1760s. The extract is found in MARC, EMV-134, 5–6. Robert Webster has produced a transcript of Walsh's letter to Charles Wesley as Appendix 2 in his *Methodism and the Miraculous*, 209–225.

[2] Numeral missing—manuscript cut.

To Lady Huntingdon[1]

Everton, November 16, 1762

My Lady,

I received your letter from Brighthelmstone,[2] and did not return

---

[1] The letter is taken from CHCA (Letter 1) and is a copy made by A.C.H. Seymour. He included an extract in his *Life of Huntingdon*, 1:323–324. No letters to Lady Huntingdon are included in the first edition of *WB* (1838). The extract is also included in the second edition of *WB* (1864), 445, and stopped at "my Master's business." It was also published in *The Free Church of England Magazine and Harbinger of the Countess of Huntingdon Connexion* (1867), 248–249. The Countess of Huntingdon (1707–1791) was one of the outstanding leaders of the Evangelical Revival. After the death of her husband in 1746 she devoted her money, property and energy to the cause. Her houses were preaching stations; she appointed chaplains, built chapels on her property, founded a college, and knew and helped most of the Evangelical leaders and clergy of the time. During the early revival at Everton in 1759 she had sent two of her chaplains to give her a report on the work, and in 1760 she visited Everton herself to meet Berridge and hear the preaching. She persuaded Berridge to return to London with her to preach in her house. The letters of Berridge to Lady Huntingdon reveal an open and frank relationship, which was most unusual against the eighteenth-century background of rank, class and propriety. R.A. Knox comments: "In all that galaxy of Evangelists there is only one (apart from Wesley himself) who writes to her with no hint of approaching her on all fours—Berridge of Everton" (*Enthusiasm*, 488). Lady Huntingdon was strong-minded, but Berridge had his own will. For a modern sympathetic biography, see Faith Cook, *Selina, Countess of Huntingdon: Her Pivotal Role in the Eighteenth-Century Evangelical Awakening* (Edinburgh: Banner of Truth, 2001). For her influence through the groups associated with her, see Alan Harding, *The Countess of Huntingdon's Connexion: A Sect in Action in Eighteenth-Century England* (Oxford: Oxford University Press, 2003). Edwin Welch, *Spiritual Pilgrim: A Reassessment of the Life of the Countess of Huntingdon* (Cardiff: University of Wales Press, 1995) is also valuable.

[2] Lady Huntingdon established her first proprietary chapel in Brighton (Brighthelmstone) in 1761, a town she had initially visited in 1757, seeking the benefits of sea-bathing for one of her children who was sick. The small chapel was next to the house that she had acquired in North Street. It was enlarged in 1767 because of the success of the work. Berridge had spent some time at

a speedy answer because I would not send a hasty determination. I have now had time to weigh the contents, and the more I weigh them, the less heart I find to the journey. Indeed, I cannot see my call to Brighthelmstone; and I ought to see it for myself, not another for me. Was any good done when I was there? It was God's doing, all the glory be to him. This shows I did not then go without my Master, but it is no proof of a second call. Many single calls have I had to villages when some good was done, but no further call. I am not well able to ride so long a journey, and my heart is utterly set against wheel-carriages in these roads.³ Indeed I see not my call; I cannot think of the journey; and therefore pray your Ladyship to think no more of it. I write thus plainly, not out of frowardness,⁴ I trust, but to save your Ladyship the trouble of sending a second request, and myself the pain of returning a second denial. You threaten me, Madam, like a Pope, not like a mother in Israel, when you declare roundly, that God will scourge me if I do not come; but I know your Ladyship's good meaning, and this menace was not despised. It made me slow in resolving, and of course slow in writing: it made me also attend to the state of my own mind during its deliberation, which was as follows.

Whilst I was looking towards the sea, partly drawn thither with the hope of doing good, and partly driven by your *Vatican Bull*,⁵ I found nothing but thorns in my way; but as soon as I turned my eyes from it, I found peace. And now, whilst I am sending a peremptory denial, I feel no check or reproof within, which I generally do, when I am not willing to go about my Master's business.

How hard it is to look unto Jesus! So to look as to see him full of grace! To see him all fullness and beauty, and self all emptiness and deformity. My heart has been roaming after baubles (for everything is a bauble but Christ), and much perplexed with care, since I saw your

---

Brighton even before the opening of the chapel in July 1761. He may have been there in the previous autumn or winter.

³ The editor of *WB* (1864) misses this line out. Daniel Defoe, in *A Tour Through England* (1724–1727), and Arthur Young, in *English Tours* (1768–1771), described the hazards of travel, with ruts several feet deep and the constant risk of being thrown or breaking down. However, due to the growth of the turnpike trusts, where tolls were levied on the users, main roads witnessed a vast improvement as the century progressed.

⁴ Being perverse or unreasonable.

⁵ A command or edict issued by the Pope. See October 20, 1771, where Berridge speaks of Pope Joan (Lady Huntingdon) and Pope John (John Wesley).

Ladyship. Again I have been in Moses his chair, and again in Moses his school. I have loved him and preached him again, and he has flogged me again and again for my pains.[6] All my errands to Jesus have been to steal, and to steal spices and flowers from him, to garnish my own chamber and perfume my own nostrils. But the dear Emmanuel has lately detected me in the theft, and to show his indignation thereat, has given me some glimpses of his own adorable righteousness. They were transient, indeed, but, oh! they have ravished my heart. I love him, and hate myself. What a thief and a villain I am! Give me, Lord, a little more and more of thine eye-salve,[7] for I am yet very blind. I have seen the grapes of Eshcol,[8] and the sight has made my mouth water. And surely nothing kills sin and humbles self like such a sight. Lord, I would see more of thee—I would see the King in his beauty. Haste, and show thyself to a poor sinner—to every one that is ignorant of thy righteousness; to John Wesley,[9] as well as to

John Berridge

---

[6] Berridge is referring to seeking sanctification from the law rather than Christ.

[7] Revelation 3:18.

[8] Evidences of wonder of the Promised Land for the children of Israel. Numbers 13:23. Berridge desires to see more of the glory and righteousness of Christ. Such an appreciation will sanctify.

[9] A reference to Wesley's perfectionist views. See July 16, 1759.

To Lady Huntingdon[1]

Everton, May 18, 1763

My Lady,

Every day for this fortnight I have been purposing to write to you but could not pluck up a heart to take hold of my pen, so weak and slow are my spirits. It is shame, mere shame that goads me now to the task; and a task it now is, rather than a free-will offering. Weak spirits and a weak faith are very tottering companions; one blast of wind blows them both down. How hard it is to be brought out of self, that harlequin,[2] which puts on a thousand shapes, plays a thousand tricks, and though ever undressing has always a doublet left behind: an harlequin that will never cease to play the fool, till the scene of life is over. Long have I sought to get rid of self, that I might find some rest in myself. What folly, what absurdity, what contradiction was here! Get rid of self, to rest in self! And yet every man is guilty of this absurdity who takes comfort in himself through anything in himself. He may seem to deny himself, but it is only to please himself, just as the miser tormenteth self by a starving table, in order to please self by a thriving purse. And are there not thousands of such spiritual misers, who are daily pinching off ruffles,[3] and pinching off tempers, and pinching off tea, daily stripping self of something, that self may glory in this stripping? Oh, what a labyrinth is the heart of man! Blessed be God for a good Christ. But how little do I know of him, how little can I trust in Him. Lord, show me thy glory; then shall I live to thy glory. Oh, this self, self, self! I am weary of it—very weary, Lord, thou knowest. Turn mine eyes and mine heart unto thee, and to thee only. Heavy laden I come to thee; help me, O my God. What a

---

[1] This letter is found in CHCA (Letter 2), copied by Seymour, and *FCEM* (1867), 291–292. The letter is addressed to "The Right Honourable the Countess of Huntingdon, Hill Street, Berkeley Square, London."
[2] Harlequin is a clown-like figure in the theatre, a precursor of a pantomime role, who, through his dance, costumes, tricks, and masks, frustrates the other players on-stage.
[3] Ornamental frills on a garment.

monster of absurdity is self, which can glory in fine grace as much as in a fine coat, and feed as heartily on a sweet temper as on a swinish lust. Nothing comes amiss to self, except Christ. Self can be a tyrant or a slave, a spendthrift or a muckworm,[4] an ant or a drone[5]; and to enrich itself with temporals or spirituals, can take up with a hair shirt or a bed of boards, can take up with anything but Christ.

I have not forgotten Lady Selina[6] in my poor prayers. Has the Lord remembered her? I have never been on horseback since I saw your Ladyship, and never free from pain since I wrote to you. The visitation and confirmations will be held next month[7]; and my attendance here will not be wanted after next month, till Michaelmas; my hay-harvest[8] will also be over by that time, so that if I am wanted anywhere I am able to stir. I shall be at leisure the beginning of July. May the Lord make me ready to every good word and work. I am, with all due respect, your Ladyship's obliged and dutiful servant,

John Berridge

---

4 Worm that lives on muck. Figuratively a money-grubber.

5 Non-worker.

6 Lady Selina Hastings, Lady Huntingdon's youngest daughter, who was born on December 3, 1737, and died on May 12, 1763. She was taken ill on April 26, 1763, although at first it was not thought to be serious. Lady Huntingdon was very close to her youngest daughter, particularly in the light of her family circumstances: her older daughter, Elizabeth, had married and moved to Ireland; three of her other children had died (George and Ferdinando in 1743 and more recently Henry in 1758); and her relationship with her eldest son, Francis, was strained. Selina Hastings had been a solace to her mother, and they were rarely apart. Services at Oat Hall, where she was staying, were suspended during her daughter's illness. They recommenced in June. Obviously the news of Lady Selina's death had not yet reached Berridge.

7 The new bishop of Lincoln (1761–1779) performing the inspection and confirmations was none other than John Green, who had led the theological criticism of Berridge's account of his conversion and his exposition of justification by faith alone. See July 14, 1758.

8 Berridge's income (living) came chiefly from the tithe on the produce of the parish and from glebe land that was farmed or rented out.

To Lady Huntingdon[1]

Everton, June 23, 1763

My Lady,

I received your letter from Brighthelmstone,[2] and hope you will soon learn to bless your Redeemer for snatching away your daughter so speedily.[3] Methinks I see great mercy in the suddenness of her removal, and when your bowels have done yearning for her, you will see it too. Oh, what is she snatched from? Why, truly, from the plague of an evil heart, a wicked world, and a crafty devil—snatched from all such bitter grief as now overwhelms you—snatched from everything that might wound her ear, afflict her eye, or pain her heart. And what is she snatched to? To a land of everlasting peace, where the voice of the turtle is ever heard,[4] where every inhabitant can say, "I am no more sick," no more whim[5] in the head, no more plague in the heart, but all full of love and full of praise, ever seeing with enraptured eyes, ever blessing with adoring hearts that dear Lamb who has washed them in his blood, and has now made them Kings and Priests unto God for ever and ever.[6] Amen.

Oh Madam! What would you have? Is it not better singing in heaven, "Worthy is the Lamb that was slain"[7] etc., than crying at Oat Hall, "O wretched woman that I am?"[8] Is it not better for her

---

[1]   This letter is found in CHCA (Letter 3), a copy by Seymour; *Evangelical Register, or Magazine for the Connexion of the Late Countess of Huntingdon* (1828), 14–15; Seymour, *Life of Huntingdon*, 1:356–357; *WB* (1864), 446–447; and *FCEM* (1867), 292–293. *WB* (1864) edits the letter into longer sentences. The letter is addressed to "The Right Honourable the Countess of Huntingdon at Oat-Hall, near Cookfield, Sussex." It must be one of the most unusual consolation letters ever written.

[2]   See November 16, 1762.

[3]   Lady Selina Hastings died after a short illness.

[4]   Song of Solomon 2:12.

[5]   I think he means lightness, folly, and stupidity.

[6]   Revelation 1:6.

[7]   Revelation 5:12.

[8]   Romans 7:24.

to go before, than to stay after you? and then to be lamenting, "Ah my mother!" as you now lament, "Ah my daughter!"[9] Is it not better for her to go as she did, than tarry a while with you, to fill you with anxious concern, lest she should turn to the world again?[10] Is it not better to have your Selina taken to heaven, than to have your heart divided between Christ and Selina? If she was a silver idol before, might she not have proved a golden one afterwards? How many fears and cares are you released from by her removal! Yea, how much creature idolatry! And can you wish her in a better place, can you wish her in better company? Should you not like to be there yourself? How can you then be so abominably selfish as to wish her away? How can you wish her so much misery as to be at Oat Hall?[11] She is gone to pay a most blessed visit, and will see you again by and by, never to part more. Had she crossed the sea and gone to Ireland,[12] you could have borne it; but now she is gone to heaven 'tis almost intolerable. Wonderful strange love this! Such behaviour in others would not surprise me, but I could almost beat you for it; and I am sure Selina would beat you too, if she was called back but one moment from heaven, to gratify your fond desires. I cannot soothe you, and I must not flatter you. I am glad the dear creature is gone to heaven before you. Lament, if you please, but glory, glory, glory, be to God, says

John Berridge

---

9 Elisha's response to Elijah going up to heaven: "My father, my father…" (2 Kings 2:12).

10 Seymour, *Life of Huntingdon*, and *WB* (1864) both cut this sentence.

11 Seymour, *Life of Huntingdon*, and *WB* (1864) both cut "How many fears… at Oat Hall." The owner of this house some eight miles north of Brighton approached Lady Huntingdon with the idea that she rent it and use it as part of her mission to this part of Sussex. She converted it into a place of worship, using part of it for herself and visiting preachers. Berridge, along with any others, stayed there. It is near Wivelsfield.

12 Lady Huntingdon's daughter, Elizabeth, the Countess of Moira (1731–1808), lived in Ireland. See May 18, 1763.

To Lady Huntingdon[1]

June 27, 1763

Dear Lady,

I received your letter of the 20th the day after I wrote to you, which letter was delayed because I could send you no intelligence about my coming to Oat Hall. I cannot stir till Mr. Madan[2] or Mr. Haweis[3] comes to Everton; and when either of them may come I cannot say, though I expect one of them soon. As soon as they send me notice I will inform you of it. Seldom anything succeeds to my mind, whilst I am anxious about it. And I fancy you will scarce hear me preach at Oat Hall, till you are grown mighty indifferent about me.

My poor clay ever wants to teach God how to be a good potter;

---

[1] This letter is found in CHCA (Letter 4) as a copy by Seymour; ex. in Seymour, *Life of Huntingdon*, 1:357–358; *WB* (1864), 447; and *FCEM* (1867), 308–309. *WB* (1864) misses out the first and last paragraphs, and changes the odd word. It seems that Berridge feels that his letter four days previously may have been too blunt and caused unnecessary pain.

[2] Martin Madan (1725–1790) was a barrister who was converted through hearing a sermon by Wesley, having attended in order to mock and mimic him. He was chaplain of Lock Hospital from 1750 until 1780 and was sent by Lady Huntingdon with Romaine to investigate the work at Everton in 1759. He was an unusual man with many gifts, who later disgraced himself by advocating polygamy in certain cases—he believed a seducer should be compelled to marry his victim even if he was already married. He put forward his ideas in his book *Thelyphthora; or, a treatise on female ruin, in its causes, effects, consequenes, prevention, and remedy; considered on the basis of the divine law*, 2 vols. (Dodsley, 1780), as a solution to the problems of prostitution. For an account of his life, the controversy that ruined him, and a bibliography of his extensive writings, see Falconer Madan, *The Madan Family and Maddens in Ireland and England* (Oxford: Oxford University Press, 1933).

[3] Thomas Haweis (1733/4–1820) formed the second Holy Club while at Oxford. He moved to Aldwincle, Northamptonshire, in 1764 after success at Oxford, helping Joseph Jane, vicar of St. Mary Magdalen, and assisting Madan at Lock Hospital. He attracted immense congregations at Aldwincle and became executor and trustee to Lady Huntingdon and a founder of the London Missionary Society. See A. Skevington Wood, *Thomas Haweis, 1734–1820* (SPCK, 1957).

and may not your Dresden[4] have something in it which resembles my delf?[5] You would not, like Uzzah, lay your hand on the ark of God[6]; but may you not be too solicitous about a driver of the cart? and a blinder hobgoblin than myself you need not desire.[7] Indeed I am so dissatisfied with my own carting, that, if I durst, I should throw the whip out of my hands. Every hour I lose my way; every day forget what I learnt the day before; neither instruction nor correction mends me. Yea, verily, though I know myself to be a most stupid ass, yet at times I am a most conceited ass also. Though not fit to drive a dung-cart, yet at some certain seasons I can fancy myself qualified to be the King's coachman. And nothing so much discovers to me the sovereign hypocrisy of my heart, as when anyone is so cruelly kind as to tell me that all the mean things I say of myself are very true. Nay, if your Ladyship should send me word, that you really think me that hobgoblin which I seem to think myself, and fully think myself to be, it might put me so much out of conceit with you as to fancy that your Dresden was no better than my delf. Oh! I am sick, sick, mighty sick of this self. How can you but rejoice for that happy creature who was delivered from this self, almost as soon as she felt the curse of it?

If I should come soon to town, and take a place in the Brighthelmstone coach, where must it set me down? At Lewis or Brighthelmstone?[8] And how must I come from thence to Oat Hall? By your last I find your heart is yet very sore. May the Lord bind up your wounds. I am, your much obliged and dutiful servant,

John Berridge

Low I am in body, and daily sinking lower.

---

4   A delicate white porcelain from Dresden in Saxony. Higher-class clay!
5   Either a kind of glazed earthenware made at Delft in Holland or a sod dug out of the ground. Lower-class clay! *FCEM* changes to "myself."
6   Uzzah reached out to stop the ark from falling from a cart and was killed. 2 Samuel 6:6.
7   Berridge thinks that Lady Huntingdon cannot question the purposes of God, but she can criticize and question Berridge.
8   Presumably the coach travelled down a route a little away from Wivelsfield, perhaps taking in Tunbridge Wells and Uckfield, Lewes being the last stop before Brighton. Lewes is eight miles north-east of Brighton.

To Lady Huntingdon[1]

Everton, July 3, 1763
My Lady,

I received your letter of the 30th of June this minute, and wait for a supply from London to send me packing to Oat Hall. I have written to Mr. Madan[2] this post to know positively when he or Mr. Haweis[3] can come to Everton. I cannot have an answer till Friday, and when the answer comes, you shall know its contents. I have not written to Mr. Dyer[4]; because his coming down would not help me to Oat Hall—it would only bring me to Tottenham.[5] The exchange with him must be when I return from Oat Hall to London. I dare not write to Mr. Dyer now, because I know the Tottenham congregation would grumble exceedingly to have the whole care of the chapel devolve on

---

[1] This letter is found in CHCA (Letter 5), as copied by Seymour. There are very short extracts in Seymour, *Life of Huntingdon*, 1:358, and in *WB* (1864), 448. *FCEM* (1867), 309–311, has the full letter. It has the same address as the preceding letter. Written Sunday evening.

[2] See June 27, 1763.

[3] See June 27, 1763.

[4] George Dyer. After a short curacy in Birmingham he served the chapel in Tottenham Court Road and the Tabernacle in Upper Moorfields during the illness of Whitefield and was associated with that work for several years. In 1766 he took charge at Everton while Berridge was absent. Berridge was not pleased with his influence at Everton. See March 6, 1766. In 1770 he was appointed to a lectureship at St. George's, Southwark.

[5] Whitefield built Tottenham Court Road Chapel in 1756 as a result of violent opposition at Long Acre Chapel, on the edge of London's theatre district, which he had been using since his return from America in 1755. The new congregation could attend beyond the reach of the rioters. "The building was of double brick construction and appears to have had two galleries on each of three sides. It immediately proved to be too small, and before three years had passed an addition was built, thus giving the total edifice a breadth of 70 feet, a length of 127 feet and a height to the top of the dome of 114 feet. In this completed form it was the largest non-conformist church building in Britain and probably in the world" (Arnold Dallimore, *George Whitefield*, 2 vols. [Edinburgh: Banner of Truth, 1970, 1980], 2:386).

Mr. Green[6]; and neither of the Hospital chaplains,[7] nor the Lecturer of St. Dunstan's[8] care to peep into Tottenham pulpit, there are so many snakes on the stairs. I think it is scarce possible for me to leave Everton till Monday, the 19th of July, because I have no hope of a supply till then; but I trust it will not be delayed longer. And if Mr. Madan or Mr. Haweis, or both of them successively, can stay two months at Everton, I am willing to stay the same time at Oat Hall, provided there is any appearance of success. I find my heart more at liberty to ramble than usual, and much more disposed to come to Oat Hall than before; but your expectation of success from my foolish preaching discourages me greatly. For God has generally disappointed my expectations every way, to show that the work is his, and his only. When I looked for success, I found none; when I let down the net, expecting nothing, I had a good draught. When I go to preach empty and disheartened, I am sure to be helped; when full and fearing nothing, as sure to be confounded. When I go empty, the Lord fills the hearers; when I go full, the Lord tapps[9] the preacher, and lets out his own dropsy.[10] Oh how many painful tappings have I met with since Christmas, yea, a very dreadful one this morning; and all to show me that I am a fool; but I am extremely awkward at learning this lesson, and mightily apt to forget what I have learnt. I pray to be nothing, and yet would be something; fain would be empty, and yet want a dropsy. Oh heart! heart! heart! what art thou? a mass of fooleries and absurdities! the vainest, foolishest, craftiest, wickedest thing in nature! And yet the Lord Jesus asks me for this heart, woos me for it, died to win it. O wonderful love! adorable condescension!

---

6 John Green (d.1774). After being in connexion with the Wesleys, preaching at the Foundry and other places, he left them in 1746 and became an Independent minister in Churchyard-alley, Fetter-lane, as well as running a school in Denmark Street. On leaving the Wesley connexion he wrote *An Appeal to the Oracles of God: or reasons of disagreement from the doctrine of the Rev. Mr. Wesley* (Hart, 1746), giving his reasons. For many years he was an occasional preacher at both the Tabernacle and Tottenham Court Road Chapels. Some details of his life are given in William Jay, *Life of the Rev. Cornelius Winter* (Bath: Gye, 1808).
7 Martin Madan and Jonathan Reeves. See June 27, 1763, and September 2, 1763.
8 William Romaine. See July 16, 1763.
9 Drains, empties.
10 Swelling due to fluid—thus, figuratively, being swollen with self-importance and self-sufficiency.

Take it, Lord, and let it be
Ever clos'd to all but thee.[11]

I am, your Ladyship's obliged and affectionate servant, for Christ's sake,

John Berridge

---

[11] The second verse of John Wesley's hymn "I thirst, Thou wounded Lamb of God," which is itself based on Zinzendorf. See George Osborn, ed., *The Poetical Works of John and Charles Wesley*, 13 vols. (1868–1872), 1:265. Berridge used this verse in Hymn LXIX in his *Divine Songs*, 64.

To Lady Huntingdon[1]

Everton, July 9, 1763

My Lady,

The same post which brought your last letter brought another from Mr. Madan,[2] in which he acquaints me with his purpose of setting off for Brighthelmstone on this day, and further declares that he will send me word when he can come to Everton. As soon as I have his determination, I shall prepare for another outcry over the Sussex mountains. I believe there is work to be done at and about Everton by Mr. Madan, for there is a general inquiry after him; and if you can coax him to tarry six weeks, or six months, at Everton, I now seem willing to bawl on your mountains, or beat the cushion at Oat Hall, or clamber up Tottenham stairs the meantime.[3] Only I should have a week's time to prepare for my journey, because I give notice a week beforehand where I intend to preach the week after; and disappointments after notice given are attended with great clamour. I went out last Monday, and did not return till Friday afternoon, which prevented my answering your letter by Thursday's post. Next, I am engaged to go out on Monday, and shall not return till Friday evening or Saturday morning. And the rides are pretty long—thirty miles endways, and sometimes forty. However, as soon as Mr. Madan has fixed his time, I will prepare for my journey with all speed, and send you the earliest notice of it.

Mrs. Bateman[4] has sent me a mighty pretty letter to coax me into

---

[1] This letter is found in CHCA (Letter 6), as copied by Seymour; short extracts in Seymour, *Life of Huntingdon*, 1:358, and WB (1864), 448; and given fully in *FCEM* (1867), 346–347.

[2] See June 27, 1763.

[3] Preaching on the Sussex Downs, in the pulpit at Oat Hall, and at Tottenham Court Road Chapel.

[4] Miss Bateman became Lady Huntingdon's companion after being driven from home by her father because of her attachment to Whitefield's teachings. She returned home after her father's death, and in 1765 she married Thomas Adams of Ashby, a friend of Lady Huntingdon. "Mrs." is used as a form of courtesy. See August 21, 1765.

Sussex, and withal acquaints me that your Ladyship has been ill of a fever, but is now better. I was glad to hear of both. Nothing expels undue grief of mind like bodily corrections.[5] Nothing makes the child leave crying like the rod; at least I find it so by experience. However, I dare not send such consolation to many Christians, because they are not able to see the truth or bear the weight of it. I found your heart was sorely pained, and I pitied you, but dare not soothe you. For soothing, though it eases grief for a moment, only makes Lady Self grow more burdensome, and occasions more tears in the end. A little whipping from your Father will dry up your tears much sooner than a thousand lullabies from your brethren.[6] And I now hope you will be well soon.

Since Christmas I have been growing more lusty in body,[7] which gave me much grief. I prayed often that my carcase might be lessened, to make me more fit for travelling and exercise and the Lord has answered my prayers in great wisdom and mercy, by making me grow fatter still. Oh, what a fool I am, and how wise is God! Now I seem somewhat contented with my load, only by having it increased. What a wonderful way of teaching God has!

I beg my hearty love to Mr. Madan, and remain, your Ladyship's much obliged and dutiful servant,

John Berridge

---

[5] Lady Huntingdon is still grieving because of the death of her daughter on May 12. See June 23, 1763.

[6] Some letters of condolence written to Lady Huntingdon are given by Seymour, *Life of Huntingdon*, 1:335–338.

[7] See September 7, 1767: "my bulky vessel."

To Lady Huntingdon[1]

Everton, July 16, 1763

My Lady,

I received your letter of the 9th, and find you to be in higher mettle at the time of writing it than ever I knew you. A good sign your grief is wearing off; for an excessive load makes the spirit silent and lumpish, whilst a lighter load makes it plaintive and waspish. I am sure you are better, though perhaps you may not feel it and own it. Indeed, I was mightily pleased with your letter; it was quite a metzotinto print[2] of my own heart, and let me see you can be sometimes what I am frequently. Thank you, thank you, for the consolation you undesignedly sent me. I hope to see you soon at Oat Hall, and then I will thank you again.

Mr. Madan[3] sent me word yesterday that he would come to Everton as soon as Mr. Romaine[4] came to Brighthelmstone. But in order to

---

1 This letter is found in CHCA (Letter 7), as copied by Seymour, and in *FCEM* (1867), 347. It has the same address as preceding letters. The letter was written on a Saturday, presumably after returning from his weekly preaching tour.

2 Mezzotint is a print made from a roughened copper or steel plate that has been engraved, the untouched parts giving the deepest shadows. Berridge recognized in Lady Huntingdon's account of her heart the workings of his own nature.

3 See June 27, 1763.

4 William Romaine (1714–1795) became the leading Evangelical clergyman in London after he secured the afternoon lectureship of St. Dunstan's in Fleet Street in 1749. In 1766 he finally, through the help of Lady Huntingdon, became minister at St. Anne's, Blackfriars, which quickly became a focus of Evangelicalism. He was the only Evangelical incumbent in London until the arrival of Newton and Thomas Scott. He was a scholar and a preacher who had a real concern for the poor. He first met Berridge as a result of being sent with Madan by Lady Huntingdon to assess the initial revival at Everton. He was one of the friends of Berridge who raised money on behalf of Berridge's preachers. Their relationship lasted the rest of their lives. John Newton said in his funeral sermon that Romaine "was fifty-eight years in the ministry, an honourable and useful man, inflexible as an iron pillar in publishing the truth, and unmoved either by the smiles or the frowns of the world. He was the most popular man

hasten my journey, he advised me, if Mr. Romaine called upon me in his return from Yorkshire, to ask him to stay a Sunday or two here,[5] and come away myself directly to Oat Hall. See now how groundless your suspicions are![6] But heavy grief, and disappointments on the back of it, are apt to give us a jaundiced eye, and a feverish spirit. Am not I a trimmer[7] now? Don't I trim too close? Do not I go to the quick? Indeed, I am a strange, blunt fellow, and have always been thought a blundering fool; so that I could not help smiling at your leaving Great Britain when I became a trimmer; especially because I have had many thoughts of late, and some desire, of going to New England myself. And oh, what a fine mortification it would be for you to leave Old England on account of my trimming, and then to find me close at your heels in Canada! In truth, I am apt to think we shall both see New England before we die, though perhaps not both at the same time; and what you said in your last letter with some hastiness, may be put in practice with real seriousness. Can you forbear laughing now? Well, time will show; in the meantime Oat Hall must be your Canada, and I am willing, very willing, to emigrate to Oat Hall, as soon as I can get a lawful discharge from Everton. I am now much out of conceit with my own children, as you are with the hospital chaplains, and I want to leave them for awhile, that I may love them the better at my return. I propose to set out the very first opportunity I can get, and in the meantime remain your Ladyship's much obliged and dutiful,

John Berridge

Please to present my respects to Mrs. Carteret and Mrs. Cavendish.[8]

---

of the Evangelical party since Mr. Whitefield, and few remaining will be more missed" (quoted by Peter Toon in an account of his life in William Romaine, *The Life, Walk and Triumph of Faith* [Cambridge: James Clarke, 1970], xxiii). Tim Shenton, *"An Iron Pillar": The Life and Times of William Romaine* (Darlington: Evangelical Press, 2004) is sympathetic and informative.

5   Romaine did arrive at Everton on August 1.

6   It seems that Lady Huntingdon did not think that Berridge would go to Oat Hall.

7   "Trimmer" has many possible meanings. Is it used here in the figurative sense of reprimand or scold?

8   These two sisters had married well. They had been converted through Lady Huntingdon's gospel work among her own class and were often her companions on her travels. See November 23, 1789.

To Lady Huntingdon[1]

Everton, Wednesday evening, July 20 [1763]

My Lady,

I received your letter of the 18th just now, and purposed to set off for London on Monday next in a hired chaise,[2] and after having preached at Tottenham on Tuesday, and at the Tabernacle[3] on Wednesday (notice of which is sent along with this letter), to proceed to Oat Hall on Thursday. Don't grumble when you read this, I pray; and yet I am terribly afraid you will because you have been in a sad grumbling fit of late. I expect a storm when I see you, and it may be a heavy one, for it will have a week's time from this day to gather in. However pray let it out as soon as I enter your doors, that it may be presently over. For a hasty tempest with sunshine after it, is much preferable to a whole louring[4] hazy day. I will not inform you where I lodge in town, but I should have another letter from Oat Hall to beat up my quarters. Do now let me preach quietly in town for two days, and you may scold me for it afterwards, if you will. Only I must inform you, that I am mighty apt to laugh when a scolding is over, especially if it be performed without ill-nature. I put the best face upon the matter I can; but how I shall look when I see you, I know not. Oh that I may come attended with my Master, feeling his presence, and receiving his blessing! Gird me, O Lord, with thy strength, and put

---

[1] This letter is found in CHCA (Letter 28), copy by Seymour. The date is July 20, Wednesday evening (no other date). From examining Wesley's *Journal*, Wednesday, July 20 occurred in 1763, and the short letter fits the context perfectly.

[2] A light open carriage for one or two persons.

[3] Called the Tabernacle by Whitefield because it was originally built in 1741 as a temporary shed to shelter his hearers from the elements. The permanent building was erected in 1753, and Whitefield made the chapel house his headquarters. The building was eighty feet square with a gallery on each wall and was capable of holding four thousand people. For a history, see Edwin Welch, ed., *Two Calvinistic Methodist Chapels, 1743–1811: The London Tabernacle and Spa Fields Chapel* (London Record Society, 1975), xiii–xvi.

[4] Threatening and gloomy appearance of the sky.

thy spirit within me. Give me a message to many souls and make me faithful in delivering it. May the Lord give you peace, and send tidings of peace along with your much obliged and dutiful servant,

John Berridge

To Lady Huntingdon[1]

Everton, September 2, 1763

My Lady,

I reached the Tabernacle on Monday, about six, safe and well (God be praised), heard Mr. Edwards[2] preach, and found some power in the sermon, especially at the latter end. He is a sensible man, and seems alive, but a wonderful adorer of method, and has swallowed John Calvin[3] whole, at a mouthful. However, when his method was totally exhausted, and Calvin wholly disgorged, then the Redeemer began to show himself; and as soon as Edwards had done flourishing his weapons, the Lord Jesus fought his own battles. On Tuesday I grew as mopish as a cat, preached at Tottenham[4] in the evening, and more than once thought both the pulpit and preacher were tumbling down on the clerk's head. The audience was very attentive, but very phlegmatic. There seemed to be sorrow in their looks, and mourning on their backs, but mighty unfeeling, much like the mien and garb of an undertaker—rather

---

1   This letter is found in CHCA (Letter 8), a copy by Seymour, and *FCEM* (1868), 25–27, which incorrectly has the date as September 3, 1762. Berridge is writing to Lady Huntingdon, who is still at Oat Hall. Seymour, in *Life of Huntingdon*, 1:359, gives a summary and background to the letter and correctly dates it September 2, 1763. He describes how Berridge had spent the first part of August at Oat Hall, Sussex, where Lady Huntingdon had adapted a mansion for preaching, before preceding to London and preaching at the Tottenham Court Road Chapel, and then returning suddenly to Everton at the end of the month in response to the sudden death of Hicks's wife.

2   John Edwards (1714–1785) was converted under Whitefield in Ireland. Before he settled in Leeds he had success as an itinerant preacher, including in Ireland, where he experienced some persecution. He later withdrew from Wesley's connexion and for thirty years (1755–1785) led a society meeting at White Chapel, Leeds. As Berridge notes, he had strong Calvinist leanings. See "Memoirs of the Late Rev. John Edwards," *EM* (December 1793), 221–231.

3   John Calvin (1509–1564), French Protestant Reformer whose theology of the sovereignty of God in nature and salvation was foundational in the development of Protestantism.

4   Tottenham Court Road Chapel.

dismal than dolorous. On Wednesday more vapourish than ever, and several times expected to fall backwards as I stood in the Tabernacle pulpit, but grew better as I grew warmer in preaching.[5] Nothing helps the spleen like a waistcoat well moistened by a sermon.

Sent a note on Thursday morning to Mr. Haweis,[6] acquainting him that I would wait on him the next day to settle accounts, but was prevented by a letter received from Mr. Hicks,[7] of Thursday afternoon, informing me that his wife was dead—well, and dead in half-an-hour, and beseeching me for Christ's sake to come down to him immediately. Accordingly I preached at Tottenham in the evening, set off for Everton on Friday morning, and arrived here about six. What a vapour is life! it rises and swells, —it looks gay and florid, and then bursts in a moment.

Mr. Reeves[8] and Mr. Prior are chosen afternoon lecturers at

---

[5] One difficulty in understanding Berridge's description of "mopish" and "vapours" is the reference to the spleen, which was regarded as the seat of both melancholy and laughter. Is this a reference to Berridge's humour that was controlled as he got into his preaching or is he speaking of being raised out of low spirits as he spoke? Again, are the illusions to "falling" literal, which would point to Berridge suffering some form of giddiness that improved as he preached? Another difficulty is that "vapours" had a wide range of meanings as a medical term and became a fashionable disease when the new medical language of the nerves developed. See Roy Porter's modern introduction to George Cheyne, *The English Malady, or a treatise of nervous diseases of all kinds, as spleen, vapours, lowness of spirits, hypochondriacal, and hysterical distempers, &c* (Routledge, 1991). Anne C. Vila says: "The symptoms associated with the vapours consequently covered quite a range of complaints, including melancholic lethargy, spasms and convulsions, humoral plethora, excessive nervousness, overactive imagination, nausea, headaches, and indigestion" (*Enlightenment and Pathology* [John Hopkins University Press, 1998], 231). Certainly from later references to "vapours" (August 16, 1774; April 26, 1777; October 20, 1780), Berridge's "nervous fever" (June 3, 1771; November 7, 1786; November 1, 1786) and "exhaustion" (September 17, 1782)—set against the background of chronic asthma—point to the periods of depression and lethargy that Berridge often seems to have experienced.

[6] See June 27, 1763.

[7] See May 1759.

[8] Jonathan Reeves (d.1787). He was chaplain of the Magdalen Hospital—which had been set up to care for prostitutes—from its founding in 1758 until 1764. See H.F.B. Compston, *The Magdalen Hospital: The Story of a Great Charity* (SPCK, 1917), 44. He later was lecturer at West Ham. *The Gentleman's Magazine* (May 1787), 454, in recording his death, states that he was "18 years lecturer of that parish, in which he succeeded Dr. Dodd, and joint lecturer of Whitechapel…."

Whitechapel—chosen by a great majority, and against mighty opposition. Salary, £50 a-piece; duty, a sermon alternately on Sunday afternoons.

Maxfield[9] preaches again, and grows more violent. Bell[10] recovers his delusion apace, and bids fair for a greater enthusiast[11] than ever. The minister of Whitehall told a trembling communicant very lately that she need not be afraid, if she came to the altar[12] as a poor sinner, stripped of all.

I have heard a good character of Mr. Richardson[13] and Mr. Tilney. The former is in Yorkshire, the latter in town. The latter preaches with notes, the former without. Mr. Charles Wesley says, "No one

---

Seymour states that while at Magdalen Hospital, "...the governors forbad his preaching after his own manner, and constrained him to read from time to time a sermon of Archbishop Tillotson. When he became a lecturer of Whitechapel his ministry was more popular and useful, and he often preached at Brighton, Oathall, Everton, &c. with success" (*Life of Huntingdon*, 1:359).

9   Thomas Maxfield (d.1784) was converted while Wesley was preaching in Bristol in 1739 and became one of his first lay preachers. He was later ordained by the bishop of Derry. In the 1760s he was an embarrassment to Wesley as he supported George Bell in his extreme teaching on Christian perfection and his prophetic forecasts of the end of the world. He led a breakaway group from Wesley, publishing *A Vindication of the Rev. Mr. Maxfield's Conduct* (1767), which was very critical of both Wesleys. Although there was no reconciliation, Wesley visited Maxfield in his last illness and preached in his chapel in Moorfields. He was a man of ability who came to preach against the doctrine of Christian perfection, which he had once held so strongly. See Compston, *Magdalen Hospital*, 226–269.

10   George Bell (d.1807) joined the society at the Foundry (Wesley's headquarters) in 1758 and became associated with Maxfield, who led the group in the absence of Wesley. In the early 1760s Bell claimed full sanctification, infallibility, and miraculous healings. He prophesied that the end of the world would come on February 28, 1763, which forced Wesley to disown him and belatedly speak out against his enthusiasm, although about one-fifth of the members left the society with him. After the failure of his prophecies he seems to have turned his attention to politics. See Kenneth G.C. Newport, "George Bell, Prophet and Enthusiast," *Methodist History* (January 1996), 95–105.

11   See April 1758.

12   Published letter changes to "table."

13   John Richardson (*c*.1733–1792) joined the Methodists in 1762, when John Wesley appointed him an assistant at the Foundry. He was in the process of being appointed curate of Haworth (September 10) and was to prove William Grimshaw's successor, Grimshaw having died in April. He conducted Wesley's funeral and was himself later buried in the same vault.

approaches so near Mr. Fletcher[14] as Mr. Richardson." Mr. Conyers[15] preached at many churches in London, and among the rest at St. James's Church. I purpose to return to the Tabernacle on Friday next.

I thank your Ladyship for all favours, beg my respect to Mrs. Carteret and Mrs. Cavendish,[16] and remain your Ladyship's obedient servant,

John Berridge

---

[14] John Fletcher (1729–1785), Methodist vicar of Madeley in Shropshire, who collaborated for a time with the Countess of Huntingdon but whose closest affinity was with John Wesley. See August 18, 1771, for details of his relationship with Berridge.

[15] Richard Conyers (1725–1786), Methodist vicar of Helmsley, Yorkshire, was converted a year after Berridge in December 1758. It occurred without human agency through the realization that he did not understand what the "unsearchable riches of Christ" (Ephesians 3:8) were. He found peace through comparing Hebrews 9:20 and 1 John 2:7. At this time not only was he vicar of Helmsley, he had just been appointed rector of Kirby Misperton and domestic chaplain to the bishop of London, which may explain the comment about him preaching in many churches. See October 22, 1775, for the issue of Evangelical succession when he left Helmsley in 1776.

[16] See July 9, 1763.

To Mr. Reynolds[1]

Tottenham Chapel, September 23, 1763

Dear Friend,

If through mistake or mishap my church should want a preacher on any Sunday in my absence I must exhort you to preach in my orchard[2] both morning and afternoon—or if a preacher should come, who can take care of my church only on one part of the day then I must beg of you to preach [? ?][3] in my orchard. On Sunday, October 3, Mr. Hicks[4] purposes to help me, whether in the forenoon or afternoon I know not, but whatever noon he takes, do you take the other. I expect Mr. Madan[5] at Everton on Sunday, October 10 and purpose to be at Everton myself on Sunday, October 17. If anything material happens, please acquaint me with it by sending a line directed to me at Mr. Whitefield's Tabernacle,[6] near Moorfields, London. Give my love to your wife, and take the same to yourself. The grace of our dear Lord be with you both, and with

John Berridge

---

[1] This short note in manuscript is held in MARC, PLP 8 43.2. Not all the words are decipherable as the manuscript has been torn. It was written from Tottenham Court Road Chapel while Berridge was preaching in London.

[2] If this is a literal reference, was this because Mr. Reynolds was not an ordained minister, and therefore unable to preach inside the church building, or did the afternoon meetings take place outside because of the crowds? Or was Berridge using "orchard" as a metaphor for the church itself?

[3] About half a line (maybe six words) is completely illegible because of the condition of the manuscript.

[4] See May 1759.

[5] See June 27, 1763.

[6] See July 20, 1763.

To Lady Huntingdon[1]

Tabernacle, London, September 27, 1763

My Lady,

I find you have been under the Physician's hand again, I mean the good Physician. By and by he will put a finishing hand to the work, and heal you effectually. The days of your mourning will soon be ended, and sorrow and sighing fly away. Canaan is before you; and all the inhabitants of that land do say "I am no more sick." But whilst we abide in this hospital, it is no marvel, if physic be as duly administered as our food. And though I should sympathize with every patient, I dare not be sorry for any medicine that is given them. This were to arraign the skill and tenderness of the good Physician; and I know he is just as kind when he giveth me tears to drink, as when he brings me the best wine in his cellar but I am not equally pleased with both. Like a foolish child, I like that which suits my palate better than that which agrees with my health. Preaching about the cross is a mighty pleasant thing, but nature shrugs[2] and shrieks when once it begins to be nailed to it. And self, I find, will endure much and long torture before it is happily taught to die in the Lord and rest from all its legal labours.

Since I left Oat Hall a word was given me in my sleep, "Thou shalt know the Lord." My spirit eagerly replied, "When, Lord?" An answer was returned, specifying the time, which when I awoke, I forgot. It is not nigh at hand, I fear; and at present I am a mere vagabond, seeking rest but finding none. Everything in a hour and nothing long. Light and frothy, when the sun shines; sad and moapish, when it rains. Without a dram of discreet worldly conduct, and scarce a grain of Christian faith; consequently, even saying what I wish unsaid, and doing what I wish undone. Utterly dissatisfied I seem with my whole conduct, and yet not rightly dissatisfied: rather displeased because I find nothing in self to content me, than truly hungering after Christ.

---

[1] This letter is found in CHCA (Letter 9), a copy made by Seymour. It is addressed to "The Right Hon. the Countess of Huntingdon at Brighton."
[2] Shivers for fear.

I can scarce tell you what a wilderness the world is to me, and how sick, how wondrous sick I am of myself and every other self. My heart is evermore an aching void, panting sometimes insatiably after Christ, and ready to burst the ribbed bars that confine it—at other times mighty sullen, and caring not at all for the Redeemer.

I never saw anyone like me, except it be your Mrs. Bateman[3]; and though she does not equal me, I think she does resemble me as nearly as one friend can resemble another. May the dear Redeemer exorcise us both! Last night I preached at the Tabernacle from Isaiah 30:15 and besought the people to lay aside all legal striving, and to seek for rest wholly in Christ. The audience were alarmed and one of the labourers intreated me after sermon to speak with more caution. What must we do, my Lady, with this Moses? He has hoisted his tables on every church wall,[4] and now we hoist them in every tabernacle. Dearly indeed I once loved him, and now from my heart I could stone him. May the dear Redeemer continually display his banner to you, and be more and more the support and joy of your heart. Amen.

John Berridge

---

[3] See July 9, 1763.
[4] Many Church of England buildings had a display of the Ten Commandments, the Lord's Prayer, and the creed on the wall.

To Rowland Hill[1]

Grandchester, December 18, 1764

Sir,

Mr. Thomas Palmer[2] was at my house last week, and desired me to call upon you when I went to Cambridge. I am now at Grandchester, a mile from you, and where I preached last night and this morning,

---

[1] This short note of introduction was written on Tuesday morning, December 18, from Grantchester, only a mile from Cambridge, and one of Berridge's preaching stations. It is taken from Edwin Sidney, *The Life of the Rev. Rowland Hill* (Baldwin and Cradock, 1834), 21. It is included in *WB* (1864), 449. Rowland Hill (1745–1835) was the sixth son of Sir Rowland Hill of Hawkstone in Shropshire. He was converted at Eton through the influence of his elder brother. At Cambridge he found his position as an Evangelical lonely and difficult, although he soon collected a small flock of students and townspeople. Hill, who had only been at Cambridge a term, accepted Berridge's friendly invitation and as a result spent Christmas at Everton. His family was concerned about his involvement with such a disreputable character as Berridge. His sister, after expressing her pleasure at Rowland's happy experience at Everton over Christmas, warns him not to go too frequently to Mr. Berridge, "for should that be discovered, I need not tell you the storm it would raise" (Sidney, *Life of Rowland Hill*, 22). Hill was not discouraged by such advice, however, and spent practically every Sunday at Everton, riding over early in the morning and making sure that he returned in time for college chapel in the evening. Berridge had a close relationship with Hill and encouraged him in evangelistic work. Although committed to the national Church, he failed to be ordained as a priest largely because of his evangelistic itinerations. He became famous for his work at Surrey Chapel in London, which he had built for himself. See Sangster, "Life of the Rev. Rowland Hill," and Tim Shenton, *The Life of Rowland Hill: "The Second Whitefield"* (Darlington: Evangelical Press, 2008). For subsequent correspondence, see January 19, 1770; October 31, 1770; May 8, 1771; October 20, 1771; February 27, 1772; September 3, 1773; June 17, 1776.
[2] This may be Thomas Fyshe Palmer (1747–1802), who was just in the process of starting as a student at Cambridge and who lived not far away from Everton in the village of Northill. He later became a well-known Unitarian and founded the Unitarian Church at Dundee in 1785. He was an advocate for political reform and was transported for sedition in 1793. As a result of this experience he published *Narrative of the Sufferings of T.F. Palmer and W. Skirving, during a voyage to New South Wales, 1794, on board the Surprise Transport* (Cambridge: B. Flower, 1797).

and where I shall abide till three in the afternoon—will you take a walk over? The weather is frosty, which makes it pleasant under foot. The bearer of this is Mr. Matthews,[3] who lives at Grandchester Mill,[4] at whose house I am. If you love Jesus Christ, you will not be surprised at this freedom taken with you by a stranger, who seeks your acquaintance only out of his love to Christ and his people. I am, for his sake, your affectionate servant,

John Berridge

---

[3] Matthews became a friend of Hill. The following year, two Danish visitors record in their diary a visit with Hill: "The 26th June he conducted us to a pious friend, Mr. Matthew, at Grandchester, where we met with the revered Berridge, at Everton, and in the evening setted off for Nottingham" (Sidney, *Life of Rowland Hill*, 31).

[4] There is a model of the mill in Cambridge Folk Museum. The mill had existed from 1270 and belonged to Merton College, Oxford. There is a picture of this substantial building, which was burned down in 1928, in Mary Archer's *Rupert Brooke and the Old Vicarage, Grantchester* (Cambridge: Silent Books, 1989), 33.

To the Rev. Walter Shirley[1]

[January?] 1765

Family[2]

Prayers at nine in the morning, and nine in the evening: first reading a chapter, and singing a hymn, the hymns always sung standing. On Saturday evenings the serious people of the parish come to my house about seven. I first sing a hymn, then expound a chapter, then sing another hymn, then pray, and conclude with singing on my knees, "Praise God from whom,"[3] &c.

Diet

You must eat what is set before you, and be thankful. I get hot victuals but once a week for myself, viz., on Saturday: but because you are an honourable[4] man I have ordered two hot joints to be got each week

---

[1] Walter Shirley (1725–1786) was a nephew of Lady Huntingdon and one of her chaplains. He was rector of Loughrea, Co. Galway, Ireland, from 1746 and was converted in the early 1750s when he encountered the Methodists. He divided his time between Ireland and England, basing himself at Bath, from where he served some of the chapels built by Lady Huntingdon. He was to play a prominent part in the Calvinistic controversy of the 1770s, writing an account of the 1771 Bristol conference. While Berridge was preaching in London he came to Everton during January and February 1765. Berridge usually left Everton in early January. He had presumably departed Everton before Shirley had arrived and so he left him a letter to help him adjust to the country situation. The note is found in *WB* (1838), 491, and *WB* (1864), 533–534.
[2] Berridge was unmarried but he regarded his household of servants, housekeeper and gardener, etc. as his family.
[3] "Praise God from whom all blessings flow; Praise Him, all creatures here below; Praise Him above, ye heavenly host; Praise Father, Son, and Holy Ghost." The concluding verse of the nonjuring bishop Thomas Ken's (1631–1711) "Evening" hymn from his *A Manual of Prayers for the Use of the Scholars of Winchester College* (1674). The hymn starts "All praise to thee, my God, this night."
[4] Reference to Shirley being a member of the aristocracy.

for you, with a pudding each day at noon, some pies and a cold ham; so that you will fare bravely; much better than your Master with barley bread and dry fish. There is also ale, port, mountain,[5] and a little madeira to drink: the liquor suits a coronet. Use what I have just as your own. I make no feasts, but save all I can to give all I can. I have never yet been worth a groat[6] at the year's end, nor desire it. I hope you will like your expedition: the people are simple hearted. They want bread and no venison; and can eat their meat without sauce or a French cook.[7] The week-day preachings are in the evening at half-an-hour past six. If you can preach in a house, the method with us is, first to sing a hymn, then pray, then preach, then sing another hymn, then pray again, then conclude with 'Praise God from whom,' &c.

The Lord bless you, and make your journey prosperous! Your affectionate servant,

John Berridge

---

5   A variety of Malaga wine made from mountain grapes.
6   Medieval coin that ceased to be issued in 1662. It was equal to four pence and was taken in the eighteenth century to be a small sum.
7   Berridge is recommending simple and solid teaching, nothing fanciful or hard to digest.

To Mr. Adams[1]

Everton, August 21, 1765

Dear Sir,

Your brother was so kind as to call upon me, and I would not let him depart without a token of my love for you. Such as it is you have it now in your hands; a pepper-corn[2] payment, bringing you little, but wishing you much, even grace, mercy, and peace, with a daily increase of them, both to yourself and your new partner.[3] I wish you both joy, yea much joy, but all in the Lord. Perhaps you do not know that you have married my sister. Indeed she is as like me as if we had been born of one mother. Well—you are married into a good family, but, I trust, adopted into a better; and though you have given your hand to my sister Bateman,[4] I hope your heart, as well as hers, is given to my Lord Jesus. Remember who is your Master, who, with all the tenderness of a Father, says, "Son, give me thine

---

[1]   The letter is taken from Housman, *Life of Housman*, lix–lx, and *WB* (1864), 526–527. It was not to Housman as listed in *WB* (1864) but to Mr. Thomas Adams, an Ashby merchant owning a number of stocking-frames. See Edwin Welch, "Lady Huntingdon's Chapel at Ashby," *Transactions of the Leicestershire Archaeological and Historical Society*, 66 (1992), 137. Robert Housman (1759–1838), who was at Cambridge from 1780 to 1784, was Charles Simeon's first convert and was called by Simeon his "eldest son." See Housman, *Life of Housman*, xviii. In 1788 he married Jane Adams after going to Leicester in 1787 to assist Thomas Robinson (1749–1813), the well-known Evangelical vicar of St. Mary's. Jane Adams was the daughter of Mr. Adams, who seceded from the Church of England and was intimate with the leaders of the Evangelical Revival. In 1765 Adams had married a friend of Berridge's, Mary Bateman, who had been forced as a result of her conversion to leave her family and her inheritance, her father having a great fear of Methodism, and had become a companion of Lady Huntingdon, who had offered her asylum after hearing of her plight. See July 9, 1763.

[2]   A small or insignificant rent.

[3]   Adams had just married Miss Bateman. This is a congratulatory letter with a spiritual challenge.

[4]   Spiritual sister.

heart."[5] Love *him* above all, and *her* as yourself. If your family should increase, I hope that will not induce you to enlarge your business immoderately. The cares of the world are as fatal as its pleasures. The former, like cancers, eat up the heart; the latter, like syrens,[6] bewitch it. You will remember for what purpose labour was appointed: not for the sake of thriving, but of eating, "In the sweat of thy face shalt thou *eat bread*."[7] And "they that will be rich" (are willing, are desirous to be rich, trade with this view, though ever so honestly) "fall into many snares."[8] Labouring for bread to eat is part of the curse, therefore make it not a greater curse than God intended.

Mr. Janson is with you, I hear, or near you. Pray tell him I shall be glad to see him on his return, and that I do expect him some Saturday, to stay at least till the Monday following. Present my respects to your mother and wife, and to all your society. I am, dear Sir, your affectionate servant,

John Berridge

---

5   Proverbs 23:26.
6   Fabulous creatures who, according to classical mythology, lured sailors to their destruction by their enchanting singing.
7   Genesis 3:19.
8   1 Timothy 6:9.

To Lady Margaret Ingham[1]

Everton, January 28, 1766

Madam,

Thursday last, I received a bill value fifteen pounds, conveyed by Mr. Romaine,[2] but presented by your Ladyship, which was immediately

---

[1]   Lady Margaret Hastings (1700–1768) was a daughter of the Seventh Earl of Huntingdon by his second wife. In 1739, while at Ledston Hall—the home she shared with her half-sister Lady Elizabeth Hastings (1683–1739) in Yorkshire— she heard the preaching of Benjamin Ingham and was converted. She quickly introduced the preacher and his message to her sister-in-law, Selina, Countess of Huntingdon. Lady Margaret and Ingham were married on November 12, 1741, and many in society were amazed at her marriage to an itinerating preacher. After their marriage they lived at Aberford Hall near Tadcaster, and their relationship seemed one based on real affection. Like her sister-in-law, she was fully committed to the work of the revival. She died two years after this letter in 1768, aged sixty-seven. Romaine, in a letter noting her death, says: "Many a time my spirit has been refreshed with hearing her relate simply and feelingly how Jesus was her life" (Seymour, *Life of Huntingdon*, 1:302). The first edition of *WB* (1838), 366–369, correctly identifies the letter as written to Lady Margaret Hastings. The second edition of *WB* (1864), 355–358, uses the version in *Cheerful Piety*, which erroneously entitles it "To the Countess of H." A handwritten copy of the letter is held in the Cowper Museum and a version appeared in *GS* (1842), 165–166. The context of the letter appears to be Berridge's financial difficulties. William Romaine writes to a friend on January 16, 1766: "Yesterday I dined with Mr. Berridge. He was making great complaint of his debts, contracted by his keeping, out of his own living, two preachers and their horses, and several local preachers, and for the rents of several barns, in which they preach. He sees it was wrong to run in debt, and will be more careful. But it is done. My application is to Lady Margaret. Will you stand my friend with her, and tell her Berridge's case?" (*The Whole Works of the Late Reverend William Romaine, AM* [Tegg, 1837], 710–711).

[2]   See July 16, 1763. William Romaine had a strong attachment to both Ingham and his wife. He highly valued their work and the churches associated with them. He often visited them to help in their evangelistic efforts and the churches associated with them, and tried to counter the detrimental influence of Sandemanian views (faith as a purely intellectual assent) on Ingham. Robert Sandeman (1718–1771), attacked the doctrine of imputed righteousness, stressing a more intellectualist and non-experiential view of faith.

converted into cloth for the use of lay preachers[3]; and for their donations. I return you my hearty thanks. The Lord has promised to return it with a hundred fold into your bosom, and I believe you can trust him.

I wish you had sent along with your bill[4] a few minutes of your life of faith, you might then have taught me whilst you were clothing others. For, indeed, I am one of those strange folk, who set up for journeymen[5] without knowing their master's business, and offer many precious wares for sale without understanding their full value. I have got a Master too, a most extraordinary person, whom I am supposed to be well acquainted with, because he employs me as a riding pedlar to serve near forty shops[6] in the country, besides my own parish; yet I know much less of my Master than his wares. Often is my tongue describing him as the fairest of men, whilst my heart is painting him as the Witch of Endor[7]; and many big words have I spoken of his credit; yea, I am often beseeching others to trust him with their all, whilst my own heart has been afraid to trust him with a groat.[8] Neither, Madam, is this all. Such a profound ignoramus am I, that I know nothing of myself as I ought to know, having frequently mistaken rank pride for deep humility; and the working of self-love for the love of Jesus.

When my Master first hired me into his service, he kept a brave table, and was wondrous free of his liquor. Not a meal passed without roast meat and claret; then my heart said, I love Jesus. I was ready to boast of it too. But at length he ordered his table to be spread with only bread from above and water out of the rock.[9] This my saucy stomach could not brook; my heart thought it pernicious fare, and my tongue light food. Now my love for Jesus disappeared, and I found I had followed him only for the loaves and fishes, and that, like a true worldling, I loved his cellar and larder better than his person.

Presently after, my Master detected me in a very dirty trick, which discovered the huge pride and amazing impudence of my heart. Hitherto I had been a stranger to the livery which my Master gives his

---

3   Berridge supported both part-time and full-time preachers who supplied his preaching stations. See May 3, 1773.
4   Bill of money—gift.
5   One who has served an apprenticeship for a trade.
6   Berridge's preaching stations.
7   The medium who brought up Samuel from the dead. 1 Samuel 28.
8   See January 1765.
9   See 1 Corinthians 10:3,4 and Exodus 17.

servants to wear,[10] only I knew he had many rarities, such as diamonds and pearls in plenty to dispose of; accordingly I had begged a bracelet of him, a necklace, an earring, a nose-bob, and many other pretty things, which he readily parted with, being of a generous and noble nature. And will it not amaze you to hear? I had the vanity to fix these ornaments on my old rags, intending thereby to make a birthday suit to appear at court with. To be sure, while I was putting on my pearls and mending my old rags in comes my Master, and giving me a sudden gun[11] which went to my heart, he said in an angry tone, "Varlet, follow me."[12] I arose and followed trembling whilst he led me to the house of correction, where having first made my feet fast in the stocks, and stripped off my ornaments, he then took up his rod,[13] and laid on me very severely. I cried for mercy, but he declared he would not lay aside his rod till he had scourged every rag off my back. And indeed, Madam, he was as good as his word. Think then how confounded I must be to stand naked before my Master, and especially when I now first saw myself with an Ethiopian skin, which the rags had concealed from me before. For a while I kept upon my legs, yet overwhelmed with shame, till at length being choked also with the dust and poisoned with the stench that came out of the rags in the beating, I fell down at my Master's feet. Immediately the rod dropped from his hand, his countenance softened, and with a sweet voice he bid me look up. I did so, and then I got a fresh view of his princely robes, the garments of salvation.

I think, Madam, it was a lovely sight! A charming robe reaching from the shoulders down to the feet, well adapted for covering and defence; yea, excellent for beauty, and glory. "There, prodigal Jack," said he with a smile, "put this robe on thy back, and then thou mayst come to court, and shame an angel; it was wrought with my

---

[10] Is this a reference to the teaching of the imputed righteousness of Christ in opposition to Wesley's perfection doctrine? Or is this letter speaking about Berridge's efforts to justify himself by works before his conversion? He says on his epitaph that he lived proudly on faith and works for salvation until 1754. In conversion he fled to Jesus alone for refuge. It seems to me that Berridge is speaking about his experience since his conversion.

[11] WB (1838) has "gripe." WB (1864) has "grip."

[12] I have followed the Olney copy in this sentence.

[13] WB (1838) has "nine-tailed rod"; WB (1864) has "afflictive rod"; GS (1842) has "affliction rod." Olney copy just has "rod."

own hands, and dyed with my own blood; wear it and embrace me."[14] I thanked him and bowed. But, Madam, I must tell you (though I do not desire you to credit it because I say so) when my Master opened his robe he gave me a hasty glance of his person; it was so divinely sweet and glorious, and exceedingly humane so that I fell in love with him; and now, would you think it of me, old fool as I am, and swarthy as a negro, nothing will content me but a wedding; nay, I have frequently proposed the match to my Master, who sometimes replies "when I can leave all others he will take me." The other day, having asked him, "when He would take me to himself." He answered, "when I could lie at his feet"; and then he promised also to set open his cellar and larder again, and to keep them open.

I have now removed out of the book of Proverbs into the Canticles, but have got no farther than the first chapter, and second verse: "Let him kiss me with the kisses of his mouth."[15] I seem to want nothing now but a close communion with the dear Redeemer. The world at times diverts my attention from this chief object, but my soul is ever panting after him. Yes my flesh and my heart cry out for the living God. O that he may come quickly.

May the Lord daily strengthen your union, and thus increase your communion with the Prince of Peace. I send my kind and brotherly love to Mr. Ingham,[16] and am, Madam, your Ladyship's much obliged and affectionate servant, for Christ's sake,

John Berridge

---

14 *WB* (1838) has "remember me."

15 Song of Solomon 1:2.

16 Her husband, Benjamin Ingham (1712–1772). He was an early Methodist at Oxford and went as a missionary alongside Wesley to Georgia. With Wesley he joined the Moravian society in London, and although independent, he remained on intimate terms with the Moravians, inviting them to supervise the societies he had formed in Yorkshire and the north of England, until 1755. In 1759 he adopted Sandemanian views, which split the societies, with most leaving him. Perhaps some of Berridge's letter with its strong emphasis on his own experience of saving truths of justification and sanctification can be understood in the light of Ingham's own spiritual pilgrimage. For a recent account of Ingham, see H.M. Pickles, *Benjamin Ingham: Preacher Amongst the Dales of Yorkshire, the Forests of Lancashire and the Fells of Cumbria* (Coventry: Pickles, 1995). For an older work, see Luke Tyerman, *The Oxford Methodists: memoirs of the Rev. Messrs. Clayton, Ingham, Gambold, Hervey and Broughton, with biographical notices of others* (Hodder and Stoughton, 1873), 57–154.

To Lady Huntingdon[1]

Everton, March 6, 1766

Dear Lady,

Your letter of February 12, I received in due time, but could not answer it sooner for want of certain intelligence from Mr. Hicks.[2] Yesterday he told me positively, that he could not go at this time, and today I send you advice of it. As to myself, I am now determined not to quit my charge again in a hurry. Never do I leave my bees, though for a short space only, but at my return I find them either casting[3] and colting,[4] or fighting and robbing each other; not gathering honey from every flower in God's garden, but filling the air with their buzzings, and darting out the venom of their little hearts in their fiery stings. Nay, so inflamed they often are, and a mighty little thing disturbs them, that three months' tinkling[5] afterwards with a warming-pan[6] will scarce hive them at last, and make them settle to work again. They are now in a mighty ferment, occasioned by the sounding brass of a Welsh Dyer,[7] who has done me the same kind office at Everton that he has done my friend at Tottenham.[8] 'Tis a pity he should have the charge of anything but wasps; these he might allure into the treacle pot and step in before them himself, but he never will fill a hive with honey. If you see not already, you will very soon find, the mischief arising from leaving a family[9]—all the elements will break in upon you in

---

1   This letter is found in CHCA (Letter 10), as copied by Seymour: "To the Right Honourable the Countess of Huntingdon at Bath." Seymour, *Life of Huntingdon*, 1:366, has a short extract from this letter: "As to myself…hive of honey."
2   See May 1759.
3   Throwing things away.
4   Running wild.
5   Possibly means repairing. The work of a tinker was to repair pots.
6   A long-handled pan of brass which held warm coals and was used for warming beds.
7   Rev. G. Dyer. See July 3, 1763.
8   Whitefield; Tottenham Court Road Chapel.
9   In this section Berridge is speaking of the problems that have come on

their turn. Water has bereaved you of your children at Hampston, and fire consumed them at Bath. Dropsies are now ripe at the Sea, and malignant fevers will kindle at the Spa. Your other house has been robbed, and your present mansion will be plundered too, unless you leave a good barking dog behind you, when you quit it. During your absence, the ravens, so we call them in Leicestershire, will certainly send an old clucking hen to pick up your chickens. These have got, as you know, a fine syren[10] note and large downy wings, but no scratching feet: they come with their bagpipe and spread their umbrella, but no barley-corns; and cuckoo-like, hatch no chickens themselves. They are building a hen-roost, I find, near your chickens' house; and will make fine work with your poultry by and by, clipping many of their wings, stripping some of their feathers, and brooding others to death.

But whither am I going? Blessed be God, there is a keeper of Israel, who never slumbers nor sleeps; and but for this keeper all our labour were vain. Happy servants who are taught the blessed art of goading on the oxen continually, and then leaving the Master to guard his ark in the cart.[11] Into this Master's service have I been hired eight years, and scarce know his name yet. Often have I ran up into the garret to view him, but either saw nothing there, or mistook a meteor for the sun: of late I have gone down into the cellar to find him. It is a dark and perplexed passage; but when I can venture down, my Master always meets me at the bottom, and opens a bottle for me. And nothing sure exceeds the goodness of his wine, but the sweetness of his heart. Three weeks ago I fell into such deep poverty of spirit as amazed, and frightened, and shamed me much; but I soon found this door of poverty led into the chamber of grace, and filled me with a fragrant sense of the Saviour's presence, making it like unto ointment poured forth.[12] For the space of twelve hours I could scarce hold up my head for shame, nor hold in my tears for joy. Oh! what a mystery is godliness! How much do we prate about our tools before we learn anything of our trade! How long do we preach or hear of Jesus; before we sink into his spirit! Indeed, nothing but a total shipwreck can make us lay, like Paul,

---

Lady Huntingdon when she has been absent from her causes. Seymour says Berridge figuratively warns "her Ladyship against Independents, and Baptists, and other Dissenters, who were at that time alluring the congregations from her Ladyship's chapels" (*Life of Huntingdon*, 1:366–367).

[10] An alluring and deceiving sound. See August 21, 1765.

[11] 2 Samuel 6:6.

[12] Songs of Songs 1:3.

one day in the deep[13]; and nothing but daily shipwrecks can make us lie there every day. My good Lady, though I use you very ill, in omitting at some times, and in delaying at all times the payment of my epistolary debts, yet you are much upon my heart, and I believe upon the heart of every well wisher to our Sion. That the Lord may refresh your own soul, and prosper every labour of love undertaken for his sake, is the hearty prayer of your Lady's obedient and affectionate servant for Christ's sake,

John Berridge

Mr. Sellon[14] is not arrived.

---

[13] 2 Corinthians 11:25

[14] Walter Sellon (1715–1792), a baker and lay preacher, had his antagonism to Methodism removed when he met John Wesley in 1745. He became a master at Kingswood School (1748–1750) and later was ordained by the bishop of Lincoln on his appointment as curate at Breedon on the Hill, a few miles from Lady Huntingdon's residence. He later became vicar of Ledsham, Yorkshire, the home of Lady Huntingdon's half-sisters (Ledston Hall) in 1770. He strongly supported Wesley's cause in the Calvinistic controversy, writing books against James Hervey in 1767 and Jerome Zanchius in 1771.

To Lady Huntingdon[1]

Everton, July 28, 1766

My Lady,

Your second letter filled me with shame indeed, the former being unanswered. "And well it might," you reply "What! Has not Jesus Christ taught you at least good manners—to return a civil answer to a civil question?" In truth, my Lady, I have learned nothing yet, but that I am a wayward ass, and a conceited dunce. Still I abide in my dungeon, and all the light which comes through its chinks, only shows me the frightfulness of it. Eight years I have been to Christ's School, and so far from learning good manners, I have not yet learned my letters. Indeed I am not got to great A, but am still fumbling at the Christ's cross which is before it. What a frightful character it is, and how hard to learn! Some horn-books[2] have not this cross, I am told; and there the scholars learn at a wondrous rate. I have often wished it was out of mine; but there it is, and a frightful large one truly, just as big as my*self*. Sometimes I take it up, and then it weighs me down: sometimes I stumble over it, and then it breaks my shins: sometimes I run away from it: and then my master flogs me; sometimes I am out of all heart, and cry like a child, then he gives me a sugar-plumb,[3] and were it not for some kindness I have for my master, I should certainly burn his cross and Horn-book together. But what is all this, you ask, to the Sussex journey? A very pertinent reply, though a very sorrowful one: I have not yet learned the cross—and now having given what may be the true reason, Master *Self* desires to be heard in

---

[1] This letter is found in CHCA (Letter 11), a copy by Seymour. It is addressed to "The Right Honourable Countess of Huntingdon at Lady Gertrude Hotham's New Norfork House, Grosvenor Square, London." This letter was directed to Oat Hall and then redirected to London.

[2] A book for children containing the alphabet, the Lord's Prayer, and Roman numerals, which was covered with a thin piece of transparent horn. It was often attached to the child's belt and was in use in England well into the eighteenth century.

[3] A small oval sweetmeat made of boiled sugar.

his own cause. He declares then, that elderly as he is, and somewhat corpulent, and mighty subject to the vapours,[4] yet he travels five days in the week, and sometimes six, both in summer and winter, to the no small discomposure of his ease, and therefore thinks it very hard that he may not lay quiet and snug in the harvest. Besides, he avers, that he has never been from home these last three years, but at his return he always found his family scolding and fighting, with maimed limbs, broken heads, and bloody noses in abundance.[5] And though he would not intrude upon the masters' office, which is both to make and keep the peace; yet he finds by experience, that *absence* is one of these times, wherein men are said to *sleep*, and the enemy comes to sow tares. Matt. 13:24,25. Don't you think Master *Self* pleads notably? Indeed he has quite overcome me: and if you are not convinced by his arguments, I must impute it to your aversion to his cause.

I did not receive your last letter till Saturday afternoon, having been out the whole week; so that I am very fleet in answering this letter, if you can overlook my neglect of the other. Yesterday I heard from the Archdeacon of Tottenham,[6] who complains, dear man, of his bellows;[7] and well he may, for they have been put to notable use, and blown up many a flame: but now they lose wind and begin to wheeze. However, so long as any nozzle and leather remains, I believe he will clap their sides together. By his account Mr. Beckman[8] lays a dying. What a deal of stuff have I written about this thing and the other thing; and nothing yet about Jesus. He gave me a good day, yesterday; and made me often weep for him. What a miracle of mercy He is! What a prodigy of folly and phrenzy[9] I am! Lord, how canst thou bear with me? How canst thou love me! Thou art always the same! I, always different! Thou, unchangeable as the rock; I, wavering and

---

[4] See September 2, 1763, for a discussion of the "vapours," and October 23, 1779, for details of the nervous fever that afflicted Berridge most years.

[5] Whenever Berridge had travelled to help Lady Huntingdon he had returned to problems at Everton.

[6] Whitefield.

[7] Lungs.

[8] A close friend of Whitefield, who had cared for him in his own house in the suburbs of London when he collapsed in 1761. Whitefield had made him a trustee along with Keen and Hardy in order to help manage the affairs of the Tabernacle and Tottenham Court Road Chapels.

[9] Frenzy—literally, madness—was later used to describe the excitement produced by mania.

whirling as the weather-cock! Misfit for any office within thy house; only fit for an outward pane of thy temple. Neither care I much what I am, high-priest, Levite, [?], or weather-cock, only let me be near thee; and whilst I am whirling, keep me from falling. I cannot bear to be separated from thee, much less forever, that is hell indeed. Full of folly, phrenzy, megrimes,[10] old and ugly too, still my soul longs for thee. Ever roving, wavering, whirling, still I find no rest, till I turn again to thee. That the kind Master may daily feed you with his own bread, and the good Shepherd watch over your flocks, is the hearty wish of your very affectionate, not not [sic] very dutiful servant,

John Berridge

---

[10] Severe headache, vertigo, whim or vapour—low spirits. The term "migraine" was first used in 1777.

To William Lee[1]

Everton, September 7, 1767

Dear Sir,

"The Lord reigneth; let the earth rejoice."[2] Your vicar cannot remove you, till his Maker and your Master say, "Depart hence in peace." All your times and ways are in his hands. If it is for his glory, and the welfare of his people, that you should stay where you are, no vicar or diocesan[3] can remove you. But if he has other work, and large employment for you, he will call you away; and you must give up Ishmael, as Abram did, for Isaac's sake; and Ishmael, though given up by Abram, shall not be deserted by the Lord, but become a nation.[4]

I love the people much, and left my heart in Lakenheath church and chapel (that is, in the house and pantry) when I took myself away. If you can only be quiet, and daily commit yourself to the Lord, begging his direction and superintendence, all things will be ordered right, and end well. But if you stir a finger in the matter, you will be sure to disturb the Lord's hand, and discompose your own soul. The

---

[1] William Lee was curate of Lakenheath and was expecting shortly to be dismissed by his vicar. L.E. Elliott-Binns says Lee (or Ley), who was a Methodist itinerant before his ordination, went to Lakenheath as a result of openings made by Wesley and Madan. See *Early Evangelicals*, 269. It is in the context of his relationship with Berridge, formed as a result of Berridge preaching at Lakenheath, that he asks for advice. The following year he was in London and introduced Professor John Hendrik Liden to the Wesleys. See "John Wesley and Professor Liden, 1769," *WHS*, 17:1 (1929), 1–4. He was still a preacher in the Wesley connexion in the mid-seventies. See Wesley, *Letters of John Wesley*, 6:5, 73. Lakenheath is situated in the north-west tip of Suffolk, about forty-five miles from Everton. It is now the site of the largest United States Air Force base in Britain. Copies of the letter were published in *Gospel Magazine* (1827), 363–364; *GH* (1835), 278–279; *GS* (1843), 179–180; *WB* (1864), 450–452; and *S* (1893) 262–263.
[2] Psalm 97:1.
[3] Bishop.
[4] Genesis 21.

Captain is now teaching his cornet[5] how to stand still, and see the salvation of God.[6] A Christian soldier must learn to halt as well as march. One is as much a piece of exercise as the other, and can only be learnt by practice. Preaching may show it, but cannot teach it. Then pray be still, and use no other weapon but the shield of faith.

If your vicar send you notice to quit your cure,[7] look upon it as a *bene decessit*[8] from the Lord, and go in peace. When Jesus sent the devil to blow down Job's house, and slay his children, and plunder his cattle, he did not rail at the instrument, but cried out, like a wise man, "The Lord gave, and the Lord hath taken away; blessed be the name of the Lord."[9] Yet he lost more than sixty pounds[10] by his disaster; he lost all. Nothing was left except a froward piece of furniture in his house, without a name, but not without a tongue; a very crooked rib, and much unlike yours.[11] And what was the end of Job? Twice as much as the beginning.[12]

My advice, then, is this. Do not expect to leave Lakenheath till you have actual warning to go. Clouds will often gather in the lower region, and move over our head, without wetting our feet. But if a storm falls, Jesus sends it. Have you warning to go? Go in peace. Rail not at the hand that writes your mittimus.[13] Jesus employs very strong hands sometimes to do his work and to carry his messages. Take heed of railing. Jude tells us, that Michael durst not bring a railing accusation,[14] even against the devil himself; much less ought we against any of his servants. Are you discharged, and know not whither to go? So was Abraham, who went out, not knowing whither he went.[15] So must all his children. Be not anxious; be not fretful; be a little child, and your

---

5   Commissioned officer who carried the colours. Jesus Christ is teaching his commissioned officer.

6   Exodus 14:13.

7   Office of a curate.

8   *GM* (1827) and *S* (1893) have *"bene decessit"* (a good dismissal from the Lord—providential), which suggests they have the manuscript. *WB* (1864) has "as being direct."

9   Job 1:21.

10   Lee's salary. Many curates were paid less than this.

11   Job's wife, who was little help to him in his troubles. Notice Berridge's greetings and affection for Lee's own wife at the end of the letter.

12   See Job 42:10.

13   The first word of a writ in Latin "we send." Thus, a notice of dismissal.

14   Jude 9.

15   Hebrews 11:8 and Genesis 12.

Lord will lead you. Acknowledge the Lord alone in all your ways, and he will direct your paths.[16] What you seek after will blight and wither. Where the Lord leads you, he will follow you. This is strong meat, but very wholesome. The Lord will help you to digest it.

I know not how to transport my bulky vessel to Lakenheath and back again in one week. As soon as the world beats a drum for arms, the Christian should fall upon his knees, and not upon his foes. Give my kind love to your little dame, and to all Christian friends, and believe me to be your affectionate friend and servant,

John Berridge

---

[16] Proverbs 3:6.

TO CORNELIUS WINTER[1]

[Winter?] 1767

Dear Sir,

...Pray frequently, and wait quietly, and the Lord will make your way plain. Jesus trains up all his servants to waiting, and if you are called to the ministry, he will exercise your soul beforehand with sharp conflicts. Joseph must be cast first into a pit by his own brethren,[2] then into a prison by his master,[3] before he rules the kingdom; and David must be hunted as a flea upon the mountains,[4] before he gets the sceptre. How can you tell what others feel, unless you have felt the same yourself? How can you sympathize with a prisoner, unless your own feet have been fast in the stocks? How can you comfort those who are cast down, unless you have been often at your wits' end? Expect nothing but conflicts day after day to humble and prove you, and teach you

---

[1] Cornelius Winter (1742–1808) was converted on hearing Whitefield in 1760. He joined the Tabernacle and started preaching at Sheerness, Chatham, and other places. In 1766 he paid his third visit to Berridge and sought an introduction to Mr. Whitefield with a view to a situation in America. Berridge gave him a letter of introduction, and as a result Winter was asked to preach for Whitefield. He helped Whitefield with occasional preaching and office work. At his own request he accompanied Whitefield to America to preach among the negroes and returned to England on the death of Whitefield in 1770, seeking ordination so that he might return to America. He later became a minister at Painswick, Gloucestershire. In Jay, *Life of Winter*, 84–86, these two extracts are introduced by the following: "In my situation, hitherto described, letters with which I was favoured from dear Mr. Berridge, were of great use indeed; an extract I will here insert from two of them." The circumstances fit the time before Winter accompanied Whitefield to America. The extracts are erroneously printed in WB (1838), 121–122, and WB (1864), 442–443, as one complete document. Besides giving the letter (1892), 262–263, S prints the first of these extracts with a description of the circumstances, in an account of Winter's life ([1902], 11). See February 12, 1771.

[2] Genesis 37:24.

[3] Genesis 39:20.

[4] 1 Samuel 23:26.

to speak a word in season to one that is weary. This is indeed the high road to the kingdom for all, yet a minister's path is not only narrow and stony like others, but covered also with bushes and brakes;[5] and if you labour to remove them by your own hands, they will quickly tear your flesh and fill your fingers with thorns. Let your Master remove them at your request, and remember it is always his work, as it is ever his delight, to clear our way, and lead us on till sin and death are trodden down. Undertake nothing without first seeking direction from the Lord, and when anything offers that is plausible and inviting, beg of God to disappoint you if it be not according to his mind. You cannot safely rely on your own judgment, after God has told you, "He that trusteth in his own heart is a fool."[6] This advice relates to all important changes in life. Go nowhere, settle nowhere, marry nowhere, without frequent usage of this prayer....

...I find your heart is yet looking towards America; this inclines me to think God will some time send you thither; in the meanwhile be thankful you have a pulpit in England to preach Jesus Christ in, and health to preach him. Be not in a hurry to go, lest you go without your passport,[7] and then you go on a fool's errand. Do not wish to be anywhere but where you are, nor anything but what you are. It is want of communion with God that makes our thoughts run a gadding. Daily beseech the Lord to make your way plain, then leave it to him to direct your steps. Wish not to do good in America next summer, but to do good in England every day you continue here....

---

5   Bracken, brushwood, and briars.
6   Proverbs 28:26.
7   He must have God's authorization to travel.

To Lady Huntingdon[1]

Everton, December 26, 1767

My Lady,

I had a letter from your Ladyship last Saturday, and another from Lord Buchan.[2] His letter required an immediate answer, which I sent on Monday, and then went out preaching.[3] I am now returned, and sit down to answer yours. But what must I say? Verily you are a good piper; but I know not how to dance. I love your scorpion letters dearly, though they rake the flesh off my bones; and I believe your eyes are better than my own, but I cannot yet read with your glasses. I do know that I want quickening every day, but I do not see that I want a journey to Bath.[4]

---

[1]   Lady Huntingdon had obviously written another letter demanding his presence at Bath. This letter is found in CHCA (Letter 12), as copied by Seymour, and *WB* (1864), 502–503, which misses out the last section—"Furthermore, my Master…sake"—and the section in brackets. The bracketed section in the middle gives Berridge's views on Lady Huntingdon's College at Trevecca. Work on adapting one of the buildings at the Howell Harris settlement in Mid Wales had just begun on December 1. See December 28, 1768. It may be that this response had already been written, and Berridge folds the added pages into the letter. This would explain the reference to the length of the letter and the saving of double postage. In *WB* (1864), 449–450, this section is included as a separate letter with the explanation that it is an answer to Lady Huntingdon's plan for examining students to be admitted. The explanation and extract in *WB* seem to be taken directly from Seymour, *Life of Huntingdon*, 2:92.

[2]   David Stuart Erskine (1742–1829), the Eleventh Earl of Buchan. His father, Henry David Erskine (1710–1767), a Scottish nobleman, had moved to Walcot near Bath with his daughter, Lady Anne Erskine, and was converted through Lady Huntingdon's circle. His son "succeeded to the earldom in 1767, and seems almost immediately to have appointed Venn, Berridge, and Fletcher of Madeley as his chaplains. His later life was spent in literary retirement in Scotland, but his adhesion to Lady Huntingdon seems to have created great excitement in fashionable circles" (John Venn, *Annals of a Clerical Family* [Macmillan, 1902], 92).

[3]   See May 18, 1763, for Berridge's normal pattern of preaching, leaving Everton on Monday and returning on Friday or Saturday.

[4]   Lady Huntingdon had one of her chapels at Bath, a spa town known for its

I have been whipped pretty severely for fighting out of my proper regiment, and for rambling out of the bounds of my rambles[5]; and whilst the smart of the rod remains upon my back, it will weigh more with me than a thousand arguments. All marching officers are not general officers; and everyone should search out the extent of his commission. A gospel minister, who has a church will have a diocese annexed to it, and is only (*episkopoς*) an overseer, or Bishop of that diocese: and let him like faithful Grimshaw[6] look well to it.[7] An evangelist who has no church[8] is a metropolitan, or cosmopolitan, and may ramble all the kingdom, or all the world over; and these are more highly honoured than the other, though they are not always duly sensible of the honour. They are nearest to the apostolical character of any.

But whom do you recommend to the care of my church? Is it not one Onesimus who ran away from Philemon?[9] If the Dean of Tottenham could not hold him in with a curb, how shall the Vicar of Everton guide him with a snaffle?[10] I do not want a helper merely to stand up in my pulpit, but to ride round my district; and I fear my weekly circuits would not suit a London or a Bath divine, nor any tender evangelist that is environed with prunello.[11] Long rides and miry roads in sharp

---

hot springs, which attracted the rich and famous. She was often there herself.

5   His own circuit.

6   See July 16, 1759. Frank Baker comments: "Berridge delighted in outlandish figures of speech that sometimes obscured rather than illuminated his thought, but probably Berridge was in this instance paying a tribute to Grimshaw's concentrated ministry within his own parish, a tribute the more noteworthy coming from such a notorious invader of the parishes of others. If Berridge did mean this, however, he was wrong. He was wrong even if he implied simply that Grimshaw had carved out and faithfully served a little diocese of his own among the parishes immediately surrounding Haworth. For although William Grimshaw was one of the most conscientious parish priests of the century, he was at the same time one of the most confirmed itinerants, on occasion travelling very far afield on pastoral and preaching journeys" (*William Grimshaw, 1708–1763* [Epworth Press, 1963], 103). I think Berridge is arguing that Grimshaw kept to his own circuit (diocese) in his preaching.

7   This sentence has been tidied up in *WB*.

8   Like Wesley or Whitefield.

9   Philemon 10.

10   The snaffle was a simple bridle-bit, which had a lot less controlling power, than the more complex and strong "curb," which fixed the lower jaw to the bridle and was used for checking unruly horses. Whitefield had obviously been let down by one of his preachers.

11   A dark woollen material of plum colour used to make clergymen's gowns.

weather! Cold houses to sit in, with very moderate fuel, and three or four children roaring or rocking about you! Coarse food and meagre liquor; lumpy beds to lie on, and too short for the feet; stiff blankets, like boards, for a covering; and live cattle in plenty to feed upon you! Rise at five in the morning to preach; at seven, breakfast on tea that smells very sickly; at eight, mount a horse with boots never cleaned; and then ride home, praising God for all mercies.[12] Sure I must stay till your academy[13] is complete, before I can have an assistant.[14]

(The soil you have chosen is proper, Welsh mountains afford a brisk air for a student and the rules are excellent. But I doubt the success of the project and fear it will occasion you more trouble than all your other undertakings besides. Are we commanded to make labourers or to "pray the Lord to send labourers?"[15] Will not Jesus choose, and teach, and send forth his ministering servants now, as he did his disciples aforetime; and glean them up when and where he pleaseth. The world says, no; because they are strangers to a divine commission and a divine teaching. And what if these asses blunder about the Master's meaning for a time, and mistake it often, as they did formerly. No great harm will ensue, provided they are kept from paper and ink, or from a white wall and charcoal. Do you like to see cadelambs[16] in a house, and suckling with a finger, or to view them skipping after their dams in their own proper pasture? We read of a school of prophets in the Scripture,[17] but we do not read that it was God's appointment. Elijah visited the school, which was at Bethel, and seems to have been fond of it. Yet the Lord commands him to fetch a successor, not from the school, but, as the Romans fetched a dictator, from the plough.[18] Are

---

[12] For a contrast in circuit accommodation see Jonathan Rodell, "'The Best House by Far in the Town': John Wesley's Personal Circuit," *Bulletin John Rylands Library*, 85 (Summer and Autumn 2003), 111–122.

[13] See December 30, 1768.

[14] At this point Seymour incorporates another letter on the academy. He does this by using brackets. The letter is the usual length without the extra material. See Spring 1768.

[15] Luke 10:2.

[16] Lambs cast off by their mothers and brought up by hand.

[17] 2 Kings 2:3.

[18] Elisha was called by Elijah while ploughing with twelve pairs of oxen. 1 Kings 19:19. Cincinnatus in 458 BC was appointed dictator at Rome in order to rescue the army, which was surrounded and threatened with defeat. He was working on his farm when he received the call. After defeating the enemy he resigned and went back to his farm.

we told of a single *preaching* prophet that was taken out of this school or do we find any public employment given the scholars, except once sending a light-heeled young man, when light heels were useful, with a horn of oil, to anoint Jehu, 2 Kings 9. That old prophet who told a sad lie to another prophet was of this school, and might be the master of this college, for he was a grey-headed man, 1 Kings 13:11. Whilst my heart is thus prattling to you very simply, like a child, it stands in no fear of offending you; and if your project be right, the Master will keep you steadfast, and you will only smile at my prattling. Indeed I am the most dubious man in the world about my own judgment, and will stickle[19] for nothing, excepting to love and to trust in my Lord.)

But enough of these matters. Let us now talk of Jesus, whom I treat in my letters, as I deal with him in my heart, crowd him into a corner; when the first place and the whole room belongeth of right to himself. He has been whispering of late, that I cannot keep myself, nor the flock committed to me; but has not hinted a word as yet, that I do wrong in keeping close to my fold. And my instructions, you know, must come from the Lamb, not from the Lamb's wife, though she is a tight[20] woman. He has taught me to labour for him more cheerfully, and to loathe myself more heartily, than I could before. I see myself nothing and feel myself vile, and hide my head, ashamed of all my sorry services. I want his fountain every day, his intercession every moment; and would not give a groat[21] for the broadest fig-leaves, or the brightest human rags to cover me. A robe I must have, of one whole piece, broad as the law, spotless as the light, and richer than an angel ever wore, the robe of Jesus.[22] And when the elder brother's raiment is put on me, good Isaac will receive and bless the lying varlet Jacob.[23] Furthermore, my Master is learning me, but I learn slowly to take him for my only portion; lean and feed upon him, delight and wrap myself up in him. Martha yet calls me brother, but I love dear Mary better, and am seeking her good part, "to lay at Jesus's feet and hear his word."[24] I believe he will indulge me with a nearer and sweeter acquaintance, because my heart often cries out for him. At present I

---

[19] To strive or contend.

[20] Competent, able, skilful, smart. Of course Berridge is being ironical. This sentence has shocked many people's sensibilities.

[21] See January 1765.

[22] Berridge wishes to be dressed in Christ's righteousness.

[23] The scheming Jacob was accepted in the clothes of another. Genesis 27.

[24] Luke 10:39.

seem a mere wild ass in the wilderness, but the ass has some love for Jesus, and the Master has rode upon his back a hunting without bridle or saddle, for he does not love human furniture or equipage.

If I was a letter in debt, the length of this will handsomely pay off arrears, and save double postage. I am glad to hear of Miss Orton's[25] welfare; and of your removal, one step at least, from the gates of death. May the Lord keep you evermore at his feet, where I want to lay living and dying, and then neither harm nor fear of harm can befall you. So prayeth your affectionate servant, for Christ's sake,

John Berridge

---

[25] Jennett Payne Orton, intimate friend and companion of Lady Huntingdon. See March 20, 1771, and March 2, 1776. She married Thomas Haweis in 1788. She was very rich, with extensive property in the West Indies.

PART 2

1768–1775

Years of difficulty

To John Wesley[1]

Everton, January 1, 1768

Dear Sir,

I see no reason why we should keep at a distance, whilst we continue servants of the same Master; and especially when Lot's herdsmen[2] are so ready to lay their staves on our shoulders. Though my hand has been mute, my heart is kindly affected towards you. I trust we agree in essentials, and therefore should leave each other at rest with his circumstantials. I am weary of all disputes, and desire to know nothing but Jesus; to love him, trust in him and serve him; to choose and find him my only portion. I would have him my meat, my drink, my clothing, my sun, my shield, my Lord, my God, my All. Amen.

When I saw you in town, I gave you an invitation to Everton; and I now repeat it, offering you very kindly the use of my house and church. The Lord accompany you in all your journeys. Kind love to your brother.[3] Adieu.

John Berridge

---

[1] See November 22, 1760. There is no record of Wesley ever renewing his relationship with Berridge. Wesley visited places nearby but did not visit Everton. The Calvinistic controversy during the 1770s in which Berridge took part reinforced their separation. From this letter, which was published in 1783 in Wesley's magazine, *AM* (1783), 616, it seems that Berridge was at this stage unhappy with their division.

[2] Genesis 13:7 records the strife between Abraham's and Lot's herdsmen. Obviously the Evangelical leaders faced common enemies and needed a united front.

[3] Charles Wesley. See November 22, 1760.

To Lady Huntingdon[1]

Everton, December 30, 1768

My Lady,

When the frost broke up, I became a scald[2] miserable indeed; just able at times to peep into my Bible, but not able to endure the touch of a quill. I am now reviving, but not revived, and can venture to take up a pen. You shall have its first-fruits, such as they are.

I am glad to hear of the plentiful effusion from above on Talgarth.[3] Jesus has now baptised your College, and thereby shown his approbation of the work. You may therefore rejoice, but rejoice with trembling. Faithful labourers may be expected from thence, but if it is Christ's college a Judas will certainly be found amongst them. I believe the baptism will prove a lasting one, but I believe the sensible comfort will not last always nor long. Neither is it convenient. In

---

[1] This letter seems to show a complete change in Berridge's ideas about the value of the college. It is found in CHCA (Letter 17), a copy by Seymour; *ER* (1824), 74, with a cut section; Seymour, *Life of Huntingdon*, 2:94–96; *GS* (1842), 165–166; and *WB* (1864), 504–505, with minor differences. It is addressed to Lady Huntingdon at Brighton. Berridge is just entering a long period of illness that would virtually stop his itinerancy.

[2] Is Berridge referring to having a fever or is he just irritable? *WB* (1864) has "scalled."

[3] Two miles from Trevecca, Breconshire, Wales, where Lady Huntingdon founded a college in 1768 in order to train Evangelical ministers. Trevecca was in the parish of Talgarth. The background was the expulsion for Evangelical views of some students from St. Edmund Hall, Oxford. Lady Huntingdon leased a country house about a mile from Howell Harris, and the college was opened on her birthday, August 24, 1768. For a time she lived at the college. For a succinct account of the college and Lady Huntingdon's relationship to it until her death, see Edwin Welch, ed., *Cheshunt College—The Early Years: A Selection of Records edited with an introduction by Edwin Welch* (HRS, 1990), viii–ix. See also Geoffrey Nuttall, *The Significance of Trevecca College, 1768–1791* (Epworth Press, 1968), and Dorothy Eugenia Sherman Brown, "Evangelicals and Education in Eighteenth-Century Britain: A Study of Trevecca College, 1768–1792," Ph.D. thesis, University of Wisconsin–Madison (1992).

the present state of things, a winter is as much wanted to continue the earth fruitful as a summer. If the grass was always growing, it would soon grow to nothing; just as flowers, that blow[4] much and long generally blow themselves to death. And as it is thus with the ground, so it is with the labourers too. Afflictions, desertions, and temptations are as needful as consolations. Jonah's whale will teach a good lesson, as well as Pisgah's top[5]; and a man may sometimes learn as much from being a night and a day in the deep, as from being forty days in the mount.[6] I see Jonah come out of a whale and cured of rebellion[7]; I see Moses go up to the mount with meekness, but come down in a huff and break the tables.[8] Further I see three picked disciples[9] attending their Master to the mount, and fall asleep there. I believe you must be clad only in sackcloth, whilst you tarry in the wilderness, and be a right mourning widow till the Bridegroom fetch you home. Jesus has given you a hand and a heart to execute great things for his glory, and therefore he will deal you out a suitable measure of afflictions, to keep your balance steady. Did Paul labour more abundantly than all his brethren? He had more abundant stripes than they all. The Master will always new shave your crown, before he puts a fresh coronet upon your head; and I expect to hear of a six months' illness, when I hear of building a new chapel.

I cannot comfort you with saying that I think your day is almost spent; but it is some encouragement to know that your noon is past, and that your afternoon shadows lengthen. Go on, my dear lady, build and fight manfully, and believe lustily. Look upwards and press forwards. Heaven's eternal hills are before you, and Jesus stands with arms wide open to receive you. One hour's sight and enjoyment of the Bridegroom in his place above, will make you forget all your troubles on the way. Yet a little while, and he that shall come will come, and receive you with a heavenly welcome. Here we must purge and bleed,[10] for physic is needful, and a tender Physician administers all.

---

4   Bloom.
5   The mountain from which Moses saw the Promised Land before he died. Deuteronomy 34:1.
6   Paul's experience (2 Corinthians 11:25) compared with Moses on the mountain with God (Exodus 24:18).
7   Jonah 3:1.
8   Exodus 32:19.
9   Peter, James, and John on the Mount of Transfiguration (Luke 9:32).
10 Medical treatments of the day.

But inhabitants of heaven cry out and sing,

"We are no more sick!"
"Ah! Lord, with tardy steps I creep,
And sometimes sing, and sometimes weep;
Yet strip me of this house of clay,
And I will sing as sweet as they."[11]

A very heavy time have I had for the last three weeks; cloudy days and moonless nights. Only a little consolation fetched down now and then by a little dull prayer. At times I am ready to wish that sin and the devil were both dead; they make such a horrible racket within me and about me. Rather let me pray, Lord, give me faith and patience, teach me to expect the cross daily, and help me to take it up cheerfully. Woefully weary I am of myself, but know not how to live and feast daily upon Jesus. A treasure he is indeed, but lies hid in the field,[12] and I know not how to dig in the dark.

Your franks[13] are all spent, I find, and so poor Jack[14] must now be like Marget[15] in a cage, have all the chatter to himself. This looks mighty civil, but is not wondrous honest, for good folks should pay their debts, as well as give gifts. May daily showers from above fall upon you and refresh you, and the dew of heaven light upon your chapels and college. I remain your affectionate servant in a loving Jesus,

John Berridge

Kind respects to Miss Orton.[16]

---

[11] This is the last verse of Berridge's own hymn: "O happy saints, who dwell in light." See Hymn 143, *Sion's Songs*, 193–194.

[12] Matthew 13:44.

[13] Berridge has used up his paper and Lady Huntingdon will pay for the letter when she receives it. He can now only talk to himself. *WB* (1864) changes to "frames."

[14] Berridge himself.

[15] This may be a short form of Margaret, which was the country term for a magpie. A tame magpie was kept in a cage to attract other magpies, which were then killed.

[16] See December 26, 1767.

To George Whitefield[1]

Everton, May 22, 1769

Dear Sir,

Your kind note was received yesterday, which tells me where you have been and what you were doing. You have got your wings again, I find. 'Tis well. I wish I could send you a congratulation without envy, but I cannot. Whilst you are winging your way from county to county, and perching, like an eagle, on the cupola[2] of every tabernacle, I am sitting at home solitary, like a sparrow on the house-top, or rather like an owl in the desert.[3] Able I am, through God's mercy, *fruges consumere terrae*,[4] and scarce fit for anything else.[5]

At present I have no prospect of going anywhere from home to preach, and but for these words, "Wait the Lord's leisure"[6] and "thy

---

[1]   George Whitefield (1714–1770). One of the greatest itinerant preachers of all time, he took a leading role in the eighteenth-century revival. He came to preach at Everton soon after Berridge's conversion, and a little later, in early 1761, Berridge was happy to preach for him in London when Whitefield was on the verge of a physical breakdown. After this he preached most years during the winter months at Whitefield's Tabernacle until 1792, the winter before he died. This note shows their close relationship and the fact that they were kindred spirits. For a detailed and sympathetic approach to Whitefield, see Dallimore, *Whitefield*. Harry S. Stout, *The Divine Dramatist* (Grand Rapids: Eerdmans, 1991) provides a more critical and analytical account. Berridge is depressed as he writes this letter. Besides *WB* (1864), 443–444, the letter is found in *ST* (1879), 476, which I think is more faithful to the original punctuation and includes some extra phrases. The letter is introduced: "A friend at Devonport has sent the following characteristic letter by John Berridge. The original is dated May, 1769."
[2]   The dome forming the roof of a building.
[3]   Psalm 102:6,7.
[4]   "To eat the produce of the earth." From 1768 recurring illnesses and disabling asthma confined the once energetic preacher to his own home for long periods.
[5]   This sentence is omitted in *ST*.
[6]   Isaiah 40:31.

137

youth shall be renewed like the eagle's,"[7] I should never expect to go out again. Everything is apt to hurry and disquiet me, and at times I am scarce able to bear company. Indeed, if I may tell you the truth, I do not look for a speedy end of my troubles, because my heart is not humbled under the affliction. I cannot kiss the rod, nor let the Master quietly tumble and seize me, whip or kick his poor sorry whelp, just as he pleases. Sometimes I bark and howl, and sometimes grin and snap,[8] and whilst matters are at this pass 'tis no marvel that he keeps my feet in the stocks. I wish and pray for a resigned will, but have it not; yea, wish more for resignation than for health. Dear Lord, bestow it on me.

Oh, how churlish is my heart at times, much harder than a nether[9] millstone; then I sit and squat like some poor toad under a tile, and spit at everything that vexeth me. Anon, my heart is broken down with some sweet contrition, and then I get such charming sights of grace, such cheering gleams of love, as make me think I never shall grumble more. But these visits oft are short, and when they end I slide at once from heaven to earth, and downward still to hell, the hell of my own bosom. Weary I am of myself, right weary, and ashamed. Eleven years at a gospel school,[10] and have not yet half learnt the first lesson of the lowest form "Take up thy cross."[11] What a booby! None but Jesus could bear such dunces in his school. 'Tis well for me that he is God as well as man, else I should weary him out, and his compassions would fail.

But enough on this subject. Perhaps I may disquiet you, if you are a little sunk into the scald-miserable order.[12] Well, you are returned with a cold and hoarseness. Proper physic, after a five weeks Pentecostal feasting.[13] We are like children, always wanting the treacle pot, but a wise man says, "It is not safe, eating too much honey,"[14] and therefore

---

7 Psalm 103:5.
8 "nor let...grin and snap" only occurs in *ST*.
9 The lower stone on which the corn is ground.
10 Berridge was converted in late 1757.
11 Matthew 10:38.
12 Berridge is concerned that his own depression may affect Whitefield.
13 Whitefield had been touring the West Country. He reports to Robert Keen from Bristol on May 4: "I designed to go to Plymouth, but I have such a cold, and the weather begins to be so warm, that I know not how the issue will be. Hitherto, blessed be GOD, we have had golden seasons" (*A Select Collection of Letters of the Late Reverend George Whitefield*, 3 vols. [Dilly, 1772], 3:386).
14 The wise man Solomon. Proverbs 25:27.

thorns in the flesh[15] usually follow close at the heels of heavenly manifestations and succours. These thorns often seem to us a mere dead weight, but prove an excellent ballast, and keep our ship from oversetting. When we get into port we shall drop our ballast, this house of correction, and take our leave of the old man of sin, that hearty friend and cousin-german[16] of the devil.[17]

Oh for a safe passage and a happy landing, to be met and welcomed by Jesus, and embrace in the arms of this faithful and unchangeable Friend. Come, my brother, let us trudge on—whilst I creep do you run, and the Lord direct our feet, and quicken our pace, and prosper our work continually. Peace be with thee, and with all that love the Lord Jesus,

John Berridge

---

[15] 2 Corinthians 12:7.
[16] First cousin.
[17] "and take…devil" is only found in *ST*.

To Lady Huntingdon[1]

Summer 1769

...Mr. Glascott[2] has arrived—a very acceptable person to myself and to my flock. Not a dozing face, with a hoarse doctrinal throat; but a right sharp countenance, with a clear gospel pipe. He is going about Everton this week. Afterwards he goes out on Mondays and returns on Saturdays. In six weeks' time he will be able to visit not all, but most of my churches. I hope you can spare him so long at least. I thank you most heartily for sending. The Lord multiply his grace, mercy, and peace upon yourself and upon your churches....

---

[1] Lady Huntingdon had written to Berridge, asking him to come to the anniversary meeting at Trevecca College, thinking that the change of air might help him physically. Berridge wrote, declining the invitation because of his illness, which had reduced him to a state of great weakness. He also took the opportunity to thank her for sending Glascott to him. The extract and the context of the letter come from Seymour, *Life of Huntingdon*, 2:28.

[2] Cradock Glascott (1743–1831) had served as a curate at Shovel in Berkshire but after being dismissed had become an assistant chaplain to Lady Huntingdon and worked in her connexion until 1781, when, to Lady Huntingdon's great distress, he broke off formal relations with the connexion. He then became vicar of Hatherleigh in Devon for fifty years. He regularly helped Berridge at Everton during Berridge's long period of illness. Glascott was valued by Berridge and the church at Everton. See March 23, 1770; June 8, 1771; and January 28, 1788. In 1776 Glascott writes to a friend: "I shall stay with my old Everton friend a day or two" (C. Glascott to Mr. Sparke, November 30, 1776, Cheshunt College Archives, F1/0427, Westminster College, Cambridge).

To Lady Huntingdon[1]

Everton, January 9, 1770

My Lady,

…You complain that every new work, after a season, becomes a lifeless work. And was it not in the beginning as it is now? Do not the Acts and the Epistles show that the primitive churches much resembled our own? In their infancy we find them of one heart and soul, having all things common. But presently read of partiality in the distribution of their church-stock,[2] then of eager and lasting contentions about circumcision, coupling Moses with Jesus, and setting the servant on a level with his master. And Gentile churches were much on a footing with Jewish. The Corinthians soon fell into parties about their leaders,[3] into errors about the resurrection,[4] and into many gross immoralities.[5] The Galatians seemed ready at first to present Paul with their own eyes,[6] but grew desirous at last of plucking out his. The Ephesians had been much tossed with winds of doctrine.[7] The Colossians had fallen into will-worship,[8] etc. and the Thessalonians had some of our gossips among them,[9] who would not work, but sauntered about picking up news and telling tales. St. Paul's labours were much employed in Asia, and many churches were gathered there; yet I hear him complaining in a certain place, that they in Asia were turned aside from

---

[1] Lady Huntingdon had written, expressing her disappointments with some of her churches. After initial interest and success there was now deadness among those who had seemed to have such life and zeal. It is in the light of these concerns that Seymour, *Life of Huntingdon*, 1:386–387, chose this extract from Berridge's reply. It is included in *WB* (1864), 506–507.

[2] Acts 6:1.

[3] 1 Corinthians 1:12.

[4] 1 Corinthians 15:12.

[5] 1 Corinthians 5:1.

[6] Galatians 4:15.

[7] Ephesians 4:14.

[8] Colossians 2.

[9] 2 Thessalonians 3:11.

him.[10] The General Epistles,[11] which were written late, unanimously show that errors and corruptions had broke into all churches during the Apostles' lifetime; and the seven Epistles dictated by Jesus in the Revelation confirm the same.

Scripture mentions a former and a latter rain[12]; between which there must of course be an interval of drought and barrenness. The former rain falls just after seed-time, when there is plenty of manna coming down from above, plenty of honey flowing out of the rock, and plenty of joyful hosannahs rising up to Jesus. After this rain comes the interval, during which most of the stony and thorny grounds sheer off, taking a final leave of Jesus; and the good grounds are scarcely discernible, so barren they appear and full of weeds, and so exceedingly cold and swampy. Now one soars up into the cloud of perfection,[13] crying out, I am a queen! and becomes the devil's goddess. Another falls asleep and snores hard in election[14]; God's truth, indeed, is often made the devil's cradle. A third drops plump into a pond, and then keeps roaming day and night about the devil's wash-pot. A fourth gets bemired in the world, and lies quite contented, though nearly choked in the devil's quagmire. At length the Lord arises in just indignation to chastise and vex his people, continuing his plagues till he has broken their bones and humbled their hearts, causing them to see, and feel, and loathe their backslidings, and raising up a sigh and a cry in their hearts for deliverance. Then comes the latter rain to revive and settle; after which they learn to walk humbly with God....

John Berridge

---

[10] 2 Timothy 1:15.
[11] James, Peter, Jude, and John.
[12] Joel 2:23.
[13] Sinless perfection teaching of Wesley.
[14] Calvinistic teaching on the sovereignty of God in personal redemption.

To Lady Huntingdon[1]

Everton, March 23, 1770

My Lady,

Your letter just suited my case. It was bleeding plaster for a bleeding heart. These many months I have done little else but mourn for myself and others, to see how we lie among the tombs contented with a decent suit of grave clothes. At times my heart has been refreshed with these words, "On the land of my people is come up briars and thorns...until the Spirit be poured out upon them from on high,"[2] but the comfort soon vanishes, like gleams of a winter sun. I cannot wish for transports, such as we once had,[3] and which almost turned our heads, but I do long to see a spirit poured forth of triumphant faith, heavenly love, and steadfast cleaving to the Lord.

Before I parted with honest Glascott,[4] I cautioned him much against petticoat snares.[5] He had burnt his wings already. Sure he will not imitate a foolish gnat, and hover again about the candle? If he

---

[1]   Lady Huntingdon had recently written to Berridge, and she had made a slight allusion to the withdrawal of the help of Richard de Courcy (1743–1803) from her connexion. De Courcy was refused ordination in Ireland after serving as a curate to Walter Shirley at Loughrea. He came to England in 1768 and was connected with Lady Huntingdon. He was ordained in 1770, receiving the Crown living of St. Alkmund in 1774 and remaining there until his death. She was obviously seeking direction. Lady Huntingdon received Berridge's letter at Brighton on March 26! The letter is printed in Seymour, *Life of Huntingdon*, 1:388–390, and *WB* (1864), 507–510.

[2]   Isaiah 32:13,15.

[3]   Berridge, I think, is referring to the great success of the early days of the revival at Everton when many flocked to meetings and the gospel message spread around the whole area. He may be referring to the physical accompaniments of that early period. See April 20, 1770, for another retrospective view.

[4]   See Summer 1769 and January 28, 1788.

[5]   For Berridge's views on women and marriage, see ch. 14, "Berridge and Women," in Pibworth, *Gospel Pedlar*. He had a warm and positive relationship with women but he thought that an itinerate evangelist like himself would be hindered by marriage.

should fall into a sleeping-lap, he will soon need a flannel nightcap, and a rusty chain to fix him down, like a church-bible to the reading-desk. No trap so mischievous to the field preacher as wedlock, and it is laid for him at every hedge corner. Matrimony has quite maimed poor Charles,[6] and might have spoiled John and George,[7] if a wise Master had not graciously sent them a brace of ferrets.[8] Dear George has now got the liberty[9] again, and he will escape well if he is not caught by another tenterhook.[10]

Eight or nine years ago, having been grievously tormented with housekeepers, I truly had thought of looking out for a Jezebel myself. But it seemed highly needful to ask advice of the Lord; so falling down on my knees before a table, with a Bible between my hands, I besought the Lord to give me a direction. Then, letting the Bible fall open of itself, I fixed my eyes on these words, "When my son was entered into his wedding chamber, he fell down and died."[11] This frightened me heartily, you may easily think, but Satan, who stood peeping at my elbow, not liking the heavenly caution, presently suggested a scruple, that the book was Apocryphal,[12] and the words not to be heeded. Well, after a short pause, I fell on my knees again, and prayed the Lord not to be angry with me,

---

6   Berridge thought that Charles Wesley's happy marriage had blunted his evangelistic desires. It is true that after his marriage he undertook little itinerant preaching, but this may have been due to his views about the national Church and obedience to it.

7   John Wesley and George Whitefield.

8   Ferrets were used to drive rabbits out of their holes. Hence, this is a reference to Berridge's belief that Wesley and Whitefield were glad to itinerate due to their unhappy marriages. Dallimore is offended at this slur on Whitefield's marriage, saying: "All in all, there is much evidence that throughout many years the marriage was tolerably happy and that therefore Berridge's reference to her as 'a ferret' is grossly misleading" (*Whitefield*, 2:473). Henry Rack says that the description "was perhaps unfair to the former though less so to the latter. But Charles was less guilty than some of his brethren of subordinating domestic life to the exigencies of gospel ramblings" (*Reasonable Enthusiast*, 259). For a modern analysis of the Wesley marriages, see Anna M. Lawrence, "'A Most Solemn Season of Love': Charles Wesley and Marriage in Early Methodism," in Newport and Campbell, eds., *Wesley: Life, Literature and Legacy*, 465–485.

9   Mrs. Whitefield had died on August 9, 1768.

10   One of a set of hooks used in a frame (tenter) that stretches and dries cloth to make it even and square.

11   2 Esdras 10:1.

12   Those books not regarded as having the authority of Scripture by the Protestant Church, although read for profit and instruction.

whilst, like Gideon,[13] I requested a second sign, and from the Canonical Scriptures. Then letting my Bible fall open as before, I fixed my eyes directly on this passage, "Thou shalt not take thee a wife, neither shalt thou have sons or daughters in this place."[14] I was now completely satisfied, and being thus made acquainted with my Lord's mind, I make it one part of my prayers. And I can look on these words, not only as a rule of direction, but as a promise of security, Thou shalt not take a wife, that is, I will keep thee from taking one.

This method of procuring divine intelligence is much flouted by flimsy professors, who walk at large, and desire not that sweet and secret access to the mercy-seat, which babes of the kingdom do find. During the last twelve years I have had occasion to consult the oracle three or four times,[15] on matters that seemed important and dubious, and have received answers full and plain. Was not this the practice of the Jewish Church? God gave laws and statutes to them as well as to us; but when dubious cases arose they consulted the oracle,[16] which gave directions how to act. Joshua and Israel are blamed for not consulting the oracle before they made a league with the Gibeonites.[17] Yea, in the Patriarchal times, we find Rebecca inquiring of the Lord concerning her twins[18]; and are there not now, as well as formerly, many dubious cases? And can we think that God will deny that direction to the Christian Church which he freely granted to the Jewish? Is not access to the mercy-seat more free and more open than before? I believe perplexed cases are often sent on purpose to teach us to enquire of the Lord. But leaving the oracles of God we make an oracle of man. A dozen wise heads are consulted, and their sparkling opinions usually prove as various as the

---

[13] Gideon asked for another sign. Judges 6:39.

[14] Jeremiah 16:2.

[15] In the fly-leaf of his Bible Berridge notes the "Passages of Holy Writ given me, when in trouble or perplexity. I Chron. xvii. 1,2. June 22, 1758, when I began to itinerate, and when my Squire and Potton Vicar complained of me to the bishop. Revel. iii. 8,9,10,11. July 24, 1758, when my Squire complained to my College. Job. xi. 16,17,18,19—also Isaiah liv. 7,8,9,10—also Psal. xci. 14,15,16, after a long illness, much wanted to humble my heart, greatly lifted up. Jeremiah i. 19. Often given, as fresh troubles came. Jeremiah xvi. 2, given when I consulted the Lord about marriage." The editor, William Wileman, adds: "These passages are all marked in the text, and are the only portions in the Bible thus distinguished from others" (*Gospel Gems*, iv). See also August 10, 1774.

[16] The Urim and Thummim.

[17] Joshua 9.

[18] Genesis 25:22.

colours of the rainbow. Thus we are plunged into greater perplexity than before. A very proper chastisement for our folly! At my first setting out, I trudged on in this old beaten dirty track, and many wise folks perplexed me soundly, as I in my turn have perplexed yourself; witness the Welsh College.[19] At length I found the method little better than "seeking to familiar spirits, and to wizards that peep and mutter; should not a people seek to their God."[20] Daniel sought to his God, and got out the secret of Nebuchadnezzar's dream. "Oh yes" cries a casuistical professor, one of Isaiah's muttering wizards, "but this was a most extraordinary case." True, and yet David affirms that "the secret of the Lord is with all them that fear him."[21] Where is faith? Buried under mountains and not removing them.[22]

However, this oracular enquiry is not to be made on light and trifling occasions, and much less with a light and trifling spirit. Whoever consults the oracle aright will enter on the enquiry with the same solemnity as the High Priest entered into the Holy of Holies. Neither must this be done upon any day but a high day; not on trifling occasions, but on very important concerns. And whoever thus consults the word of God as his oracle, with a hearty desire to know and do God's will, I believe he will receive due information. Some people, I am told have had answers on their first enquiries, but afterwards have received no answer at all. The reason may be easily guessed. We begin our enquiries with momentous matters, and receive satisfaction. We naturally slide into matters of no moment, which are either plainly resolved by the word, or require only common faith and waiting; and thus we make the consultation [a] matter of amusement, like the drawing a picture-card out of a Scripture pack, which is not pleasing unto God. For though He is willing to be consulted, he is not willing to be trifled with, and much less to be made the subject of amusement or diversion.

John Berridge

---

[19] See Spring 1768.
[20] Isaiah 8:19.
[21] Psalm 25:14.
[22] Matthew 21:21.

To a Friend in London[1]

Everton, April 20, 1770

Dear Friend,

John Harding is returning to London and brings you this letter. The Lord take him under his protection and guidance. You have lived to see, I make no doubt, many hopeful plants wither, many soaring professors dwindle away and many Christian mariners wrecked. What a mercy it is we are yet in the ship, and bound for Canaan! Well, hitherto the Lord hath helped us; glory be to his grace. Not unto us, not unto us, but unto him be all the praise. How charmingly the blossoms look, and how pleasantly they smell, in a gospel spring. But how little fruit is found at the vintage! Some are running back to Egypt for its onion and garlic.[2] Others are living upon doctrines, sucking the shell and never cracking the nut. And a few, oh very few, are feeding on Christ. Some are wholly withered, some are mighty confident, and a few are watchful and prayerful, walking and looking like men that are waiting for the Lord. Indeed where the gospel comes it makes or mars often effectually, proves a savour of life or of death; either makes men the salt of the earth or the refuse of all things. Come, my friend, let us trudge on with circumspection. There are many pillars of salt[3] on our right hand and left which bids us be cautious; and a good Christ is before us, who bids us be bold. Let us lean on his arm, and tread in his steps; taking his word for our rule, and his Spirit for our guide. We run for a crown. The race is but one heat, and the further we run the more strength we shall get. Much of the course is now past, and then heavenly hills are in view, and Jesus stands at the goal, with crowns in his

---

[1] This letter in manuscript is held in the MARC, PLP 8 43.3. During Berridge's long illness he had opportunity to review the past and reconsider his own theology. This is very much a personal letter of encouragement in the light of his own experience. We do not know the recipient.

[2] Faced with difficulty and trial, the children of Israel wanted to return to Egypt rather than enter the Promised Land. Numbers 11:5.

[3] When Lot's wife was fleeing from Sodom she looked back and became a pillar of salt (Genesis 19:26).

147

hands, ready to place them upon the conquerors' heads. Oh for wings of faith and wings of love to speed our flight. We are running through a wilderness to paradise; are flying from hell to heaven, parting with self and sin to embrace a God and Christ in Glory. All the saints triumphant were once on earth as we are, wrestling, struggling, fighting, praying as we do. Now their warfare is over. Jesus has brought them safe through, and "Jesus is the same yesterday today and for ever."[4] He can make us also more than conquerors through his love.

Dear Christian, salutations to all your shepherds and the flocks. Kind love to yourself and your wife. Grace and peace be with you both, and with

John Berridge

---

4   Hebrews 13:8.

To James Berridge[1]

Everton, June 9, 1770

Dear Brother,

I have been pretty well in the winter, but am now worse again, and scarce able to bear company. These afflictions will be over by-and-by, and if they are sanctified I shall have reason to bless God for them. Dear brother, you and I are growing old apace. Is it not time to think seriously of that world to which we are hastening? What will your farms and your money profit you when you are laid in the cold grave, and appear naked at Christ's bar? The Lord bless you, and give you to think of these things....

Believe me, your affectionate brother,

John Berridge

---

[1] I think this is an extract with personal details removed, leaving the spiritual challenge. See July 9, 1759. Taken from S (1893), 29. Berridge sold part of his family inheritance (see May 3, 1773). James was two years younger than Berridge and was to die in Sutton Bonnington, Nottinghamshire, two years later. See July 9, 1759, for details of the rest of the family.

To Rowland Hill[1]

Everton, October 31, 1770

Dear Sir,

When God designs any for special service he prepares them for it by special trials. Joseph must be hated by his brethren, banished [from] his country, villainously accused, and then imprisoned, before he becomes the ruler of Egypt.[2] David must be despised by his brethren, banished [from] the court, and hunted like a flea in the wilderness, before he takes Judah's sceptre.[3] I look upon your present trials as a happy omen of future service, and if you continue waiting and praying, a door will be

---

[1] We have several accounts of this letter as well as the manuscript held in JWFP MARBL, Box 1 Folder 70. The copy in the *Methodist New Connexion Magazine* (1817), 300–301, removes the odd phrase that might cause offence, such as "must be hated by his brethren" and "be despised by his brethren," because of its implications for Hill's family. *CM* (1841), 601, removes the section about Scotland and Lady Glenorchy being a prop and the section on the Master sending out his old ass again. The account in *GS* (1852), 147–148, occasionally removes a phrase. The letter is addressed "For Mr. R. Hill at The Rev. Mr. Buckley's at Kippax near Ferry-bridge, Yorkshire." Edward Buckley (1743–1783), a college friend of Hill, had obtained ordination, becoming the curate at Kippax in 1767 (vicar in 1770), a substantial parish near Pontefract in Yorkshire and the home of Lady Huntingdon's niece, Mrs. Medhust. He was concerned with Hill's failure to secure ordination and a post in the national Church. Buckley had written to Hill as follows: "My dear friend, I had the favour of yours, and know not whether to say I am sorry or not for the refusal you have lately met with, since I doubt not it is the will of a good and gracious God that it should be so. It would be conferring an honour and pleasure upon me, if you would make my house your home, and the sooner you come, the greater will be the obligation. Let the next post inform me that you are on your journey northwards; perhaps the Bishop of York, who is one of the most candid men in the world, will do for you what the Bishop of Lichfield has refused; we probably can muster up some friends for you here, who will stir and interest themselves more in your behalf than any of your own relations" (Sidney, *Life of Rowland Hill*, 49).
[2] Genesis 37–50.
[3] 1 Samuel 23 – 2 Samuel 2.

opened by and by. Be not solicitous about orders.[4] As soon as they are wanted they will drop into your lap. In the meantime, be the Lord's running footman, a gip[5] of Christ's college, ready to run at every man's call. And perhaps you may find more pleasure in this rambling service than in any other. Jesus loves his scouts[6] dearly, for he was once such himself; and all that can perform the office of a gip cheerfully shall have many a kind look and many a good bit[7] from their Master. The spaniel that has been hunting all day is allowed to come between his master's legs at night, and gets kissed, and stroked, and fed; while old Sly, the house dog, is kicked from the fire, and goes supperless to bed.

I observe further concerning your present situation, it may possibly grow more dusky before it clears up. The darkest moment in the whole night is just before the day-break. Be not therefore discouraged, if your sky becomes more dark and cloudy. Your affairs must come to a crisis, and at that crisis the Lord comes. Your Abraham must go to the summit of the mount, bind his dear Isaac, take the cruel knife in his hand, and point it at the poor child's throat, and then the Lord appears. In the mount He will be seen.[8] Oh for faith and patience; the Lord has good reasons to delay his coming; and blessed are they that wait for him.

How kindly has Jesus stopped your journey to Scotland, and shown, I think, that you have no business there, at least not for the present. Perhaps Lady Glenorchy[9] has been your prop of late; if so, it is very friendly in Jesus to kick away that wooden leg. And when he has dried up all your earthly cisterns, and your own pitcher of water is spent too, He will conduct you to a spring as he conducted Hagar.[10] Fear not, only believe. Stand still, and let the Lord work his own work

---

4   Ordination.
5   A Cambridge name for a college servant and bed-maker.
6   The Oxford term for a college servant.
7   Old form for "bite." The working dog gets fed more than the house dog.
8   Genesis 22:14.
9   Viscountess Willielma Glenorchy (1741–1786) adopted Evangelical views in about 1765 after her religious concern was aroused through her friendship with Rowland's sister Jane. On the death of her husband in 1771 she became very wealthy and later founded chapels for her followers in Exmouth, Newton Burhill, Edinburgh, Carlisle, Matlock, Buxton, and Strathfillan. See D.P. Thomson, *Lady Glenorchy and Her Churches—The Story of 200 Years* (Crieff: Barnoak, 1967) and T.S. Jones, *The Life of the Right Honourable Willielma Viscountess Glenorchy, containing extracts from her diary and correspondence* (Edinburgh: White, 1824).
10   Genesis 21:19.

and take his own time, and you shall see his salvation.

I have had a miserable summer; Jesus flogging and poor Jack pouting and snarling. I am now better, and can preach once a week, blessed be God, and have some hope that the Master will send out his old ass once more to alarm the devil and the minor prophets of Cam[11] with his bray by and by.

Give my dear love to Mr. Buckley.[12] He must be honest and bold for Jesus if he can welcome you. What a mercy it is there are some left who are not afraid of the cross, nor ashamed to receive a stigmatised pilgrim. Go on, dear Sir, and may your coat be more bespattered for Jesus. The more muck the more money, says the farmer, and so says the Christian. Nothing so scandalous in his eyes as a clean coat, clean shoes, and a flannel nightcap. The Lord bless you both and be gracious to

John Berridge

---

[11] The river Cam flows through Cambridge; thus the area. *GS* changes this to Canaan.
[12] The Rev. Edward Buckley (1743–1783), in whose house Hill was staying. See introductory note to letter.

To Rowland Hill[1]

Everton, January 19, 177[1]

Dear Sir,

As the eyes of a servant wait upon the hand of his master, so should our eyes wait upon the Lord. A servant is guided by his master's hand as well as his word; and the servants of God must be guided by providences as well as by the written word. Your situation and conduct, I think, must be regulated altogether by the providential hand. It behoves you to stand still, and not to hurry; keep your eyes upon Jesus; and pray much that he may give you a spiritual eye to discern his providential finger, and a spiritual heart to follow its direction. When the cloud *seems* to move towards any place, prepare to follow it, but pray still to be kept from the delusions of your own spirit, and from the wrong counsel of others. If you walk in this path, neither guided by your own, nor mine, nor any other foolish judgment, but simply waiting upon the Lord, he will certainly direct your way. And if, to mortify your pride, he suffer you at any time to mistake his mind and act indiscreetly, as he suffered Peter in the affair of Malchus,[2]

---

[1] Rowland Hill (see December 18, 1764) had spent the winter at his father's house at Hawkstone. His family were against his field preaching, and although he was strongly attached to the articles and liturgy of the Church of England, Hill, because of his irregularity, failed to achieve from the bishop of Lichfield the ordination that he was seeking at this time. We have this letter in manuscript form held at JWFP MARBL, Box 1 Folder 69. This gives us the chance to examine the editing of *CM* (1841), 600–601, which published the letter. Large parts that deal with personalities (his elder brother, Richard; Pentycross's scruples; Venn coming to Yelling; Mr. Lyon moving away from Everton; and Johnny Stittle's visit) are excluded. Sidney, *Life of Rowland Hill*, 50–53, gives parts of the letter, including the background. However, there must be a mistake with the date, as Berridge says in the postscript that "Penty has published a monody on the death of Mr. Whitefield: it is poetical and pretty." Whitefield died on September 30, 1770, and thus the date must be 1771 and not 1770 as on the manuscript. It seems that, writing in January, Berridge used last year's date by mistake, or he dated it in accord with the old standard, under which years commenced on March 25.

[2] John 18:10.

when he has rebuked you, he will soon heal Malchus's ear, and set all matters right again.

Be not anxious about orders, they will come as soon as wanted, nor be anxious about anything, but to know the Lord's will, and do the Lord's work. One of your Master's titles is "Counsellor" and a wonderful counsellor he is. Therefore, ask no counsel, and take no counsel, but of the Lord; so shall you walk more evenly, than if you had the whole congregation of Gospel divines at your elbow every moment to advise you.

Your late successful expedition seems a providential prelude for field preaching next summer; and if Yorkshire is to be the field of action, Wales must lay out of your way; and as the Master has set his young ass a braying, it seems not likely that he should send him to Wales for a schooling.[3] However, this is all but conjecture, and I would not give a groat[4] for a hat brimful of such wisdom. The cloudy pillar[5] must direct you; keep to that and you are safe. I called you an ass,[6] and I would have you always think yourself one, and always pray the Master to ride on his ass when you go to preach; there will be plenty of hosannas, and you will go on triumphantly. Oh, 'tis a glorious thing to dance before the ark, and make ourselves vile, as David did.[7] What if you are taunted by a relative[8] as David was, mind it not. Jesus will kiss and bless you. I long to see you a right gospel ass, kicking up your heels and braying before a deluded people and their mad prophets.

Avoid no dirt, refuse no shame, but part with all your honour for Jesus as freely as He parted with heaven for you. As Paul was, so be thou, a fool for Christ's sake, yea, the very scum and offscouring of all things.[9] I believe the Lord Jesus, who has a peculiar love for your family, intended this honour for your elder brother, but through bad advice he has declined it; and the Lord now seems to be conferring this honour upon you; which will make the younger brother prove at length

---

[3]   Presumably a reference to Lady Huntingdon's college at Trevecca.

[4]   See January 1765.

[5]   The children of Israel were led in the wilderness by a cloudy pillar. See Numbers 9:17.

[6]   Berridge referred to himself as the Everton ass. He goes on to make a reference to Christ riding on the donkey.

[7]   When the ark was brought back into Jerusalem David was leaping and dancing. His wife Michal despised him for his behaviour. 2 Samuel 6:16.

[8]   His brother, Richard Hill, had been an active lay evangelist, but he had recently been persuaded to stop.

[9]   1 Corinthians 4:10–13.

the better gentleman. I am glad you find a peaceful refuge for the present, and good winter quarters at Hawkstone; but if the Lord makes you take the field in the spring, and gives success, you may expect that friends and foes will fasten on you, like leeches; and needfully fasten to draw out the hot and bad blood which a successful expedition will occasion.

Poor Penty,[10] I fear, will not take a degree, or not take it honestly.[11] He came to my house about a three weeks ago, and brought two pockets full of doubts and scruples, relating to the Articles and Liturgy. I would fain have had the scruples left at Everton, but he took them all back with him to college, and seemed determined not to part with them. However, from the precipitate step he formerly took in signing a college paper, I apprehend it possible he may take a flying leap into a degree still. There is something very amiable in dear Penty. I believe the Lord loves him and designs him for great things. Perhaps he may be intended for a spiritual comet, a field preacher, as well as yourself. This seems to be his aim and ambition. If he cannot subscribe Church Articles, he does not mean to settle amongst Dissenters. He wants to raise a flock of his own, and I hope the Lord will give him one. When he left me, he talked of going to the Welsh college.[12] May the Lord direct him.

I am now able, blessed be God, to preach twice on a Sunday and once a Wednesday. A very small matter, indeed; but I am become somewhat thankful for a day or a week of small things. Whether this strength will continue, when the hot season returns, I know not, nor is it needful to know at present. This only do I know, that all my troubles are of my own procuring. My pride set my feet in the stocks, and brings fresh rods and more harrows on my back. I know Jesus loves

---

10 Thomas Pentycross (1748–1808), a close friend and ally of Rowland Hill, while at Cambridge. His scruples about the national Church and his itinerating for Robert Robinson, the Baptist minister at Cambridge, delayed his graduation. He overcame his objections to taking orders and was made deacon by Berridge's old bishop, now at Winchester, John Thomas, on September 9, 1771, becoming the curate of Horley in Surrey. He later served as vicar of Wallingford (1774–1808), where he had great success. For a modern account of his life, see Tim Shenton, "Thomas Pentycross (1748–1808): Faithful to One Cause," in *Forgotten Heroes of Revival: Great Men of the 18th Century Evangelical Awakening* (Leominster: Day One, 2004), 166–89.

11 In order to obtain a degree one had to subscribe to the articles and Prayer Book of the national Church. Pentycross took his BA degree in 1771.

12 Trevecca. See December 26, 1767 and December 30, 1768.

me, and therefore takes the trouble to scourge me soundly. I feel the furnace humbles my heart, and yet I seem full of pride still.

Mr. Venn[13] has got a new living, which is but 8 miles from Everton. This is [a] matter of joy to me, and I hope will be serviceable to my flocks. I send my best Christian respects to your brother; and give him a hearty invitation, which I believe he cannot accept, to Everton. May Jesus bless him, and direct you, and lift up the light of his countenance on us all. Grace be with you, and with your,

John Berridge

P.S. Mr. Lyons[14] and family intend to settle at Bath in the summer. John Stittle[15] preached at my house in the holidays. He is a wonderful

---

[13] Henry Venn (1724–1797) came to Yelling as a dying man, or so he thought, after twelve years of great success at Huddersfield. He had been appointed as rector at Yelling on December 24, 1770. His own conversion occurred gradually in the early 1750s as he came to realize that his guide, William Law, seemed to undervalue the atonement as the sacrifice for sins. See F.W.B. Bullock, *Evangelical Conversion in Great Britain, 1696–1834* (St. Leonards-on-Sea: Budd and Gillatt, 1959), 83–86. He already knew Berridge from university days and had visited Everton during the early days of revival. In 1763 Venn had published *The Complete Duty of Man: or, a system of doctrinal and practical Christianity; with prayers for families and individuals* (Glasgow: Collins, 1829), stressing the need to trust Christ alone for salvation in contrast to the popular *The Whole Duty of Man*. See November 24, 1781, for Berridge's high view of Venn's family. See August 10, 1774, for their common perspective, although Venn seems to have had more of a conscience over itinerating than Berridge. This is shown later in Venn's discouraging Simeon from adopting Berridge's pattern. For accounts of Venn's life, see Venn, *Life and Letters of Venn*; Loane, *Cambridge and the Evangelical Succession*; and Bill Reimer, "The Spirituality of Henry Venn," *Churchman* (Winter 2000).

[14] John Lyons (1731–1775) lived in Tetworth from the early 1760s. His first two children were born in Antigua, which suggests he had property there. He was presumably ill and was going to Bath for medical reasons. See March 20, 1771.

[15] Johnny Stittle (1727–1813), one of Berridge's helpers. Born at Madingley and by trade a hedger and thatcher, he was converted through the preaching of Berridge and later became minister of the newly formed Green Street Independent Meeting House in Cambridge from 1781 until his death in 1813. He could read well but could not write. When Simeon became more moderate in his Calvinism some of those who attended his church transferred themselves to Stittle's chapel. Simeon very generously gave him a quarterly allowance for looking after his stray sheep! See Courtney S. Kenny, "A Forgotten Cambridge Meeting-House," *Transactions of the Congregational Society* (1909), 4:228–229, and Andrew Adam Smith,

man, indeed; somewhat lifted up at present, I think, but his Master will take him by the nose by-and-by. Penty[16] has published a monody[17] on the death of Mr. Whitefield; it is poetical and pretty.

"Nonconformity in Green Street, Cambridge," *Presbyterian Historical Society of England* (1969), 64–5.

[16] Pentycross.

[17] A poem in which the mourner bewails someone's death. Whitefield died on September 30, 1770. Pentycross was acquainted with Thomas Gray at Cambridge and had poetical gifts; his poem "Wittenham-Hill" (1777) received a third edition in 1812. I have failed to find any record of the monody.

To Cornelius Winter[1]

Everton, February 12, 1771

Dear Sir,

I have been exceeding low the last summer, unable to preach, unable to write. When I felt somewhat better, then I heard of Mr. Whitefield's death and did not know but that accident might bring you back to England. You are come over for orders, and if they are needful to promote the Redeemer's interest, they will be granted; if not needful, they will be withheld. Lay the matter daily before the Lord, leave it with him. Such circumstances are designed to show that your whole life must be a life of faith. I wish you would desire Mr. Gould of Hoxton Square[2] to pay the lenths[3] of my living. He has often done this for me and sent the receipt in a letter. If it suited your convenience, I should be glad to see you at Everton. Let me know how you succeed about the orders, and what success you met with in your ministry at Georgia. The Lord bless you and your truly affectionate friend,

John Berridge

---

[1] This letter is taken from the Wesley Historical Society Library Manuscript Book, 70–71, and was copied into it from the original manuscript by George Stampe on March 4, 1904. It is addressed to "Cornelius Winter at the Tabernacle near Moorfields, London." Winter had just returned to England from America on the death of Whitefield, whom he had been helping, and was seeking to be ordained. The copy date looks like 1776 but the letter is obviously 1771.

[2] Laid out in 1683, the square became fashionable in the eighteenth century. It was the home of the Nonconformist Hoxton Square Academy.

[3] I think this is "tenths." The tenth part of the annual profit of every living originally paid to the pope but transferred to the Crown by Henry VIII. In 1704 the fund was established by Queen Anne for the relief of the poorer clergy and was called Queen Anne's Bounty. It was merged with the Ecclesiastical Commission in 1948. See G.F.A. Best, *Temporal Pillars: Queen Anne's Bounty, the Ecclesiastical Commissioners, and the Church of England* (Cambridge: Cambridge University Press, 1964). Although the amount was not great to Berridge, because the tax was rated according to the valuation made in the time of Henry VIII, he was relieved of the burden through this friend in London.

To John Newton[1]

Everton, March 13, 1771

Dear Sir,

In November I gathered strength enough to preach, and through mercy have continued preaching ever since. For the last month I have shared with my neighbours in a cold, which has kept me wheezing and coughing, and pulled me down, but not laid me up. Oh, how needful is the furnace both to discover our dross, and to purge it away! How little do we know of ourselves of the pride, sensuality, and idolatry of our hearts, till the Lord lays us down on a bed, and searcheth all our inward parts round with his candles. My heart, I knew, was bad enough, but I scarcely thought there was half the baseness in it which I find, and yet I know not half its plague. How sweet is the mercy of God, and how rich is the grace of Jesus, when we have had an awful peep into our hearts! This makes us prize the gospel, embrace the Saviour, and fly to his cross. At times I am so overwhelmed with the filth and mire of my nature, that I can scarcely look through it unto Jesus. And when he has put on a little of his eye-salve, and scoured off my films, I stand amazed to think he can touch such a leper. And yet when the sun shines clear for a season, and my dung hill is covered with snow, I forget my leprosy, or become a leper only in speculation. I think it perhaps, but do not feel it, nor am humbled by it.

---

[1]   John Newton (1725–1807), the converted slave trader who became one of the leading Evangelical clergy of his day. A close friendship is revealed by their letters. In 1764 Newton became curate at Olney in Buckinghamshire, twenty-six miles from Everton, where he befriended the poet William Cowper. Newton occasionally visited Everton, and Berridge had friends at Olney. See Bruce Hindmarsh, *John Newton and the English Evangelical Tradition* (Oxford: Clarendon, 1996); Jonathan Aitken, *John Newton: From Disgrace to Amazing Grace* (Continuum, 2007); and Richard Cecil, updated by Marylynn Rousse, *The Life of John Newton* (Fearn: Christian Focus, 2000). The manuscript is in LPL, MS 3972 f.13. The letter is included in *WB* (1838), 369–371, and *WB* (1864), 362–364. They show only minor punctuation editing.

What a heap of absurd contradiction is man, and most of all the perfect man cast in the foundry![2] Well might the Redeemer say, "I am God, and not man; and therefore ye children of Jacob are not consumed."[3] After an affliction, I think I can say with David, It is good for me to have been afflicted[4]; I can see and feel some profit attending it. Indeed, I never grow really wiser or better, unless when I am baptised both with the Holy Ghost and with fire. If the dove comes without a furnace, my heart is soon overset; pride steals in and heaven's blest beams turn everything sour within me.

The volume of sermons[5] which you sent, I was possessed of before; and wanted the first small volume of sermons,[6] which you published. This volume being small you may bring it with you to Everton, when you visit us again, which I hope will be in spring. I have no prospect of going abroad at present, for though my flesh has revisited my bones, my breast and stomach remain weak, and my body is tender.

I like your *Ecclesiastical History*[7] much; but am rather sorry you have undertaken to carry it through; sorry for your sake, not the readers'. I fear it will chill your spirit and deaden your soul. Much writing is pernicious. Besides, you just read over many dry and barren histories; you must bring to light many controversies, foolish or noxious, which had better lie buried fifty fathoms deep; and from the fourth century to the Reformation you must be rooting in kennels[8] continually. However, study to be concise.

I have enclosed half a guinea in the letter for the Sermons and History. Present my Christian respects to Mrs. Newton,[9] and to such

---

[2]   John Wesley's society met in an old foundry. Hence, a reference to John Wesley's doctrine of perfectionism.

[3]   Malachi 3:6.

[4]   Psalm 119:71.

[5]   *Sermons Preached in the Parish Church of Olney in Buckinghamshire* (1767).

[6]   *Six Discourses (or Sermons) as Intended for the Pulpit* (Liverpool: 1760).

[7]   *A Review of Ecclesiastical History, so far as it concerns the progress, declensions and revivals of Evangelical doctrine and practice with a brief account of the spirit and methods by which vital and experimental religion have been opposed in all ages of the church* (Edward and Charles Dilly, 1769).

[8]   The hole or lair of a fox—thus, looking in dark and dirty places for that which is profitable.

[9]   Mary Newton (née Catlett; 1729–1790). John and Mary were married in Rochester on February 12, 1750, and had a very close and committed relationship.

of your flock as know me. The Lord bless both the shepherd and the sheep, enriching all your souls with active faith, fervent love, and deep humility and may dear Jesus bless poor

John Berridge

To Miss Orton[1]

Everton, March 20, 1771

Dear Madam,

I have eaten up all your ginger, and it is now high time to thank you for it. My gratitude is long in coming, but it was not mislaid or forgot; I have been thinking to send it every week for these four months, but sometimes real sickness prevented and sometimes strong vapours overcame me. At length my gratitude comes, and being too bulky for the post, is sent by the waggon packed up in a hamper.

I am the same lazy, crazy fellow as usual, chattering a little on a Sunday, then wounded and groaning most of the week after. My breast is weak and tender, my head fanciful and roving, my mind much disposed to be fretful, and my feet ready to quarrel with the weight of my carcase. 'Tis well I have such a Saviour as Jesus; for none but Jesus could make anything of me, or bear with me. I am growing violently out of conceit with myself every year, and hope soon to be one of Job's scholars, and loathe myself in dust and ashes. I do long for that gospel brokenness of heart, which will make me vile in my own eyes, and bring me weeping, like my sweet-heart Molly Magdalene, to the feet of Jesus. Dear Jesus! Do not you love him, Madam? Sure he is precious in your eyes, and dearly welcome to your heart. Do you not look and sigh for him after and sometimes drop a tender tear for him? If he gives a flourish at your window, or plays around your heart he will certainly moisten your eyes,

---

[1] The manuscript addressed to "Miss Orton at Bath" is held in FBC, Box CO10. Jennett Payne Orton (d.1799) was an intimate friend of Lady Huntingdon who travelled often with her in her Christian work. See December 26, 1767. She was born in the Island of St. Christopher in the West Indies, where her family held substantial property. She supported many Evangelical causes from her means. Lady Huntingdon left all her chapels and houses to her and her husband, Thomas Haweis (whom she married in 1788), along with Lady Anne Erskine and John Lloyd. See Seymour, *Life of Huntingdon*, 2:490. She died at Bath following a long illness that was the result of a carriage accident.

and turn the rock into a river. I am never well, but when I am thus weeping; never happy but when my eyes are drowned in tears; and I could wish these eyes were a fountain of tears, that I might weep day and night.

My heart, through grace, has been following Jesus for some years, but of late it has chiefly delighted to attend him at Gethsemane and Calvary. Christ is everywhere precious, but on a cross he is glorious. His love appears great when he is preaching or healing, but it shines forth godlike indeed when he is bleeding and dying. No sight of Christ humbles the soul, and melts down the heart, like this. If you would be well out of conceit with the world, yourself, and sin, learn to look on a crucified Jesus, and dwell at his cross. It seems a very barren tree and a naked prospect to self-righteous man, but is the Christian's tree of life, and opens his view of heaven.

Pray, what is become of our good Lady?[2] Is she gone to Georgia, or gone to Wales, or gone to heaven? I hear nothing of her, and the papers are silent about her. If she is upon earth, I suppose she has got some work in hand for her Master; and I scarce think she is fled to the skies, because I lately received some salt of amber[3] from her. When you write to her, pray inform the Countess that poor Jack of Everton is still alive, but mightily crazy; has received her amber, and thanks her heartily, and loves her dearly. All blessings attend her.

My heart is in deep mourning at the thought of parting with Mr. Lyon's family, but it seems needful. May the Lord bless the waters to Mr. Lyons, and make the removal prove beneficial to the souls of all the family. Why, Mr. Shirley has got a gospel wife,[4] I hear; great luck indeed! Pray give my dear love to them both. I have got a budget[5] full of kindness for Mr. Glascott,[6] but I send none. The budget shall not be opened, till he comes to Everton.

Dear Madam, press forwards; you are in the right road to glory. Honour and immortality are before you, and Jesus is waiting to receive you. May you daily grow more bold in his service; more simple,

---

[2] Lady Huntingdon.

[3] A natural antibiotic containing succinic acid that was used as a general curative for centuries.

[4] See January 1765. Walter Shirley had married Henrietta Maria Phillips (d.1792) on August 27, 1766. A gospel wife would be a committed Christian who fully supported her husband's gospel preaching.

[5] A bag or wallet made of leather.

[6] See Summer 1769.

loving and childlike in your conduct. May your union with Jesus grow stronger, and your communion grow sweeter and closer, till the bridegroom sends for you home, and puts the crown on your head.

Grace and peace be with you and with your affectionate servant,

John Berridge

To Rowland Hill[1]

Everton, May 8, 1771

Dear Rowly,

My heart sends you some of its kindest love, and breathes its tenderest wishes for you. I feel my heart go out to you whilst I am writing, and can embrace you as my second self. How soft and sweet are those silken cords which the dear Redeemer twines and ties about the hearts of his children! How different from mere natural affection, and much more from vicious self-love. Surely it is a pleasant thing to love with a pure heart fervently, and something of this love I feel for you, which brings a melting tear into my eye, and refreshes my very body as I write. Grace, mercy, and peace be with you. May heavenly truth beam into your soul, and heavenly love inflame your heart.

I suppose you are now arrived in the West, and are working as a labourer in your Master's vineyard. Be faithful and diligent, and look up to your Master continually for direction and assistance. Remember his gracious promise, "Lo, I am with you always, even to the end of the world."[2] He will supply you with wisdom, strength, and courage: for he sends none upon a warfare at their own cost. I think your chief work for a season will be to break up fallow ground. This suits the accent of your voice at present. God will give you other tongues when they are wanted; but now he sends you out to thrash the mountains, and a glorious thrashing it is.

Go forth, my dear Rowly, wherever you are invited into the devil's territories; carry the Redeemer's standard along with you; and blow

---

[1] The background of this letter is a preaching tour that Hill made around many parts of Gloucestershire, Somerset, and Wiltshire. His headquarters were in Bath at the house of Lady Huntingdon. This was a difficult period in Hill's life as he faced opposition from his family, problems obtaining ordination, and a lack of money. Hence Berridge's encouragement. The letter is in Sidney, *Life of Rowland Hill* (1834), 57–58; Seymour, *Life of Huntingdon*, 2:50–51; *CM* (1841), 601–602; and *WB* (1864), 510–511. It was addressed "For R. Hill, Esq. to be left with the right hon. the Countess of Huntingdon, at Bath, Somersetshire."

[2] Matthew 28:20.

the Gospel trumpet boldly, fearing nothing but yourself. If you meet with success, as I trust you will, expect clamour and threats from the world, and a little venom now and then from the children. These bitter herbs make good sauce for a young recruiting sergeant, whose heart would be lifted up with pride, if it was not kept down by these pressures. The more success you meet with, the more opposition you will find; but Jesus sitteth above the water-floods and remaineth a King forever. His eye is ever upon you, and his heavenly guards surround you. Therefore fear not; go on humbly, go on boldly trusting only in Jesus, and all opposition shall fall before you.

Make the Scriptures your only study, and be much in prayer. The apostles gave themselves to the word of God and to prayer. Do thou likewise; labour to keep your mind in a heavenly frame; it will make your work pleasant, and your preaching and your conversation savoury. Now is your time to work for Jesus; you have health and youth on your side, and no church or wife on your back. The world is all before you, and providence your guide and guard. Go out therefore, and work whilst the day lasteth: and may the Lord Jesus water your own soul and give ten thousand seals to your ministry.

I am with great affection, your friend,

John Berridge

To Lady Huntingdon[1]

Everton, May 8, 1771

...I find you have got honest Rowland[2] down to Bath; he is a pretty young spaniel, fit for land or water, and has a wonderful yelp. He forsakes father, and mother, and brethren, and gives up all for Jesus; and I believe will prove a useful labourer, if he keeps clear of petticoat snares. The Lord has owned him much at Cambridge and in the North, and I hope will own him more abundantly in the West....

...Mr. Winter,[3] who went to Georgia with Mr. Whitefield, and returned last Christmas, called lately upon me, and acquainted me with the state of the Orphan-house. He says there are but few Orphans in the house, and no symptoms of grace in any. Mr. Wright[4] has the whole management of the house, who, according to my little knowledge of him, seems neither to have zeal nor grace enough for the work. Mr. Whitefield, when at Georgia, made a sumptuous feast on a Sunday for all the better dressed people,[5] intending to renew this every year by way of commemoration; but I hope you will put a stop to this guttling

---

[1]   Seymour, *Life of Huntingdon*, 2:49, 255, gives two extracts of a letter. Only one extract is dated the 8th, although because the other is given as May it is more than likely they are part of the one letter. It is the same date as the letter to Hill.

[2]   Rowland Hill. See May 8, 1771 and December 18, 1764.

[3]   See Winter 1767 and February 12, 1771. Cornelius Winter's role at Bethesda, which had been founded by Whitefield as an orphan home in Georgia but was being expanded with a view to becoming a college, was educating the negroes on the plantation. Edward J. Cashin says that Winter "took a jaundiced view of what he considered to be the secularization of Bethesda" (*Beloved Bethesda: A History of George Whitefield's Home for Boys, 1740-2000* [Macon: Mercer University Press, 2001], 103).

[4]   Ambrose Wright, the manager at Bethesda, had been sent out by Whitefield to improve and extend the buildings in order to support a college.

[5]   Whitefield had invited the rulers and legislators of Georgia to Bethesda and had supplied "a handsome and plentiful dinner" and entertainment. There were eulogistic reports of Whitefield's work in the Assembly of Georgia and in the newspaper. For an account of this event based on the *Georgia Gazette*, see Stout, *Divine Dramatist*, 273-274.

business.[6] I wish the Orphan-house may not soon become a mere Blue-coat Hospital and Grammar school.[7] If Mr. Fletcher[8] could go to Georgia for a year, things might be on a better footing. Indeed, I never could relish Mr. Wright, he seems a mere cabinet maker,[9] without godliness. Mr. Winter, who gave me this intelligence, is a zealous, prudent, godly youth, and is now settled at Bristol, in the room of Mr. Adams, so that you may easily obtain all needful intelligence from him....

---

6   Whitefield had left Lady Huntingdon the responsibility of the orphanage in his will. "In respect to my American concerns, which I have engaged in simply and solely for His great name's sake, I leave that building, commonly called the Orphan-house, at Bethesda, in the province of Georgia, together with all the negroes, books, furniture, and every other thing whatsoever, which I now stand possessed of, in the Province of Georgia aforesaid, to that elect lady, that mother in Israel, that mirror of true and undefiled religion, the Right Hon. Selina, Countess Dowager of Huntingdon..." (Seymour, *Life of Huntingdon*, 2:256).

7   Charity schools founded in the sixteenth and seventeenth centuries were sometimes started as hospitals and wore blue uniforms, the traditional colour of charity.

8   See August 18, 1773.

9   Berridge is saying that Wright had been sent for his building skills not for his spiritual qualities. Whitefield writes in a letter to a friend in February 1770: "Mr. Wright is the main spring, with regard to the buildings..." (John Gillies, *Memoirs of the Rev. George Whitefield* [Middletown: Hunt and Noyes, 1841], 203).

To Mr. Adams[1]

Everton, June 3, 1771

Dear Sir,

I received your letter and thank you for your kind invitation. I am glad your zeal for Christ and his gospel continues; may it increase more and more. My desire is still to go out as usual, but, alas, I am become a mere broken vessel. This time three years I was seized with a high fever, which laid me up for five months; this was succeeded by a nervous fever,[2] which has hung on me ever since. In the winter I am somewhat braced, and can make a poor shift to preach on the Sabbath, but nothing more. As soon as the hot weather comes in, I am fit for nothing but to sigh and yawn. Last summer I did not preach for four months. I feel myself now growing very feeble, and how much longer I shall be able to preach I know not. My breast is so weak that I can bear very little exercise of walking or riding, and I am so tender that I cannot stir out of doors in summer without a cloak, when there is a wind.

---

1 See August 21, 1765, for the erroneous designation in *WB* (1864), 527–528, to Rev. R. Housman. This letter is taken from Housman, *Life of Housman,* lxi–lxii.

2 In the eighteenth century "nervous" could either mean a stubborn illness that did not yield to medicine or disordered, excitable, timid feelings. "'My complaints,' complained Colonel Ellison in 1744, 'are what the Modern Physicians term nervous, a cant word the Gentlemen of the Faculty are pleased to make use of when a distemper proves obstinate and does not yield to their medicines'" (E.N. Williams, *Life in Georgian England* [Batsford, 1962], 62). For Berridge's use of "nervous" in this sense in a literature context, see April 3, 1773. However, here the term does seem to refer to some form of melancholic lethargy. George Dyer, writing three years after Berridge's death, notes that Berridge was "oppressed with weak nerves and an occasional melancholy..." (*Memoirs of the Life and Writings of Robert Robinson* [G.G. and J. Robinson, 1796], 54). In the context it seems physical illness had left him very low, suffering some form of nervous exhaustion, which was a recurring factor in his life—"weak nerves." See October 23, 1779, where Berridge says that he and his nervous fever had been "housekeepers every summer for forty years." See also November 1, 1786. This seems to be linked with the chronic asthma from which Berridge suffered. See April 11, 1775, for the hint of some form of hysteria. See September 2, 1763, for a discussion of "vapours."

My disorder is nearly the same with dear Mr. Whitefield's,[3] and from tokens received I expect to continue in this state for two years longer.[4] Do think of me, dear Sir, daily, and beg of God to strengthen me to preach on the Sabbath. The Lord gave me notice of this sickness nine months before it came, following me first with these words, "Thou shalt be dumb for a season,"[5] and then with these words "Thou must have fellowship with Christ in his sufferings."[6] Well, Lord, be it so; only grant me patience, a resigned will, and a sanctified rod. I find we know but little of ourselves, and gain but little of the gospel-broken heart, till we have been emptied from vessel to vessel,[7] or fried like a cake in a pan, and turned a hundred times over. Our malignant humours lie hid in the sunshine, and squat like a toad under a tile; but when David's iron harrows are drawn over our Ammonitish backs again and again,[8] then the toads will spit and swell. I wish you and Mrs. Adams[9] much joy in the Lord. May Jesus bless you and keep you, and lift up the light of his countenance on you,[10] and on your affectionate servant,

John Berridge

P.S. Pray give my love to Mr. Sellon[11] when you see him.

---

3   Whitefield suffered from asthma.
4   This is an interesting prophecy. See August 10, 1774.
5   Gabriel's word to Zechariah after he had expressed doubts concerning the prophecy to his wife. Luke 1:20.
6   Philippians 3:10.
7   Jeremiah 48:11.
8   David punished the sons of Ammon by cutting them with sharp instruments. 1 Chronicles 20:1–3.
9   See July 9, 1763.
10   Numbers 6:26.
11   See March 6, 1766.

To Lady Huntingdon[1]

Everton, June 8, 1771

My dear Lady,

I am coming early with another letter, because I am yet able to write, and do not know how long I shall be able. My health and strength are declining apace since the warm weather came in. My legs are almost gone; and my horse is almost useless. As yet I have been able to do whole duty on the Sabbath, but fear I shall be laid up soon. Do, my dear Lady, wrestle with me in prayer that I may be strengthened to labour; and get the men and women of Israel to help. The same fervent prayer that opened Peter's prison door[2] may open the door of my mouth. Jesus loves to bring His disciples to His feet, and His heart is so tender He cannot resist much importunity. I would fain prattle a little for Him in the pulpit this summer; for we have now large congregations, and it is sad, very sad, to have them broken up, and to be laid aside myself altogether, as a broken vessel. If my Lady could spare Mr. Glascott[3] for six weeks in the hottest part of the summer, it might be of great use. He is very dear to me, and very acceptable to my flock, and the best marching soldier in the King's Cassock regiment,[4] which regiment, like the King's guard, is usually more for show than for service.

Mr. Venn[5] is coming to Yelling, nine miles from Everton, but he is weakly himself, and cannot dismiss the old curate at present, without quarrelling with his whole parish; so that I can expect no Sunday help

---

[1] The letter is from Seymour, *Life of Huntingdon*, 2:51–52, and *WB* (1864), 511–513. Seymour says: "The health of that good old man was declining rapidly as the warm weather advanced; and fearing he should soon be entirely laid aside, wrote to entreat her Ladyship to send her chaplain, Mr. Glascott, to supply his church, as the congregations were unusually large during the summer months, and it would grieve him to see them as sheep without a shepherd" (*Life of Huntingdon,* 2:51).

[2] Acts 12:12.

[3] See Summer 1769.

[4] Member of the clergy.

[5] See January 19, 1771.

from him. Mrs. Lyons has dropped a hint about providing me with a curate by subscription. The proposal is very agreeable to me, and might be very useful. Doors are open, and ears are open everywhere, but messengers are wanting. There are several serious students at both Universities, but I fear they are very prudent, and very doctrinal, and such would not suit me. If one of your college[6] could be ordained, he might make a good field-fighter; and if it is my Lord's mind, he will soon put a gown on his back, notwithstanding all opposition.

But enough of this matter. I weary you, and weary myself with writing about it. Every subject proves barren but Jesus; and my poor feeble heart droops when I think, write, or talk of anything but him. Oh! that I could get near unto him, and live believingly upon Him, looking up to His eye for direction, leaning on his arm for support, fed with the milk of His word, quickened by the breath of his spirit, and clothed with the robe of his righteousness. I would walk, and talk, and sit, and eat, and lie down with him. I would have my heart always doating[7] on him, and find itself ever present with Him. The work is thine—Lord, help me. I cannot come to thee, but thou canst come to me. A welcome lodging thou hast provided in my heart; why standeth my Lord without?[8] Come in, come in, thou heavenly guest, and abide with me day and night for ever. May this Angel of the covenant guide,[9] guard, and bless you, and prosper every labour of love undertaken for His sake.

Grace be with you, and with

John Berridge

---

6   One of the students at Trevecca. See December 26, 1767.
7   Old form of "doting."
8   Revelation 3:20.
9   Malachi 3:1.

To John Newton[1]

Everton, June 10, 1771

Dear Sir,

Mr. Coetlogon,[2] a faithful brother, has paid me a kind visit, and intends to call upon Mr. Newton in his return to Aldwincke,[3] where he officiates in Mr. Haweis'[4] absence. I could not omit this opportunity of testifying the sincerity of my love and esteem for you, which, like other good fruits, are growing riper with age. Though I write but seldom to you, for writing almost oversets me, yet I frequently converse with you, and receive instruction from you. I have read over your Sermons and History[5] twice, and am now perusing them a third time without weariness.

When the warm weather first set in, I began to sink apace, and was apprehensive I should soon be laid aside, but through mercy I am somewhat braced up again, and again enabled yet to do whole duty

---

[1] See March 13, 1771. The manuscript is held at LPL, MS 3972 ff.15–16, showing that the publication in *WB* removes personal names and also cuts two sentences (from "I can bear..."). See *WB* (1838), 373–374, and *WB* (1864), 366–367.
[2] Charles Edward de Coetlogon (1746–1820). While at Pembroke College (1766–1770) he joined the Evangelical group of students associated with Hill. He was not ordained at the time of this letter. In 1772, after being ordained deacon and priest on the same day on March 15, he became assistant chaplain of Lock Hospital, where he became well known for his eloquent preaching. Venn comments while in London: "His discourses are all I would wish to hear—judicious, doctrinal in a proper degree, very experimental, and faithfully applied. In the midst of caresses and admiration, more than any preacher fixed at the Lock ever met with, may he be kept vigilant and humble!" (Venn, *Life and Letters of Venn*, 224). He finished his life as vicar of Godstone, Surrey (1794–1820).
[3] Twenty miles south-east of Olney in Northamptonshire.
[4] Thomas Haweis (1733/4–1820). See September 2, 1763. Haweis is at Cambridge finishing a degree that he had started at Oxford. He was under the Regius Professor of Civil Law, Samuel Hallifax, later bishop of Gloucester, who had preached three sermons before the university in 1760 against Berridge's preaching on justification by faith alone. For Haweis's positive relationship with Hallifax and Hallifax's move towards Calvinism, see Wood, *Haweis*, 147.
[5] See March 13, 1771.

on the sabbath. I can bear very little exercise in walking or riding, and a gentle hurry overturns me, but I can still bear quiet company, and am refreshed by it. I hope a gale of grace is now blowing my furnace and purging out some of my dross. I see clearly the utter need I stood in of rods and scorpions, and can thankfully say, it is good for me to have been afflicted.[6] By a token received, I expect to be kept an invalid two summers more.[7] Well, I am out of hell, and it is a mercy to be on mercy's ground, and under the correction of a merciful Jesus. Dear Lord, let every stroke of Thy rod be received with meekness, and convey heavenly instruction to my heart. We know but little of ourselves, and gain but little of gospel-broken heart, till we have been emptied from vessel to vessel, or fried like a cake in a pan, and turned a hundred times over. Perhaps Mr. De Coetlogon might reside at Olney when you come to Everton, and be ready to do your occasional duty, or preach your weekly lecture. This would set your mind at ease; and you might ride over, if you thought proper, to Mr. Venn,[8] who is expected this week at Yelling, which is only nine measured miles from Everton.

When you send a letter by your cheesemonger, order it to be left with Mr. Alderman William Parker,[9] at Bedford. Your last packet came safe. Your first sermons are good; but there is no comparison between the first and the second publication. It is pleasant to behold the improvements of a Christian. May your heart keep pace with your understanding. I find a great difference has arisen between two old clerical friends, who have been long connected. A quarrel must be bad in either, but the separation may be good for both. May Jesus water your soul, and water your flock, and water all the dry grounds belonging to

John Berridge

P.S. Kind respects to Mrs. Newton and all friends.

---

6 Psalm 119:71.
7 See June 3, 1771.
8 See January 19, 1771.
9 William Parker (1708–1785) lived in Angel Street (now Harper Street), Bedford. One of the first preachers of the Methodist society in Bedford, he was buried in St. Peter's churchyard, with the inscription: "Sacred to the memory of William Parker, late an Alderman of this corporation, and one of the first preachers in the Methodist chapel in this town; who departed this life March 27, 1785, in the 80th year of his age" (he was actually seventy-seven). For details of Parker, see Joan M. Anderson, *Early Methodism in Bedford* (Rush and Warwick, 1953).

To John Newton[1]

Everton, October 18, 1771

Dear Sir,

It is now high time to return my thanks, and I return them heartily for the kind visit you made me. I trust your labour of love is not in vain. Removing from camp to camp is of use to a Christian soldier, and more especially to a Christian sergeant. It shakes dust from our clothes, and rust from our joints, and promotes activity, the true spirit of a soldier. Without excursions we are apt to grow timid, and to settle on our lees. Grace's motto is *criscit eundo*.[2]

Mr. Hill,[3] who went to Bristol to chide his brother, and fell a prophesying,[4] has, since his return to London, sent a very severe letter to poor Rowland. Oh, what is man! But how easily we spy the vanity and inconsistency of the creature in another, and how hardly we discern it in ourselves. The foulest stain, and highest absurdity in our nature is pride, and yet this base hedgehog so rolls himself up in his bristly coat, that we can seldom get a sight of his claws. It is the root of unbelief. Men cannot submit to the righteousness of Christ. It cleaves like a pitched shirt to the skin, or like leprosy to the wall. No sharp culture of ploughing and harrowing will clear the ground of it. The foul twitch[5] will be sure to spring up with the next kindly rain. This

---

1   Berridge thanks Newton for his visit in the light of Newton not sharing Berridge's enthusiasm for itineration. Besides *WB* (1838), 374–376, and *WB* (1864), 367–368, the letter, except for the first and final paragraph, is found in William Jones, *Memoir of the Rev. Rowland Hill* (Fisher, 1837), 144–145.

2   It increases as it goes.

3   Richard Hill (1732–1808), the older brother of Rowland Hill, had been persuaded by his father to stop preaching irregularly and was sent to Bristol in an attempt to get his brother to cease preaching irregularly. On arriving at Bristol he found Rowland preaching to the miners at Kingswood and agreed to preach himself the next day. He was a leading Evangelical on the Calvinist wing. He became MP for Shropshire in 1780. See E. Sidney, *The Life of Sir Richard Hill* (Seeley, 1839).

4   See 1 Samuel 10:10.

5   Couch-grass. Before the days of chemicals it was very difficult to eliminate

diabolical sin has brought more scourges on my back than everything else; and it is of so insinuating a nature, that I know not how to part with it. I hate it, and love it. I quarrel with it, and embrace it. I dread it, and yet suffer it to lie in my bosom. It pleads a right, through the fall, to be a tenant for life; and has such a wonderful appetite, that it can feed kindly both on grace and garbage; will be as warm and snug in a cloister as a palace; and be as much delighted with a fine prayer as a foul oath. But whither am I running? Why, running into pride, whilst I am abusing it. Lord, save me! If it must dwell with me, let it not be a lordly master, but a loathed domestic; if it will follow me here, like my shadow, let it not entail a curse upon me. Oh, that I could once say unto thee, foul pride, farewell forever.

Half an hour after you left Everton, a messenger from Mr. Woolmer[6] inquired of me, what stranger preached in my church the night before. It seemed a strange message; but who, that knows the plague of his own heart, can wonder at anything. Through mercy I grow stronger as the weather grows cooler, and purpose setting up a weekly lecture. The Lord increase you more and more, you and your children; and bless the dear partner of your bosom. Kind love to all Christian friends at Olney. Grace be with you and with your,

John Berridge

---

in sandy soil since any small piece remaining in the ground grew back again.

[6] Possibly Joseph Woolmer (c.1719–1784), who had just been sent out as an evangelist by a local church on October 7, 1771. See Reginald Denness Cooper, *The History of the "Old Meeting House," St. Neots, 1691–1890* (Thomson, 1890), 38, and Jacob Stanley, "Memoir of the Rev. Samuel Woolmer," *The Wesleyan Methodist Magazine* (May 1830), 291.

To Rowland Hill[1]

Everton, October 20, 1771

My dear Rowly,

Your letter refreshed me much. Go on, and fear nothing but your own heart. You are in the high road to everlasting honour, pursuing the very track of your Master, and highly favoured by him. Your ship is now in full sail, and of course will require much ballast to keep her steady and upright. This ballast will be thrown into your ship providentially, just as it is wanted, by ill-judging kindred,[2] lukewarm professors of a crazy world. When Jesus sees your heart elevated, though secretly unknown to yourself, he will throw in a fresh skep[3] of ballast, to sink your bark a little lower. When you need but a little depression, the world may give it; when you want more; professors may bring it; when more still, your kinsfolk may give a blow. They are all your friends when they use you ill; and you ought to be as thankful to the heavenly Physician for thus paring off the proud flesh from your heart as to an earthly surgeon for paring off the proud flesh off your limbs. Did not the world scourge your Master, spit in his face, crown him with thorns, and crucify him? Did not chief priests and Pharisees insult him, mock him, tempt him and defame him? Did not his kinsfolk come and lay hold of him, to stop his ministry when He first set out, thinking him beside himself (Mark 3:21).

Well, you know the servant must be as his Master. Yet, fear none of these things; Jesus will make you more than conqueror. Needful support and comfort will be given you here, and everlasting glory crown thy head hereafter. (The late contest at Bristol seems to turn upon this

---

1 The accounts in *CM* (1841), 868, and *GS* (1856), 57, both remove references to Hill's family and references to the Calvinistic controversy. The manuscript is held in JWFP MARBL, Box 1 Folder 24. Berridge is encouraging Hill to continue preaching. The letter is addressed "For Rowland Hill Esquire at the Tabernacle house care of Mr. Benjamin Jones Linen Draper in Bristol."
2 Hill's family were against his preaching activities.
3 A wicker basket used in agriculture.

hinge, whether it shall be Pope John, or Pope Joan.[4] My dear friend, keep out of all controversy. Wage no war but with the devil. Your old friend and great admirer Dr. Rutherforth[5] is dead. *"Sic transit mundi pompa."*[6])

If your old college friends drop their correspondence heed it not: only seek a closer communion with Jesus. Our cisterns must dry up, before we can lie wholly at the fountain. Through mercy, I have been so kept on my legs this summer, as to preach every Sabbath, and intend setting up a weekly lecture again. Keep on praying and preaching again; let nothing stop you. The Lord be with your spirit and mine,

John Berridge

---

[4] John Wesley and Lady Huntingdon. At the conference for his preachers in 1770, Wesley reminded the movement of the 1744 warning that it had leaned too far towards Calvinism. Lady Huntingdon attended the 1771 conference in August at Bristol in opposition to the 1770 minutes, which seemed to contradict the doctrine of justification by giving a more prominent place to works. A compromise was reached but there was no real peace and the controversy lasted several more years, with Berridge himself taking part.

[5] Thomas Rutherford, DD (1712–1771) was a contemporary of Berridge at Cambridge. He was a distinguished scholar holding the Regius Chair of Divinity from 1745 until his death. Although giving no lectures as the other eighteenth-century holders of the post, he was active in moderating (examining publicly) in the divinity school and in writing. See Winstanley, *Unreformed Cambridge*, 106, where Rutherforth receives positive comments. To understand Berridge's perhaps ironical comments one needs to understand Rutherford's attack on the revival as seen in the first three of his *Four Charges to the Clergy of the Archdeaconry of Essex. I Some plain arguments to prove that Christianity does not reject the aid of human learning. II An examination of the doctrine of the Methodists concerning inward feeling. III An examination of the doctrine of the Methodists concerning assurances.*

[6] So passes away the show of the world.

To David Edwards[1]

Everton, November 26, 1771

Dear Brother,

Mr. Winter[2] informs me of the loss of your dear wife. You once knew she was mortal; but she has now put off mortality, and is become immortal. Can this grieve you? Oh, that I was where she now is!

Safe landed on that peaceful shore
Where pilgrims meet, to part no more.

She was once a mourning sinner in the wilderness; but she is now a glorified saint in Zion; the Lord has become her everlasting light; the days of her mourning are ended. Does this trouble you? She was once afflicted with bodily pains and weakness, encompassed with cares, and harassed with a crowd of anxious needless fears; but she has now arrived at her Father's house, and Jesus, dear Jesus, has wiped away all tears from her eyes, and freed her in a moment from all pains, cares, fears, and wants. And shall this affect you?

---

[1] Written to David Edwards (1731–1795) of Ipswich on the death of his wife, Mary. Edwards had got to know Berridge when he was based at St. Neots. See Seymour, *Life of Huntingdon*, 1:365. In 1763 he went to Ipswich as the minister of the Congregational church meeting in Tucker Street and was there until 1791, when he retired to Wotton-under-Edge in Gloucestershire. He authored *Sermons to the Condemned* (J. Hawes, 1775). The letter is found in *WB* (1838), 371–373; *WB* (1864), 364–5; and Ryle, *Christian Leaders*, 250–251, all of which date this letter March 26, 1771. However, the *New York Missionary Magazine and Repository of Religious Intelligence* (1801), 454–6; *MissM* (1801), 113–114; *EM* (1812), 128–129; *Evangelical Magazine and Missionary Chronicle* (1814), 504–505; *Methodist New Connexion Magazine* (1802), 355; and *S* (1892), 96–97 have the date as November 26, 1771, which makes more sense in light of the postscript. Also *S* has an added section not found in the other transcriptions—"Well, my friend…my hymns and sermons"—which suggests it came from a manuscript, the title in the magazine being "An Original Letter from Mr. Berridge to Mr. David Edwards."

[2] Cornelius Winter. See Winter 1767.

179

She ranges on the heavenly plains,
And sings with sweet heart-melting strains;
And now her soul begins to prove
The heights and depths of Jesus' love.
He cheers her with eternal smile;
She sings hosannas all the while;
Or, overwhelm'd with rapture sweet,
Sinks down, adoring at his feet.[3]

You have not lost your wife; she has only left you for a few moments—left an earthly husband to visit a heavenly father, and expects your arrival there soon, to join the hallelujah for redeeming love. Are you still weeping? Fie upon you, brother! Weeping, because your wife can weep no more. Weeping, because she is happy; because she is joined to that assembly where all are kings and priests! Weeping, because she is daily feasted with heavenly manna, and hourly drinking new wine in her Father's kingdom! Weeping, because she is now where you would be and long to be eternally! Weeping, because she is singing, and singing sweet anthems to her God and your God! Oh, shameful weeping!

Jesus has fetched your bride triumphantly home to his kingdom, to draw your soul more ardently thither. He has broken up a cistern, to bring you nearer, and keep you closer to the fountain; has caused a moment's separation, to divorce your affections from the creature; and has torn a wedding-string from your heart, to set it a bleeding more freely, and panting more vehemently for Jesus. Hereafter you will see how gracious the Lord has been in calling a beloved wife home, in order to betroth the husband more effectually to himself. Remember that the house of mourning becomes and befriends a sinner; that sorrow is a safe companion for a pilgrim, who walks much astray until his heart is well broken up.[4]

Well, my friend, I hope your mind is somewhat composed, and can bear to part with your wife for a season. What a mercy she was not left a widow, but went before! What a mercy we must follow soon after! She is only gone to pay a visit to the Friend you love, and who will send for you by and by. Your day, like mine, is wearing off apace,

---

3   Both quotations are from Berridge's own hymn "O happy saints, who dwell in light." See Hymn 143, *Sion's Songs*, 193–194.
4   *EM* and *S* include "up."

and your Bridegroom cometh quickly. Do not stand weeping over cold clay, but trim your lamp, and go forth to meet him. One half of yourself is gone before, and your passage over Jordan will now be lighter. The curtain will soon be drawn, and then you will see your wife again, and Jesus.

I have got a sight of the Calvinistical doctrines at last.[5] Awful, indeed, they are, and very humbling and joyful to a believer. However, through grace, I am not run mad with doctrines. I do not preach or sing of John Calvin, but of Jesus Christ; he is the dear subject of my hymns and sermons.

May all your tears flow in a heavenly channel, and every sigh waft your soul to Jesus. May the God of all consolation comfort you through life, and in death afford you a triumphant entrance into his kingdom! So prays your friend and brother in the gospel of Christ,

John Berridge

I have sent a few lines to be inserted on your wife's tombstone.

September, 1771, the Body of Mary Edwards, Wife of David Edwards, fell asleep, and was laid in this bed as a resting-place till the resurrection.

A loving and beloved wife she was;
A tender mother and a lowly Christian:
Who lived in the faith of Jesus,
And died triumphant over death.
"Weep not for me," the ashes cry,
"The spirit sings with saints on high;
But go and learn the life of faith,
Or thou wilt die the second death."

---

5 See June 9, 1773.

To Rowland Hill[1]

Everton, February 27, 1772

Dear Rowly,

Your letter of the 14th January was obliged for want of a passport to perform quarantine at Cambridge which delayed its arrival hither. I am glad you can find such comfortable winter quarters at Hawkstone.[2] Is not this mercy from the Lord who prevents the expulsion.[3] After nine months' itineration the Lord's advice to the twelve seems applicable to you; "come into a desert place and rest awhile."[4] Rest, and look into yourself; rest, and look with stillness to Jesus. But your retreat must have its trials too, and kindly they are provided lest you should love a retreat too well, and tarry too long. A messenger of the Lord must have no paradise on earth; no peace but in Jesus. Every good[5] meal he finds must be eaten with bitter herbs. Whilst your friends and others oppose your itineration stoutly your heart will be stirred up more eagerly to proceed; when their opposition ceases a reluctance through weariness will be ready to spring up in your own bosom. Everywhere, and at all times, trials will attend you from within or without.

---

[1] The copy from the original manuscript was made by George Stampe on March 4, 1904, into the WHSLMB, 71–73. There is a cut version both in *CM* (1841), 869, and a short extract in Sidney, *Life of Rowland Hill*, 68. The letter is addressed "For Rowland Hill Esq., at Hawkstone, near Whitchurch, Shropshire," the family home where Hill was resting from his preaching during the winter months.

[2] Richard Hill (1655–1727) established the house in the early eighteenth century but it was his nephew and heir, Sir Rowland Hill, the first Baronet Hill of Hawkstone (1705–1783) and father of Richard and Rowland Hill, who built the reputation of the estate with follies and landscaping, which was further developed by his son Richard. The park became one of the top attractions of the late eighteenth and early nineteenth centuries. Today after being restored in the 1990s it is again becoming a popular tourist attraction.

[3] His father had threatened to exclude him from the family home because of his preaching.

[4] Mark 6:31.

[5] *CM* adds "good."

You need not doubt of your being in God's way because he owns your word abundantly, and gives you much favour with the people. And indeed, my dear Rowly, these are the best days you will ever meet with, and the richest harvest you may ever reap. Learn to prize them, and adore the mercy of God, both in calling you to the work, and in making you faithful. The Lord has put a treasure into your hands, and given you an heart to use it; and by a blessed traffic you are storing up for yourself abundant honour, glory and immortality. And why this favour bestowed on you? Grace! Grace! The Lord loves you; be humble and thankful. The Lord delights to honour you; may your heart delight in the Lord and in his service. Oh what is grace? I see and taste a little of it, but want a daily better sight, and sweeter taste. Well might our apostle say, "Oh the depth!"[6] In this depth I want to plunge, and lose myself, that I may find and know Jesus. But his love is unfathomable. Eternity will scarce unravel it. So much the better; then it is just what it should be to make me happy, infinite and endless. Hallelujah!

I am better this winter than last, blessed be God, and preach at some adjacent village once a week and also in my own house, but am still good for nothing. I can bear no severity of weather nor a long ride. I have reason to hope I shall be fitted for more labours but not yet. Make the best of your time; and whilst the Master affords travelling health and strong lungs, blow your horn loudly. I do not invite you to Everton when you come to Cambridge,[7] because a man who has got possession of my heart may enter my house without a call. Hearty love and respectful salutations to your brother;[8] I hope when he visits Yelling[9] he will not forget Everton. I have a chapel and a cathedral at his service.[10] Grace be with you and with your,

John Berridge

---

6   Romans 11:33.
7   Hill came to Cambridge in the summer to collect his M.A. and he visited many of his friends in the neighbourhood of the university.
8   Richard Hill. See October 18, 1771.
9   New home of Henry Venn. See January 19, 1771.
10 See January 1781.

To John Thornton[1]

Everton, September 29, 1772

Dear and honoured Sir,

I received your kind letter yesterday, accompanied with a parcel of books for others, and some parcels of physic for myself; and attended with what you are pleased to call a trifle. May the Lord remember you for this kindness, and multiply his mercy upon you.

My Master has been tying me to a whipping-post for four years, and has chastised me smartly with rods and scorpions. Indeed, they were both sorely wanted; for I have a very saucy will, and a sad proud heart, and was grown in my own conceit almost as good a man as my Master. He sent me out to preach; and because he was pleased to do

---

[1]   John Thornton (1720–1790) was one of the richest men of his day. His obituary in *Gent Mag* declared him "the greatest merchant in Europe, except Mr. Hope of Amsterdam" (December 1790, 1056). He made his money through trade with Russia and had an office in the city and a villa at Clapham, Surrey. Berridge, as well as other Evangelical leaders, had a close relationship with him. He used his wealth for charitable purposes, and in this first extant letter he sets the pattern for future correspondence, in which he thanks Thornton for the supply of money, medicine and books. The letters show Berridge's frankness as well as Thornton's generosity. Venn estimated that Thornton gave away £150,000 in his lifetime (about £15,000,000 in today's money). Smyth calls him "the Nuffield of the Evangelical revival" (*Simeon and Church Order*, 246). Ford K. Brown regarded him as the one "who has more claim than any other to be thought of as the founder of the Evangelical Reformation" (*Fathers of the Victorians: The Age of Wilberforce* [Cambridge: Cambridge University Press, 1961], 78). A modern study showing his American connections is Milton M. Klein, "*An Amazing Grace*": *John Thornton and the Clapham Sect* (New Orleans: UPS, 2004). See Ernest Marshall Howse, *Saints in Politics: The "Clapham Sect" and the Growth of Freedom* (Allen and Unwin, 1953), 15–16, and ch. 1, "John Thornton," in M. Seeley, *The Later Evangelical Fathers* (Thynne and Jarvis, 1913). The letter is from *GM* (1837), 125–126, and *CM* (1842), 218. This is the first of twenty-seven letters published by *GM* between 1837 and 1839. They note that "a series of letters has been sent us by a friendly correspondent, written by that eminent servant of God, John Berridge, formerly vicar of Everton in Bedfordshire." The editors incorrectly ascribe the addressee as Henry Thornton instead of his father, John Thornton.

wonders by his word and Spirit, I stole all his laurels from him and girt them around my own temples. But the Lord was jealous of his honour, and has taken me to task roundly, and made me willing not only to throw the pilfered laurels at his feet, but to cast my scoundrel self there. He has lowered my top-sail, beaten down my masts, ransacked my vessel, and battered its sides so wonderfully, that I am escaped like a mere wreck into haven. I can now feel as well as call myself vile, and can submit to lay my hand upon my mouth, and to thrust my mouth in the dust.

Dear Sir, how sweet is poverty of spirit and brokenness of heart! It makes me weep kindly tears, and open all my bosom freely, for Jesus. It brings him nigh unto my heart, and makes me clasp him eagerly; it teaches me what grace is, and helps me to prize it. It sinks me down to nothing, and makes me fall as a drop into the ocean; and when I am nothing Jesus is my all, and fills me, and wins me. Then I become a little child, and my heart is all hosannah. I could die for Jesus. Something of this state I know, but, alas, I am not settled in it, and what I know, was learnt in a house of correction; this house suits me well. I cannot thrive but in a furnace; nor even there, unless it is well blown with the breath of grace.

I trust my dear Master loves you, and hope he keeps some favourite rod for you. Your situation is lofty, and of course perilous, exposing you to slips and falls. You sail in a very stately vessel; Oh, my Jesus grant you ballast to keep it steady! All the glories of the world are like that painted cloud, which Satan brought upon the eyes of Jesus on the mountain of temptation.[2] I believe you do condemn these tinsel glories; and yet without a gracious rod, you might grow proud of that contempt. You are indebted unto Jesus more than ten thousand others; a very rich man, and yet very likely to be saved! What a miracle of mercy! Oh love the Lord with all your heart, and serve him well with all your strength. Grace and peace be with you, and with your affectionate servant,

John Berridge

---

2   Matthew 4:8.

To John Thornton[1]

Everton, April 3, 1773

Dear and honoured Sir,

Your first paper on 2 Kings 22:8, is pertinent and striking. I can find nothing here to pick a quarrel with, except a poor little *then*, at the conclusion, which occurs thrice in four lines. The last *then* may be turned out of doors, without ceremony, for his company is not wanted; and his note, by frequent repetition, groweth troublesome.

Your remarks on 2 Chron. 32:24, are ingenious, and the reflections at the close are weighty. But there is a fly or two in this pot of ointment,[2] which may be picked out. The word *craftily*, seems rather too strong and base a word for Hezekiah; it denotes a fraudulent purpose, as well as carnal policy. And though Hezekiah acted unfaithfully to the God of Israel, he meant no treachery to the king of Babylon. Suppose the sentence ran

---

[1] John Thornton was seeking to publish a new edition of *Bogatzky's Golden Treasury*, a book of daily devotional readings. Carl Bogatzky (1690–1774) was a German pietist who first published his *Golden Treasury* in 1718, the completed form appearing in 1734. He revised it many times, and it obtained a vast circulation. The first English translation appeared in 1754, and it is upon that translation that Mr. Thornton's adaptation is based. *CM* (1842), 218, says that Thornton "undertook himself to edit the *Golden Treasury* which was enriched with some compositions of Cowper and Newton, that afterwards were published in *Olney Hymns* (W. Oliver: 1779). Conscious of his own deficiencies as a writer, it appears he submitted portions of the work, in manuscript, to his friend Berridge, and gave him full liberty to criticize the same." Berridge's notes and comments were published at the end of the nineteenth century in *Bogatzky's Golden Treasury: a reprint of Mr. John Thornton's edition of 1775 together with critical notes hitherto unpublished, by John Berridge, vicar of Everton, and important corrections by the same hand*, ed. Charles P. Phinn (Elliot Stock, 1891). For Bogatzsky and the history of the treasury, see John Kelly, *The Life and Work of Charles Von Bogatzky, author of "The Golden Treasury": a chapter from the religious life of the eighteenth century* (Religious Tract Society, 1889). This letter is found in *CM* (1842), 218–220; *GM* (1837), 126–127; *WB* (1838), 376–378; and *WB* (1864), 368–370. *GM* misses out the first paragraph.

[2] Ecclesiastes 10:1.

thus: "Hezekiah foolishly sought to avail himself of this false notion of the king of Babylon; and by not affronting their god, hoped to gain," etc. Again, *worldly wisdom* occurs twice, and *carnal wisdom* once, in the space of five lines: but short comments should contain *multum in parvo*,[3] and of course, be free from repetitions, or identical expressions. Suppose the sentence was expressed in some such manner as this: "Carnal policy and pride of heart proved a snare to Hezekiah, and prove the ruin of all sinners, that perish. They are too wise to be taught of God, and too lofty to lie at the feet of Jesus."

Your comment on Deut. 33:26, is nervous,[4] and your reflections are pertinent; but an application at the close seemeth wanting, to give the comment proper length, and full weight. I have some objection against your double "verily." No prophet used it before Christ, nor any apostle after Christ. It seems an expression, peculiarly belonging unto him, who is truth itself; and therefore only fit for him to use. I am persuaded the text was originally wrote thus; "There is none like unto the God of Jeshurun, who rideth on the heavens for thy help, and on the sky for thy excellence," i.e., to make thee excellent. Thus the two expressions tally; and the 26th verse perfectly corresponds with the 29th, "Happy are thou, O Israel! Who is like unto thee, O people, saved by the Lord who is the shield of thy help, and the sword of thy excellence."

What follows is sent as a supplement to the third paper, which you may alter, curtail, or reject at pleasure; making as free with my ink, as I do with your pen. I begin with your reflections. How safe then must they be, who are under the wing of the God of Jeshurun, who find him reconciled to them by the death of his Son, and feel themselves reconciled to him by the power of his grace! He rideth on the heavens for their help, and none can outstrip his progress, or obstruct his purpose. Verily, he it is that giveth strength and victory to his people; blessed be God! Is he, who rideth on the heavens, thy help? Does thy heart trust in him alone; and does his grace subdue thine outward iniquities, and thine inbred corruptions? Is he, who rideth on the sky, thine excellence?

---

3   Much in a small space.
4   Muscular, vigorous, strong, free from weakness. Toplady speaks of "Dr. Gill's excellent and nervous tract on predestination" (*The Works of Augustus Toplady, BA, late vicar of Broad Hembury, Devon. A new edition, complete in one volume printed verbatim from the first edition of his works* [Chidley, 1794], 4), and Thomas Scott says in *The Force of Truth: an authentic narrative* (Seeley, 1836), 63, that in his unconverted state he was not able "to receive the following nervous passage concerning justification." See June 3, 1771.

Does he seem only excellent in thine eyes, and cause thee to excel in virtue? Has he planted thee among his excellent ones of the earth, and made thee to abound in faith and love, and fruits of righteousness? If the Lord is not thy help, alas thou wilt be slain by sin, and prove a ruined soul. If the Lord is not thine excellence, thou art still an apostate spirit, a stranger unto God, and to his Christ. Awake, arise and call on God. His ear is open unto prayer, and thou art yet on mercy's ground. Oh, call upon him speedily, and cry unto him earnestly, that thou perish not![5]

Mr. Cowper's[6] hymn needs no advocate to plead its cause; it speaks sufficiently for itself; but the poor author cannot take the comfort of his own hymn, being now in much deplorable distress. How dark and feeble is a Christian's understanding without the light and comfort of God's Holy Spirit.

Dear Sir, you have much business on your hands, and will need much prayer, beside family worship, to keep the world at your feet, and God in your heart. Where many irons are in the fire, a live coal had need be in the heart continually; else whilst we are waiting on other vineyards,[7] we may impoverish our own spirits. I find you walk much, and I hope you can wear your shoes out praying, as well as walking. Praying walks are healthful walks indeed: they fetch down corruption as well as carcase.[8] I wish you right Christian cheer every day, a gentle cup of tribulation, and full cup of supplication, sweetened with divine communion. The good will of him that dwelt in the bush,[9] dwell with you and yours, and with

John Berridge

---

[5] "How safe…perish not" is included in Thornton's completed manuscript that he later sends to Berridge for evaluation. See Bogatzky's *Golden Treasury*, ed. Charles P. Phinn, reading for November 5.

[6] William Cowper (1731–1800), a major Evangelical poet who at this time was living at Olney in close association with John Newton. Cowper's contributions to what was later published by John Newton under the title *Olney Hymns* were written during 1771–1772. Cowper had recently entered his third derangement earlier in the year and would in fact go to stay at Newton's house on April 12—a few days after Berridge wrote this letter—in order to escape the noise of the annual fair. For Berridge's evaluation of Cowper's poetry, see April 13, 1782 and September 17, 1782. For a sympathetic account of Cowper, see George M. Ella, *William Cowper: Poet of Paradise* (Darlington: Evangelical Press, 1993). For a critical biography, see James King, *William Cowper: A Biography* (Durham: Durham University Press, 1986).

[7] Song of Songs 1:6.

[8] Some spiritual benefit as well as physical benefit.

[9] Exodus 3.

TO MR. WOODGATE[1]

Everton, April 20, 1773

Dear Sir,

Through a cloud of visitors, a weak body, and weaker spirits, I had neither leisure nor inclination to write in London; but being now returned into the country I must take up my pen, else you may think me defective in brotherly respect. From the little conversation I had with you, I found my heart united unto you, and feel a brother's kindness for you.

Gowns, bands, and academical learning weigh but little with me. What I look for in a preacher, is the Spirit's baptism and a spiritual ordination. Where these are found, I care not whether the preacher comes in a leather jacket or a cassock. If he brings a Christ in his heart, he will warm his audience, and prove his divine commission. But Sir, I find it no easy matter to walk with Christ, and keep up close communion with him; and a sad work it is to mount a pulpit without a sense of Jesu's presence. It is not mere thinking upon a subject, that will make a good Christian orator. If we would pray and preach well in a pulpit, we must pray much out of it. The closest walkers prove the closest and warmest preachers. A man may have much to say, but will speak to little purpose, unless Christ is with him; and we must not think that Jesus Christ will follow us into a pulpit, unless we follow him out of it, and follow with a gospel-broken heart. I always ask the dear Redeemer's presence, when I stand up to preach, but often preach without it, because I did not seek it heartily before I came to preach.

---

[1] This letter is addressed to "Mr. Woodgate, Near the Market, Chatham, Kent." The manuscript is held in the Simon Gratz Autograph Collection (c.12 b.2), the Historical Society of Pennsylvania, Philadelphia. Richard Woodgate (1730–1787) is asking about the qualifications and opportunities for preaching. He worked in the dockyards at Chatham before becoming in 1774 the pastor of the church that met in Jewin Street, London, a meeting house that was founded by the famous hymn writer Joseph Hart a few years before, in 1760. Thomas Wright says that he is the Mr. Ardent of William Shrubsole's allegorical work *Christian Memoirs* (Rochester: Fisher, 1776). See Wright, *Joseph Hart* (Farncombe, 1910), 107. He was buried in Bunhill Fields. See April 21, 1775 and April 28, 1779.

You are placed much alone, and have but little help from your brethren; but this need not grieve you. When help is truly wanted, Jesus Christ will surely send it. How can he well do otherwise? And when he sends no help, whatever we may think, it is not wanted. Let this reconcile you to your situation; and be assured, though alone, with the presence of your Master, you will find help enough. We are often contriving help for the Master, when we should be only praying to him for his help.

Give my hearty love to all among you that seek and follow Jesus Christ. Grace and peace be multiplied upon you all. The Lord be with your spirit, and with the spirit of your affectionate brother and fellow servant,

John Berridge

To John Thornton[1]

Everton, May 3, 1773

Dear and honoured Sir,

Your papers keep up a good spirit, and do not evaporate on the reading—the former pieces were good, but your last bottle, I think, is best of all. It is well brewed for the stomach, and much disposed to whet the appetite and quicken digestion. Happy it is, when both a bride[2] and her groom have the heart to become common brewers for Jesus Christ.

I cannot relish doctrinal preaching, or doctrinal printing: it leaves a careless sinner and a formal professor just where it found them. Discourses are likely to do good, when, like your paper, they stimulate reflection, force a reader to rummage his bosom, set the sinner a quarrelling with himself, and push a lazy pilgrim on a trot. I perused your paper with such a cavilling heart, as you would wish, and searched diligently to pick some hole in your coat, but no rent can I find, only a stitch or two seems to be let down. The sentiments are lively and proper, but, perhaps the words of one sentence might be altered, as follows, "If thy peace with an offended God is not already made through the blood of atonement, or is not earnestly seeking after"—thus the two part of the sentence tally (is not made, or is not seeking after,) which should be regarded in writing. Further, "to have fellowship and communion," is the same thing as to have fellowship and fellowship, or communion and communion—both the words have the same meaning, only one is English and the other Latin. Either would do well, if the other was rejected. These little niceties are overlooked in common talk, or from a pulpit, but are not well received from the press.

Well, dear Sir, these two stitches belong to the lady's gown,[3] the next belongs to your coat. "Alas! for the fir trees, when the cedars shake!"

---

[1] Berridge is still working on Thornton's papers, and it seems that he has received a fresh supply for criticism. See April 3, 1773. The letter was printed in *GM* (1837), 168–170, and *CM* (1842), 220–221.

[2] Mrs. Thornton wrote some of the papers herself. Phinn suggests that perhaps three are included in Thornton's 1775 edition of *Bogatzky's Golden Treasury*.

[3] Mrs. Thornton's contributions.

Here is a point of admiration too much—only one can be admitted at the end. The particle "for" should be governed by "alas" but is cut off from that government by the point of admiration, which always makes either a full period, or a distinct member of a sentence. I suppose this was only a hasty dash of the pen, which might readily be made, because the word "alas" is commonly followed by a note of admiration. Your paper consists of five paragraphs, and if a short black line was added at the end of each paragraph, it would make the transition more observable to a common reader. Mr. Newton's hymn is, like himself, sensible, serious, and pithy; and, if he has got a barrow full of such hymns, I wish he would wheel them into the world. Perhaps the twentieth line of the Raven hymn[4] may need a little quickening;

By ravens He sends them their food,

the words, "sends them their food," being monosyllables, and very long quantities, and following each other close, make the line drag heavily, which might easily be remedied, as follows;

By ravens He sendeth their food.

I can despair of no serious Arian,[5] after the change which has been wrought in myself. Near thirty years I was an avowed enemy to Christ's divinity, and when God had given me some knowledge of his Christ, and sent me forth to preach his gospel,[6] it was three years before I was fairly rescued from this quicksand. You judge exceedingly right, to stand still, and avoid disputings; they only gender strife, and stir up pride. A sweet behaviour, joined with secret prayer, will do more in this matter than a thousand eager disputations. Perhaps, before you have worn another pair of shoes out in supplication,[7] Mrs. Thornton[8]

---

[4] The hymn is in the Olney Hymn Book 1, Number 35: "Elijah fed by ravens." The line has become "He sends them by ravens their food."
[5] Someone who subscribes to the heresy of Arianism. Arius (d.336) denied the eternality of Jesus Christ, the Son of God, as the Logos. Berridge struggled for many years with a subordinationist Christology before regaining orthodox views on the nature of Christ. This of itself did not lead to his spiritual renewal.
[6] Berridge may be referring to his ordination or his starting as a curate at Stapleford.
[7] Thornton prayed during his walks. See April 3, 1773.
[8] Lucy Watson (1722–1785) was the only daughter and heiress of Samuel

may behold her Saviour's Godhead, and exult in it. The paper shows she is endued with a vein of manly sense, and, what is better still, a strain of serious piety.

I return you hearty thanks for the enclosed paper and will now tell you what I do with my money, and how the paper will be applied. My living is £160 a year: £100 of which defrays the expense of house-keeping, horse-keeping, servants' wages, my own raiment, and Sunday food and liquor for poor pilgrims who come to church from afar. I keep no company; pay no visits, but preaching ones; and receive no visits but from travelling Christians, who are welcomed with some hashed[9] meat, unless they chance to come on boiling days, which are twice a week. The work of God has extended itself from Everton, by means of field-preaching, into four counties, viz., Bedfordshire, Hertfordshire, Essex and Cambridgeshire. Near forty towns have been evangelised, many of which lay at a great distance from each other, and two lay preachers ride from town to town, preaching morning and evening every day. These are yearly allowed £25 a piece, to provide themselves with horses and clothes, and defray turnpike[10] expenses. There are also six Sunday preachers, who often want support, and receive it from me. By this means the gospel is preached without charge to the hearers. No collections are made, which mightily stoppeth the world's clamour. But, Sir, besides these constant outgoings, I have a thousand other occasional demands upon me. The flocks in every place are very poor, and often distressed, on account of their religion. Labouring men have been turned out of work; and some who are unable to work, through sickness, lameness, or old age, have been deprived of parish collection,[11] or received a very scanty one, because they are Methodists.[12] These you may think will apply to me for relief—true, you reply, but how are you able to relieve them? I will tell you, Sir. When I began to preach the gospel, I was possessed of £140 in money, and a paternal inheritance of

---

Watson, a rich merchant and landowner in Kingston upon Hull. They had been married on November 28, 1753.

[9] Meat already cooked and cut up into small pieces and mixed with vegetables.

[10] Turnpike companies were a private initiative to improve the often unmaintained roads.

[11] The government had put the responsibility for maintaining the poor onto the parish. The local overseers would take any opportunity to reduce their expenses in a system that was failing to meet ever growing demands.

[12] Methodists was not used as a denominational name but as a name for a movement.

£24 a year. The money was first expended—then I sold some needless plate and books for £50—this also was expended—and, lastly, I sold my inheritance, which is not half expended. I scatter my mites about, because I am trading for another world. What silver and copper is left behind me, will profit me nothing; but what is given for Christ's sake will find a gracious recompense. The world would call me a fool for this traffic,[13] but they will see and own hereafter, that I carried my goods to the best market.

The walls of my house are made of plaster, and very leanly in some parts and I fear the wood-work is decayed; they have wanted repairing for some years, but I could not find a heart to repair them, because of the expense. Some part of your donation shall now be applied to this purpose, and the rest to Christ's poor. My health, through mercy, is better, and I am able to travel two or three days in a week to preach. It would delight you to see how crowded my cathedrals are, and what abundance of hearers they contain, when the grain is threshed out. I believe more children have been born of God in any one of these despised barns, than in St. Paul's Church or Westminster Abbey. The Lord direct you in all your concerns, and keep you travelling right forward in the way to Canaan, with a warm heart, a cool head, a nimble foot, and praying lip. Grace and peace be with you, and with your obliged and affectionate servant,

John Berridge

---

[13] Dealings, business. See April 8, 1774.

To Mr. Adams[1]

Everton, June 9, 1773

Dear Sir,

I received a very kind letter from you about a twelvemonth ago. "Aye," says Mrs. Adams,[2] "so you did, and it is a shame for you not to answer it sooner. If I had the care of you I would teach you better manners." Indeed, if anyone could help me, I believe Mrs. Adams might, for she has both sense and spirit, and has long been a great favourite with the Vicar of Everton. But, alas, the Vicar has grown grey, and very vapourish; and old asses, though they have long ears, are very hard of hearing.

When your letter came to hand I was deep in the suds,[3] and continued so for five months; during which time I did not stir out of my parish, and could not bear the thought of writing. As the winter drew on I grew better, and might have written; but then shame prevented me. So I threw your letter into the fire, that it might not reproach me. At length, Thomas Clark,[4] an old Nottinghamshire friend, comes up to Everton, and I determined to write (better late than never), and retrieve my character if possible. Pray tell Mrs. Adams I am very sensible of my fault, and ask pardon, and hope to do better another time; and let her know that I am become a moderate Calvinist.[5]

---

[1] See August 21, 1765, for an explanation why the letters addressed to Mr. Housman in *WB* (1864) are really to Mr. Adams. This letter is in Housman, *Life of Housman*, lxii–lxiii, and is included in *WB* (1864), 528–529.

[2] See August 21, 1765, for a note on Mrs. Adams.

[3] In difficulties through his illness.

[4] Thomas Clark, a farmer in West Leake, Nottinghamshire, who died in 1781. In his will he left land in Great Grandsen, a village about six miles from Everton, to his sons John and Robert. See July 21, 1781.

[5] Berridge had moved to a Calvinistic theology during these years of illness, and it is on his mind because he has just completed a book on the subject (see August 18, 1773), in which he says how he arrived at his views. "A furnace is the proper school to learn this doctrine in, and there I learnt it. Nor men nor books could teach it me; for I would neither hear nor read about it. A long

My health, through mercy, is much better than it has been for five years; and I now retain some hope of visiting your parts again, but not this summer. If my body groweth able to endure a journey, and the clergyman you mentioned continues willing to exchange churches, I may yet see Ashby.[6] Pray give my kind love to him.

I hope, the older you grow, the more you become sensible of your vileness, and lay your mouth lower in the dust.[7] The more grace you have, and the holier you are, the viler you will be in your own eyes. Mercy will be your pleasant food and song, and a gospel-broken heart your sweet companion. Young pilgrims are often soaring to the moon, and talking much of their own graces; but an old traveller drops into the dust, and sings hosannas unto Jesus.

Present my kind love to Mrs. Adams, and to all Christian friends. Grace and peace be with you all, and with him who is the least of all,

John Berridge

---

and rancorous war I waged with it; and when my sword was broken, and both my arms were maimed, I yet maintained a sturdy fight, and was determined I would never yield; but a furnace quelled me. Large afflictions, largely wanted, gave me such experience of my evil heart that I could peep upon *electing grace* without abhorrence; and as I learnt to *loathe* myself, I learnt to *prize* this grace. It seemed clear, if God had mercy for me, it could be for this gracious reason, because *he would have mercy*: Romans 9:18; for every day and every hour, my desert was death.... I know the rancour of the human heart against this doctrine, for I have sorely felt it; and *charitably* thought that all its teachers were the devil's chaplains" (*Christian World*, 181–182).

6   Ashby-de-la-Zouch, twelve miles south of Derby, where the Adamses lived.
7   Lamentations 3:29.

To John Thornton[1]

Everton, August 18, 1773

Dear and honoured Sir,

I have just received your *Golden Treasury*[2] by the hands of my dear brother of Yelling,[3] and thank you kindly for the pretty little valuable present. It is much improved in its present dress. The Lord bless the book and the editor.

In May I began to itinerate, after a five years' discontinuance through illness, and kept on, though with much feebleness, for two months, when I was seized with a smart attack of my old complaint. I am now, as the world accounts, a scald miserable, but lying at Jesus's gate, and am reduced to a mere Sunday preacher; the Lord be praised that I am not wholly laid aside. What a fund of corruption is lodged in the human heart! Every stripe I receive, my Master's word tells me, I have procured for myself. Lord, I own it; sanctify the rod, and make the furnace purge away my dross. I trust the Lord has taught me to hate sin, and to hunger after righteousness; yet I am often seeking after holiness in such a manner, as stiffens my heart, brings a dry and lean soul, and makes my eyes lose the sight of Christ's salvation. This convinces me there is a mystery in the manner of obtaining sanctification, that we are not soon acquainted with; we are apt to consider sanctification as a separate work from justification, following after it, and wholly independent of it; whereas they seem to be connected works, and inseparable from each other, one resulting from the other.

---

[1] There are several sources for this long letter in which Berridge deals with some major theological issues. Thornton must have asked him for his views on sanctification, an issue that was at the heart of the Calvinistic controversy then raging. The letter is found in *GM* (1837), 170–172; *WB* (1838), 378–382; *CM* (1842), 821–823; *GS* (1848), 78–80; and *WB* (1864), 370–374. *GM* has some underlining for emphasis.

[2] It seems that Thornton's new edition of *Bogatzky's Golden Treasury* had just been published. Was this an earlier publication before the 1775 edition? See April 3, 1773.

[3] Henry Venn. See June 8, 1771.

The clearer sight we get of Christ, and the sweeter views we have of our adoption, the more our hearts are filled with love, joy, peace, and all the fruits of the Spirit, which is sanctification. When Jesus gives a clearer view of his dying love, he always accompanies that view with the graces of the Spirit. The heart is filled at the same time with pardon and holiness, with justification and sanctification; so that if we desire to be holy, we must seek to be happy in the Saviour's love, must seek a clear evidence of our adoption, and labour to keep it clear. As our views of Christ are more cloudy and discouraging, our bosoms will be more barren of heavenly tempers.[4] A man may be constitutionally meek as the lamb, constitutionally kind as the spaniel, constitutionally cheerful as the lark, and constitutionally modest as the owl, but these are not sanctification. No sweet, humble, heavenly tempers, no sanctifying graces are found but from the cross.[5] Jesus says, "He that eateth my flesh and drinketh my blood, hath (or possesseth) eternal life."[6] Where he sheweth how eternal life (which must comprise the whole of spiritual life) is obtained, viz., by eating his flesh and drinking his blood, i.e., by feeding on his atonement. Thus all divine life, and all the precious fruits of it, pardon, peace and holiness, spring from the cross. And is not this intimated by John, when he says, "One of the soldiers pierced his side, and forthwith came there out blood and water."[7] They did not follow one another, but came out together; the blood betokening pardon, the water sanctification. Carnal men make the water come out first, and the blood follow: they seek a little obedience first, and then hope to have the benefit of the blood. Professors often make the blood come first, and the water follow; i.e., seek first to be justified, and then to be sanctified. But I believe experienced Christians make the blood and water flow together; get holiness by clear views of the cross, and find eternal life by feeding on the Saviour's flesh and blood. Was not a lamb sacrificed every morning and evening in the Jewish temple? And was not this intended to show us, that we must feed on Christ's atonement every day, and derive all our life, the life of peace and holiness, from his death? Upright people are often coming to me with complaints, and telling me, that since they received pardon, and have been seek-

---

4 Influences or feelings.
5 *GM* has "The graces of the Holy Spirit are found but from the cross."
6 John 6:54.
7 John 19:34.

ing after sanctification (as a separate work) their hearts are become exceeding dry and barren. I ask them how they find their heart when Jesus shows his dying love. They tell me, full of peace, and love, and every heavenly temper. Then I answer, Jesus hereby shows you, that holiness as well as pardon is to be had from the blood of the cross.

Labour therefore to get your conscience sprinkled every day with the atoning blood, and sanctification will ensue of course; the blood and water flow together. When Jesus only gives a smile, and seals some promise on the heart, though it be not the seal of pardon, it occasions a sweet transforming change in the soul; and all fancied sanctification, which does not arise wholly from the blood of the cross, is nothing better than Pharisaism; and if persisted in, will end in Pharisaism. For when sanctification is considered as a separate work from justification, and wholly independent of it, by and by it is considered as a justifying work itself; and men profess and preach they are first to be justified by the blood of Christ, and then by their own obedience.

Oh, dear Sir, if we would be holy, we must get to the cross, and dwell there; else notwithstanding all our labour and diligence, and fasting and praying, and good works, we shall be yet void of real sanctification, destitute of those humble, sweet, and gracious tempers, which accompany a clear view of the cross. But mere doctrinal knowledge will not give us this view; it only proceeds from a lively faith wrought in us by the Prince of Life. A legal spirit helpeth forward our mistake in the matter of sanctification. We would fain divide the water from the blood, fain would separate sanctification from justification, that we may make merit of it, as the Foundry people[8] do. Whereas, if they are inseparably connected, and both pardon and holiness spring from the blood of the cross, the root of merit is dug up thereby, and Christ is all in all. Another thing confirms our mistake, which is, that all heavenly graces are called fruits of the Spirit. Hence we conclude, that pardon must spring peculiarly from the blood of the cross, and holiness be a separate work of the Spirit. But though all gracious tempers are the Spirit's fruits, yet that fruit is bestowed at the foot of the cross; eternal life is found at Calvary by eating the Saviour's flesh and drinking his blood.[9]

---

8   Those who met at the Old Foundry, Moorfields, the headquarters of Wesley's work.
9   *GM* rewrites some of this paragraph with the likely motive of clarifying. *CM* is probably from the manuscript, which includes the postscript.

In my pamphlet,[10] I wrote something against what the world calls sincere obedience, and with a twofold view; first to expose that *insincere* obedience which is commonly cloaked under the name of sincere obedience, or doing what we can. Secondly, to show that obedience, where it is sincere, and the fruit of the Spirit, is no ground of merit, or cause of justification, and I thought no professor could misunderstand me; but in a letter just received from Mr. Fletcher,[11] he writes thus, "What you have said about sincere obedience, has touched the apple of God's eye, and is the very core of antinomianism.[12] You have done your best to disparage sincere obedience, and in a pamphlet, ready for the press, I have freely exposed what you have written." Then he cries out in a declamatory style, "For God's sake, let us only speak against insincere and Pharisaical obedience." Indeed, I thought I had been writing against insincere obedience throughout the pamphlet; and that everyone who has eyes must see it clearly: but I suppose that Mr. Fletcher's spectacles invert objects, and make people walk with their heads downwards.

May the Lord Jesus bring and keep you and yours at the cross, to see and sing the wonders of redeeming love, till you are called up higher

---

[10] *Christian World.* Berridge's "pamphlet" extends to two hundred pages. There were two editions during 1773 and one in the following year with minor additions. The reason Berridge entered the Calvinistic controversy, in spite of his advice to keep out of all controversy, was that he felt the whole nature of the gospel was at issue. See ch. 16, "The Christian World Unmasked," and Appendix 2, "Sincere Obedience," in Pibworth, *Gospel Pedlar.*

[11] John Fletcher (1729–1785) had known Berridge since the early days of revival at Everton; he visited Everton in 1760. Since that time he had become the designated successor of Wesley and acquired the parish of Madeley in Shropshire. Berridge and Fletcher moved apart theologically during the 1760s over the issues of perfectionism and Calvinism. Fletcher engrossed himself in the Calvinistic controversy, and his defence of Wesley was to last six years and run into many hundreds of pages. Fletcher devoted the second half of *Logica Genevensis Continued, or the first part of the Fifth Check to Antinomianism* (R. Hawes, 1773) to attacking a character in Berridge's book. Afterwards he produced *Logica Genevensis Continued, or the second part of the Fifth Check to Antinomianism* (Bristol: W. Pine, 1774), explicitly criticizing Berridge. Any break in their relationship was later restored; Fletcher visited Everton in 1776, and Berridge saw him in London the following year. See *WB* (1864), xliv–xlv. Mrs. Carteret, in an undated letter to Lady Huntingdon at Trevecca, reports that Fletcher, who she thinks is dying, was "very weak and emaciated to a great degree, we found Mr. Berridge with him at prayer" (CCA, F1/1118). For a modern study on Fletcher, see Patrick Streiff, *Reluctant Saint? A Theological Biography of Fletcher of Madeley* (Peterborough: Epworth Press, 2001).

[12] The idea that Christians are not restrained by the law.

to sing eternal praise with all the saints. Grace, mercy, and peace be with you, and with your much obliged and affectionate servant,

John Berridge

P.S. The papers tell me, that the Orphan-house[13] in Georgia is burnt down; but the papers are mistaken. It has long ceased to be an orphan-house, and was wholly converted into lumber house for human learning. The first laudable intention was perverted, and God has cast a mark of his displeasure on it. Yet how compassionate the Lord has been to Mr. Whitefield, in sending the fire after his death.

---

[13] See Berridge's letter to Lady Huntingdon on May 8, 1771. Whitefield had left the care of the institution to Lady Huntingdon, who sent over students from the college to help. The two wings of the college were just completed when the fire struck and destroyed Whitefield's dream of a college linked with the orphanage. The property lay in ruins until 1870, when a new building was constructed. There is a short undated extract to Cornelius Winter in *WB* (1864), 531, on this subject, probably written at the same time: "It excites in me no surprise that the Orphan House is burnt down. It was originally intended for orphans, and as such, was a laudable design, but has ceased to be an Orphan House, in order to become a timber-house for human learning, and God has cast a brand of his displeasure upon it; but how gracious has the Lord been to Mr. Whitefield, in preserving it during his life time. We all live to lay plans; and you laid one last winter, but your Master has shown you He will not employ you as his counsellor."

To John Thornton[1]

Everton, August 31, 1773

Dear and honoured Sir,

Your favour of the 26th came duly to hand, with an inclosed paper, which brought me on my knees for a blessing upon you and yours. A hundred *Golden Treasuries*[2] are also received, and more than half were disposed of last Sunday; the rest will follow quickly.[3] My stock of Bibles and Testaments is almost gone, and when it suits I should be glad of a few of the smallest Bibles and Testaments. The labouring poor, who go to work, may carry these in their pockets, and peruse them at meal times; and the type of the smallest Bibles is nearly as large as that of the 12mos.

I thank you for the friendly admonition you gave me respecting Mr. Fletcher.[4] It made me look into my heart, and I found some resentment there. What a lurking devil this pride is! How soon he takes fire, and yet hides his head so demurely in the embers, that we do not easily discover him! I think it is advisable to write to Mr. Fletcher, though despairing of success. His pamphlet will certainly be published now it is wrote. Indeed I have wrote to him aforetime more than once, and besought him to drop all controversy, but he seems to regard such entreaties as flowing rather from a fear of his pen than a desire of peace. His heart is somewhat exalted by his writings, and no wonder. He is also endowed with great acuteness, which, though much admired by the world, is a great obstacle to a quiet childlike spirit. And he is at present eagerly seeking after legal perfection which naturally

---

[1] Thornton had replied to Berridge's letter of August 18, not only sending more gifts but also criticizing Berridge for his comments about Fletcher. It is recorded in *GM* (1837), 214–215; *WB* (1838), 383–385; and *WB* (1864), 374–376.
[2] See August 18, 1773.
[3] Berridge's attitude toward the value of Christian literature had changed since the early 1760s. See November 22, 1760. Much literature was distributed in Berridge's area through the generosity of Thornton.
[4] See August 18, 1773.

202

produceth controversial heat. As gospel and peace, so law and controversy go hand in hand together? How can lawyers live without strife. In such a situation, I know from my own former sad experience, he will take the Scotch thistle[5] for his motto, *"noli me tangere."*[6] But his heart seemeth very upright, and his labours are abundant; and I trust the Master will serve him, by and by, as he has served me, put him into a pickling-tub, and drench him there soundly, and when he comes out dripping all over, he will be glad to cry grace, grace, and a little child may lead him. We learn nothing truly of ourselves, or of grace, but in a furnace. Whatever Mr. Fletcher may write against my pamphlet, I am determined to make no reply. I dare not trust my own wicked heart in a controversy. If my pamphlet is faulty, let it be overthrown; if sound, it will rise up above any learned rubbish that is cast upon it. Indeed, what signifies my pamphlet or its author? While it was publishing I was heartily weary of it; and have really been sick of it since, and concluded it had done no good because it had met with no opposition.

I thank you heartily for the kind offer of your assistance, but no more will be wanted of a long season; and till I am sunk in a deep slough, I dare not ask you, or anyone, to help me out. God has given me a free heart to dispose of my substance, and I am no more indebted to myself for this liberality, than a nightingale is for his wings or voice. But I feel a backwardness sometimes to be another's almoner, lest my honesty should be suspected. And this, perhaps, ariseth from the pride of my heart. A liberal mind was given me from a child, which made my carnal relations prophesy of me, that if I lived to be a man, I should surely prove a beggar. But I find, "He that watereth, shall be watered again."[7] And though I am possessed of a good vicarage, and some substance besides, I know of no effectual way to keep me from starving, but by giving. When Jesus opened mine eyes, my heart was so enlarged, that I gave away money and books without discretion; and was frequently imposed on, chiefly by the borrowing people, who all forgot to repay me, excepting one. Upon my own credit I once borrowed twenty pounds for a person, paid the interest for two years, and then was forced to pay the principal. These impositions are everywhere met with by benevolent people, and are trials for benevolence; for every virtue must be tried; and where benevolence is not rooted in

---

5   The cotton thistle is an emblem of the Scottish nation.
6   Do not touch me.
7   Proverbs 11:25.

the heart by grace, such trials overset it. I suppose such impositions are intended also to teach us caution. They have made me cautious, but I am afraid of growing suspicious, for we are apt to run into extremes; and it is better to be imposed on sometimes, than turn away a real needy person unrelieved from our door.

Mr. Williams' case showeth, that when the Lord has brought his people into extremity, He is near at hand to relieve them. And by the providential steps to bring Mr. Williams into the living, and his antecedent trials, it should seem that a great door of usefulness will be opened. In reading over your *Golden Treasury*, I found the same paper, with a little addition, in Nov. 5 and Dec. 12. May the good will of him, who dwelt in the bush, dwell with you and yours, and with your much obliged and affectionate servant,

John Berridge

To Rowland Hill[1]

Everton, September 3, 1773

Dear Sir (I mean, my dear Rowly),

Your kind letter was long in coming, but it brought good tidings and refreshed my heart. The motto of your seal[2] rejoiced me much; it gave me a peep into your bosom, and a taste of your letter before I read it. Indeed I was somewhat afraid lest orders[3] and a petticoat[4] would cure you of rambling; but my fears were groundless, and all is well. The lampoon published against you is a blessed omen for good that God intends to honour you. It seems to me a happy token that you will remain an itinerant, and that much good will arise from your ministry. Luther used to say, when the Lord had fresh work for him, a strong trial was always sent beforehand to prepare him for it by humiliation.

Study not to be a fine preacher. Jerichos are blown down with rams' horns.[5] Look simply unto Jesus for preaching food; and what is wanted will be given, and what is given be blest, whether it be a barley or a wheaten loaf, a crust or a crumb. Your mouth will be a flowing stream, or a fountain sealed, according as your heart is. Avoid all controversy

---

1   A copy of the letter was made by George Stampe on March 4, 1904, in WHSLMB, 69–70. This shows the defective nature of the printed sources. *WB* (1864), 513, has the last half of the letter missed out as well as the odd sentence. *CM* (1841), 870, has the erroneous date 1774 and again misses out the second half of the letter, although it gives most of the last paragraph. Sidney, *Life of Rowland Hill*, 91–92, gives much of the letter but omits the last two paragraphs. The letter is addressed to "The Rev. Mr. Rowland Hill at the Tabernacle House, Old Orchard, Bristol."

2   Hill's family motto was *"En Avant"* (go forward), which was presumably embossed on the seal.

3   Hill was ordained deacon in the national Church at the end of May by the bishop of Bath and Wells. He had obtained a curacy at Kingston in Somerset and had been preaching around this whole area. He had met with all kinds of opposition, including being stoned, having his effigy burned, and being the subject of virulent satire.

4   He married Mary Tudway on May 23, 1773, at Mary-le-bone Church, London.

5   Joshua 6.

in preaching, talking, or writing; preach nothing down but the devil, and nothing up but Jesus Christ. Mr. Fletcher[6] has sent me word that my pamphlet contains the core of antinomianism and that he is going to preach another Check[7] in answer to it. So he may, but he will not draw a reply from me.

What is become of my dear Nely Winter.[8] Is he got into petticoats too? I have not heard from him since Xmas. When you see him or write to him give my kind love to him. I purpose, God willing, to spend six weeks at the Tabernacle after Xmas and should be glad of your supply at that time, or at any time. You need not ask my leave to come, but come when you can. When you are in full orders, get it advertised in the public papers that all the kingdom may know of it. I have a good reason for this, for in May and June I was able to itinerate two days in the week, but have been laid up since; able indeed to preach, through mercy, on a Sunday, but no more.

I saw your other half once in London, and liked her hugely. She wept prettily and I hope her tears are not yet dried up. Give my kind love to her and a hat-full of kind respects to Mrs. Lynn, Miss Hermer and take a heart full of affection for yourself. Grace and peace be with you both and with your,

John Berridge

---

6   See August 18, 1773, and August 31, 1773.
7   *Logica Genevensis Continued.* See August 18, 1773.
8   Cornelius Winter. See Winter 1767.

To an Unknown Enquirer[1]

Everton, September 14, 1773

Dear Sir,

I received your kind letter, and thank you for it. You want nothing but an opened eye to see the glory of Christ's redemption; and he must give it, and will bestow it, when it is most for his glory and your advantage. Had you Daniel's holiness, Paul's zeal, John's love, Magdalene's repentance (and I wish you had them all), yet altogether they would give you no title to a pardon. You must at last receive it as a ruined sinner, even as the Cross-thief received it. No graces or services of your own can give you a right to pardon; you must come to Jesus for it, weary and heavy-laden[2]; and if you are afflicted for sin, and desirous of being delivered from its guilt and power, no past iniquities in your life, nor present corruptions of your heart, will be a bar to pardoning mercy. If we are truly seeking salvation by Jesus, we shall be disposed, as we are really bound, to seek after holiness.

But remember, though holiness is the walk to heaven, Christ is the way to God; and when you seek for pardon, you must go wholly out of your walk, be it good or bad, and look only to him who is the way. You must look to him as a miserable sinner, justly condemned by his law, a proper brand for hell, and look to be plucked from the fire by rich and sovereign grace. You have just as much worthiness for a pardon as the Cross-thief had, which is none at all; and in your best estate you will never have any more. A pardon was freely given to him upon asking for it freely, and given instantly because no room was left for delays; and a pardon is as ready for you as for him, when you

---

[1] The letter is found in *GS* (1869), 364–365; Ryle, *Christian Leaders*, 251; *GTOP* (1878), 200–201; and *S* (1907), 63. From the preface in Ryle, *Christian Leaders*, iv, we can see that he was the first to publish this letter in the *Family Treasury* in 1866–1867. The letter was written to someone who was seeking Christ and was presumably a member of Romaine's congregation at St. Ann's Blackfriars, London. It provides an excellent insight into Berridge's view on the relationship between faith, works and assurance.

[2] Matthew 11:28.

can ask for it as he did, with self-loathing and condemnation; but the proper seasons for bestowing the pardon are kept in Jesus' own hand. He makes his mercy manifest to the heart when it will most glorify his grace and benefit the sinner. Only continue asking for mercy; and seek it only through the blood of the cross, without any eye to your own worthiness, and that the blood in due time will be sprinkled on your conscience, and you shall cry, Abba, Father.[3]

Present my kindest love to my dear brother Mr. Romaine.[4] The Lord continue his life and usefulness. Kind respects and Christian salutation to Mrs. Olney. Grace and peace be with both, and with your affectionate and obliged servant,

John Berridge

---

[3] Romans 8:15.
[4] See July 16, 1763.

To John Newton[1]

Everton, September 20, 1773

My dear brother,

I write this letter, expecting an opportunity of conveying it to you by my dear neighbour, Mr. Venn[2]; and I wrote another some months ago, intending to send it to Bedford; but before an opportunity offered, yours came to hand, acquainting me with your purpose of coming to Everton speedily, so I burnt my own. I was heartily grieved to be absent, when you came to my house, but durst not omit my own journey; and I knew you would excuse my absence, when it was occasioned by our common Master's business.

For two months I was able to travel and preach two days in a week, and then had a return of my old complaint; not so violent as usual, but enough to confine me at home. Since the cool weather set in I am growing better, through mercy, and hope to be on horseback shortly, and preach a little in the neighbourhood; but I fear I shall not be able to reach Olney. My midway preaching at Bedford[3] seems to be foreclosed by the stench which my pamphlet has occasioned, and I cannot reach Olney in one day. However, I hope Mr. Venn's visit will provoke a returning visit from you this autumn, and I entreat you not to pass by Everton without warming a bed and a pulpit. If the Lord gives me strength, I will pay off all my debts; but if I am forced to be insolvent, do you act like a generous Christian, and continue your loans. My Master will repay you, if I cannot.

The Vicar of Madeley[4] has sent me word, that my prattle in my pamphlet of sincere obedience "is the core of Antinomianism, has exposed St. James, and touched the apple of God's eye," and that he

---

[1]   Because Henry Venn is visiting Olney, Berridge takes the opportunity to write to Newton. It is found in *WB* (1838), 385–386; and *WB* (1864), 376–377.

[2]   See June 8, 1771.

[3]   There was a Methodist society at Bedford. For its history, see Anderson, *Early Methodism in Bedford*.

[4]   John Fletcher. See August 18, 1773.

intends to put my head in the pillory, and my nose in the barnacles[5] for so doing. How fierce a tiger is zeal without knowledge, and I have been that tiger myself! And what utter destruction the Lord's own servants would make in his vineyard if the Lord himself did not hold the vines in his right hand! Oh, for that world, where all will say, I am of Christ; and oh, for more of Christ, while we live in this world! Kind Christian salutation to Mrs. Newton, and true hearty love for yourself. Grace and peace be with you both, and with your flock, and with your affectionate servant,

John Berridge

---

[5] An instrument placed on the nose of a restive horse.

To John Thornton[1]

Everton, September 25, 1773

Dear and honoured Sir,

I have received[2] the Bibles, Testaments and Watts' songs,[3] a most acceptable present for God's children. May the God of grace give a recompense, by filling you with all joy and peace in believing. You know the promise, "He that watereth, shall be watered again"[4]; how gracious is God! He grants ability to give, and bestows a heart to give, and then recompenses the gift. Oh, how little mine eyes behold the riches of grace; yet my heart longs and prays to behold it more, and to adore and glorify it more. The *Golden Treasuries* are dispersed among my flocks, some in one town, and some in another, and are much valued. About a dozen are yet left to drop into people's hands, as I shall find occasion. Watts' *Songs* are tempting things for children, and well adapted to season their minds with religion. The sight of your Bibles and Testaments filled my heart with joy. For my hearers are Bible readers, and prefer the word of God to everything. In general, they are people of great simplicity, and are Calvinists, but unpractised in disputes, and so happy as not to know what a Calvinist or Arminian means.

I have written to Mr. Fletcher,[5] and told him what was my intention in speaking against sincere obedience, and that my intention was manifest enough from the whole drift of the pamphlet. I have also

---

[1] The manuscript is held at LPL, MS 3096 ff.114–115. It seems that Thornton sent Berridge's letter to John Newton at Olney. The letter was printed in *GM* (1837), 215–216; *WB* (1838), 386–388; and *WB* (1864), 377–379.

[2] In *WB* the editor adds the details "six dozen of Bibles, as many Testaments, and 386 Watts' Songs" and misses out the last sentence.

[3] Isaac Watts (1674–1748), Nonconformist hymn writer whose *Hymns and Spiritual Songs* first appeared in 1707 and ran through many editions. His *Divine and Moral Songs for the Use of Children* was published in 1715 and had a constant sale over the next century. See Harry Escott, *Isaac Watts, Hymnographer* (Independent Press, 1962).

[4] Proverbs 11:25.

[5] See April 3, 1773.

acquainted him that I am an enemy to controversy, and that if his tract is published, I shall not rise up to fight with him, but will be a dead man before he kills me. I further told him, I was afraid that Mr. Toplady[6] and himself were setting the Christian world on fire, and the carnal world in laughter, and wished they would both desist from controversy. A letter seemed needful, yet I wrote to him without any hope of success, and it appears there is not any.

Mr. Jones,[7] an expelled Oxonian, has just been with him, and called upon me last Saturday, as he returned to his curacy. Mr. Fletcher showed him what he had written against my pamphlet, which has been revised by Mr. Wesley, and is to be published shortly, and bound up, I hear, with another tract, which he has written against honest John Bunyan.[8] Mr. Jones says, he considers and treats

---

[6] Augustus Toplady (1740–1778), Anglican vicar, poet, editor, controversialist, and famous hymn writer ("Rock of Ages"; "A debtor to mercy alone"). He was a strong Calvinist and vigorously opposed John Wesley. He wrote major books in the debate, *The Church of England Vindicated from the Charge of Arminianism* (Joseph Gurney, 1769) and *Historic Proof of the Doctrinal Calvinism of the Church of England*, 2 vols. (Keith, 1774). Of the latter George Lawton speaks of no one being able to push back the tidal-wave of evidence that beats through the book. See *Within the Rock of Ages: The Life and Work of Augustus Montague Toplady* (Cambridge: James Clarke, 1983), 117. Thomas Wright, speaking of Toplady's friendship with Berridge, says: "In London he occasionally met the Rev. John Berridge, with the clay of Bedfordshire still on his boots. They used to chat together in some particularly inconvenient coffee-house, which Berridge, who objected to comforts because they saddled him with self-sufficiency, had at considerable trouble discovered; and at such times Berridge would regale Toplady with accounts of his apostolic journeys, made in defiance of the bitter enmity of the hard-riding parsons and drinking squires, his neighbours, and in illustration of his favourite saw, 'Prudence is a rascally virtue'" (*Toplady and Contemporary Hymn-Writers*, 92).

[7] Thomas Jones (c.1744–1817) was one of the six Evangelical students who were expelled from St. Edmund's Hall, Oxford, in 1768 for holding the doctrine of election, consorting with Methodists, attending unlawful meetings, and being destitute of scholarship. Whitefield, with others, protested and wrote in their defence, and this was the start of the Calvinistic controversy of that time. Jones had been a hairdresser and had received help from John Newton before going to Oxford. He was later ordained and became curate of Clifton Reynes near Olney and married Lady Austin's sister, a relative of Cowper's. There are five letters to Mr. Jones in Newton's *Cardiphonia* (Edinburgh: Waugh and Innes, 1824).

[8] John Bunyan (1628–1688), author of *The Pilgrim's Progress; Grace Abounding; Holy War*; etc. A tinsmith of Elstow near Bedford, Bunyan was imprisoned for

me as an antinomian; but why should I resent it, when my Master was so considered and treated by the Pharisees, who called him a friend of publicans and sinners. I believe it is a healthful thing for every author to have his head in the pillory, and the barnacles on his nose; it may help to chill his vanity, and make him sick of scribbling. I seemed sick of my pamphlet before, but my Master knew my heart, and saw I was not, and He is now sending me a puke,[9] to make me cast it all up.

Well, let me have Jesus near my heart, and let the world take my reputation; which is not worth keeping. A sinner I am, and a miserable one too; and the reputation of such a sinner must be a miserable thing at best; yet poor as it is, we are loath to part with it, till Jesus hooks it away from us. A fund of vanity is lodged in the heart, and we perceive it not till the filthy pool is stirred by some dabbling hand. A Saviour of infinite compassion well becomes us; we know not how to bear with each other, and none but Jesus can bear with us all. He is God, and therefore we are not consumed. A Smithfield[10] fire would unite the sheep, and fright the goats away; but when the world ceases to persecute the flocks, they begin to fight each other. Indeed the worst part of the sheep is his head, which is not half so good as a calf's head, and with this they are butting at each other. Until the millennium[11] come, and perhaps until the resurrection, Judah will be vexing Ephraim, and Ephraim will be envying Judah.[12]

Teach me, Lord, to become a child and to have no part in this envy or vexation. I only add, what I have abundant cause to add, the Lord bless you, and unite his upper springs with your nether springs,[13]

---

many years for unlicensed preaching and was a major figure in seventeenth-century Puritan literature. For an appreciation of Bunyan from a Christian perspective, see Barry E. Horner, *Pilgrim's Progress: Themes and Issues* (Darlington: Evangelical Press, 2003). For a modern academic analysis, see Anne Dunan-Page, ed., *The Cambridge Companion to Bunyan* (Cambridge: Cambridge University Press, 2010).

9   An emetic.
10   Cattle market in London associated with the gibbet and the stake. Most of the Marian Martyrs suffered death there.
11   The time of victory as portrayed in Revelation 20. The postmillennialist expects the resurrection after the millennium.
12   Israel became two kingdoms after the death of Solomon, and their subsequent history was characterized by constant conflict.
13   Lower springs—your life here.

causing them to water well your own heart, and the hearts of all your family. Grace and peace be with you, and with your much obliged and affectionate servant,

John Berridge

Mr. Bentley[14] returned from Yorkshire last night and left our friends as well as usual.

---

[14] Roger Bentley (*c.*1733–1795) had been made vicar of St. Giles, Camberwell, through the efforts of John Thornton in 1769 after failing to obtain a living since his ordination in 1760 in York. When Thornton died in 1790 he was made a trustee of Thornton's Trust. After Bentley's death in 1795 those in his congregation who were dissatisfied with the preaching of his successor founded Camden Chapel, Peckham.

To John Newton[1]

Everton, November 2, 1773

Dear Sir,

I received your kind letter by the Sandy gardener, but could not return an answer by the same conveyance, because he intends no more journeys to Olney[2] for some weeks. My housekeeper has been ill of a fever for three weeks, and is so weak she cannot sit in a chair, and so fainting on her bed, that life is scarcely kept in her. There is a hope of recovery, but a distant one. This circumstance, with the approach of winter, has induced me to put off my visit till the spring. It is an easy matter, I find, to get into debt,[3] but no easy matter to get out. Yet what are my debts to you, in comparison of my debts to God: these are numerous indeed, and attended with every kind of aggravation; and the weight of them so presseth down my spirit at times, that I can scarcely look up. However, when they have well broken and melted my heart, the Surety[4] appears, and cheers up my spirit; and then, with a tear in mine eyes, I sing hosannas to the lovely Jesus.

Ten years ago I expected to be something before this time, and seemed to be in a very hopeful way, but Jesus has copped my locks,[5] and sawed my horns, and harrowed my back so stoutly, that scarce anything is left me besides the skin of my teeth, and that I suppose must go by and by, for he will have all. Well, though I sometimes snarl and snap at my Master, I think the more He whips me, the more I love him. Solomon says, a rod for a fool's back[6]; and I am sure no instructions suit me like rods and scorpions; for my heart is a quintessence of

---

[1]   LPL holds the manuscript, MS 3972 ff.17-18. Printed in *WB* (1838), 389–390; *WB* (1864), 379–381; and *Gospel Banner* (1885), 359–360.
[2]   Newton was curate at Olney. See March 13, 1771.
[3]   See September 20, 1773.
[4]   Christ as the one who takes to himself the sinner's responsibilities to God. He is the sinner's personal guarantee of the new covenant.
[5]   Samson lost his power when he had his hair cut off by Delilah, thus forfeiting the symbol of Nazarite separateness. Judges 16.
[6]   Proverbs 26:3.

215

folly and madness. A furnace seems a hot atmosphere to breathe in, and a deadly path to walk in, but is really a place of liberty. Like the furnace of Nebuchadnezzar,[7] it only burneth our bonds, our earthly and selfish attachments, and consumeth no other flesh but proud flesh. A handful of grace, sprinkled into a furnace, changeth its nature, like the handful of meal thrown into a pot,[8] and maketh fire, in its nature destructive, prove a salutary heat.

I need not tell you that I love you, nor that Jesus has taught me to do so; and the less cause you can find in yourself to be esteemed, the more cause I shall have to love and esteem you. Kind Christian salutations to Mrs. Newton and your guests, unknown indeed to me, but known to Jesus, I trust, else they would not seek a place in your house.[9] If the good centurion, Captain Scott,[10] is with you, let him know he has long had a corner, and large one too, in my heart; and may have when he please a corner in my house for a lodging, and my horse-block[11] for his pulpit. As I am but an awkward old bachelor, I must beg of you to speak a handsome word, and make a leg up to me to his lady, a deaconess, I suppose. The Lord bless her. Jesus Christ bless you all, and the smallest of you all,

John Berridge

---

7   Daniel 3.
8   2 Kings 4:41.
9   On April 12, 1773, William Cowper and Mrs. Unwin had moved in with Newton for a few days' rest as Cowper had entered a deeper depression at the beginning of the year. They stayed, being cared for by the Newtons, for fourteen months!
10   Jonathan Scott (1735–1807), a convert of Mr. Romaine while at Lady Huntingdon's congregation at Oat Hall. In 1769 he sold his commission and devoted himself to preaching, particularly in Cheshire, Staffordshire, and Shropshire. J.H.Y. Briggs says: "to him more than any other, the existence of evangelical congregationalism in Staffordshire owes its existence, some 22 churches tracing their origins to his labours. Beyond this, some five churches in Shropshire, six in Cheshire, four or five in Lancashire, and others in Derbyshire were profoundly influenced or started by him" (Donald M. Lewis, ed., *Blackwell Dictionary of Evangelical Biography, 1730–1860*, 2 vols. [Oxford: Blackwell, 1995], 2:988). He was one of the regular supplies for twenty years at Whitefield's Tabernacle. Towards the end of Berridge's life, Berridge refers to a visit of Scott to the Tabernacle and says that he is "a truly spiritual man." See February 21, 1788.
11   A small platform of stone or wood for mounting a horse.

To John Thornton[1]

Everton, November 10, 1773

Dear and honoured Sir,

I owe you many thanks and many prayers, and a letter beside; but the debts I owe my God are without number, and a daily increasing sum, and exceedingly heinous. Everlasting thanks for a Surety, whose blood is of infinite value, and who can save to the uttermost.[2] Ten years ago[3] I hoped to be something long before this time, and seemed in a promising way; but a clearer view of the spiritual wickedness in my heart, and of the spiritual demands of God's law, has forced me daily to cry, O wretched man that I am![4] God be merciful to me a sinner.[5] I am now sinking from a poor something into a vile nothing; and wish to be nothing, that Christ may be all. I am creeping down the ladder from self-complacence into self-abhorrence; and the more I do abhor myself, the more I must hate sin, which is the cause of that abhorrence.

A legal heart may strive against sin, through fear of hell; or strive against sin to glorify himself, as laying a foundation for merit; but a gospel-broken heart strives against sin, through a loathing of it, as the filthiness of his spirit, the image of the devil, and a contradiction to God's holiness. From experience I know there may be grace, where there is no fixed abhorrence, but it must be grace in the bud; and till men are brought with Job to this state of self-abhorrence,[6] I believe their righteousness is merely Pharisaical, a Dagon[7] in the Lord's temple, a rival set up against Jesus. And I am confident, where grace

---

[1] This is found in *GM* (1837), 217–218; *WB* (1838), 390–392; and *WB* (1864), 381–383.

[2] Hebrews 7:25.

[3] This whole passage is important in understanding Berridge's move away from Wesley's teaching on sanctification.

[4] Romans 7:24.

[5] Luke 18:13.

[6] Job 42:6.

[7] The Philistines set up the ark of God beside their idol Dagon, which fell on its face toward the ark. 1 Samuel 5:2.

is, it will reign, and cast this Dagon down; and though set up again, and yet again, will surely break his legs and bones at last. God[8] says, He will dwell with a broken heart; but a heart cannot be broken where there is a sense of merit[9]; it is only broken down by a dread of sin, or by a loathing of it. First, we are made to dread past sin, on account of its guilt; and as grace thriveth, we are taught to loathe ourselves, on account of our sinful nature. As the heart is more washed,[10] we grow more sensible of its remaining defilement; just as we are more displeased with a single spot on a new coat, than with a hundred stains in an old one.

The more wicked men grow, the less ashamed they are of themselves; and the more holy men grow, the more they learn to abhor themselves. You desire me to become a friendly monitor[11]; but am I qualified for the office? I seem to be sent forth as a reprover in the gate,[12] rather than a chamber counsel. I have so many beams in my own eye,[13] that I can scarcely see, or find a heart to pluck a mote from a brother's eye. What I can do, I will do; but I fancy you will prove the best monitor; and I must thank you for the hint you gave me about my foxes.[14] Others have given the same hint. I thank them also for their kindness, and confess to you that I am growing sick of my kennel, and intend to go no more a fox-hunting.[15]

Alas, dear Sir, you know the man, and his communication. My pamphlet[16] and my letters testify sufficiently that I was born with a fool's-cap[17] on my head,[18] and the fool is ready to show his cap, not

---

[8]   *GM* has "At last God."
[9]   The place works play in sanctification was a key point of disagreement in the Calvinistic controversy.
[10] *GM* has "And as the sinfulness of the heart is felt."
[11] I think Thornton must have appealed to Berridge to keep order among those involved in the controversy, like a senior pupil would in school.
[12] Amos 5:10.
[13] Matthew 7:3.
[14] A reference to the Song of Solomon 2:15: "the little foxes that spoil the vines." Hence, Berridge's own faults that Thornton had obviously mentioned. One of these foxes was Berridge's use of humour.
[15] One fault Thornton seems to highlight is that Berridge has been too critical of others.
[16] *Christian World.*
[17] A cap with bells that was worn by fools and jesters.
[18] Two years later, on October 17, 1775, Thornton refers to this phrase. "I remember you once jocularly informed me you were born with a fool's cap on:

only in a parlour, but sometimes in a pulpit; for which he has had many drubbings[19] from his Master when he came down. But this is not the worst. Through mercy, I know myself to be a fool, and can lament my folly to my friends; but my pride is such, that I do not like the world should call me what I call myself.

In my family[20] I now have a strong proof of the power of grace. My housemaid has been ill for many weeks of fever and jaundice, and when she seemed near death, would cry out, Lord, I am ready, I am coming, I am coming! Her fever and jaundice are abated, but we are now apprehensive of a dropsy.[21] She is feeble, and faint, and swollen, but meek, and patient as a lamb. Oh, sir, though our breath is in our nostrils, and we know not what an hour may bring forth, yet how faintly do eternal things affect us, and how little we live as on the confines of death! The Lord bring eternity nearer our minds, and Jesus nearer our hearts. May God bless you and yours with covenant blessings, and make you a truly royal family, even heirs of a crown that fadeth not away. Grace and peace be with you, dear Sir, and with your much obliged and affectionate servant,

John Berridge

---

pray, my dear sir, is it not high time it was pulled off? Such an accoutrement may suit a natural birth, and be of service, but surely it has nothing to do with a spiritual one; nor ever can be made ornamental to a serious man, much less to a Christian minister" (*WB* [1864], 523). See October 22, 1775, for Berridge's defence.

19 Beatings with a stick.
20 See January? 1765.
21 An accumulation of fluid in the body's tissues.

To John Berridge[1]

Everton, November 12, 1773

Dear Jacky,

My housemaid has been ill for many weeks, with a fever and jaundice. I am obliged to have a nurse to look after her. My brother Matty[2] has lately sent me a letter, in which he seems to write like a penitent man, but I feel he is not duly convinced of sin. I hope you do not forget to read your Bible, and pray to Jesus Christ frequently. If you neglect prayer and the word of God, you will soon lose all seriousness and become conformable to the world. You had need be very watchful, else youth and health and worldly business will soon draw off your heart from God; and going from God is like going downhill, when you once set off you know not how to stop. Though you are young, you may be called away before me; and if you lose your own soul, it will profit you nothing, though you had gained the whole world; seek the kingdom of God and his righteousness, and all earthly things that are needful shall be added unto you.[3] While you seek diligently after the Lord, everything will prove a blessing to you; but if you forsake him, everything will prove a curse. Oh, may the Lord bless you and delight in you to do you good, and may you delight to serve him. I love you much; may you be taught to love the Lord and serve him. Grace and peace be with you, and with your affectionate uncle,

John Berridge

---

[1] Written to his nephew, John Berridge (b.1750), of Scarrington, Nottinghamshire, son of his brother James. See May 30, 1780; July 21, 1781; and May 24, 1792. The letter is from *S* (1893), 29–30.

[2] Matthew, Berridge's third brother.

[3] Matthew 6:33.

To John Thornton[1]

Everton, January 14, 1774

Dear and honoured Sir,

Your kind favour of the 10th came duly to hand, but the 50 *Treasuries*[2] and 300 *Admonitions*[3] are not yet arrived. The former *Treasuries* are dispersed, and the little Testaments are marching off apace, both of them sweet pocket companions for the labouring poor. If beggars might be choosers, I should wish for 200 only of the *Admonitions*, and a few more of the small Testaments, instead of the 100 other *Admonitions*. My hearers are of a sound gospel delf,[4] very poor and simple hearted, and cry out for the Bible. They think, and rightly think, that one little Testament is worth one million of the *Christian World Unmasked*.[5] However, human writings are of use to carnal men, who care not for the Scripture. For although the children love the honey of God's word, and tasting, feel it is divine; yet strangers must be caught with human treacle; and many a wasp has been taken by it and conveyed to Jesus' beehive.

Your letter will afford materials for a sermon. I say no more of it, because of the tinder mentioned in your last, enveloping the heart;

---

[1] This letter is taken from *GM* (1837), 254–255; *CM* (1845), 27–28; and *GS* (1849), 116–118. This theological letter follows on from the letter of November 10, 1773. *GS* says: "The above has been sent us, with two or three others, as an original letter of old John Berridge"; it has some words in italics.

[2] *Bogatzky's Golden Treasury.* See April 3, 1773.

[3] Joseph Alleine, *An Admonition to the Unconverted*, also published as *An Alarm to the Unconverted* and *A Sure Guide to Heaven*. It was first published in 1671, three years after his death at the early age of thirty-four, his health having suffered due to imprisonments during the Restoration. A passionate evangelist, an excellent teacher, and a caring pastor, he was ejected from the national Church in 1662. It is a compelling manual on conversion, covering mistakes about conversion; its nature, necessity, and marks; the miseries of the unconverted and directions to the unconverted; and finally the motives for conversion. Countless editions of this book have been issued. It has been reprinted over 500 times and a modern edition is in print today.

[4] A piece of basic earthenware or a pit or quarry. *CM* has "class."

[5] See August 18, 1773.

but shall add, by way of supplement, a few remarks on a noted text: "Christ is made to (or for) us wisdom, righteousness, sanctification, and redemption."[6] Paul is not here speaking of what Christ worketh *in* us by his grace, but of what he hath wrought *for* us, as our legal Surety. The four capital blessings mentioned in the text, were procured for us without any contrivance or concurrence of our own; and therefore the conclusion in the next verse is weighty: "Let him that glorieth glory in the Lord." Laws, human and divine, not only demand obedience, but require from the subject a right knowledge of the laws. God's law demands an atonement for sins of ignorance (Lev. 4 and 5), and he who breaks a human law will not escape punishment by pleading ignorance.

Now, man at his first creation had a perfect knowledge given him of God's law; but through sin he lost that knowledge. His faculties were darkened, and he became a stranger to the spiritual nature and extent of his Maker's law. However, God, as our great creditor, has a right to demand full payment of that knowledge he had lent us, though we through misconduct are unable to pay, having squandered it all away. And thus we become debtors for the loss of *knowledge*, as well as for the loss of *innocence*. On which account we need a Surety for wisdom, and one is provided: "In whom are hid all the treasures of wisdom and knowledge."[7] And without a Surety for wisdom, the wisest Christian would have perished, on account of his knowing but in part.[8]

Again: "Adam was created in righteousness and true holiness."[9] Now, righteousness in its strict meaning is an outward conformity to the law, and sanctification or holiness is an inward conformity to it, or devotedness of heart to God. Both the outward and inward conformity are required by the law, and in a perfect degree: but in both we are utterly defective. On these accounts a Surety is wanted both for righteousness and sanctification; and one is provided, who "fulfilled all righteousness,"[10] and could say, "Thy law is within my heart,"[11] and it is "my meat and drink to do thy will."[12]

Lastly, we are insolvent debtors for wisdom, righteousness, and sanctification; and as such, we are fallen under the curse of the law,

---

6 1 Corinthians 1:30.
7 Colossians 2:3.
8 1 Corinthians 13:12.
9 Berridge's commentary on Ephesians 4:24.
10 Matthew 3:15.
11 Psalm 40:8.
12 John 4:34.

and need a Surety to redeem us from it. Jesus is that Surety, "in whom we have redemption, even the forgiveness of sins."[13] Thus we are shown in this noble text all the debts Jesus Christ undertook as our Surety, and discharged for us. The commentators I have seen make a sadly confused work of this passage. They are puzzled to keep the parts distinct; and some parts are supposed to be wrought for us, and some wrought in us. But Paul makes no such distinction, nor will his words allow it. He only declares in this passage what Christ was made for us; a Surety for wisdom, and righteousness, and sanctification, and redemption; a Surety to discharge every claim the law had upon us.

Now, when Jesus opens a sinner's eyes, to behold the multiplied guilt of his ignorance, unrighteous conduct, and unholy heart, and of his lying under a law curse thereby, he quickly flies to the Surety for relief. And when by faith he is enabled to view a finished salvation, and steadfastly to rely upon the Surety, redemption is found; he feels the sprinkled blood, the love of God is poured into his heart,[14] which hallows it, making self-denial an easy yoke and obedience a cheerful service. And while believers keep simply looking to a crucified Christ, and the eye of faith is kept open, love and peace flow on sweetly like a river, and the heart becomes more lowly, more childlike, and more devoted unto God. By feeding *only* and daily on the flesh and blood of Christ, eternal life springs up in them as a well of water.

I suppose your Christmas pies are all eaten, though mine are not yet made. However, may the true Christmas cheer attend you all the year[15]—a sweet Christ in your heart, the hope of glory. Grace and peace be with you, dear Sir, and with your fire-side, and with all that love our common Lord, and with a poor limping traveller called

John Berridge

---

13 Colossians 1:14.
14 Romans 5:5.
15 *GM* has "may the true head of the Church send you all the year a sweet Christ in your heart...."

To Mr. N__[1]

Everton, January 15, 1774

Dear N__,

The first pages of your letters are usually much illuminated with compliments. I wonder where you pick them all up, and how you find storage for them. Indeed the old ass of Everton cannot discern his own features when you have cropped his ears and tail, and powdered and spruced him up in a letter. I am daily praying to know more of my blindness, helplessness, and vileness, and you are kindly contriving to put a mask on my face. Is this Christianity, or have I provoked you to it by sweetly begriming your own face? Leave this varnish, dear N., to the world, who love to gild a base metal and make it look like gold. Henceforth, when you write to me, consider yourself as a poor frog who is croaking to a poor toad, and then your frogship may compliment my toadship as much as you please.

The uncovenanted mercy mentioned in my pamphlet was not an inadvertent mistake, as you politely call it, but a mere blunder, resulting from gross ignorance. I wrote without illumination. It was a relic of Arminian dregs, and, as such, would not be overlooked or maltreated, but caressed by the Vicar of Madeley.[2] In the second edition of my pamphlet the whole paragraph where uncovenanted mercy appears is left out, but in the first edition it must stand as a public cryer to proclaim my foolishness. I did not like the cryer's bell at first; it sounded mighty harsh, but grows much more melodious by frequent ringing, and seems now more melodious and mellow than the pretty set of chimes in the preface of your letter. Our Jesus shows his wisdom and his mercy when he leaves us to ourselves at times, and lets us blunder on that he may fetch our crests down, and rub our noses well with our

---

[1] There is a short extract of this letter in J. Gadsby's *Memoirs of the Principal Hymn Writers and Compilers of the 17th and 18th Centuries* (Gadsby, 1855), 34–35. The full letter is found in *GS* (1852), 148–149. This may be to Cornelius Winter, whom Berridge called Nel(l)y. See September 3, 1773.

[2] Mr. Fletcher. See August 18, 1773.

ignorance. A pot of ointment with no putrid flies in it might refresh the public much by its fragrance, but would make the author smell and stink like a polecat.

I am glad to hear of your frequent preaching. It is with preaching as with praying; the more you do preach the more you may preach and the easier you will preach. Thrice a week is all that I do, and sometimes not even that; and because I preach but seldom, I think a little more than usual about my sermons. But I find it to my sorrow, the more I think about my sermons the less liberty and power I have in preaching. Indeed, my disorder so relaxes my body, and weakens my memory, and eats up my faculties, that I am little more than the stump of a methodist parson. I have no thought of publishing anything more, except a few hymns, and that is certain. Writing so shatters my frame, that I seem as glad when a letter is finished as a naughty schoolboy does when a whipping is over.

Improve your health, dear N., while it lasts, and your sands while they run, and make the best of them both for Jesus. Be not anxious to lay in a stock beforehand for the pulpit; it shall be given you in the hour. Hot bread from the oven[3] and roast meat from the spit are better far than old cooked victuals from the pantry. Grace and peace be with you, and with your much affectionate servant,

John Berridge

---

[3] See October 22, 1775, for Thornton's criticism of Berridge's public prayer for new bread not stale.

To Samuel Wilks[1]

Everton, April 8, 1774

Dear Sir,

I received a kind letter from you in town, which I laid in a drawer along with some others, and intended to call upon you before I left London; but a cold, attended with much feebleness of body, prevented my going out some weeks. When my cold was somewhat removed, your letter had wholly escaped my memory, and did not occur to my thoughts till it presented itself to my view on rummaging the drawers to pack up my things for my journey. Well, dear Sir, though you have had a very forgetful preacher you have a kind remembering God, a faithful Jesus, who watches over his vineyard day and night, lest any should hurt it. And what a mercy it is, that your beloved partner and yourself are both looking and drawing the same way. The Lord draw you both near to his side, and keep you there.

Troubles you need, and troubles will sprout up every day from within or without but a sweet view of Jesus will make rough ways smooth, and rough winds calm. Our business is to follow Christ with the heart as well as life, in the affections as well as actions, and to culti-vate a closer acquaintance and stricter union with him. The nearer

---

[1] Samuel Wilks (d.1803) was appointed to the post of Examiner of Indian Correspondence for the East India Company in 1769 in order to relieve the secretary of the company. See William Foster, *A Guide to the India Office Records, 1600–1858* (India Office, 1919). This was a well-paid and very responsible position conducting the secret correspondence of the company, for which he was awarded a pension for life. He retired in 1785 after a three-year absence through illness and was subpoenaed as a witness of the trial of Warren Hastings (1732–1818), the English administrator who played a major role in the development of India as governor of Bengal but was subsequently impeached on his return to England in 1785 for his unscrupulous methods. Wilks's wife was converted through Berridge's preaching. His grandson, Samuel Charles Wilks (1789–1872), became a well-known Evangelical in the nineteenth century in the Clapham Sect and edited the *Christian Observer* (1816–1850). The letter is found in *WB* (1838), 392–393, and *WB* (1864), 383–384.

our union is, the sweeter will be our communion; and the end both of tribulation and consolation is to drive us or lead us nearer to Jesus. Old pilgrims, I find, are apt to talk of past attainments, and to nestle in them; by which they soon become dry-skinned, and footsore, and formal. Oh, dear sir, let us be ambitious of the best things, and daily covet more of the true riches; pursuing our heavenly calling as men pursue a worldly one, with all our might. No traffic so sure and so gainful as Christian traffic; and no laziness so shameful as Christian laziness. The Lord help us to gird up our loins, and trim our lamps! The Lord make us watchful and prayerful, looking and longing for the coming of the Bridegroom!

I feel a Christian affection for you; but you must not be jealous when I tell you honestly, I find a stronger affection for your wife. My love for you is brotherly; for her, is fatherly; and none but a spiritual father knows what affection he bears to his children. The Lord bless you both. Grace and peace be with you, and with your affectionate servant, for Christ's sake,

John Berridge

To a Fellow Preacher[1]

Everton, April 14, 1774

Dear Brother,

I am now at Everton, and free from London visitors; yet not alone as I wish, for a troublesome guest has followed me down from London, and abides in my house and teases me daily. It is an impertinent acquaintance of yours whom I long to shake off, but cannot tell how; he has got footing in my house, and neither soft words nor hard ones will drive him away. When awake, he is continually complaining or yawning, and if crossed or put out of his way will hector and bully, and swears he will murder me. Dear Sir, what must I do with him? He vows he will be used like a gentleman, because one of his ancestors, it seems, was a nobleman; yet I find the name of his father was Sin, and his godfather's name is Satan; and the man's name is Esau,[2] as sorry a rascal as ever was born. With the look and temper of Cain he minds neither law nor justice, and threatens, if he can, to stab me in the wilderness or drown me in Jordan. He tells me also that he has many brethren, and one of his name is acquainted with you and heartily hates your preaching. So much for Esau.

Now for your preaching and mine. Do we not wish to excel, and wish to have the preaching effectual? That blessed effect does neither depend upon genius nor learning, but on the unction from above, which may be had for asking, and had in abundance for asking abundantly; so that in every dry preaching we may say, "have I not provided this for myself? There was water enough in the fountain to

---

[1] GS records this letter twice: (1851), 168, and (1871), 287–288. The *Christian Cottagers' Magazine* (1851), 308–309, varies the punctuation. Berridge is writing to a fellow preacher who is probably Richard Woodgate, to whom there are several surviving letters. See April 20, 1773; April 21, 1775; and April 28, 1779. The latter part of the letter seems to be missing.

[2] Berridge is taking Esau as a picture of the old man, the man concerned with this life, in comparison with the man with spiritual aspirations and desires. See Genesis 25:31 and Hebrews 12:16 for details of how Esau sells his birthright for a meal.

moisten my subject, but I did not draw it enough by supplication." Much thought on a subject beforehand may make it palatable to a hearer, but will not make it profitable except it smells of much prayer, as well as tastes of meditation. Our sermons will savour of our walk. If our walk is close, the sermon will be close; if the head be well anointed with oil, it will drop from the lip, and the tongue will tell what communion we keep....

John Berridge

To John Thornton[1]

Everton, August 10, 1774

Dear and honoured Sir,

Through mercy I have been able to itinerate thirteen weeks this summer, and am now resting my old bones during harvest, and sitting down to pay my epistolary debts, which have risen to a large amount. Indeed they have lain too long unnoticed (but writing does not suit when I ramble), and they now threaten me with letters of attorney unless due satisfaction is made before harvest is out. It is therefore high time to call for paper, and to mend up my pens.[2]

In most places I find very large auditories. My cathedral barns are much crowded, and the cathedral yards well sprinkled with hearers. No outrage or mocking as usual, but silence and attention. Inside and outside passengers, the living and lifeless professors receive me with more favour since my Master has cropped my ears, and turned his old ass out of doors again, which confirms a sweet passage given me in my illness. Job 11:16–19.[3]

I have been recruiting for Mr. Venn,[4] at Godmanchester, a very populous and wicked town near Huntingdon, and met with a patient hearing from a numerous audience. I hope he also will consecrate a few barns, and preach a little in his neighbourhood, to fill up his fold at Yelling. And sure there is a cause, when souls are perishing for lack of knowledge. Must salvation give place to a fanciful decency, and sinners go flocking to hell through our dread of irregularity?[5] Whilst irregularities in their

---

[1] *GM* (1837), 310–312; *WB* (1838), 394–396; and *WB* (1864), 384–386. *WB* edits into paragraphs while *GM* includes italics.

[2] A quill pen needed sharpening to retain its shape and efficiency.

[3] See June 3, 1771, and June 10, 1771. This was one of the Scriptures that Berridge wrote on the fly-leaf of his Bible. "Job xi: 16,17,18,19—also Isai. liv: 7,8,9,10—also Psal. xci. 14,15,16, after a long Illness much wanted to humble my Heart, greatly lifted up"(*Gospel Gems,* iv).

[4] Henry Venn was now at Yelling. See June 8, 1771.

[5] It seems as if Venn had a conscience about being preaching in other men's parishes. Berridge had to argue the case. Later, however, Venn was to come

\text{230}

worst shape traverse the kingdom with impurity, should not irregularity in its best shape pass without censure? I tell my brother Venn, he need not fear being hanged for sheep stealing, while he only whistles the sheep to a better pasture, and meddles neither with the flesh nor fleece. And I am sure he cannot sink much lower in credit; for he has lost his character right honestly, by preaching law and gospel without mincing.[6] The scoffing world make no other distinction between us, than between Satan and Beelzebub. We have both got tufted horns and cloven feet, only I am thought the more impudent devil of the two.

Your three hundred and fifty Alleines[7] are dispersed about the country, thirty miles round. The Lord attend them with a blessing. I have lately received two hundred hymn books, and a dozen of *Omicron's letters*,[8] for which I return you hearty thanks; as also for your account of the Indian woman of Tuscurora.[9] How sweet is Christian simplicity, and how much preferable to mere human eloquence! I suppose by the matter and style that shamefaced Omicron is Mr. Newton.[10] He wears a mask, but cannot hide his face. Pithiness and candour will betray the curate of Olney, notwithstanding his veil of a Greek signature. I expect him at Everton today, and a covey from Yelling Rectory, if they can bear to ride in a baker's coach.

It is much rumoured that Mr. Jobson[11] has an offer of a minor canonry in the church of Ely, and is going to leave his present curacy,

---

down against irregularity, much to the disappointment of Berridge, and would influence Simeon against irregularity. See July 2, 1785.

6   Without restraint.

7   *An Alarm to the Unconverted*. See January 14, 1774.

8   Omicron, *Twenty Six Letters on Religious Subjects* (Oliver, 1774).

9   Since 1768 Thornton had been treasurer of a board of trustees supporting missionary work among the Indian tribes. He had already become a close friend of the Mohegan Samson Occom after Occom visited England on a preaching tour collecting money for work among the Indians. On top of the financial assistance from the board, Thornton supported Occom privately, sending him many gifts. For an account of Thornton's interest in the Indians, see ch. 6, "Thornton and America," in Klein, *"An Amazing Grace,"* 67–90.

10 See March 13, 1771.

11 Rev. Abraham Jobson (1731–1831)—the eleventh wrangler in 1772, gaining his DD in 1810—was an intimate friend of Thomas Robinson during his undergraduate time at Trinity College, Cambridge. He was made a priest by John Hinchcliffe, bishop of Peterborough, on June 14, 1772, having been made curate of Doddington in March of that year. He later became vicar of Wymeswold (1776–1802), rector of Wardley with Belton (1778–1802), and finally vicar of Wisbech (1802–1831).

and reside there. Alas for him, he had need of Daniel's faith before he steps into a den of lions![12] When young gospellers change their quarters speedily, and without constraint, I mistrust they are growing lousy, and will soon be eaten up with vermin.

I have little to write in respect of myself. Enough of temporals to supply my own proper wants, but in spirituals poor indeed! And the older I grow, the poorer I seem. From an imaginary something, I am sinking into mere nothing, and a perfect scold miserable. I am ashamed of the little I do for Jesus, and of the poverty of that little. Worms are eating holes in my duties, as fast as I do them; and flies are blowing their maggots into all the pots of my ointment.[13] No prayer sits so well on my stomach now, as "God be merciful."[14] I hope you give the Lord daily thanks for your ability and inclination to do good, and take nothing to yourself but the character of an unprofitable servant.[15] The Lord increase you more and more, you and your household, giving you bread from heaven, and water from the rock, to sanctify and sweeten all the nether springs. So prayeth your much obliged and affectionate servant,

John Berridge

---

[12] Daniel 6.
[13] Ecclesiastes 10:1.
[14] Luke 18:13.
[15] Luke 17:10.

To Samuel Wilks[1]

Everton, August 16, 1774

Dear Sir,

I have been itinerating for thirteen weeks; and when I ramble about to preach, I have neither leisure nor inclination to write; but the harvest is now come forward, which affords me some rest, and I am set down to pay my epistolary debts. Indeed, my spirits have been so weak and shattered since my late long illness, that writing of letters is a real burden to me, and makes me a very tardy correspondent. At times, when I am very low, a letter that demands a speedy answer will vapour[2] me as much as a large bill requiring prompt payment would a sinking tradesman.

The Lord has led you through a variety of scenes, but he knows what he does, and does all things well. Sitting safely on the beach is very sweet after a stormy voyage; but I fancy you will find it more difficult to walk closely with Jesus in a calm than a storm, in easy circumstances than in strait. A Christian never falls asleep in the fire or in the water, but grows drowsy in the sunshine. We love to nestle, but cannot make a nest in a hard bed. God has given you good abilities.[3] This, of course, will make you respected by men of business, and tempt you at times to admire yourself, and thus bring a smart rod upon your back. Sharp genius, like a sharp knife, often makes a wrong gash, and cuts a finger instead of food. We scarcely know how to turn our backs on admiration, though it comes from the vain world; yet a kick from the world does believers less harm than a kiss. I apprehend a main part of your trial will lie here; and when you are tempted to think gaudily of yourself, and spread your feathers like a peacock, remember too, that fine parts, in themselves, are like the fine wings of a butterfly, which garnish out the moth or grub underneath.

---

[1]   See April 8, 1774. The letter is from *WB* (1838), 396–397, and *WB* (1864), 386–387.

[2]   Worry.

[3]   Reference to Wilks's position in the East India Company.

Remember, too, that a fiend has sharper points than the sharpest of us; and that one grain of godly fear is of more worth than a hundred thousand heads-full of attic wit,[4] or full of philosophic, theologic or commercial science.

Kind Christian love to Mrs. Wilks. The Lord bless you both, and bless your children. Grace and peace be with you all, and with your affectionate servant, for Christ's sake,

John Berridge

---

[4] Greek philosophy.

To Messrs. Dilly,
Booksellers in the Poultry,
Near the Mansion House, London[1]

Everton, August 30, 1774

Sir, I have carefully revised my pamphlet[2] and corrected it and have sent you a table of contents. It could not be conveyed to your hands sooner, because I was rambling out a preaching before harvest and I make all business give place to itineration. The interleaved letter you sent me of justification by faith[3] is utterly unfit for publication. It is often pert and saucy, and in general lean and raw—just the chirping of a chicken newly hatched, and scribbled over in a day. I desire you will not reprint it, unless you are resolved to put me into the booksellers' pillory, and make me stand there to be pelted by all the fraternity of Grub Street.[4]

Desire Mr. Pasham,[5] the printer, to get a good pair of spectacles before he corrects the third edition. His former pair was very dim, or had lost an eye. When the impression is printed off send me a single

---

1   The letter is taken from the *Christian's Monthly Record* (1890), 210. Charles Dilly (1739-1807) was born at Southill, a village in Bedfordshire, a few miles from Everton. After visiting America he went into partnership in a very successful business with his brother Edward. Their hospitality was famous, with many famous authors attending their dinner parties. They produced a wide range of books—their catalogue extended to thirty-two pages in 1787—publishing, for example, Boswell's works, Chesterfield's works, and many other standard books. Both brothers were committed Dissenters and thus naturally dealt with many of the works of that school.

2   This was Berridge's contribution to the Calvinistic controversy, *Christian World*. There had been two editions in 1773 and Berridge had sent the corrections for the third edition.

3   Justification by faith alone. See July 3, 1758. Berridge does not want to see his early account of his conversion reprinted.

4   Former name of a London street in the ward of Cripplegate. Dr. Johnson says that it was "much inhabited by writers of small histories, dictionaries, and temporary poems; whence mean production is called grubstreet" (E. Cobham Brewer, *Brewer's Dictionary of Phrase and Fable*, revised by Ivor Evans [Book Club, 1977], 492).

5   John Wheeler Pasham (d.1783), printer of St. Ann's Blackfriars.

copy by the Potton[6] carrier, and I will examine it carefully and return it in a week. A correct edition furthers much the sale of a book, and in order to further the sale I hope you will present me with a dozen copies, not to sell but to give away, which will much oblige your humble servant,

John Berridge

---

6   The text has "Polton."

To Samuel Wilks[1]

Everton, April 11, 1775

Dear Sir,

I received your very friendly letter, and thank you for it; but is it not rather too profuse of honour conferred—upon whom? Why, truly, on a miserable sinner, like yourself. One toad may croak to another but, sure, it would raise a smile on your face to hear one toad compliment another, and speak very handsome things of his toadship. I do not love hard words, yet am much afraid of kind ones; they have procured me many a whipping. Sweet words are to the heart what sweetmeats[2] are to the stomach; unwholesome, producing sickliness. Children may bear such sweet things, but elderly people cannot digest them.

I make no visits to London; my weak body, and still weaker spirits, will not bear it. My late long illness has made preaching in large congregations exhaust me wholly; and I am forced to sit still, and keep close in my chamber, to recover myself for the next preaching. However, though I do not go out myself, some few of my friends pay me short visits; and if the Lord should bring me again to London, I cordially invite Mr. Wilks, his dear partner, and children, to drink tea or coffee along with my toadship, on any afternoon, excepting Tuesday or Wednesday, which are my preaching days, when I must be alone. I perceive by your letter, that your constitution is breaking up, as well as my own. It is well when a cottage gives a crack before it falls; this, like the warning of a clock, prepares for the stroke; the stroke of death.

The nearer you come to Canaan, expect the more rubs[3] in your way. They are designed to rub off your rust, to wean you from transitory things, and to wing your soul for its passage. It is a great thing to live in faith, but greater still to die in faith, full faith, bearing a glorious

---

[1] See April 8, 1774. It is included in *WB* (1838), 397–398, and *WB* (1864), 388–389.

[2] Sweet foods such as sugared cakes and candied fruits or nuts.

[3] A term from the game of bowls. An impediment in the grass by which a bowl is hindered or diverted.

testimony to the love and faithfulness of God in Christ. The first work of our heavenly potter is to fashion the vessels of mercy by the finger of his Spirit; but the vessel is of little use yet for want of fire; therefore his last work is to cast the vessels into a furnace; and when baked well there, they come out meet for the Master's service. Afflictions, in the hand of the Spirit, are of excellent use; therefore be not afraid of them. Our Master's honey is very pleasant, but his rod is most profitable. Since writing hurts my breast, and wearies my spirit exceedingly, my London friends demand no more than a single letter a piece; and I trust Mr. Wilks can be as moderate in his demands as the rest.

Through mercy, I got home to Everton safe and well, but found my congregation cast into a spiritual lunacy, by the Newfoundland tales of Mr. Coughlan.[4] Present my heart's love to Mrs. Wilks. The Lord accept her, and bless her dear other half, yourself, and bless the children. Grace and peace be with you all, and with your affectionate servant,

John Berridge

---

[4]   Laurence Coughlan (d.1785) was converted at Drummersnave, Ireland, in 1753. In 1755 he was recruited by Wesley as an itinerant preacher and two years later moved to England, where he had success at Colchester. He had gone to Newfoundland in 1765 as a missionary and returned after a year for ordination. He was sent out again by the Society for the Propagation of the Gospel. After three years without visible results there was a revival around Conception Bay. He returned to England in 1773 exhausted in mind and body and was a preacher in Lady Huntingdon's connexion, finally becoming minister of Cumberland Street Chapel, London, for which congregation he published a hymn book. He wrote *An Account of the Work of God in Newfoundland, North America* (W. Gilbert, 1776). Charles Atmore says that he died whilst "engaged in conversation with Mr. Wesley in his study" (*Methodist Memorial, being an impartial sketch of the lives and characters of the preachers who have departed this life since the commencement of the work of God among the people called Methodists* [Bristol: Edwards, 1801], 83). See April 11, 1775.

To John Thornton[1]

Everton, April 11, 1775

Dear and honoured Sir,

I have received six dozen Bibles, six dozen of Testaments, one hundred Alleine's *Alarms*,[2] one hundred *Treasuries*,[3] and a Scotch Bible, for which I return you my hearty thanks. May the Lord remember the donor for good, and accompany the books with a blessing!

At my return to Everton, I found my congregation cast into a spiritual lunacy, easily mistaken for spiritual liveliness, and such gospel junketing[4] introduced, as made Methodism exceedingly palatable to a carnal taste; and this occasioned by the sermons and conduct of Mr. Jonathan Coughlan,[5] a Newfoundland divine. Such a light-spirited, vain-glorious, and *Canterbury Tales* man,[6] never stepped into my pulpit before; and if Mr. Foster's[7] account of him be true, which I do not doubt, because it comes from Mr. Foster, a pillory would suit him better than a pulpit. He claims some acquaintance with you, and talks of the books you have sent him, and therefore I send this short history of him, to prevent any further deception in him. I could let a carnal cheat pass by me, and be thankful that I passed him safely, but would tear a sheep's

---

[1]   The letter is found in *GM* (1837), 354–355; *WB* (1838), 399–400; and *WB* (1864), 389–390. *GM* has January 14, 1774, which seems to be a printer's error, as the context is April, with Berridge returning from his winter's preaching in London.

[2]   See August 10, 1774.

[3]   See April 3, 1773.

[4]   Feasting, merrymaking.

[5]   He is referring to Laurence Coughlan. See April 11, 1775, a letter written on the same day to Samuel Wilks.

[6]   Storyteller. Chaucer's *Canterbury Tales* describes pilgrims relating stories to each other to pass away the boredom of the journey.

[7]   Henry Foster (1745–1814) was for a time curate to William Romaine at Blackfriars and held several lectureships in London. He became minister of Long Acre proprietary chapel in 1780 and in 1807 vicar of Clerkenwell. One of the original members of the Eclectic Society, he was a friend of John Newton.

coat[8] from any wolf's back that I met, and pursue a gospel-cheat with hue-and-cry.

How insensibly our hearts are drawn away from the right object; and when once seduced, how easily we can mistake frothy mirth, for gospel-joy; and yet how wide the difference! Joy in the Lord, as it is the most delightful, so it is the most serious thing in the world, filling the soul with holy shame and blushing, and drawing tears of sweetest love. Merriment and laughter compose the syllabub[9] of human joy; and where no better can be had, this may be thought excellent; but an angel's mouth is out of taste for such syllabub; and so is a saint's mouth, when his harp is well in tune. Laughter is not found in heaven; all are too happy there to laugh; it is a disease of fallen nature, and as such infested me sorely when sunk into the lowest state of a nervous complaint.[10] It forced itself on me without provocation, and continued with such violence, as quite to overwhelm me; and nothing could check it, but choking it, viz., filling my mouth with a handkerchief.

I dare say Adam never laughed before he fell; and am sure he had no cause to laugh after; nor do we read that the second Adam[11] ever laughed. Laughter sprung with sin; and as it makes the life of Esau's joy, it often proves the death of Jacob's comfort.[12] More prayer would cure us of this itching disease; and make us exchange our treacle for honey, that honey which flows from the rock. The lightness and barrenness, that is found in ourselves, is owing to the want of more prayer. No divine communion can be had without it; and when the heart is destitute of that communion, it snaps[13] at any worldly comfort. The Lord encompass your heart evermore with that piece of armour, called all-prayer![14] Grace be with you, and yours, and with your much obliged and affectionate servant,

John Berridge

---

8   False prophets come in sheep's clothing but in reality they are wolves. Matthew 7:15.
9   A drink of milk curdled by adding wine or cider then sweetened, thus figuratively something unsubstantial and frothy.
10 It seems that Berridge was suffering from some form of hysteria when depressed.
11 Christ. 1 Corinthians 15:45.
12 Is he referring to the old and new man in the Christian?
13 Seizes or catches.
14 Ephesians 6:18.

To Richard Woodgate[1]

Everton, April 21, 1775

Dear Sir,

Through a multitude of visitors, and a scanty pittance of animal spirits, I have neither leisure nor strength to write letters in London, and therefore at my return to Everton, I send an annual letter to many friends, as a small token of my unfeigned respect for them.

Here below we are often meeting and parting, but above we shall meet to part no more. And, oh, what a meeting, when this noisy world and the roaring lion[2] will be far removed, and the body of sin be wholly broken down; when the soul will be all peace, all love, all joy, and become all eye to gaze on Jesus, and from his sweetness and his fullness drink eternal pleasure in. No fretful look, nor envious eye, nor jarring note is there; for every vessel is quite full, and every harp is well in tune, and every string rebounds with purest thankfulness. But we must remember, Brother, that daily tribulation comes before this blessed meeting: bitter herbs and bitter draughts are needful food as physic for a sickly stomach. And such is our condition in the present state, that all kinds of weather prove pernicious. Sunshine produces vermin, calms occasion sleepiness, and tempests breed tumours. So, we make daily work for the Physician and stand in need of all his drugs and surgery, of sweating, bleeding,[3] cupping,[4] puking,[5] purging,[6] and all little enough to cleanse the blood and stomach, so apt we are to breed ill humours.[7]

---

[1] This manuscript letter is held in MARC, PLP 8 43.6. It is addressed to "Mr. Rich'd Woodgate, a preacher at Chatham by London." Woodgate was the pastor of Jewin Street congregation, London between 1774 and 1787, which explains "the church of God around you." See April 20, 1773, and April 28, 1779.

[2] Satan. 1 Peter 5:8.

[3] Drawing blood.

[4] Drawing blood by scarifying the skin and applying a cup.

[5] Causing to vomit.

[6] Causing the stomach or bowels to empty.

[7] A person's physical and mental disposition was thought to be determined by

One gallipot[8] or more is sent me in each day, and though I have been taking physic largely many years, I am ready yet to [?] when I take a bolus.[9]

Elderly Christians are apt to grow lazy and lousy, wise and foolish, and thus we bring many stripes on our back. More secret prayer and watchfulness would prevent a deal of physic. Salute your spouse in my name, and present my hearty salutations to the church of Christ around you. Grace and peace be with you all, and with your affectionate servant,

John Berridge

---

the fluids, or humours, in the body.
8   Small earthen glazed pot used by apothecaries.
9   A large pill.

To David Simpson[1]

Everton, August 8, 1775

Dear Sir,

Your letter, for want of full direction, first rambled to Woburn, and then was remanded to London, before it visited Everton. This accounts for my tardy answer.

When I began to itinerate, a multitude of dangers surrounded me, and seemed ready to engulf me. My relations and friends were up in arms; my college was provoked; my Bishop incensed; the clergy on fire; and the church canons pointing their ghastly mouths at me. As you are now doing, so did I send letters to my friends, begging advice, but received unsatisfactory, or discouraging answers. Then I saw, if I meant to itinerate, I must not confer with flesh and blood, but cast myself wholly upon the Lord. By his help, I did so, and made a surrender of myself to Jesus, expecting to be deprived, not only of

---

1   David Simpson (1745-1799) had written to Berridge, and many others, asking for advice about itinerate preaching. He had been at Cambridge from 1765 to 1768 and had been associated with Evangelical students such as Rowland Hill, Unwin, Robinson, Pentycross, de Coetlogon, and Buckley, through whom he had known Berridge. After becoming a curate in Macclesfield in 1772, Simpson had experienced difficulties with the vicar, because of his preaching, and had his licence withdrawn. He preached in the open air and in Wesley's chapel. At the time of writing, a new chapel had been built for him by a local manufacturer, and he remained there until his death in 1799. The letter is taken from a brief life of Simpson in David Simpson, *A Plea for Religion and the Sacred Writings* (1837), xxiii–xxv. It is a copy of the original manuscript with the address: "The Rev. Mr. Simpson, at Macclesfield, Cheshire." It is also included in *CO* (1841), 721, and *WB* (1864), 529–530. See "Correspondence of Simpson with Hill, Romaine, Fletcher, and Berridge," *CO* (1841), 719–723, for details of how others responded to his enquiry. The writer makes his views clear on what he considers is an issue of morality: "Mr. Simpson's correspondence brings before the reader letters from and references to, several clergymen, who, frequently, or occasionally, violated those vows of canonical obedience by which they had voluntarily bound themselves. Assuredly it was not righteous to obtain office in a church, and then to infringe the obligations without which they could not have obtained it" (719).

my fellowship and vicarage, but also of my liberty. At various times, complaints or presentments[2] were carried to my college, to successive archdeacons and bishops; and my first diocesan[3] frankly told me I should either be in Bedlam[4] or Huntingdon gaol[5] by and by.

But, through the good blessing of my God, I am yet in possession of my senses, my tithes, and my liberty; and he who has hitherto delivered, I trust will yet deliver me from the mouth of ecclesiastical lions and the paw of worldly bears. I have suffered from nothing, except from lapidations[6] and pillory treats, which yet have proved more frightful than hurtful. If you are invited to go out, and feel yourself inclined to do so, take a lover's leap, neck or nothing, and commit yourself to Jesus. Ask no man's leave to preach Christ; that is unevangelical and shameful. Seek not much advice about it; that is dangerous. Such advice, I found, generally, comes the wrong way—heels uppermost. Most preachers love a snug church, and a whole skin; and what they love they will prescribe.

If you are determined to be evangelically regular, i.e., secularly irregular; then expect, wherever you go, a storm will follow you, which may fright you, but will bring no real harm. Make the Lord your *whole* trust and all will be well. Remember this, brother David! For if your heart is resting upon some human arm for support, or if your eye is squinting at it for protection, Jesus Christ will let you fall, and roll you soundly in a kennel, to teach you better manners. If you become a recruiting sergeant, you must go out—*"duce et auspice Christo."*[7] The Lord direct, assist, and prosper you. Grace be with you, and your much affectionate friend and servant,

John Berridge

---

2 A formal accusation.

3 John Thomas (1691–1766) was bishop of Lincoln between 1744 and 1761. Toward the end of Berridge's life Berridge gave an account to Andrew Fuller and John Sutcliff of his indictment before the bishop when his squire and other vicars complained of his itinerate preaching. See Sutcliff, "Interview with Berridge," 73–76, and Fuller's notes in *Baptist Autographs*, 53. See Introduction, pp.29–30.

4 Bethlehem Hospital, the first mental hospital, which Londoners abbreviated to Bethlam and often pronounced Bedlam.

5 Huntingdon county jail had been built in 1768 in Orchard Lane. It was closed in 1830 after a new county jail was built.

6 Stone throwing.

7 Led and directed by Christ.

To John Thornton[1]

Everton, September 21, 1775

Dear and honoured Sir,

I am somewhat shy of troubling my betters with visits or letters, which makes me a tardy correspondent, and a backward visitor. If this sprung from humility, it would have a good root; but it seems to sprout from bashfulness, a fairfaced slip of pride. The forward and the bashful temper are contraries; yet both originate from the same source. One pushes forward in hope of showing itself to advantage; the other lags behind for fear of appearing to disadvantage. One courts honour; the other dreads dishonour from fellow worms and fellow sinners. And is not self-exaltation, or pride, the common spring of both these tempers? Unlike in their features and carriage, unlike as Esau and Jacob,[2] yet are they not twins from the same mother? We are more pleased, indeed, with the bashful than with the forward, and for an obvious reason: the bashful temper flatters our pride; it is not encroaching, it is not troublesome, it keeps at a distance, and seems to look on us with reverence; and while we are mounting the ladder of worldly esteem, it stays at the bottom, not really contented with a ground station, but afraid to climb, lest it should get a fall, and be laughed at. In different constitutions the same principle produces different effects of forwardness and bashfulness; just as the same sun which softens wax hardens clay. Perhaps in our fallen state, there is not a natural temper

---

[1] WB (1864), 518–521, has this letter as 1788 but *MNCM* (1812), 168–170, and *GM* (1862), 231–232, have it as 1775. The earlier date must be correct because the context of the letter shows he had no difficulty reading or writing, whereas we know that by 1786 he had problems with both due to old age (see October 11, 1786: "I can read but little, and write less"), but also the phrase "almost sixty years have I lived" dates it as 1775. See October 27, 1787, for a description of Berridge's infirmities. Following the date 1788 I assumed mistakenly (as Phinn, *Bogatzky's Golden Treasury,* xv) in Pibworth, *Gospel Pedlar* that Berridge was still working on a new revision of Thornton's *Bogatzky's Golden Treasury* toward the end of his life. In all probability his input in the project was completed much earlier.
[2] Genesis 25:27.

but springs from pride, or a desire to exalt self; neither is there any Christian grace on earth, but pride will creep into the bosom, and mix with it as freely as oil with oil. Nor is Lady Pride ever so delighted as when she becomes intimate with humility, and by soft caresses and bland speeches, encourages the sweet damsel to think highly of herself, even when she looks and talks humbly.

No religious act can I do but pride is skulking at my elbow, and much affecting me both by her smiles and frowns. If I chance to pray or preach with a gale, she tickles up vanity; and when I am becalmed she stirreth up fretfulness. One while she whispers and tells me I am a fine fellow, and then I am cheery; by and by she calls me a fool, and then I am sullen. A weeping audience stirs up my pride, and so does a sleepy one. I am full as lofty when creeping ashamed from my pulpit with my head hanging down, as when I come away brisk with a feather in my cap. Indeed, Sir, this pride besiegeth my heart, besetteth all my steps, and meets me at every hedge corner. It has more heads than the Nile, and more shapes than Proteus,[3] and every week I discover some new prints of its foot. Henceforth if you ask my real name, it is Pride, and such an odd mysterious evil is it, I can even be proud of loathing my pride.

I am led into this train of writing by a cross, which discovered a new and bitter source of this evil. Almost sixty years have I lived, and never yet thanked God for my teeth; such a wretch I am! Nor did I know their real worth till last Friday, when I lost an upper tooth in the front of my mouth, which has made my speech so perplexed, disgusting, and painful, that I scarce know how to bear myself. Twice the labour and breath are required in speaking, yet will not suffice to articulate my words; every sentence comes out with a hiss, and I am quite ashamed to speak at all. Some concern for this loss were not amiss; but why am I ashamed? It is no crime, it is only a misfortune, or, to speak truly, a providential stroke. Yet so ashamed am I lest my lisping should make me appear ridiculous, that I cannot prevail on myself to step out a preaching. Is not this pride with a witness? Yet so saint-like is this demon, she wraps herself round with a godly cloak, and, pretending great zeal for Christ's honour, tells me gravely that a hissing tongue would make the word of God ridiculous, as if this were all her concern. Well, Sir, ever since my tooth came out, Pride and I have been laying our heads together, how to remedy this evil. I proposed filling up the cavity with beeswax. Right, says Pride, but pray let it be white wax; nothing so loathsome as a yellow tooth.

---

3 Neptune's herdsman, who was famous for assuming different shapes at will.

Accordingly we filled up the cavity on Sunday with white wax, which served indifferently well in the morning; but my pellet dropped out in the afternoon service during sermon, and made me conclude abruptly.

This sorely disgusted Pride, and made her vehemently propose a journey to London for a new tooth. I made several objections to this. The tooth must be set with golden pivots; the operator must be well paid; nor could I ride such a journey on horseback, but must take a carriage; the whole expense might amount to ten pounds; and though otherwise well enough to pass, I had not a spare sum for that purpose. Poh! Poh! says Pride. Can you not lay your case before Mr. Thornton? He will as readily help you, as offer his help. Still I objected, that the ground of my petition might appear so ludicrous, as to excite laughter, and make him cry out, "What a sad fool this Vicar of Everton is turned! Sixty years old, and wants a new tooth! Fie upon him! A new heart would suit him much better." Besides, you know, I do not love to be burdensome to others. That is right, says Pride, and you are sensible I no more love it than yourself; yet fear of shame will make even Pride become a beggar. I do therefore insist on your going to London on Monday next, the 25th, and returning to Everton when the operation is over, which may be on Thursday. Nay, do not boggle[4] at the journey; unless you comply I will certainly tease you to death, by smiting your heart fiercely every time you utter a lisping word. Well, Sir, at length I consented to put myself under Lady Pride's direction, and purpose to set out for London on Monday next.

I have lately received a box of books with a *Golden Treasury*[5] interleaved. The Lord give a blessing to the donor and the reader. After

---

[4] Be startled.

[5] This was probably the copy that became *Bogatzky's Golden Treasury: a reprint of Mr. John Thornton's edition of 1775 together with critical notes hitherto unpublished, by John Berridge, vicar of Everton, and important corrections by the same hand.* Thus the interleaved copy was probably a printed proof copy ready for Berridge's and others' final comments. Thornton had probably produced an earlier edition (see August 18, 1773, and August 31, 1773), although these may be just previous English editions. Many of the portions are new and this perhaps explains Berridge's theological criticism of some of the papers, although he welcomed the previous edition. The suggestive revisions throw light on Berridge's convictions concerning Calvinism, assurance, the gospel, and presumption in hymn singing. We do not know the dating of all Berridge's comments and additions, as Thornton was still working on his edition in the late 1780s before he died in 1790. Thornton sought help from William Bull in his final effort to complete the work. See Bull, *Memorials of Bull*, 188.

my return from London my leisure hours shall be employed on your Treasury; but itinerant preaching affords me only one spare day in the week: and sometimes I am so jaded with riding and preaching, that I seem fit for nothing on that spare day but to catch wasps, kill gnats, and count my teeth. However, I will do my best, and hope for your favourable acceptance of it. Oh, dear Sir, every year makes me more ashamed of my worthless self! Eternity is just at hand, yet how lazy and lifeless I am! Lord, quicken me! May a precious Jesus water you abundantly with the comforts of his Spirit, and enrich your family with the treasures of his grace. The God of peace be with you, and with your much obliged and affectionate servant,

John Berridge

To John Thornton[1]

Everton, October 22, 1775

Dear and honoured Sir,

Your favour of the 17th requires an answer, attended with a challenge. And I do hereby challenge you, and defy all your acquaintance to prove that I have a single correspondent half so honest as yourself. Epistolary intercourses are become a polite traffic; and he that can say pretty things, and wink at bad things, is an admired correspondent. Indeed, for want of due authority and meekness on one side, and patience and humility on the other, to give or to take reproof, a fear of raising indignation instead of conviction, often puts a bar on the door of my lips; for I find where reproof does not humble it hardens; and the seasonable time for striking, if we can catch it, is when the iron is hot; when the heart is melted down in a furnace, then it submits to the stroke, and takes and retains the impression.

I wish you would exercise the trade of a gospel limner,[2] and draw the features of all my brethren in black, and send them their portraits. I believe you would do them justice every way, by giving every cheek

---

1   This is a reply to a letter that Thornton wrote to Berridge on October 17, 1775, in which he criticizes Berridge for his use of humour both in his writing and in the pulpit. Thornton says: "I could not forbear smiling at your humorous allegory about the tooth, and was pleased at the good sense displayed in it; yet something came across my mind—Is this method agreeable to the idea we ought to entertain of a father in Israel? It would sound mighty well in a newspaper, or in anything calculated for public entertainment, but it certainly wanted that solidity or seriousness that a Christian minister should write with. What the apostle said in another sense will apply here: 'When I was a child I spake as a child,' etc. An expression of yours in your prayer before sermon when at Tottenham Court struck me, 'that God would give us new bread not stale, but what was baked in the oven on that day.' Whether it is that I am too little, or you too much, used to such expressions, I won't pretend to determine; but I could not help thinking it savoured of attention to men more than to God" (*WB* [1864], 522). There are four accounts of this letter: *MNCM* (1818), 255–257; Seymour, *Life of Huntingdon*, 1:373–374; *CM* (1845), 28–29; and *WB* (1864), 524–526.
2   A portrait painter.

its proper blush without hiding a pimple upon it. Yet I fear if your subsistence depended on this business you would often want a morsel of bread, unless I sent you a quartern loaf[3] from Everton. As to myself, you know the man, odd things break from me as abruptly as croaking from a raven. I was born with a fool's cap.[4] True, you say; but why is it not put off? It suits the first Adam but not the second. A very proper question; and my answer is this: a fool's cap is not put off so readily as a night cap. One cleaves to the head, and one to the heart. Not many prayers only, but many furnaces are needful for this purpose; and after all the same thing happens to a tainted heart as to a tainted cask, which may be sweetened by many washings and firings, yet a scent remains still. Late furnaces have singed the bonnet of my cap, but the crown still abides on my head. And I must confess that the crown so abides in whole or in part for want of a closer walk with God, and nearer communion with him. When I creep near the throne this humour disappears or is tempered so well as not to be distasteful.

Hear, Sir, how my Master deals with me. When I am running wild and saying many things somewhat rash, or very quaint, he gives me an immediate blow on my breast which stuns me. Such a check I received whilst I was uttering that expression in prayer you complained of, but the bolt was too far shot to be recovered. Thus I had intelligence from above before I received it from your hand. However, I am bound to thank you, and do hereby acknowledge myself reimbursed for returning your note.

And now, dear Sir, having given you an honest account of myself and acknowledged the obligation I owe you, I would return you the obligation in the best manner I am able. It has been a matter of surprise to me how Dr. Conyers[5] could accept of Deptford living and how Mr. Thornton could present him to it. The Lord says, "Woe to the idle shepherd that leaveth his flock."[6] Is not Helmsley flock, and a choice flock, too, left—left altogether—and left in the hands, not of shepherds

---

3   A loaf weighing 4 lb.
4   A pointed cap with bells worn by jesters.
5   Richard Conyers (1725–1786). Berridge is referring to 1767, when, shortly after the death of Conyers' wife (Thornton's sister), Thornton offered Conyers the living of Deptford. The people at Helmsley in Yorkshire, where, since Conyer's conversion in 1758, there had been much spiritual interest, did not wish their vicar to leave, and he actually left at midnight. His successor devastated the outstanding work that had been built up. See note, September 2, 1763.
6   Zechariah 11:17.

to feed, but of wolves to devour them? Has not lucre led him to Deptford and has not a family connexion overruled your private judgment? You may give me a box on the ear for these questions, if you please, and I will take it kindly, and still love and pray for you. The Lord bless you, and bless your family, and bless your affectionate servant,

John Berridge

PART 3

1776–1785

The later years

To Miss Orton[1]

Tabernacle, March 2, 1776

Dear Madam,

Your kind letter is received, and informs me that a hamper of Madeira wine[2] is travelling to the vicarage of Everton, which demands a hearty acknowledgement. I do thank you for the same, and would not content myself in merely drinking your health, without praying for my benefactress. The Lord refresh your heart by sending you many hampers of that heavenly wine, which from your own knowledge far exceedeth Madeira.

But why did you suffer such a void to remain in your letter? Your pen was excellent, your paper was roomy, your thoughts are not cramped, nor could your patience be wearied; but perhaps your ink was exhausted. Well, to be sure, says Miss Orton, what a strange creature this old vicar of Everton is! Once he complained of my bad pen, and now he complains of my short ink; and though I sent three dozen of bottles in my letter, he has the conscience to say, it was not well filled. Bottles enough, dear Madam, but the lines were too scanty; and had you consulted any casuist,[3] he must have pronounced, that three dozen of bottles did certainly require three dozen of lines to accompany them, which might have suggested some hints for a sermon. However I can easily overlook this defect, if you will only engage to send a very kind letter to a friend of mine, who loves you dearly, and wishes to make you his bride. He is a person of good birth, of excellent worth, and plentiful substance, yet through his lowly spirit, makes no great figure in the world. He has given you some hints of his kindness, which perhaps have passed unnoticed or misinterpreted by you. So, your old vicar is employed to break

---

[1] Jennett Payne Orton. See December 26, 1767. The manuscript is held in FBC, Box CO10. It is addressed to "Miss Orton at Mrs. Lyons at Paragon Buildings, Bath."

[2] A fortified Portuguese wine from Madeira.

[3] A person given to excessively subtle reasoning, intending to mislead.

the ice, and would fain put the match forward, because he knows it would prove to your comfort and credit. It is time now to tell you his name, and it may surprise you to hear, it is Jesus of Nazareth, who has long been calling and knocking at your door, and wonders you won't let him in. His sweet daily cry is, "Give me thy heart,"[4] and it grieves him to think, you should ever suspect the truth of his word, or the truth of his love. Many shy looks he has received from you, and many unkind distrusting thoughts, but he is determined to take no denial. Therefore give him hand and heart without more ado, and away to church, for he must and will wed you.

Lady Huntingdon has been ill, but is better, and ready to take wing for Norwich.[5] I think she will peep through this century, and you will join me in saying, Amen. Poor dear Mr. Peckwel[l][6] has been confined to his bed for a fortnight with a dangerous yet delicate complaint, and is attended by five surgeons and physicians. The Lord restore him. Present my hearty respects to Mrs. Lyons,[7] her sister, and children, not forgetting Miss Kitty. May Jesus bless the root and the branches, keeping them under his daily protection; grafting them into his living vine, and making them pillars in the house of our God.

---

4   Proverbs 23:26.

5   Norwich was the second largest city in England after London and the centre of East Anglia. In 1775 Lady Huntingdon had taken over the lease on the Norwich Tabernacle, which had been started by Whitefield in 1755, had come into Wesley's possession, and then had been rented by a Mr. Wheatley until 1775. In early 1777 Lady Huntingdon, accompanied by Lady Anne Erskine and Toplady, travelled to Norwich and the society was organized. Preachers were arranged and Mark Wilks was appointed over the work. For the details, see Seymour, *Life of Huntingdon*, 2:342–346.

6   Dr. Henry Peckwell (1746–1787). See November 4, 1785. While engaged in learning a business he spent much of his time at the Tabernacle. After a short time at Oxford and having experienced preaching success in Ireland, a chapel was opened for him in Prince's Street, Westminster, in 1774. Peckwell himself studied medicine, and the sermons that he preached for the benefit of the Sick Man's Friend Society, which he had founded, produced as much as £400 a year. He served Lady Huntingdon in her connexion and took an interest in those imprisoned for small debts. Henry Venn speaks of Peckwell's carriage being sent to the Tabernacle to fetch Berridge and himself. He died as a result of cutting himself while carrying out a post-mortem.

7   Mrs. Lyons (1732–1792) used to live at Tetworth but moved to Bath with her family. Her husband, John, had died there the previous year. See January 19, 177[1]. Miss Kitty is her youngest child, Catherine Anne (1764–1832), who had been born while the family were at Tetworth.

Much grace and peace be with you, dear Madam, and with your obliged and affectionate servant,

John Berridge

P.S. Please to remember me kindly to the two nannies and may the Lord keep their hearts upright.

To a Friend[1]

Everton, April 26, 1776

My dear Friend,

Your letter was a fortnight in travelling to me, partly occasioned by its tarrying five days at Tabernacle, when I was at Tottenham[2]; and I concluded you had left Hardwick,[3] or would leave it, before a letter could reach you there.

I was ill in London, most part of the time, with a cough and a cold, and very unfit for a London pulpit, though not disabled from preaching. I find the later works of a Christian are chiefly furnace work, out of one fire into another; and when we think the present furnace too hot, the way of making us think it a cool one, is by plunging us into a hotter. I pray for patience often, and should be glad to have a bushel[4] of it, but do not like the way in which it is given. God useth means to accomplish his ends, and tribulation is the means appointed to work patience[5]; but I am not very fond of such means. My old Esau[6] raises outcries at them, and says, if he must learn patience, he should like to learn it in his sleep, without the bustle of a tribulation. Yet, however unpleasing a furnace is, I find but little growth out of it; and the little I have gained, has been out of fire. Activity in well-doing is a glorious thing, but patient sufferance in well-doing exceeds it: and no man knows much of himself, till his locks have well blazed, and his bones have much crackled, in a furnace. Young cocks crow lustily, and swagger among the poultry, till they have been thrown at, and soundly banged, on Shrove-Tuesday[7]; then they come home meek enough, and are glad to hide their head in a henroost.

---

1   This letter is in *MNCM* (1818), 254–255, and *GS* (1852), 214.
2   Tottenham Court Road Chapel.
3   There are several Hardwicks. From the context it is unlikely to be the village six miles west of Cambridge but one further afield.
4   A large dry measure normally in the shape of a box.
5   Romans 5:3.
6   The old man or nature in the Christian.
7   From the twelfth to the nineteenth century cock-throwing, or throwing at cocks, was the sport of schoolboys on Shrove Tuesday.

I cannot judge of a Christian soldier, from his big words and fierce look, and tall musket, but from his being able to stand fire. Nor do I heed his hopping or kicking, or barking or bawling, in the furnace; if he can but keep in it, he is fairly listed, Jesus will still him, and teach him his exercise at length.

As I know something of itinerant troubles, I can sympathise with you; and believe, when a retreat is really wanted, it will be given; and take heed that your heart be not set upon it, else your bed, even there, will be quilted with thorns. A gourd[8] is a useful thing for the head but when made a revelling-place, it will soon breed a worm at the root. Earthly comforts, like roses, grow on a briar; and appear sweeter in the prospect, than the enjoyment. If you come into Essex this summer, I shall expect a visit at Everton, and a week or a fortnight's itineration in Cambridgeshire. Be not discouraged at your trials; Jesus will help you out, and help you through. I send you my heart's love. Grace and peace be with you, my dear friend, and with your very affectionate servant,

John Berridge

---

8 See Jonah 4:6.

To Rowland Hill[1]

Everton, June 7, 1776

My dear Rowly,

I need not say that I love you; because all who are acquainted with the old and young ass know it well and I would have them know it, and the more scandalous you grow[2]—evangelically scandalous—the more I must love you.[3]

A newspaper tells me where you are, and what you are doing, viz., turned out on Blackheath, and engaged in your old trade of devil-hunting, which is neither a profitable nor an honourable business, as the world goes, yet a more suitable employment for Gospel ministers than fox-hunting or card-hunting.[4] Success attend you—a firm seat upon the wooden horse[5]; a clear shrill horn to animate the chase; and the hasty flight of many a devil, black or white. But when the Master of the hunt is chasing the fiends of infidelity and profaneness from others, take heed yourself of the devil of pride, lest he creep into your own hive, and eat up all the honey. He is a very subtle, and a very handsome devil, I assure you; and coming always with a simpering look, a painted cheek, a dimpled chin, a nightingale's tongue, and a kissing lip—you would really take him for Gabriel,[6] unless you spy his cloven foot, which he will hide if possible, under a cassock, as well as under a petticoat.

This handsome devil, who talks as fine as any Frenchman, has often beguiled my heart, and brought me to many a whipping-post—and unless you are made of better clay, or better pottered than myself,

---

[1]   The actual manuscript is held in JWFP MARBL, Box 1 Folder 84. The manuscript is addressed to "Rev. Mr. Rowland Hill, at the Tabernacle House near Moorfields, London." The manuscript at CUL, add 8781/51, is a copy not in Berridge's hand (possibly by Seymour) and seems to read June 17, 1776. *CM* (1841), 870–871, has June 7, 1776; and *GS* (1856), 120–121, has just 1771.

[2]   *CM* and *GS* add "I mean."

[3]   CUL copy omits "you."

[4]   Berridge presumably meant card playing, as in CUL copy.

[5]   Pulpit.

[6]   An angel who stands in the presence of God. Luke 1:19,26.

he will surely, by his glozing[7] speeches, conduct you to a house of correction. Yet be not discouraged—Bridewell[8] is the common luck of Gospel ministers—the best need bitter herbs,[9] instead of mint sauce, to eat with their lamb. And if the Master brushes your back soundly with birch,[10] he will make all well again with a kiss. Nothing better for a Christian than the Master's birch-wine. I am drinking it now, to sharpen my appetite, and relieve a palsy of a spiritual kind.

My last long visit to London has almost overset the old Gospel pedlar, and my Everton friends tell me, I must go no more to Tabernacle, unless I mean to lay my bones there. Well, if Jesus receiveth my spirit, no matter where my bones are laid; and I suppose the worms at Tottenham have no sharper teeth than those at Everton, or if they have, it would not trouble me. I have had only two weekly journeys of preaching since I came down. The third laid me up without preaching and sent me home in a carriage; since then, I preach only on the Lord's day but I keep eating every day of the week so I have fourteen meals for one sermon, a poor business truly for a methodist parson. Yet I give thanks that I am not exalted to the privilege of a bishop, which is, to eat every day, and preach no day.

My dear Rowly, give up yourself wholly to Jesus, and freely employ body, and soul, and substance, in his service. Work while the day lasteth; for life and health are uncertain, and what your hand findeth to do, do it with all your might. If Esau complains of stiff-back, or sore-breast, and cries out for some ease and a lobster,[11] give him a pulpit[12] and beef tea,[13] this will quiet him and the less he is humoured the stiller he grows. Present my hearty respects to your Mary[14] and tell her I wish her much joy in the Lord. Grace, abundant grace, be with you both, and with your affectionate servant,

John Berridge

P.S. Kind love to all Christian friends.

---

7   The CUL manuscript has "fine."
8   A prison and house of correction in London.
9   The Passover was eaten with bitter herbs. Exodus 12:8.
10 Rods used in floggings were usually made of birch twigs.
11 This phrase only occurs in the manuscript.
12 *CM* adds "sweat."
13 A medical brew that was made from beef and used to treat invalids.
14 See September 3, 1773.

To J.S.[1]

Everton, September 20, 1776

Dear Sir,

Your kind letter arrived safe, but a long illness of fourteen weeks, attended by great weakness of spirits, has delayed my answer till now; and this I hope will be received, a sufficient apology for my tardy answer.

You ask, May I call Jesus mine, though I am not yet fully assured of an interest in him by the spirit of adoption? By the tenor of your letter, I think you not only may, but ought. Take David for an example, "God hath spoken in his holiness,"[2] made me a promise of victory over mine enemies; therefore "I will rejoice," in the prospect of its full accomplishment. He could already say, "Gilead is mine, Manasseh is mine"[3]; and by faith he says further, "Over Edom will I cast out my shoe, over Philistia will I triumph."[4] Let Jesus Christ answer, and rebuke your unbelief in the following precious words, "Come unto me, all ye that labour and are heavy laden, and I will give you rest."[5] If J__ S__ is laden with the guilt and filth of sin, finding them a heavy burden, and is labouring to be delivered from that burden, and is coming on seeking to Christ *alone* for deliverance, then rest, blessed rest, heavenly rest, is promised to J__ S__ from Jesus Christ, and J__ S__ may say with thankfulness, repentance is mine, faith is mine; and rejoicing in faith, should say, further, with David, "Rest will be mine, over Edom and Philistia will I triumph."[6]

Satan, it seems, is whispering in your ear, that believing before sealing is not faith, but presumption. Let Paul give the devil an answer,

---

[1] This letter is found in *CM* (1845), 271–273. Some parts may have been left out, although the dots may be Berridge's own. The letter is the normal length, which would indicate that little has been removed. J.S. is obviously a stranger who has written to Berridge concerning Christian assurance.
[2] Psalm 108:7.
[3] Psalm 108:8.
[4] Psalm 108:9.
[5] Matthew 11:28.
[6] Psalm 108:9.

262

"*After* that ye believed, ye were sealed."[7] This sealing does not make faith to be saving; it only *assures* a disciple that he is possessed of saving faith, and has a real interest in Christ…. Again, others confidently assert, you may have true faith, and perish at last. Let Jesus Christ rebuke such raw scribes. (1 John 3:18–20). Turn to your Bible for the passage…. As Jesus Christ has given a promise of rest to J__ S__ (I put your name down because Satan would thrust your name out), so he gave a promise of a child to Abraham when seventy-five years old; but Abraham waited twenty-five years for its accomplishment, and thereby gave glory to God. As Paul says, and tells you whence the glory arose, namely in this, that "Abraham did not regard his own age, nor the deadness of Sarah's womb, but overlooking human probability, or possibility, against *all* hope, he believed in hope, and *thereby* gave glory to God."[8] He would trust in God's Word, though everything made against it. Try to tread in Abraham's steps; and when unbelief says it is against all hope to believe, say with Abraham, I will believe against hope. And remember, though a sealed faith brings most comfort to a disciple, a waiting faith brings most glory to God.

I cannot doubt of your having the Spirit of Christ, because of your deep humiliation for sin, your hatred of sin, your desire of holiness, your seeking Christ alone for pardon and justification, and your consolations from above. These are evident tokens of the Spirit's indwelling, and the seal will be given when it is most for God's glory, and your welfare; and though it should not be impressed till the twelfth hour, be not discouraged but pray for it, and expect it; and by waiting patiently for the blessing while it is delayed, you give glory to God as Abraham did.

You are blessed with that brokenness of heart, which is God's gift, and with which he has promised to dwell; and that broken spirit will carry you safe over Jordan, while the perfection boasters[9] drop in…. I have read very little of Mr. Fletcher's[10] works, but enough to see that he is yet a stranger to the Gospel.[11] I cast away all controversial writers,

---

7   Ephesians 1:13.
8   Romans 4:18–20.
9   Wesley's perfectionist teaching.
10 See August 18, 1773, and September 20, 1773.
11 Given the friendly relationship Berridge seemed to have with Fletcher, this is a strange comment, even in the light of Fletcher's attack on solifidianism (the belief that only faith is required for salvation). Perhaps the previous excluded sentence would have thrown light on it. Does Berridge mean that Fletcher is a

and betake myself to the word of God and prayer. This is my chief employment, and my best delight; and I would advise you to do the same; for controversy will puzzle you, and may tincture you with a controversial spirit, which is generally a bad one, even when engaged in a good cause.... Till you have a preacher to your mind, I think you should hear Mr. Wesley's preachers, and contribute towards them, but not be a member of their society. By withdrawing from the society, you will prevent pert, raw preachers from teasing you in their society; and by continuing a contribution, you will keep on some terms with them. In the meantime, keep a society at your own house, along with those who are willing to attend. Mr. Keen,[12] one of the trustees for the Tabernacle, might possibly provide some preacher from themselves, or from Lady Huntingdon, who would visit you occasionally and frequently, but not dwell among you. If you write to him in my name, and tell him your case, he will cheerfully return you an answer, and do what he can for you. Direct to Mr. Robert Keen, No. 1 in the Minories, near Aldgate, London....

This letter has laid as a burden on my mind for many weeks, but through weakness, I had not courage to set about it till this day; and now I am soundly weary with writing. The Lord Jesus bless you, direct you, and keep you. Grace and peace be with you, dear Sir, and with your truly affectionate servant,

John Berridge

---

stranger to an aspect of the gospel? See note, August 18, 1773, for evidence of their restored relationship.

[12] Robert Keen (d.1793) was a woollen draper and a very close friend of Whitefield. Keen had much of the day-to-day responsibility for the Tabernacle and Tottenham Court Road Chapels when Whitefield was away, and Whitefield bequeathed the chapels to Keen and another trustee, Daniel West.

To a Fellow Preacher[1]

Everton, April 16, 1777

Dear Brother,

I am once more returned to Everton, in better health than usual, and a somewhat deeper sense of my nothingness, blessed be God! I am yet a stranger to Abraham's exalted measure of faith, namely, hoping against hope, and thereby giving glory to God. While frames[2] are lively, or not cloudy, I make a shift to shuffle on after Christ; but when sins are beating on my conscience, and they are daily beating, Unbelief says, "It is horrid presumption to 'hope against hope'"; and Moses tells me, with an angry look, I am making Christ the minister of sin. But has not Christ made full atonement for all believers' sins, past, present, and to come? If He has made complete atonement, we may still go with a blush, yea, a confident blush, for pardon, notwithstanding repeated and aggravated provocations; and we shall dishonour Christ, and wrong our own soul, if we go not. But suppose, through unbelief and fear, we dare not venture to go, can this mend the matter? Will it not rather beget grudgings against God, as an austere Master, and stir up enmity against him as a consuming fire? Which is most apt to kindle repentance, shame, love, and kindly obedience? Is it a dread of invincible wrath, or an assurance of pardon through the riches of divine grace. I have been prattling about the matter in the pulpit for some years, but usually clogged the subject so much for fear of abuse, as to hinder its use.

This morning I had a sweet view, in the Spirit's light, of believing in Christ for righteousness, not only without but against all comfortable feeling; and clearly saw it was not apt to stifle repentance of sin and harden the conscience, but to melt the heart of a pilgrim, and quicken his feet, and furnish his mouth with praise. And though graceless souls, like toads, will convert all meat into poison, yet a gracious

---

[1] This short letter is found in *GS* (1851), 304. It was written to a fellow preacher after Berridge's winter preaching in London.
[2] Feelings.

heart must be fed with the food of grace notwithstanding. But I forget myself, and am preaching to a preacher. Excuse the impertinence, and accept of much love from my heart, a whole bushel, to cover it.

Grace and peace be with you and with your affectionate servant,

John Berridge

To Lady Huntingdon[1]

Everton, April 26, 1777

My dear Lady,

Mrs. Carteret, a well-favoured pilgrim, tells me I owe you a letter, and your Ladyship might tell Mrs. Carteret[2] I owe you much love, which will ever be paying, I trust, and never be paid. Demands on this score, if honestly made, are always welcome, and if roguishly practised, are quickly forgiven. For whoever thought of hanging a love-thief, except a disappointed lover? A miser, who cannot open the string of his purse without pain, can part with the string of his heart freely to a bountiful friend, and the favours you have shown me call out for more than one heart-string; a dozen at least.

"Well, well, enough of this," you say, "but what have you seen or heard in London? As you are an old fellow, with a prattling tongue, I shall expect a long history, but let it be a faithful one." Indeed, my Lady, I have seen and heard some things to please me, and some things to grieve me.

---

[1] Seymour gives the background to this letter: "In the year 1776 there was some misunderstanding between Lady Huntingdon and the trustees of Mr. Whitefield's chapels, which arose from the conduct of certain individuals connected with the Gloucestershire association, some of whom had endeavoured to draw away the most popular and talented young men among the students at Trevecca. The early part of the year 1777, Mr. Berridge paid his annual visit to the metropolis, when he had abundant opportunities of inquiring into the unpleasant differences subsisting between her Ladyship and Mr. Whitefield's trustees. The result of his inquiries, with some observations on Churchmen and Dissenters, which evince the truly Catholic spirit of this excellent minister of Christ, he gives in the following letter to her Ladyship, dated Everton, April 26, 1777" (*Life of Huntingdon*, 2:421–422). It seems that Lady Huntingdon was concerned that the new chapel could become a Dissenting meeting-house similar to the Tabernacle, as she had appointed the Tabernacle trustees as trustees of the new work. She seems to have withdrawn her students as preachers at the Tabernacle itself. See Harding, *Countess of Huntingdon's Connexion*, 142–143, for the general background. The letter is taken from Seymour, *Life of Huntingdon*, 2:422–424, and *WB* (1864), 514–517.

[2] See September 2, 1763.

I have seen the Tabernacle-temple well crowded with attentive hearers, which has cheered my heart; but the Tabernacle-house[3] deserted by your students, which has grieved my spirit. Upon asking the cause, I was told the trustees were suspected of a design on your mulberry gardens.[4] What has occasioned that suspicion I know not, but I well know they had no more desire to steal your mulberries, than to steal my teeth; and I believe the profit of the mulberries, if that base thing had been in view, would no more enable them to buy a crust, than my old teeth would enable them to bite it. When the yearly accounts of the two chapels[5] are made up, I know they are sometimes below par, and have seldom £20 in hand; and the Mulberry Gardens, if under their management, were not likely to produce any other gain besides trouble. Indeed, my Lady, I am well satisfied that the trustees have been your hearty friends and faithful servants; and am sorry to find they are much offended at your suspicions. Could I discern lucrative views in them, as much as I love Tabernacle (that old bee-hive, which has filled many hives with her swarms), I would visit her no longer. But the more I know of the trustees, the more I am confirmed of their integrity, which they will give proof of shortly, by adopting Dr. Ford as a third trustee.[6]

Well, now I am prattling, I must even prattle on; an old man's tongue is like an alarm, when it's set off, though teasing enough, it will run down. But you cry, "No more griefs, pray, Mr. Grievous, unless you intend to set me a yawning." Indeed, my Lady, I have another; and beg you would seal up your lips to prevent yawning, if that is indecent out

---

3   There was a house attached to the chapel where Whitefield and visiting ministers stayed.

4   Mulberry Gardens Chapel in Wapping, East London, was built by Lady Huntingdon and opened in 1776. During the building of the chapel several clergymen and students from Trevecca preached under the mulberry trees with great success.

5   The Tabernacle and Tottenham Court Road Chapels.

6   Seymour comments: "This was in the year 1777. From this as well as from other circumstances, it would appear that the Doctor, being known as a preacher and trustee in Lady Huntingdon's connexion, was associated with Messrs. West and Keen in the Tabernacle trust" (*Life of Huntingdon*, 1:216). John Ford (1740–1806), after serving as an apprentice surgeon in Ipswich, became a very successful doctor in London, his practice yielding an income of at least £3,000 per annum. He was actively involved in the Evangelical scene. He retired early, studying Hebrew with Romaine in order to devote himself to Christian work. See "Memoir of the late Rev. John Ford, MD," *EM* (December 1806), 529–536, and *EM* (July 1806), 322, for an account of his death.

of a church. I am told, and simply tell you my tale, that since the trustees were dismissed your service, you have taken a Tory ministry,[7] are growing sadly churchified, and seem to walk with a steeple on your head, newly sprung up, but pointing very high. I regard neither high church, nor low church,[8] nor any church, but the church of Christ, which is not built with hands, nor circumscribed within peculiar walls, nor confined to a singular denomination. I cordially approve the doctrines and liturgy of the Church of England, and have cause to bless God for a church-house to preach in, and a church revenue to live upon. And I could wish the Gospel might not only be preached in all the British churches, but established therein by Christ's Spirit, as well as by a national statute; but from the principles of the clergy, and the leading men in the nation, which are growing continually more unscriptural and licentious, I do fear our defence is departing, and the glory is removing from our Israel.[9] Perhaps in less than one hundred years to come, the church-lands may be seized on to hedge up Government gaps, as the abbey lands were two hundred and fifty years ago. "But," you say, "the Lord is sending many Gospel labourers into the church." True; and with a view, I think, of calling his people out of it. Because, when such ministers are removed by death, or transported to another vineyard, I see no fresh Gospel labourer succeed them, which obliges the forsaken flocks to fly to a meeting.[10] And what else can they do? If they have tasted of manna, and hunger for it, they cannot feed on heathen chaff, nor yet on legal crusts, though baked by some starch Pharisee quite up to perfection.

What has become of Mr. Venn's Yorkshire flock?[11] What will become of his Yelling flock, or of my flocks at our decease? Or what will

---

[7] The Tory party traditionally supported the national Church and the Establishment.

[8] High Churchmen have a much more elevated view of the episcopate, priesthood and sacraments than do Low Churchmen, who regard them as relatively unimportant.

[9] A reference either to Ezekiel 10, and the glory departing from Israel, or 1 Samuel 4, where Phinehas's wife's dying words are to name her son "Ichabod"— the glory departed from Israel.

[10] Nonconformist places of worship were called meeting-houses.

[11] When Venn moved from Huddersfield many people left the church and formed a meeting with his support because of the non-Evangelical vicar who was imposed upon them. Venn himself contributed toward the cost of the new building. William R. Shenk notes that later Venn "came to regret deeply this action for it always cast a shadow over his churchmanship" ("'T'owd Trumpet': Venn of Huddersfield and Yelling," *Churchman*, 93/1 [1979], 48).

become of your students at your removal? They are virtual Dissenters[12] now, and will be settled Dissenters then. And the same will happen to many, perhaps most, of Mr. Wesley's preachers at his death. He rules like a real Alexander,[13] and is now stepping forth with a flaming torch; but we do not read in history of two Alexanders succeeding each other. "But," you reply, "some of my best preachers leave me in my life-time." Perhaps they may; and if I may judge of your feelings by my own, on such occasions this must grieve you, on the first view at least; but wait and see whether the Lord's hand be not in it. I dare not commend Barnabas for his abrupt departure from Paul; yet it might be permitted, with a view of sending him to Cyprus.[14] The Lord can, and often does, make the wrath of man, or the foolishness of man turn to his praise. However, it is good, for us, I know, to have our well meant views frequently perplexed and overturned, else we might grow headstrong, and fancy ourselves wise enough to be the Lord's privy counsellors, yea, able to out-counsel him. We had rather sit with Jesus at the counsel-board, than follow him with a string on our nose, to turn us round, or turn us back, at his pleasure.

Some years ago, two of my lay-preachers deserted their ranks, and joined the dissenters. This threw me into a violent fit of the spleen, and set me a coughing and barking exceedingly; and when the phlegm was come up, and leisure allowed for calm thought, I did humbly conceive the Lord Jesus might be wiser than the old vicar; and I did well in sending some preachers from the Methodist mint among the Dissenters, to revive a drooping cause, and set old crippled pilgrims on their legs again. Nay, it is certain that some of these deserting preachers have not only quickened the Chelsea invalids,[15] but raised up new and vigorous recruits for the King's service. Be glad, therefore, my Lady, to promote the Lord's cause in any way, in your own line, if it may be; in another line, if it must be. If your preachers abide with you, and are valiant for the truth, it is well, if they depart, let them depart, and rejoice you have been instrumental in sending them forth; if a lively preacher goes, he will prove a live coal among dying embers; if a dead one departs, he is buried out of your sight.

---

[12] Those who had separated from the national Church.

[13] Alexander the Great (336–323 B.C.), who, after crushing all opposition at home, set out to conquer the world.

[14] Acts 15:39.

[15] These were occupants of a hospital for old and disabled soldiers founded by Charles II in Chelsea and thus an image for those Dissenters who were incapacitated.

Paul tells me in one place, "All in Asia are turned aside from me,"[16] and in another he says, "Some preached Christ out of envy and strife,"[17] out of envy and opposition to him; yet "What then? Every way Christ is preached; and therein I do rejoice, yea and will rejoice."[18] Dissenters may appear wrong to you, God hath his remnant among them, therefore lift not up your head against them for the Lord's sake; nor yet for consistency's sake, because your students are as real dissenting preachers as any in the land, unless a gown and band can make a clergyman. The bishops look on your students as the worst kind of Dissenters; and manifest this by refusing that ordination to your preachers that would be readily granted to other teachers among the Dissenters.

When I consider that the doctrines of grace[19] are a common offence to the clergy, and the Bible itself a fulsome[20] nuisance to the great vulgar; that powerful efforts have been made to eject the gospel doctrines out of the church; and the likelihood there is, from the nation's infidelity, of a future attempt succeeding; there is room to fear, when the church doctrines are banished [from] the church by a national act, Jesus will utterly remove the candlestick,[21] and take away his church-bread from those hirelings who eat it and lift up the heel against him.

So you are whispering to Lady Anne,[22] "this old Vicar is very tedious, and growing pedantic too. He would fain turn a seer, and has not wit enough for a common conjurer or a strolling fortune-teller; but he is often eaten up with the vapours,[23] poor man, and I must excuse him." Indeed I am not wholly eaten up with the vapours, nor cannot, because I am much eaten up aforehand with esteem for your Ladyship.

---

[16] 2 Timothy 1:15.

[17] Philippians 1:15.

[18] Philippians 1:18.

[19] The doctrines that emphasize man's complete dependence on God's grace for salvation. They include the doctrines of unconditional election, total depravity, effectual calling, particular redemption and perseverance of the saints.

[20] Foul, offensive.

[21] Revelation 2:5.

[22] Lady Anne Erskine (1739–1804), eldest daughter of the Tenth Earl of Buchan, who got to know Lady Huntingdon and was converted while Lady Erskine's father was living at Bath for his health. After her father's death in 1767 she spent long periods with Lady Huntingdon and for the last years of Lady Huntingdon's life they lived together in the Spa Fields chapel house. As one of the trustees for the connexion, she remained at the Spa Fields house after Lady Huntingdon's death and was responsible for much of the administration.

[23] Worry, depression. See September 2, 1763.

I know your zeal for the Master's honour, and for the prosperity of his Zion, which must endear you to every honest-hearted pilgrim. The good Shepherd[24] be your guide and guard. May his cloud direct all your motions, and distil a gracious dew upon yourself, and upon your students! Please to present my respects to Lady Anne, and Miss Orton[25]; and believe me to remain your heart well-wisher and affectionate servant,

John Berridge

---

24 John 10:11.
25 See December 26, 1767.

To Mrs. Wilberforce[1]

Everton, December 19, 1777

Dear Madam,

Sometime since your newspapers announced Mr. Wilberforce's decease and being very desirous of knowing how he departed, I wrote to Mrs. ___ for information. From her pleasing account I learn that Heaven has gained a new inhabitant in the loss of your partner and that his sun set clear, after a long stormy day. Glory be to God for a good close of his journey, a rich cordial both to your departing, and surviving friend. Can you mourn, Madam? Yes, you may. Nature must pay a tributary tear for your loss of a partner who is half of ourselves, but you can mourn in hope, be sorrowful, yet rejoicing. Nature may grieve for your present separation, while grace can rejoice at his happy flight, and your blessed prospect of another meeting, which will have no second parting. Follow not his clay in your thoughts to its earthly lodging, but soar up after his Spirit to your heavenly mansion. His sins and sorrows and tears are washed away, and he is entered on eternal day. Now he knows your need of his past temptations; and the moment of his Master's joy, will make him rich amends for all your buffetings in St. James's Place.[2] Everlasting smiles are seen on your face, which was long darkened by an awful gloom, your sad symptom of a heart deep in woe. Once he could only sigh, now he can only sing. His harp is thoroughly tuned once for ever and whilst you perhaps are

---

[1]   Written to Hannah Wilberforce (1724–1788), half-sister of Berridge's friend John Thornton, on the death of her husband, William (1721–1777), aged fifty-five years. The manuscript is held in The Letters of Thomas Haweis ALS (11/2:115), Bridwell Library Special Collections, Perkins School of Theology, Southern Methodist University, Dallas, Texas. Hannah and William were aunt and uncle to William Wilberforce, the emancipator, who came, aged nine, to live with them at their house in London for three years when his father died. See December 19, 1777; February 21, 1788; and the extract [November/December 1788] to Hannah when she was dying.

[2]   A street in the St. James's district of London near Green Park. It was an area inhabited by the gentry.

dropping a widow's tear, he is singing and shouting hallelujahs to God and your Lamb. Oh, your riches of grace in giving a poor tempted, bewildered pilgrim such an exit! There is rich encouragement for all distressed Pilgrims, yet upon the road to fast[en] their dejected souls on such unfathomable mercy.

You will consider this removal no doubt as a call, to prepare for your own or rather, should I say, to quicken your preparation. You have been long travelling I trust towards Zion but the best need a spur to hasten their pace, and Jesus has called your husband away to espouse you the closer to himself. No more care, or prayer, is wanted for your deceased friend. Henceforth let your thoughts and desires centre in Jesus. He is worthy, call upon him, lean upon him, live upon him, and glory in him, make him your all. You have now an husband and a sister above; and when your angels are bringing home a new London guest, one is looking for his wife and your other for her sister; be you also looking and hasting for the coming of Jesus. Much grace and peace be with you, dear Madam.

Your affectionate servant,

John Berridge

To Mrs. Hillier[1]

Everton, April 10, 1778

Dear Madam,

A feeble frame of body, acting in concert with unbelief, often robs you, I believe, as it often robs me, of much comfort. Good frames[2] are desirable things, and to be sought after, yet we are apt to judge of ourselves too much from our frames, and too little from the Word of God. When the heart is heavy and cold, we conclude hastily there is no spiritual life and no love of Christ in the heart, and are ready to give up all hope. But in your worst frames, are not those frames a burden? This is a proof, you have some life: for the dead feel nothing.

Again, in your heaviest frames, is not the absence of Christ a trouble? Do you not desire his presence, yea prefer it before any other joy? Well, this desire of Christ's presence is a *sure* indication of love towards Christ. For we never desire anyone's company, at least not much of his company, except we love him. Why is a wife heavy and sorrowful during her husband's absence, upon a long journey? It is because she loves him. Yet perhaps her love to his person is so overwhelmed with sorrow for his absence, that she may overlook her own love; whilst only attentive to her sorrow. This is often the case with believers, who overlook their love to Jesus, whilst sorrowing for his absence. Yet a moment's recollection would assure them, they could not sorrow for Jesus, except they loved him.

Well then, in your next heavy frame, when Lady Mistrust is got to your elbow, and whispers in your ear, there is no love in your heart for Jesus; pray, ask her Ladyship, why then does my heart pine after Jesus? We cannot desire what we hate, but what we love. Stick to this answer, and it will send her Ladyship a packing: but if she desires a salute at parting, as perhaps she may, for she is an impudent

---

[1]   The manuscript for this letter is held in MARC, PLP 8 43.7. It is addressed to "Mrs. Hillier, No. 5 Pancrass Lane, Queen Street, Cheapside, London." Berridge is again answering a letter concerning assurance.

[2]   Feelings, emotional states.

baggage,[3] turn away your face, and tell her, you could have no desire for Jesus, unless he had first a desire for you; and the desires of his heart, proceeding from love, are unchangeable.

The Lord make you thankful, exceedingly thankful for what you have received, and then press on for further blessings. I am, dear Madam, in the best bonds your affectionate servant,

John Berridge

---

3   An artful young woman.

To Mrs. King[1]

Dear Betty,

Through mercy I got home safe and well; but why did I say got home? I am only arrived at my Everton Inn, and the Lord be praised for that accommodation, but I am travelling still, travelling when I sit and when I lay down; yea, when I stand still, travelling apace to my long home. Oh, that my heart may travel to Jesus fast as the minutes travel along. Every new year seems to travel faster, whilst I travel slower. Lord, quicken my tardy pace; I am weary and ashamed of myself; so near home, and so little dead to self and the world! One foot in the grave and so little still of the heavenly mind! In my sixty-third year, and the sickle at hand, yet so little ripe for the harvest! What need we have of alarms; yet how soon an alarm passeth over, like an hurricane, and we nestle in the world again! Jesus says "watch"[2]; but the carnal mind says "a little more sleep."[3] Jesus says, "Take up the cross"[4]; but the carnal mind says, "take thine ease."[5] Alas, how little do I know of Christ's self-denying doctrine. I preach of the cross, but preach about it, and about it, without taking it up. Nay, I think the taking up a cross was an easier matter, some years ago, than at present it seems. Then what have I been learning of late years, but the knowledge of doctrines? Learning how to think and talk, but not how to walk: receiving more light, and losing much love. I think, and seem to see too, that this is the case with many others, besides myself. Aged Christians had

---

1   The manuscript is held in FBC, Box CO10. It is addressed "For Mrs. King, at the Tabernacle, near Moorfields, London." On the manuscript, in another hand, was written: "Betty King was the Tabernacle house keeper and yet my [care?]— she is mentioned as dismissed from her service for reproving Mr. Piercy for suffering his carriage to be cleaned in the sight of the congregation assembling for worship on the Lord's day."

2   Matthew 26:38,41.

3   Proverbs 6:10.

4   Matthew 16:24.

5   Luke 12:19.

need be watchful and prayerful, else they quickly grow chaffy and stumpy. Instead of hungering for fresh manna, they [are][6] talking only of the food they ate[7] ten years ago. A sad symptom of a present soul-famine. Give my hearty love to all the Tabernacle brethren and sisters, and believe me your cordial friend in the best bonds,

John Berridge

---

[6] Manuscript is torn.
[7] Manuscript has "eat."

To Mr. Robert Heath[1]

Everton, April 25, 1778

Dear Brother,

I am coming once again to Plymouth, a long journey for an old man, and the carriage costly; yet come I must, to pay respect to Mr. Heath; but to make travelling charges as light as possible, I shall fold myself up in half a sheet, and come post in a letter.

I love to see Christians appear in miniature, and am labouring to contract myself. An arduous task indeed! For no sooner is one paring taken from self, but another piece of proud flesh springs up in its stead, and I feel as bulky, as lofty as ever. Many living physicians have been consulted to lessen this bulk, but the buried Doctors speak most to the point. John Baptist understood a gospel pulse well, and says positively, "Jesus must increase, but *I* must decrease," John 3:30. From him I discern, that self-will is the Pharaoh, who hardens himself against Christ, saying, Who is the Lord that *I* should serve him? And the Lord's batteries of course are planted against this great *I*. Once I thought that growing knowledge, with good frames must make children sprout up apace into Christ; but I learn from the Baptist, that good knowledge,

---

[1] This letter is found in the *Theological Magazine, or Synopsis of Modern Religious Sentiment* (10/1797), 20; *Christian Watchman*, 22 (1833), 1; and the *Baptist Magazine* (1861), 198. It is to Robert Heath, Plymouth Dock, and in *TM* it is entitled "Copy of a Letter from the Late Rev. John Berridge, Author of the Christian World Unmasked. Communicated by the Rev. Doctor Ryland, of Bristol." *BM* notes: "A Christian brother in Margate treasures the original." Robert Heath (1741–1800) came to prominence as a deacon at the Plymouth Tabernacle, a work that grew out of Whitefield's success at Plymouth Dock. He later became minister of the Tabernacle at Roborough, a village just outside Plymouth. Berridge probably met him when Whitefield introduced him to the Tabernacle in London before his death in 1770. He became well known for his help, materially and spiritually, to American sailors imprisoned at Plymouth in the American War of Independence (1776–1783). See "Memoir of the Late Rev. Robert Heath," *TM* (1801), 160–163, and chapter 5, "Robert Heath: Evangelist and Humanitarian," in Sheldon S. Cohen, *British Supporters of the American Revolution, 1775–1783: The Role of the "Middling Level" Activists* (Woodbridge: Boydell Press, 2004), 107–132.

and good frames, however desirable, may turn a child rickety, and make his great *I* grow bigger still. Yea, I learn also, whatever be my knowledge or frames, Jesus gets increase in my heart no farther, than great *I* gets decrease As I grow out of self, I grow into Christ, and no faster. Jesus rises and gains dominion, as self sinks. If, then, I wish for more of Christ, I must have less of self; and this tiger grows lean, not by feeding, but by starving; grows quiet, not by wheedling,[2] but by thumping. Hence I see the want of some daily cross, which Jesus kindly sends to crucify self. Hence, too, I find a need of much prayer, to take my cross patiently, and make it work effectually; and if a cross knife seems sharp, and cuts deep, it is sent to pare off some large carbuncle, which is ever sprouting up from proud self. I would therefore look on my Lord Wilbewill as my worst foe, insolent towards God, offensive to my neighbour, and vexatious to my own heart. May I give him no quarter, but treat him like a wild beast as he is, and embrace every cross as an appointed means for taming this tiger.

So you are preaching again, my friend says, and upon a rusty subject. True, my heart needs this preaching every day, and it will not be amiss for you, if it reunites your heart to strange treatment, and much you will meet with from the world and the flesh[3] before your warfare is finished. When you write to London, send my hearty love to Mrs. Newman.[4] Give kind respects to your family. Grace and peace be with you all and with your affectionate servant,

John Berridge

---

2 Coaxing by flattery or endearments.
3 *BM* has "church."
4 *BM* has "Newsam."

To John Thornton[1]

Everton, June 12, 1778

Honoured Sir,

I have received twelve dozen of small Bibles, nine dozen of small Testaments, and one thousand Hymns for children,[2] which I will distribute as carefully as I can. Indeed some care is needful, that your bounty may not be interrupted in its course, by passing through slippery fingers. I gave thirty of Watts' small hymns to a neighbouring Baptist minister, who sold them at half price. He had maintained a good character for many years, but is now dismissed from his flock, by the breaking out of some heinous misconduct. Such misapplications call for caution in the original giver, and in his almoner, but should not stop the current of bounty. For if good is only to be done where it cannot be misapplied, but little good can be done at all. If only half of the books, or money you give, is given to good purpose, you may think yourself well off, and shall not lose the benefit of the other hand. If only a quarter of the sermons I preach is made effectual, I need not grudge to throw in the other three quarters. Jesus Christ was an excellent fisher of men, and toiled much in letting down his net; yet the fish that He caught were but few. The most part were not gathered into his net, or slipped through the meshes. Hear his complaint: "I have laboured in vain, I have spent my strength for nought."[3] Yet he goes forward with this consideration, "My work" or my reward "is with my God."[4]

Oh, Sir, it is worthwhile to spend much money and labour, if some good, though but little, is done thereby! Misapplications of your bounty will be made, but the whole of it remaineth still your own, and your children will fare the better for it. I sometimes put a small book into the hand of a travelling beggar, and desire him to read it, but expect he

---

1   This is another thank-you letter to Thornton. It is found in *GM* (1837), 450–451; *WB* (1838), 401–402; and *WB* (1864), 391–392.
2   Watts. See September 25, 1773.
3   Isaiah 49:4.
4   Isaiah 49:4.

will sell it for a trifle to the first person he meets. Yet bread thus cast on the waters, is found again,[5] and often proves a savoury meal. Yea, such is the temper of some people, they will read a book, which cost them something, but would lay it aside, if it cost them nothing; treating man's free gift with the same neglect as God's free grace.

My spring fever is making a forcible attack, and weakening my strength and my spirits exceedingly, so that I can scarce bear company, or struggle through the fatigue of a letter. I often feel a foolish wish for stronger health, and would sanctify that wish by the hope of doing more service. But I forget that our God is called a husbandman, and that his cultivated grounds need a fallow in due season, to tumble them over, and break them well, with harrow and plough, again and again, in order to cleanse them from rubbish, and make them more kindly for after fruit-bearing. Some wealthy farmers about Everton have lately cropped their grounds every year, and thought to make the ground amends by laying extraordinary manure upon it. But they see their mistake, and return to the old method. For the grounds, being deprived of their fallow year, the proper season for cleansing them, are much overrun with foul weeds and twitch. And I know of no ground that needs more ploughing and harrowing, than the ground of my heart, so churlish it is, and full of rank weeds. Young Venn[6] is the most promising youth I have seen; great mental abilities; close application to study and much unction from the Holy One.

I am weary with writing. Accept a warm prayer, and I conclude. The Lord Jesus multiply grace and peace upon yourself and your partner, and make your whole household a household of faith. Amen.

John Berridge

---

5 Ecclesiastes 11:1.
6 John Venn (1759–1813), second child and only son of Henry Venn. He had recently commenced residence at Cambridge University. After a period as vicar of Little Dunham in Norfolk, he was appointed vicar of Clapham in 1792, becoming a member of the Clapham Sect of social philanthropists. As rector of Clapham, "he was the personal friend and spiritual guide of perhaps the most notable congregation in the whole of England in his generation" (Hylson-Smith, *Evangelicals in the Church of England*, 83). Henry Venn records that Berridge "is as affectionate as a father to my son, and gives him many valuable books" (Venn, *Life and Letters of Venn*, 233). See Michael Hennell, *John Venn and the Clapham Sect* (Lutterworth, 1958).

To John Thornton[1]

Everton, October 24, 1778

Dear and honoured Sir,

On Wednesday morning last, a dissenting minister, not a Baptist,[2] called at my house, and finding me gone abroad to preach, he left a note and pursued his journey, having engaged to preach that evening at a village, thirty miles distant from Everton. Two years ago he was settled at Oundle, in Northamptonshire, where he found a congregation, very meagre in all respects, but which is now in a thriving state. I believe him sound in faith and practice, and he loves itinerant preaching, and practises it much. He is zealous, but not furious, of a catholic spirit without lukewarmness, and his fire warms without scorching. His name is J. Wildbore.[3] We were both born at Nottingham, and are very distantly related. The purport of his note is as follows: "My congregation increaseth, and I trust the Lord is with us, but the people are very poor. My income is under[4] thirty pounds a year, which is too narrow for a wife and four children. I want ten pounds to discharge a few debts, and wish for a friend to lend me that sum. At my father's death, who is aged and infirm, an estate at Nottingham, of a few hundred pounds value, comes to me, which will then enable me to discharge the loan."

Had I seen Mr. Wildbore, I would have given him a guinea, but could not lend him ten pounds. I have many demands upon me and am often in the deep myself, with my chin under water, but the Lord keeps my nose above it, which is enough, quite enough to keep me from sinking, but not enough to save a brother from drowning. Had

---

[1] This letter is found in *GM* (1837), 492–493; *WB* (1838), 402–404; and *WB* (1864), 392–394. *GM* gives October 14, 1778.

[2] *GM* omits "not a Baptist."

[3] James Bakewell Wildbore (1742?–1822). Wildbore left Oundle in 1781 and served in Falmouth, Dublin, Macclesfield, and finally Falmouth again, retiring in 1817. For a summary of his career and the revival that was experienced at Dublin, see Seymour, *Life of Huntingdon*, 2:208.

[4] *GM* has "only."

I Mr. Thornton's heart and purse, I would not lend Mr. Wildbore a groat, but send him ten pounds immediately, and thus refresh my own bowels, by relieving his wants. I know your poor's bag is a deep one; but how far exhausted at present, I know not; yet if a ten pound bill lies skulking in some corner of the bag, I do wish and pray you would drag him out and send him to Oundle. It would occasion many thanksgivings to God, and many prayers for your welfare.

Mr. Venn[5] has informed me of your fall and recovery.[6] The latter will fill you with thankfulness, no doubt; and the former inspire you with caution, I trust. Indeed, Sir, you appear too venturesome. And since you are neither very young, nor very slender, is it not seasonable to adopt some caution, for the sake of your family, as well as yourself. Caution, in the hand does not wrangle, but harmonize with faith in the heart. And since the Lord affords you numerous servants is it not a disregard of this mercy, to travel in the dark and in danger of thieves, without an attendant? Mercies are bestowed for use, and the use creates thankfulness in upright hearts; but your leaving all the servants at home is like a miser's hoarding all his cash in a bag, to the neglect of his bodily wants. And if you persist in this track, the money-miser will claim kindred, and call you cousin; and Jesus Christ will not thank you for this new relation. The Lord bless you abundantly, and enrich your family with his choicest blessings. I remain, with much affection, your obliged servant,

John Berridge

P.S. I preached at Yelling, on Tuesday evening to a large congregation, and left the family in good health. Jacky[7] goes on well, is very studious and serious, and promises to be a polished shaft in the Lord's quiver.

---

5   Henry Venn at Yelling. See June 8, 1771.
6   Thornton had fallen from his horse. John Newton gave him the same advice that he ought to take a servant to accompany him when out riding. See Newton to Thornton, September 24, 1778, Thornton Family Papers, Cambridge University Library.
7   John Venn. See June 12, 1778.

To John Thornton[1]

Tabernacle, February 11, 1779

Dear and honoured Sir,

I have received your kind letter of the 9th instant, inclosing another with a bill in its bosom, value £25; five of which are appointed for the poor, and the rest for Mr. Kennedy.[2] Accept my hearty thanks for the same.

London congregations are almost too much for me; and I am usually in great travail, whilst I am here. My head very cloudy, my body exceeding heavy, and my thoughts frequently so fugitive and scattered, that sometimes I know not where to find them. At other times I cannot hold them, when I have them. Yet if through this travail any children are born, it is well; and if others are suckled better still. A feeble body damps my spirits, and somewhat my zeal, but not my desire to labour and die in the service of my Master; and through grace my heart pines after God, for more of his image, and nearer communion which are not obtained by mere preaching, or reading, or hearing, without much prayer and watchfulness. Formality steps into ordinances quickly, unless they are salted with prayer, before and behind. Crowded and attentive congregations are reviving sights; yet perhaps this is rather an age of much hearing, than much praying. The old puritan spirit of devotion is not kindling and breathing among us. Religious controversy[3] has hurt the work much, religious gossiping has hurt it still more, and deep-mouthed Calvinism loves sitting and hearing much better than kneeling and praying. May God make all grace abound to yourself, to your family, and to your affectionate servant,

John Berridge

---

[1] This short letter was written from the Tabernacle during Berridge's winter preaching in London. It is taken from *GM* (1837), 536; *WB* (1838), 404–405; and *WB* (1864), 394–395.

[2] Possibly Kennedy was one of Berridge's lay helpers. See May 3, 1773.

[3] *GM* has "slanderers."

To John Thornton[1]

Tabernacle, March 12, 1779

Dear and honoured Sir,

I purpose, God willing, to wait upon you at Clapham, on Sunday evening, the 21st. I shall preach at Tottenham[2] in the morning, and, when the afternoon service is over, set off in a hackney coach.[3] I had much rather travel in a hackney carriage, than in your own, because it would prevent your coachman from attending on the afternoon ordinance.

My heart is much grieved at the mighty efforts made by popish priests, and at the horrible speeches uttered by popish hearers, who rejoice in the prospect of Smithfield fires[4] and think the kingdom is their own.[5] Indeed, the land was never so rife for popery since the Reformation, as now; and unless the Lord Jesus appears for our rescue, we are like to be overwhelmed by it. The mighty ones care not what religion is established, because, through infidelity, they have discarded all religion. The bishops and clergy are become such dumb dogs, not a single one will bark at the popish beast; the mean ones, through ignorance and profaneness, are ready to take up any profession for a mess of pottage.[6] The late bickerings and literary duellings among the shepherds,[7] call for a lancet to let out the hot blood; and the much worldly conformity among professors seems to require a fan

---

[1]   This is another short note from the Tabernacle, in which Berridge makes arrangements for a visit to Thornton at his home at Clapham. The letter comes from *GM* (1837), 536–537, and *CM* (1845), 29–30.

[2]   *GM* has "Tottenham Court Chapel."

[3]   A carriage for hire.

[4]   Most of the Marian martyrs suffered death at Smithfield.

[5]   This refers to the popular excitement following on from a Catholic Relief Bill passing through Parliament in 1778. The excitement continued to increase until the Gordon Riots in June 1780.

[6]   Esau sold his spiritual privileges for a meal of lentil soup. See Genesis 25:29–34. The ordinary clergy will believe anything as long as they receive their meal ticket.

[7]   *GM* adds "in defending the leading truths of the gospel."

to separate the chaff from the wheat. What will be the issue, I know not; but this I know, the Lord reigneth, and will be a sanctuary to all his real people. May the Father of mercies bless you and yours with all spiritual blessings, and with a rich abundance of them. With much gratitude, I remain your affectionate servant,

John Berridge

To the Rev. Mr. Woodgate[1]

Everton, April 28, 1779

Dear Brother,

Do you ask after my old carcase? It is sorry, yet suitable. A better would not serve me so well. Or ask what returns I am making for mercies received? Why, truly, sometimes underrating the Lord's bounty, sometimes overrating myself for it—one while proud of what he gives, another while thinking he might give more. Mercies momentarily received get few heart-thanks, yet, if withheld, fetch many heart-risings. Seldom I value mercies aright till I want them, and seldom improve them aright when I have them. Indeed, the best return I seem to make is astonishment—astonished to see how good the Lord is, and how evil I am. Then I feel a little of that broken heart which God delighteth in—a suitable frame for believers on earth. It stirreth up duty and praise, and is sweetly enlarged in saints above, who are evermore filling God's heaven with praise.

If all were not gift and grace (gift to the needy, and grace to the unworthy), heaven would be like this earth—a subject for boast—a room for contempt. Martyrs might whistle to others who pressed too near, and bid them "Stand off! We are better than you!" Mary[2] Magdalene would have no companions in heaven but repenting prostitutes, and the cross thief[3] no associates but Tyburn penitents.[4] As for the perfectionists,[5] if Christ knows where to put them in heaven, I know not, but think they would class by themselves, and might scuffle with the martyrs for precedency.

---

[1] The *Boston Recorder*, 14 (1823), 54, and the *Investigator* (1823), 75–76, both give the addressee as "The Revd. Mr. Woodgate, No. 30, Ironmonger's Row." *S* (1885), 15, says it is addressed to "W__, Old Street, London." Richard Woodgate was an eminent Nonconformist minister at Jewin-Street Chapel. See April 21, 1775. The letter also appears in *WB* (1838), 405–407, and *WB* (1864), 395–396.

[2] *BR* has "Molly."

[3] One of the thieves crucified with Christ repented. Luke 23:42.

[4] Tyburn was the place of public execution in London.

[5] Those influenced by the complete sanctification teaching of John Wesley.

Brother, by feeling much of my own heart, I know something of yours, and believe, if God would humour your wish, you would preach yourself into hell by a run of fine sermons. How pleased we are to see a congregation in tears when we are in the pulpit! But remember, though a wet sermon breaks the hearts of hearers down, it raises the heart of a preacher up, and a dry sermon often profits him more than a wet one. I usually find, in myself and others, that a wet sermon claps a cloven foot upon the preacher.

Kind respects to your partner. Grace and peace be with you both, and with your flock, and with your affectionate brother,

John Berridge

To John Thornton[1]

Everton, July 27, 1779

Dear and honoured Sir,

By the favour of Mr. T. Astell,[2] I received a copy of the *Olney Hymns*.[3] They are experimental and sound; the language intelligible to all believers; and the sense sufficiently closing at the end of each line; a very needful thing in public worship, where many are destitute of a hymn-book.[4] They seem to want a little unction sometimes, and sometimes a little more poetic vein, and I wish there had been more hymns of praise; but on the whole I think it the most edifying hymn-book yet published. The worst fault I can find in the book is, that it proves a single copy, a private treat, without a general feast, a meal for myself without any dole for others. Methinks I see you upbraid my ravenous appetite, and indignantly ask, "Will his mouth be always gasping after my publications?" Indeed, Sir, it may unless you wisely clap a padlock on my lips, and keep the key in your pocket.

---

[1] Both *WB* (1838), 405–407, and *WB* (1864), 395–396, have the date as 1775. However, the reference to *Olney Hymns* and Mr. T. Astell date it as 1779, as does *GM* (1838), 30–31.

[2] William Thornton Astell (1733–1801), the local squire, formally William Thornton, son of Godfrey Thornton (1701–1751). He obtained permission on February 21, 1777, to change his name as he inherited his uncle's property at Everton when Richard Astell died, in compliance with the will of his grandfather William Astell. He lived at Everton until his death, producing no heirs.

[3] *Olney Hymns* were published in February 1779. The hymn book was produced by John Newton and consisted of his own compositions and those of William Cowper. In the preface he says that his "desire of promoting the faith and comfort of sincere Christians, though the principal, was not the only motive to this undertaking. It was like wise intended as a monument, to perpetuate the remembrance of an intimate and endeared friendship" (*Olney Hymns* [1847], iii). See Hindmarsh, *Newton*, 258–280, for the occasion, context and evaluation of the hymns.

[4] Hymns were often sung line by line, being repeated after the clerk. Berridge says in his withdrawn 1760 collection: "care has been taken to avoid enthusiastic rant; to throw out hard words, and to make the sense end, or nearly end, at the proper pauses" (*Divine Songs,* 5).

We have been in a state of war at Everton for two years, and have had preludes of a French and Spanish invasion.[5] The squire and the widow[6] are making incursions on each other alternately, and labouring to harass and vex each other sufficiently. A notable fruit this of the religion of nature (under Christian profession) which loves to traffic in misery, and studies hard to render unkindness for unkindness. Oh, from what wretchedness does precious grace save a true believer! The Lord fill my heart with this precious grace! Times are awful; and likely to be more so. Rods have been used without effect, and now the scorpions are coming. May their bite awake, but not destroy us! National pride, infidelity, and profligacy are growing very rampant, and will grow from bad to worse unless restrained by heavy judgments. The worst evil God can bring upon a nation is to say to it, as once he said to Ephraim, "Let him alone,"[7] but if the Lord intends our good, he will chastise sorely. This is the Bible-road to reformation. On this account, however formidable judgments are, I know not whether I should fear them more or bid them welcome. Strong physic is become needful for the body politic; and however nauseous to the palate, or griping in the operation, it must be deemed a blessing. The Lord prepare us for the tempest, and prove our hiding-place. Yes, he says, "On every dwelling of mount Zion, He will create a pillar both of cloud and fire; and on all the glory shall be a defence."[8] Amen.

I suppose you have received a letter of thanks from our society at Stretham,[9] for assisting them to build a small barn—a threshing floor for Jesus. The barn is now erected and thatched, and the people are happy and thankful. The Lord keep yourself and family under his gracious protection; and enrich you all with his choicest treasure, the blessings of salvation. Amen and Amen. I have just room to subscribe,

John Berridge

---

5   On April 12, 1779, France had entered into a secret treaty with Spain to make war against Britain. The intended large joint French and Spanish fleet never materialized, although on June 3 the French fleet sailed from Brest, and Spain declared war against Britain on June 16.

6   *WB* omits "squire" and "widow." William Thornton Astell, the new squire, and Richard Astell's (d.1777) second wife, Hannah Astell, whom he had married in 1770.

7   Hosea 4:17.

8   Isaiah 4:5,6.

9   About thirty miles from Everton, and ten miles north of Cambridge.

To the Rev. Mr. Collins[1]

Everton, September 28, 1779

Dear Sir,

Your letter came duly to hand, but could not be answer'd, till I had wrote to Mr. Keen, and received a letter from him. The cause, as follows. I am growing old, bulky and feeble, and durst not undertake another journey to London, unless the Trustees could be satisfied with preaching only twice in a week. Mr. Keen[2] informs me they shall be contented with this; and now I can acquaint you, that I heartily accept your offer to supply my Church; and some extra parochial cures[3] too, if you please. You may ramble about, or stay at home, as you please. I usually go to London in the first or second week of January; and, if no accident prevents, arrive at Tabernacle House about four in the afternoon, where I hope to see you, where also you will sleep; and the chaise which brings you up will wait upon you next morning to take you down, and the Lord come with you. Mr. Keen will give you timely notice of the day, I set out for London, and

---

[1] This was written to the "Rev. Mr. Collins, Tabernacle House, Moorfields, London. Brian Bury Collins" (1754–c.1807) was admitted to St. John's College, Cambridge, as a sizar (a poor student who received assistance, often in return for undertaking menial tasks) in 1771 and obtained his degree in 1776, being ordained as a deacon in the same year and becoming curate of Rauceby and then Cranwell, both in Lincolnshire. He was dismissed as a curate for field preaching and did not obtain priest's orders until 1781, when David Simpson of Macclesfield offered him a title as assistant curate. Wesley, Newton and Venn all counselled him against his practice of itinerating if he wished to be ordained. He preached for Wesley, Lady Huntingdon, and Rowland Hill and was concerned about the division between Arminian and Calvinistic Methodists. If Collins did "ramble about" those "extra parochial cures" would not enhance his ordination prospects at the time of this letter. Berridge is feeling his age and Collins has offered his services at Everton during Berridge's winter preaching. The letter is found in A.M. Broadley, "Correspondence of the Rev. Brian Bury Collins, MA," *WHS*, 9.2 (1913/1914), 30.
[2] One of the trustees of Whitefield's London churches. See September 20, 1776.
[3] Curates have a cure.

Mr. Venn will exchange with you on Sacrament Days.[4] *In Xto vive, et valebis.*[5] Grace and Peace be with you and your affectionate brother,

John Berridge

---

[4] Collins had not yet obtained full orders and thus Venn would take the communion on Sundays.

[5] Live in Christ and prevail.

To the Rev. Samuel Lucas[1]

Everton, October 23, 1779

Dear Sir,

Your letter of the 2nd of July came duly to hand, but has waited a wearisome while for an answer. Indeed, I have been much, yet not too much, afflicted with my old disorder for some months, a nervous fever.[2] We have been housekeepers every summer for forty years; and this fever-friend has kept me this summer twelve weeks at home, and forbade me all literary correspondence. As winter comes on, I begin to revive; and when the swallows march off, I begin to march out; as when the swallows return, I am often obliged to keep in. It is well we are not in our own keeping, nor at our own carving, since we so little know what is good for us. I do not love this fever-friend; yet he is certainly the best earthly companion I have. No lasting gain do I get but in a furnace. Comforts of every kind, in the issue, make me either light or lofty, and

---

[1] There are a variety of dates given for this letter. *WB* (1864), 396–398, and *GB* (1885), 331–332, have October 23, 1775. *GS* (1857), 311, has October 18, 1778. *GM* (1861), 482, and *Zion's Trumpet, or the Penny Spiritual Magazine* (1847), 228–229, have October 28, 1788, and *EM* (1812), 385–386; *Zion's Casket, or The Penny Spiritual Treasury* (1835), 103–104; *WB* (1838), 407–408; *GS* (1840), 193–194; *CMR* (1889), 327; and Gadsby, *Memoirs of Hymn Writers,* 34, have October 23, 1779. *GS* (1857), 311, has October 18, 1788. In a brief extract of this letter in *GM* (1862), 351, the editor records: "A friend sends us a copy of one of John Berridge's unpublished letters written from Everton in 1779, to the Rev. Samuel Lucas of Walsall." Samuel Lucas (*c.*1748–1799) presumably got to know Berridge when, as a very young keen evangelist, he preached in villages around his hometown of Bury St. Edmunds. Through the encouragement of another friend of Berridge, David Edwards of Ipswich (see November 26, 1771), he attended the Mile End Academy in 1769. After spending a vacation preaching at Walsall in 1772, he was called as the minister of the Congregational Church at Bridge Street Chapel (1773–1779), later moving to Swan Hill, Shrewsbury (1779–1797). He had a strong sense of humour, as did Berridge. See "Memoir of the Rev. Samuel Lucas of Shrewsbury," *CM* (1829), 457–469.
[2] See June 3, 1771 for the possible meanings of "nervous" and a discussion of Berridge's illness. This was probably some form of nervous exhaustion.

294

swell me, though unperceivably, with self-sufficiency. Indeed, so much dross, native and acquired, is found in my heart, that I have constant need of a furnace; and Jesus has selected a suitable furnace for me, not a hot and hasty one, which seems likely to harden and consume me, but one with a gentle and lingering heat, which melts my heart gradually, and lets out some of its dross. Though I cannot love a furnace, nor bask in it like a salamander, yet the longer I live, the more I see of its need and its use. A believer seldom walks steadily and ornamentally, unless he is well furnaced. Without this his zeal is often scalding hot; his boldness attended with fierceness, or rather rashness; and his confidence at times more the result of animal spirit than the fruit of the Spirit; but a furnace consumes these excrescences, and when sweetly blown with grace, will make a Christian humble, watchful, and mellow; very censorious of himself, and full of compassion for others.

May your congregation be increasing in numbers, and the power of the Lord be present to wound and to heal, to quicken and comfort and build. But let me add, the growth of the children will greatly depend on your conduct; for a congregation quickly drink in the spirit of the preacher. If you converse much with God on the mount, as Moses did, and the old Puritans did, your hearers will see a gospel lustre on your countenance, and stand in awe of you; and, what is best of all, like Moses, you will not be sensible of that lustre, whilst others see it and reverence it. Much secret prayer will solemnize your heart, and make your visits savoury as well as your sermons. The old Puritans visited their flocks by house-row; the visits were short; they talked a little for God, and then concluded with prayer to God. An excellent rule, which prevented tittle-tattle, and made visits profitable. May Jesus bless you, and water your flock! Your affectionate brother,

John Berridge

P.S. When you pass near Everton, call upon us and give us a sermon.

To Mrs. Elizabeth H___ [1]

Everton, March 31, 1780

Dear Madam,

Through mercy I got home safe and well, and my lame foot seems to gather strength daily. Last Lord's day I preached without a stool, and found but little inconvenience from standing all the time. I found some thankfulness for my lameness whilst I was in town, but now find it abundantly more. It is good for me that I have been afflicted. I was made to see a need of it soon after it came, and now find a blessing from it. The Lord be praised for past sickness, and returning health. Whilst we dwell in houses of corrupt clay we shall need continual correction. We cannot, therefore, wonder at the lesson written on the Lord's school door, "Take up thy cross daily." [2] It must come because it is needful; it will come because it is healthful. Expect the cross daily, and it cannot surprise you, nor much hurt you when it comes. It will come from every quarter just as it is wanted; and it comes with a rough and lowering countenance, but brings a blessing secretly in its hand for you. We are often simple enough to think that any other cross were better for us than the present; yet since Jesus is a kind and wise physician, he always sends the most suitable medicine. He lays a blister [3] on the proper part; yea, and takes it off too when it has done its work. Afflictions have been to me some of my greatest mercies.

Seek daily for a full manifestation of Christ's love; yet be not anxious lest you fall short of it. Diligence is required, but anxiety is forbidden. The times of awakening, reviving, or comforting, are acts of sovereignty, in which the Lord consults his own glory, and his people's

---

[1] This letter is found in *WB* (1838), 408–410, and *WB* (1864), 398–399. This is probably Mrs. Elizabeth Hillier, who left £1,000 to Cheshunt College when she died in 1799. See Welch, *Cheshunt College*, 145. See April 10, 1778, and June 29, 1781. Berridge is writing again on returning from his winter London preaching.
[2] Luke 9:23.
[3] Doctors used to make blisters on various parts of the body as part of medical treatment.

profit. It is enough that we are told, "Ask, and ye shall have."[4] And again, "If I tarry, wait for me."[5] And again, "Whosoever will, let him come; and he that cometh, I will in no wise cast out."[6]

You have need, and are required to rejoice in the Lord evermore. Rejoice in Jesus, that he hath quickened you. Rejoice, that you are drawn to seek his face. Rejoice for the glimpses of his countenance, and the frequent refreshings of his word. These are tokens of love. Rejoice that you can mourn for an absent Jesus. Such mourning is a sure proof of your love to Jesus, and you could not love him, unless he had first loved you. Seek on, therefore, dear Madam, and seek rejoicing, and may the Lord water your heart abundantly. I remain, your affectionate servant,

John Berridge

---

4   Luke 11:9.
5   Habakkuk 2:3.
6   Revelation 22:17 and John 6:37.

To John Berridge[1]

Dear John,

I am glad to hear that you are well in health, and diligent in business, and well esteemed and spoken of amongst your neighbours. Honesty, sobriety, and civility are blessings from God. They are his gifts; but no righteousness of our own can save us. Happy is the man who is brought to a right knowledge of Christ, and a saving acquaintance with him; who is taught of God how to believe in Jesus Christ, to love and delight in him, to pray to him and praise him, to trust in him wholly, and to cast every care and burden upon him. May you be found among these happy people.

Dear John, you will find as well as others, care and troubles enough in the world; and after a few years must be removed from it forever. Oh, think seriously of that other world which is eternal; and read the good word of God daily, and pray earnestly for the grace of Christ, and for the guidance of his Spirit. Now is your spiritual seed-time; now is the day of salvation. Be diligent whilst the day of life lasteth, for the night of death cometh wherein no man can work. Oh, let the concerns of your soul be our daily thought and prayer. Your body will soon be laid down in the dust, but your soul must live forever. Take care of the main concern; be wise for your soul, and then you are wise forever. May the Lord protect you by his providence, and direct you by his grace, and bless you in body and soul. I remain, your affectionate uncle,

John Berridge

---

[1] This is a letter to Berridge's nephew. It seems that he has little spiritual interest and this explains Berridge's challenge. See November 12, 1773; July 21, 1781; and May 24, 1792. It is recorded in *WB* (1838), 411–412, and *WB* (1864), 401.

To John Thornton[1]

Everton, October 20, 1780

Dear and honoured Sir,

I am seldom without thorns in my flesh,[2] through a peevish[3] disorder called vapours[4]; and now have a thorn in my family, through insanity. My poor maid, who has lived seven years with me, and is fifty years old, began to droop on August twelvemonths, and in February last fell distracted. For a fortnight she was very violent, rolled on the floor, tore her flesh, and endeavoured to destroy herself. Afterwards she grew calmer, and has been tolerably calm ever since, yet roaming at times, and afraid of being cast into prison for her past ravings. She tells her fellow servant I shall certainly hang her, and weekly appoints a day for her execution. These fears emaciate and enfeeble her much, and nothing I can say removes them. Yet she retains her recollection pretty well, is rational enough in many things, can do most of the housework, and seems displeased when I provide a helper. Some gracious words have been given her from the Lord, which make me pray and live in hope she will be restored, and the visitation sanctified.[5]

Oh, Sir, the partition between sane and insane is so slender, none but God can keep the partition up. What a mercy to have full use of reason, and reason preserved, and reason improved and illumined by grace; to be sane in mind, and faithful in Christ; a ready hand for the world, and a willing heart for the Lord.

Old age, with its winter aspect, creeps on me apace. My mind waxes feeble as well as my limbs; my windows grow dark, my memory leaks, and my grinders are few.[6] Much ashamed I am for loving the Lord so little, and doing so little for his name; and much out of temper with Administration for persisting in a ruinous war, and trying

---

[1] This letter is found in *GM* (1838), 113–114, and *WB* (1864), 399–400.
[2] 2 Corinthians 12:7.
[3] Fretful, childish, vexatious—this fits the sense where "vapours" means worry.
[4] See September 2, 1763; August 16, 1774; and April 26, 1777.
[5] She recovered after two years. See September 17, 1782.
[6] Ecclesiastes 12:3.

to entail poverty, popery, and slavery on us.[7] Surely the Lord's hand is in this, to scourge the nation for their contempt of his word and his Christ. Infatuation comes judicially from the Lord, which bids me lay my hand on my mouth. When I read of convoys taken, and loss by insurance, I think of Mr. Thornton[8] with more concern than he, I do suppose, feels for himself. We may live without anxiety when we are alive to God.

Mr. Astell[9] has gained much credit by his upright conduct in office; and Mr. Venn gave great satisfaction to real Christians by his assize sermon. He is gone into Yorkshire, hoping to ride off his disorder in the mountains.[10] I have no opinion of going so far from a parish to ride for health; yet some uncommon providence seemed to point out this step. I wish it may succeed; but Dr. Doddridge's[11] going to Portugal for health, and dying in his passage occurs to my thoughts, on such like occasions. You have now had a specimen of young ___,[12] and may form a judgment of him. Is any tache[13] wanting, you could wish to see

---

[7] This was probably the American War of Independence, which had begun in 1775. In 1778 Britain had declared war on France; in 1779 Spain had declared war on Britain; and in 1780 Britain declared war on Holland. Peace treaties were made in 1783 with America, France and Spain.

[8] See September 29, 1772 for Thornton's wealth.

[9] William Thornton Astell had been made sheriff of Bedfordshire on February 2, 1780.

[10] Venn had started his journey in September. See December 12, 1780.

[11] Philip Doddridge (1702–1751). After training at an academy in Kibworth in Leicestershire and moving with it to Hinckley, he became a minister at Kibworth, later moving to Market Harborough (1725) and then to Castle Hill, Northampton (1730). He attempted to unite Nonconformists but often received criticism by those who regarded him as a trimmer. He suffered from ill health and overwork from his broad commitments and extensive correspondence. He became well known for the large academy that he ran at Northampton, his *Family Expositor* (1738–1756), and his spiritual autobiography, *The Rise and Progress of Religion in the Soul* (J. Brackstone and J. Waugh, 1745). After several months of serious physical decline, he sailed from Falmouth with his wife, Mercy, on September 30, arriving in Lisbon on Sunday, October 30. He died of tuberculosis a few days later on October 26. See Geoffrey F. Nuttall, ed., *Philip Doddridge, 1702–51: His Contribution to English Religion* (Independent Press, 1951) and Malcom Deacon, *Philip Doddridge of Northampton, 1702–51* (Northampton: Northamptonshire Library, 1980).

[12] Is he speaking of John Venn? See June 12, 1778.

[13] Buckle or hook; therefore, "mental grasp" or "understanding" in this context.

in a young man, designed for the ministry?[14] A new alliance with your family is in agitation, I hear; the Lord accompany it with his blessings; and that all your branches may be grafted into the living vine, and the parent-stocks be well watered with the dews of grace, is the hearty prayer of your dutiful and affectionate servant,

John Berridge

---

[14] The two sentences "You have...the ministry" are omitted in *GM*.

To John Newton[1]

Everton, December 12, 1780

Dear Sir,

Mr. Keen[2] recommends a Mr. Mayor[3] to supply my church during my London visit, and refers me to you for a character. Is he moral? Is he also evangelical? Can he preach without notes, and will he condescend to visit some neighbouring country town once a week, and give a sermon or an exhortation in a barn or a house? Is he also a single man? A speedy answer to these queries will be esteemed a favour.

Next week I go to preach in a parish church; a high honour indeed! Mr. Peers,[4] the Rector of Ickleford,[5] near Hitchin, is newly enlightened to preach Jesus, and desires help from evangelical brethren. Sixteen years ago I preached in one of his neighbour's barns, and now am invited to preach in his church. He has driven the Squire and his family from the church, which is a mighty good symptom, and if he has any reputation still remaining among the neighbouring clerics, it cannot survive my preaching in his pulpit. Indeed, he is a bold man to ask the madman of Everton to dust his cushion.

Mr. Venn has been traversing the mountains of Yorkshire for ten weeks,[6] and is returning home this week full of power, I hear, stout in

---

[1]   The manuscript is held at LPL, MS 3972 ff.19-20. It is also recorded in *WB* (1838), 412–413, and *WB* (1864), 401–402.
[2]   One of the trustees of Whitefield's Tabernacle in London. See September 20, 1776.
[3]   See January 1781.
[4]   John Witherington Peers, LLD (1744–1835) was instituted rector of Pirton in 1873, becoming also the rector of Morden in Surrey in 1778, and was also a curate of Stadhampton and Chislehampton from 1790 until his death. He became the author of several theological works, including *Eight Sermons in Defence of the Divinity of Our Lord* (1816).
[5]   Ickleford in Hertfordshire is about fourteen miles from Everton and two miles north of Hitchin.
[6]   Venn writes to his nephew: "Though I have lost my ague since 9th of July, yet I have but little strength. I am therefore advised to try riding by short journeys, and change of air; for which purpose I intend setting out next week to

body, and vigorous in spirit. The Lord has restored my leg to perfect soundness, and strengthened my body for itinerate preaching the last three months and is crowding my church abundantly on a Sunday afternoon, glory be to his grace. I hope a latter rain is coming down; indeed, it is wanted. Our skins are growing very dry; the spiritual pulse beats very low; and grey hairs are sprinkled upon us. I hope you find some refreshing seasons in your new barn floor,[7] and some grain beating out of the straw. Present my very kind Christian respects to Mrs. Newton; and if you could peep into my bosom, you might see how much you are loved and esteemed by

John Berridge

P.S. Much grace and peace be with you all.

Yorkshire, and shall be absent two or three months. Mrs. Venn is afraid of the journey; and chooses rather to stay with my daughters. If the journey does not help me much, I am to try Bath waters" (Venn, *Life and Letters of Venn,* 311).

[7] In 1779 Newton had moved from Olney to become vicar of St. Mary Woolnoth, London.

To the Rev. Mr. Mayor[1]

January 1781

If Mr. Mayor desires to know how the Vicar of Everton proceeds in his family and church, the following will inform him.

Morning family prayer at half past seven, first reading a Psalm or chapter, and making occasional remarks; then singing an hymn, afterwards prayer and concluding with "Praise God, from whom all blessings flow," and dine at one, sup at 8, or sooner if you please, family prayer at 9, as before; and then retire to rest.

On Sundays I go to church at half past 9 in the morning, sing 6 verses of a psalm after a litany; conclude with the Nicene Creed, then sing 6 verses of another Psalm. I give out what Psalm I choose to have sung and mention the verse I begin with, and the first line of the verse, leaving the rest to the clerk. After sermon I sing a hymn in the pulpit, and give out the whole myself, making mention of the metre; then pray, and conclude with "Praise God, from whom &c." On Sunday afternoons I go to church at half past one; sing 6 verses of a Psalm after the 2d lesson, and 6 verses more at the end of the prayers; and observe the same method in the pulpit, as in the morning.

---

[1] This is a note left for the Rev. Mr. Mayor, who was substituting for Berridge while he was fulfilling his winter preaching in London. It is just entitled "For the Rev'd. Mr. Mayor." The manuscript is held in the Howard Edward's Collection at The Historical Society of Pennsylvania, Philadelphia (AM.0614 40). At the end of the letter the date of January 1781 is written in another person's hand. The paragraphs are clearly marked in this short note. John Mayor (c.1755–1826) was a Welshman who went up to Oxford in 1774 and graduated on March 4, 1778. Three months afterward he was ordained deacon by the bishop of Oxford and a year later, in September 1779, he was made priest in Westminster. Thus he was still a young man when he was to substitute for Berridge at Everton. Later in 1781 he was appointed by Richard Hill, the patron, to the living of Shawbury, near Shrewsbury, where he remained until he died in 1826. He counted as friends many of the leading Evangelicals of his day, having a particularly close relationship with Thomas Scott, whom he travelled a hundred miles to see in 1782 to consult over his problems concerning baptism.

Our sacraments are monthly, and the sacrament days are marked in the Almanac.[2] During the communion I usually sing a single verse of an hymn, two or three times. You will please to bring home the sacrament collection, and give it to my servant John Penn, to be distributed by me among the poor.

Once a month on a Wednesday I preach at my cathedral in Potton, one mile from Everton, the road always clean: I believe you would be refreshed to preach there yourself. And once a month on a Thursday I preach in a large kitchen, belonging to Mr. Lamm of Biggleswade, five miles from Everton, turnpike road. If you are a stranger to kitchen doctrine, I can assure you, that good Gospel soup may be had there. Whoever steps into my pulpit, to supply for a time, is expected at Potton and Biggleswade. 'Tis looked on as a thing of course; and the carnal neighbours would conclude you were infirm or lazy, if you did refuse. Potton cathedral and Biggleswade kitchen are considered by all people as consolidated with Everton Vicarage.

However, you are wholly left, dear Sir, to your discretion. The Lord abundantly water your own soul, and bless your labours.

---

[2] A calendar with astronomical data.

To Mrs. Hillier[1]

Everton, June 29, 1781

Dear Madam,

What with itinerant preaching, and feebleness of body, when I came home, I have long delayed writing to my London friends. At length being quite ashamed of this neglect, I stayed at home this week, and set it apart for this purpose. Many of the Lord's children are ignorant of their own blessings and under a seeming want of the favour of God, are mourning and refuse to be comforted. But could you mourn for the favour of God, unless his favour had taught you to mourn? If he had not looked upon you in love, you had been as regardless of his favour as other fluttering, slanting[2] damsels in London. But you desire a *sense* of his favour, a communication of his love; and you do well. Now the very desire of a communication of God's love is a proof that you love God; for we do not desire what we hate, but what we love; and you could not love God, unless he had loved you first.

Suppose, you had never felt a direct intimation of God's love by his spirit, yet whilst you are mourning and praying for a sense of this love, Jesus Christ declares you are one of God's blessed ones, for "blessed are they, that mourn."[3] But you have had many intimations of God's favour, conveyed to your heart, under his ordinances; and these are love tokens, bestowed on the children. Do you add, the manifestations were short, though sweet; and were but a crumb. Perhaps so, yet if they were short and sweet, they were *real* indications of love and all manifestations below are short at longest, they are but glimpses of glory; abiding manifestations are reserved for heaven. [But?] why think you meanly of a crumb? One crumb of the heavenly bread is worth more than all the spice or gems of the Indies. Such a crumb

---

1   The manuscript is held in MARC, PLP 8 43.8. It is addressed to "Mrs. Hillier, No. 5 Pancrass Lane, Queen Street, Cheapside, London." See April 10, 1778 and March 31, 1780. Torn parts of the manuscript are indicated by question marks in brackets.
2   Falling away.
3   Matthew 5:4.

is never given to a dog, a wolf, or a goat. Crumbs are the children's table-fare below, and the whole bread reserved for above. The hatred God has given you of sin, with a fervent desire after holiness, a whole reliance on Christ for salvation are a loud and abiding witness of your heavenly birth. And they, who are born from above, shall never die eternally. Come then, my dear Madam, lift up your heart [?].

To John Berridge[1]

Everton, July 21, 1781

Dear John,

I am glad to hear by John Clark,[2] that you are well in health, are sober-minded, and diligent in business. I wish also that your soul may prosper; that you may not only be sober-minded, but heavenly-minded; and whilst you are diligent in business, may be fervent in spirit, serving the Lord. If you hope to dwell with God in heaven, you must have the kingdom of heaven brought down into your bosom. Your heart must be devoted unto God and taught to delight in him as your portion, to trust in him alone, and to worship him in spirit, and in truth. But this you cannot do till you are born again. You must have a heavenly nature given, before you have a heavenly mind. My dear John, the Lord give you this heavenly nature, that you may walk with God here, and dwell with him hereafter. I remain, your affectionate uncle,

John Berridge

---

[1] This letter to his nephew is from *WB* (1838), 413–414, and *WB* (1864), 403. See November 12, 1773; May 30, 1780; and May 24, 1792.
[2] Son of Thomas Clark, an old Nottinghamshire friend, who, with his brother Robert, had land in Great Gransden, a few miles from Everton. See June 9, 1773.

308

To George Gorham[1]

Everton, November 10, 1781

Dear Sir,

Yesterday I returned to Everton, but not so well as I expected, having lost health and strength this present week. I have sent you four razors and a penknife to be set by Mr. Rutter,[2] and left a shilling in his hand for that purpose, when he came to Yelling last Friday sennight. Desire him to take some pains with them and return them to you, when they are done. And I must beg of you to bring them to Yelling, and either Mr. Venn[3] or his son[4] will convey them to me, who have promised, either father or son, to spend one day in a week at Everton, whilst I continue feeble. Present my very kind respects to your father. Grace and peace be with you [and][5] with your affectionate servant,

John Berridge

---

1 George Gorham (1752–1840) of St. Neots attended the services at Everton from childhood. He inherited a large fortune from his father and later went into banking but lost all his money and had to live on the property and income of his wife. In *WB* (1838), 60–65, George Gorham writes a letter of his memories of Berridge, based on Berridge being "intimately known to my family for more than thirty years during the last twenty of which, I also had the pleasure of his acquaintance." His wife and he saw Berridge two days before Berridge's death. He records: "Whilst we took a silent weeping Farewell, having attended his ministry from my childhood, and felt it a blessing to sit under such a minister, I experienced a shock like a surviving son, who loses a beloved Father. I was then forty years of age I loved him as my spiritual Father" (*WB* [1838], 65). In *WB* (1864), xliii, the letter is introduced as a "letter from the late Rev. G.J. Gorham." This mistake probably arises from confusion with his son the Rev. G.C. Gorham (1787–1857). The manuscript is in "The Papers of John Berridge," BER 1/1, Henry Martyn Centre, Westminster College, Cambridge. See November 21, 1781; December 17, 1781; and August 17, 1792.
2 George Rutter (1740–1803) lived in Huntingdon Street, St. Neots, and was a barber and wig-maker.
3 Henry Venn. See January 19, 1771.
4 John Venn. See June 12, 1778.
5 Manuscript is torn.

To George Gorham[1]

Everton, November 21, 1781

The bearer of this is Ellen Raven, my extempore housekeeper. She is come to St. Neots,[2] in hope of meeting with Thomas Pope, of Great Paxton,[3] and receiving an old debt from him. If she fail of meeting him at St. Neots she must travel on to Great Paxton. I sent four razors with a penknife to you by your housekeeper, with a note, desiring you to send them to Rutter, and informing you that I had paid him beforehand. I desired you also to take them to Yelling, and Mr. Venn or his son, who now come to Everton one or other every Monday, would convey them to me. Jacky Venn[4] was with me last Monday, but brought no razors, nor any tidings of them. If the razors abide with you, I beg you will send them by Ellen, which will oblige your affectionate servant,

John Berridge

---

[1] See November 10, 1781. This manuscript is held in HMC, BER 1/2.
[2] A small town four miles north of Everton.
[3] A village just north of St. Neots.
[4] John Venn. See November 10, 1781.

To John Thornton[1]

Dear and honoured Sir,

Your letter, bringing present pay, and plenty of good promises, came safe to hand, for which I do most heartily thank you, and beg of God to enrich you with his heavenly treasures. No fear of your proving a defaulter, but I must take heed lest I make a little Christ of you. The human heart loves a human prop, and is glad to see an earthly supply near at hand. I believe the children often lose a benefactor, because they hoist him up into the place of God. However God will not suffer his children to starve, but as one channel dries up, another is set a running to supply their wants, and teach them to place their whole trust in the living God.

I came from Yelling[2] not much improved in my health, but greatly delighted with their family worship, and with the gracious behaviour of the whole family. Truly it seems a little household of faith. Nelly[3] is quick and smart, and appears to advantage in company; but Jenny[4] is the most solid, and has the best abilities. She visits all the sick in the parish, makes up their medicines, delights in the work, and would make a good parson's wife. Her health is but indifferent, yet she does not seem to quarrel with the Lord on that account. Kitty[5] had a wonderful breathing of the Holy Ghost upon her three or four years ago, which continued for many months. A spirit of prayer was given in rich abundance with divine consolations, and her heart seemed wholly taken up with God. I hope this has left such a relish for divine things as will never be lost. Jacky[6] is the top branch of the tree, highest and humblest. His abilities seem equal to anything he undertakes, and

---

[1] The letter is from *WB* (1838), 414–416, and *WB* (1864), 403–404.

[2] The home of the Venns, a few miles from Everton. For a history of the Venns' children, see John Venn, *Annals,* 108–111.

[3] Eling Venn (1758–1843), eldest daughter of the Venns. See August 2, 1792.

[4] Jane Venn (1760–1852).

[5] Catherine Venn (1765–1818).

[6] John Venn (1769–1813). See June 12, 1778.

his modesty is pleasing to all that behold him. He has daily hours of retirement for waiting secretly on his God, as have his sisters, father, and mother; and he is so recollected in his talk, that I seldom hear him speak a trifling thing. His behaviour in college has turned the hearts of the Master and Fellows entirely to him, who were very averse, and even injurious for a season, on account of his being the son of a Methodist clergyman.[7] There seems not a doubt but he will be elected Fellow next Easter[8]; yet no profit will accrue to him from his Fellowship until he is Master of Arts, which will be two years after he is chosen. He talks of taking Deacon's orders next Trinity Sunday.[9] The Lord surely delights in that Yelling family to bless it; for grace reigns and triumphs over parents, children, and servants.

I feel something within which haunts me daily, and troubles me. It is an eager desire since my fever was removed of growing well presently, and of mounting my pulpit out of hand; but the Lord fits me accordingly, by sending frequent colds, which throw me back again. I have no prospect of a thorough recovery until spring; yet if two or three cheerful days come, I am expecting wings to fly abroad. Oh, for that blessed world, where every will is melted down completely into God's will, and God becomes their all in all. The Lord shine upon your heart daily, and refresh you with his mercy, and make all your children monuments of Jesus' grace. I remain, dear Sir, your much obliged and affectionate servant,

John Berridge

---

[7]   Henry Venn (1724–1797). See June 8, 1771.

[8]   Although Venn had a poor showing in his examinations the Master of Sidney Sussex College had encouraged him in his hope of a fellowship, and he had stayed on another year in college. During this time he was treated by the fellows as one of themselves. A quarrel between the college tutor and a friend of Venn ended his hope of a fellowship. See Hennell, *John Venn*, 58.

[9]   The Sunday after Whit Sunday. John Venn was not ordained deacon until September 22, 1782, by Thomas Thurlow, bishop of Lincoln, at the bishop's residence at Buckden.

TO MRS. JOHN THORNTON[1]

November 24, 1781

Dear honourable Madam,

You have a peculiar art and I trust a peculiar delight in surprising me with kindness. I no more expected to receive a basket of physic from Clapham, without any application made for it, than from the court of St. James.[2] Liberal souls experience the truth of Christ's assertion "'Tis more blessed to give, than to receive,"[3] while the selfish heart remains a stranger to this blessing, unable to taste the refined pleasure of it. But when the heart is cheerfully stirred up to good works, without any saucy claim of merit, and with a single eye to glorify God, we shall do well to remember "It is God, that worketh in us, both to will and to do."[4] The verb is in the present time, worketh, or is working; intimating thereby that of ourselves, we are nothing, as Paul declares of himself[5]; and that if let to ourselves, should have neither will nor power. If then we find a readiness to hear, to read, to pray, and do good works, God is working that readiness in us, enabling us to will and do; and the whole of our will and power must every moment be ascribed to the working of his Spirit and of course to the praise of his grace.

I am now for a time come back from the borders of an eternal world. Oh, the vast difference between thinking and preaching of

---

[1] The manuscript is found in PLFELM, GD26/13/710. The letter is addressed to "Mrs. John Thornton, Clapham, London." Written to Mrs. Lucy Thornton (1722–1785), wife of John Thornton. See May 3, 1773 and November 15, 1785. The explanation of the two separate letters written on the same day to John and Lucy Thornton may be that while Berridge wrote to Lucy at their home address he wrote to John at his business address in Lothbury Street, London. See February 22, 1785.

[2] The court of the sovereign named after St. James's Palace, where even today diplomats are formally received.

[3] Acts 20:35.

[4] Philippians 2:13.

[5] 2 Corinthians 12:11.

this border, and a new approach to it by sickness. I felt the solemnity of the border but without the terror. The Lord in great mercy (no thanks to me) so upheld my faith, though without any joy, as to keep my heart from shrinking. But I hope the solemnity will never wear off, and I feel the Lord has quickened my soul by this fatherly chastisement. May this quickening continue to increase, till I am conveyed beyond the reach of an evil heart, an evil world, and the evil one.

When the Lord laid me on a sick bed, he showed me in what a slovenly manner I had walked with him, pacing through a round of duties, and between each duty, suffering my heart to ramble into the world and round the world, till another season of duty returned. This was not looking and [waiting?] for the coming of the Son of God. [Nor?] was it running the Christian race looking continually unto Jesus.[6] In short, I did not follow on earnestly to know the Lord, but was too much content with present attainments such as they were; and this brought a rod on my back. Our fallen nature does not love dependence, at least not continual dependence, and believers, unless prayerful and watchful, are ready to walk with God by halves and quarters.

Many thanks for the physic and all favours. The Lord fill you with spiritual wisdom and multiply his grace upon you, and may the dew of his blessing descend upon all your branches. I am, Madam, your respectful and affectionate servant,

John Berridge

---

6   Hebrews 12:1–2.

To George Gorham[1]

Everton, December 17, 1781

Dear Sir,

Ellen Raven, my present house-helper will need two guineas quickly to pay her rent, and desires to know when or how she may receive that sum from Mr. Pope. A month ago and he promised to pay it in a fortnight's time. If you could speak to Mr. Pope on Thursday, perhaps she might receive some information, and that information might be brought to Everton by means of Mr. Raymond, or some market-people. My hearty respects to your Father.[2] Grace and peace be with you both, and with your affect[ionate] servant in the best bond,

John Berridge

P.S. I have thoughts of going to London on the third of January. The Lord be my guide and guard.

---

[1] The manuscript held in HMC, BER 1/3. See November 10, 1781, for the background to this letter.
[2] Stephen Gorham (1721–1789).

To Lady Huntingdon[1]

February 1782

...I am persuaded your Ladyship will rejoice that dear Rowley[2] is going, with the Lord's help, to erect a standard for the Gospel in the very middle of the devil's territories in London. What a bellowing and clamour the old enemy will make at this fresh invasion of his kingdom! But he may storm, and rage, and persecute—Christ's cause must, and will prevail over every opposition men or devils can raise. A meeting has been held, and I am told the place fixed upon is one of the worst spots in London[3]—the very paradise of devils. This much is satisfactory. Fine soil for ploughing and sowing! By and by, my Lady, we shall hear of the reaping time—the harvest—and the harvest home! How glorious will be the triumphs of the Gospel in that place! Some of the blessed fruits we may expect to meet in our Father's kingdom above. I am now looking every day to hear that the foundation stone has been laid, and the King of Zion consecrating the spot by the conversion of souls to himself. I need not remind your dear Ladyship to pour forth a volley of prayers for the success of this sanctuary....

---

[1] The first meeting to consider the building of what became known as Surrey Chapel took place at the Castle and Falcon tavern in Aldersgate Street on February 4, 1782. This is an extract from the letter. It is found in Seymour, *Life of Huntingdon,* 2:320. The work at Surrey Chapel was led by Berridge's old friend Rowland Hill, and Berridge, in London at the time because of his winter preaching, sent a report to Lady Huntingdon. Although Rowland Hill was no longer allowed to preach in her chapels, and this was the chief reason for seeking to establish a work himself, Lady Huntingdon approved of the erection of Surrey Chapel, and gave a liberal subscription. The first stone was laid on June 24, 1782.

[2] Rowland Hill. See December 18, 1764.

[3] It was built in a neglected part of Southwark.

To John Newton[1]

Everton, April 13, 1782

Dear Brother,

Accept my hearty thanks for your preface,[2] which is judicious, like all your other works, for which I greatly esteem them. Your productions, and Dr. Owen's[3] are always new to me, I can read them again and again with fresh pleasure and profit. Your sense is never withdrawn; your thoughts are your own, and your language not crippled with feeble epithets, nor encumbered with superfluous ones. But why need I tell you what you know, and what others know and acknowledge as well as myself; only there is a pleasure in telling a friend we esteem, how much we esteem him. I think your preface should be prefixed to the second edition, which is likely to be called for soon. Your name, though ranked among Methodists, is not very unsavoury, and your preface would recommend itself.

Mr. Cowper's Hymns, though poetical, did not raise expectation of such poetic vein, as his book discovers. I was amazed as well as charmed, as I read along; and think him the nation's Poet Laureate, though not

---

[1] The manuscript is held at LPL, MS 3972 ff.21–22. Published in *WB* (1838), 416–417, and *WB* (1864), 405–406.

[2] William Cowper had just published his first book, *Poems* (1782), which included his didactic poems examining the moral fabric of society: "Table Talk," "The Progress of Error," "Truth," "Expostulation," "Hope," "Charity," "Conversation," and "Retirement." Newton had written a preface, which he had sent to Berridge for his evaluation. The preface was included in a later edition. For a critical evaluation, see chapter 3, "The Moral Satires and *Retirement*," in Vincent Newey, *Cowper's Poetry: A Critical Study and Reassessment* (Liverpool: Liverpool University Press, 1982).

[3] John Owen (1616–1683), leading Reformed theologian and Nonconformist, whose books are still in print. He was prominent in the foundation of Cromwell's State Church, became Vice-Chancellor of Oxford University and helped compose the Savoy Declaration of Faith. For many years after the Restoration he was an acknowledged leader of Nonconformity. For a modern introduction to Owen, see Carl R. Trueman, *The Claims of Truth: John Owen's Trinitarian Theology* (Carlisle: Paternoster, 1998).

the King's. There is more sweet and wholesome sack[4] in his verse, than in Whitehead's,[5] my former fellow collegian. He is very happy in his descriptions and peculiarly excellent in the choice of his epithets. Perhaps a grain of insanity, not discoverable in the verse, has helped his muse, by giving her a loftier wing, a more luxuriant fancy, than she could have had without it. Do I find nothing to blame? Yes, but as a lover and a friend. His ear is not so fine as his fancy. Many of the lines are not readable, neither prose nor verse, and break old teeth inhumanly. His meaning frequently lies out of present sight, and then as much circumspection is needful to unfold him, as to develop a crabbed classic,[6] or unkennel a Hebrew root.[7] I think he makes too free use of the word "fool." It suits the petulant tongue of pride, but not the humble lips of a Christian; and poetry cannot authorize what Scripture reproves.[8] The last thing I would mention is a typographical fault, running more or less through the whole book, which should be remedied in the next edition. The comma is often left out in passive verbs or participles, which makes the line a syllable too long. Thus, in the fourth page, line 18, you read, "How seldom used," instead of "how seldom us'd." So in page the sixth, line 12, you read, "Indeed? replied the Don," instead of, "Indeed? reply'd." This matter will require some care in the corrector. In page 280, line 1, is a double fault; point it thus, "As he that slumbers in pavilions, grac'd," &c.

What need bedaubing the Chancellor[9] with eulogium, unless a sinecure is wanted? In page 280, universal censure is cast on all squires

---

4   A white wine from Spain.
5   William Whitehead (1715–1785), poet and playwright. Both Berridge and Whitehead were elected fellows at Clare College in 1742. Whitehead became Poet Laureate in 1757 after Thomas Gray (1716–1771) had declined the post. His *Plays and Poems* was published in two volumes in 1774. See Kenneth Hopkins, "William Whitehead," in his book *The Poets Laureate* (Bodley Head, 1954), 79–91.
6   To give the meaning of an intricate piece of Latin or Greek.
7   To trace a Hebrew word back to its root.
8   Matthew 5:22.
9   Berridge is referring to the poem "On the Promotion of Edward Thurlow, Esq. to the Lord High Chancellorship of England." Berridge is suggesting Cowper is praising the chancellor unnecessarily unless he is looking for some monetary support. It contains such verses as "Discernment, eloquence, and grace, Proclaim him born to sway The balance in the highest place, And bear the palm away." Edward Thurlow (1731–1806) was Lord Chancellor from 1778 to 1783 and Cowper had previously had a close relationship with him when both were clerks in the same solicitor's office. Cowper thought that Thurlow had said that if he ever became Lord Chancellor he would remember him. See note, Letter to

and parsons.[10] Is it liberal, or Christianly? And a great statesman is made to pass his time altogether with a mechanic[11] and a hobby.[12] Is this at all likely? But you say I am become a mere wasp. So it seems, but without a sting.

When I first looked on your frank, it appeared to me a desirable thing, that all senators who could not learn to speak, should yet be taught to write; and that a master, with a handsome stipend, be appointed to instruct all those who cannot make a legible scrawl. I suppose your franker, by his characters, must be a Chinese.[13] Present my very kind respects to Mrs. Newton, and remember me to Sally.[14] Much grace and sweet peace be with you all; and the Lord water your pulpit and parlour discourses. Yours very affectionately,

John Berridge

Joseph Hill, February 20, 1783, in Thomas Wright, *The Correspondence of William Cowper*, 4 vols. (Hodder and Stoughton, 2004), 2:47. Also see Ella, *Cowper*, 326–328, for Cowper's failed attempt to re-establish his relationship by sending him his poems.

10 "Retirement," ll. 437–440: "He chooses company, but not the squire's, Whose wit is rudeness, whose good breeding tires; Nor yet the parson's, who would gladly come, Obsequious when abroad, though proud at home."

11 Manual worker. See "Retirement," ll. 449.

12 A buffoon.

13 The letter was franked—signed by the sender—to ensure it was sent free of charge to the receiver. Obviously Newton or the person giving the authorization had difficult handwriting.

14 Sally Johnson, the Newtons' maid. There are seven letters to Sally in Newton's *Cardiphonia*.

To John Newton[1]

Everton, September 17, 1782

My dear Sir,

Your kind letter refreshed my spirit once and again, and may refresh me still more when it has received an answer; but for the last month I durst not peep into it for fear of the date, so disdainful it looked for want of an answer. During my latter years I have been continually making apologies for slack returns to my corresponding friends, and am not one jot better yet. No one can be ashamed more, or grieved more, or repent more, or resolve more, than I have done, yet no reformation ensues. My heavy constitution weighs down shame, and grief, and repentance, and buries all resolution. Indeed, I am now sinking into the dregs of life, just able to preach once in a week, and for two or three days after preaching my mind seems so weakened, and my thoughts so scattered, I scarce know how or where to pick them up. My outward case, the soul's coffin, is well to look at, only rather too portly; and my health is better than usual in the summer, but my strength is soon exhausted by preaching, and my breast complains long afterwards.

I have now a curate,[2] but not an assistant; a good man, I hope, but without a mouth. He can neither preach without notes, nor read handsomely with notes. So my congregation is crumbling away, and Everton Church is transporting to Gamlingay Meeting[3]; however, we

---

1   The manuscript is held at LPL, MS 3972 f.23. It was published in *WB* (1838), 418–419, and *WB* (1864), 407–408.

2   Richard Whittingham (1785–1845) was licensed curate at Everton on September 5, 1782 (see September 24, 1782: "until following Easter"), having been made a deacon the previous day in Temple Church, London (Clergy Database). See October 3, 1783. It seems that these lines were possibly an embarrassment to Whittingham, who edited them out of *WB*.

3   The Baptist fellowship at Gamlingay, which dated from 1652, became a formal church in 1710 when it separated from the Bedford congregation. At the time of this letter there was no fixed pastor, and membership may have thinned after the village suffered a terrible epidemic of smallpox in 1777. See Garwood

shall keep the Bells and Steeple, I suppose. Decaying ministers must expect decaying churches for lively curates are not readily found, at least not at Everton, a Church of ill fame. Such medicinal draughts though not toothsome,[4] may prove wholesome; and if Christ must increase, we must decrease; but we are somewhat awkward in learning the art of sinking. Longinus περι υψος suits the old man far better than Christus περι βαθος.[5]

I read your letter to Mr. Venn,[6] who seemed to be affected with it, and has returned an answer, I hope, to your content. His son,[7] a very gracious youth, has gone to Buckden for orders,[8] and prays earnestly for the Lord's unction along with the Bishop's hands on Sunday next. He seems intended for a polished shaft, and has been much in the furnace of late, a good school for Christian experience. Mr. Simeon,[9] a young Fellow of King's College, in Cambridge, has just made his appearance in the Christian hemisphere, and attracts much notice. He preaches at a church in the town, which is crowded like a theatre

---

S. Tydeman, *A Brief History of Gamlingay Old Meeting Baptist Church* (1981) and Roy Gibbons, *The Tale of a Village Chapel: A Brief History of Gamlingay Baptist Church, 1652–2009* (2009).

4 Delicious and appetizing.

5 The Greek is literally "around the heights" in comparison with "around the depths." Longinus, an unknown author who probably lived in the first century A.D., wrote a treatise on aesthetics and literary criticism, *On the Sublime* (περὶ ὕψους), which promoted an elevated style both in writing and thought. Berridge is saying that everything going well suits the old nature but, with the new nature, it is possible to live with Christ in the difficulties and troubles of life.

6 Henry Venn at Yelling. See June 8, 1771.

7 John Venn was ordained deacon a few days after this letter, and the following day became curate at Yelling. See November 24, 1781.

8 See November 24, 1781.

9 Charles Simeon (1759–1836) was appointed vicar of Holy Trinity in Cambridge in 1782, where he remained until his death. He became the leader of the Evangelical movement in the Church of England by firmly establishing Evangelicalism within the establishment, influencing and training students at Cambridge, giving impetus to the missionary movement, promoting ordered and relevant preaching, and forming Evangelical patronage trusts as a solution to the secession issue. He became strongly committed to order and obedience to the canons and thus opposed itineration. Berridge encouraged him to preach irregularly, but this was stopped by Henry Venn. See Spring 1785 and the letter to Thornton on July 2, 1785, where Berridge refers to Simeon's feet being "often put in the stocks by the Archdeacon of Yelling." Simeon preached at Berridge's funeral.

on the first night of a new play. A gospel curate is also sprung up at Royston, a market town, ten miles south-east of Everton. Thus Christ is opening many doors to spread his gospel. May he open many hearts to receive it.

I did not expect a reply from Mr. Cooper,[10] but came off as well as I could expect. It is beneath a good poet to heed the vituperation of a crazy old Vicar. My strictures will not harm him; I wish his muse may hurt him no more.[11] Poetic fame is a sweet morsel for the mind to feed upon, and will try to beguile his heart into idolatry. Indeed, the muses[12] are all wanton girls, with meretricious[13] heart, and quickly draw Helicon[14] hunters into their embraces.

I have no doubt of your skill to form a plan for an academy[15]; but where will you dig up academical tutors, and how will you create academical patrons to support the work? You need not only a pencil to design, but the philosopher's stone[16] to make money, with good store also of *lignum vitae*[17] for academical blocks; and neither the stone nor the wood are readily found. Your eye is fixed, I perceive, upon a fine bull,[18] but how will you pair him, except with wild bullocks?

After two years of insanity,[19] my housemaid is perfectly restored, better in health now than ever, and thus enabled to do her work with

---

[10] Manuscript has "Cooper." See April 13, 1782.

[11] Referring to Cowper's mental illness.

[12] In Greek mythology the Muses were the nine daughters of Zeus and Mnemosyne who were associated with the arts and sciences.

[13] Alluring by a false or empty show. Unreal.

[14] The mountain sacred to the Muses.

[15] Because Nonconformists were excluded from the universities they established their own institutions of higher education. They were often linked with a prominent minister and were used to train ministers. Newton wrote out his ideas for an academy in May 14, 1782, but they were not printed until 1784 under the title *A Plan of Academical Preparation for the Ministry, in a Letter to a Friend.* The plan covered the topics of choice of place, choice of tutor, choice of pupils, and choice of studies.

[16] The hypothetical substance, which, according to alchemists, would convert all base metals into gold.

[17] Literally "living wood," i.e., spiritual and stimulating tutors, by whom the students are moulded.

[18] William Bull (1738–1814), pastor of the Independent Chapel at Newport Pagnell and a friend of Newton, Cowper and Thornton. A college was opened at Newport Pagnell in the following year. See Bull, *Memorials of Bull.*

[19] See October 20, 1780.

ease. The Lord be praised for this mercy. Church-work goes on heavily here. Many of the old sheep are called home, and few lambs drop into the fold. The wealthier sort seem to be growing downward into the earth, and find solid gold a more tempting idol than poetic fame. Sometimes I am ready to be offended at them, but this is stifled by finding more cause to be offended with myself.

I hope this will find Mrs. Newton, your dear other self, perfectly recovered. The Lord continue her life for your comfort, and your health for the church's profit. Many blessings of every kind attend you both. Give my love to Mr. Foster,[20] when you see him. Yours very affectionately,

John Berridge

---

[20] Henry Foster (1745–1814). See April 11, 1775.

To Benjamin Mills[1]

Everton, September 24, 1782

Dear Sir,

Your kind letter, with the enclosed, came safe to hand, for which I return you my hearty thanks; and yesterday bought a great coat for one that needed it much. Your letter not only brought seasonable advice, but made a seasonable purchase; and the Devonshire Plane[2] will keep the wearer's back warm for some years.

Many merchants, though with a mercantile genius, are not apprised of the best way of traffic. They can venture their substance on a ship's bottom, but dare not cast it on the waters: whereas the waters surely bring back what is cast upon them[3]; whilst a ship's bottom, like the *Royal George*,[4] oft goes to the bottom. But the Lord has taught you the Christian art of improving your substance, and bringing a blessing upon it. Many professors, with a rich head, are so poor in faith, and of course so poor-spirited, they dare not trust the Lord with any of their cash, except it be copper, and that coined at Birmingham. Twenty charity sermons, delivered by the best begging mouth, could not induce them to take the Lord's paper for even ten pounds, paid into his bank. Is it not shameful, that the London Bank, or even a

---

[1]   This letter was printed in *CM* (1845), 273. It is addressed to "Mr. Benjamin Mills, No. 15 Middle Moorfields, London." Benjamin Mills was presumably a merchant who was involved in the work of Whitefield's chapels. He was or later became a trustee. In his farewell sermon at the Tabernacle in 1792, Berridge makes a reference to Mills's recent death: "And one of the trustees has lately been removed from them (note Mr. Mills), the Lord direct them in the choice of another" (*Last Farewell Sermon*, 33). For other letters, see October 3, 1783; November 20, 1784; November 4, 1785; November 1, 1786; October 9, 1788; and November 23, 1790.

[2]   Devon wool fleece was excellent for woven fabrics because of its fineness.

[3]   Ecclesiastes 11:1.

[4]   The *Royal George* was the flagship of Admiral Kempenfelt. It had sunk suddenly in the harbour at Portsmouth a few weeks before on August 29, 1782, with the loss of 800 lives.

private bank, should have more credit than the Lord's bank, and this among Christians and believers, too, as they are called? Is it not ominous that the *Royal George* should sink, and cannot be buoyed up?

My church at present is in a decline, and seems consumptive. Mr. Hicks[5] supplied my church from September last till the following Easter; and fairly drove away half my congregation. My present curate is a stop-gap, but no assistant.[6] He cannot preach without notes, nor read handsomely with notes; so my hearers are dwindling away, and transporting from Everton Church to Gamgay Meeting....[7]

I am sorry to hear that Mr. H__ [8] is busy, as you call it. I suppose in collecting money for the chapel. It is a beggarly business, indeed: and he has been too engaged in that business of late years. If he had prudence or compassion he would do otherwise: but poor Job and Lot are anyone's plunder.[9] All people who meet rigging,[10] think they may successfully unrig the two sisters for their purpose, and care not if they strip them naked....[11] I am glad Margate has helped your little wife.[12] She is a favourite of mine, and give my love to her, but do not be jealous. The Lord bless and keep you both, and embrace your children in the arms of covenant mercy. My love to the trustees, the preacher, and the doctor. Your much obliged and affectionate servant,

John Berridge

---

5   Samuel Hicks, vicar of Wrestlingworth. See July 16, 1759.
6   See September 17, 1782.
7   See September 17, 1782.
8   This could be Charles Hardy, one of the trustees of the Whitefield's chapels as well as Whitefield's executor.
9   Job and Lot lost their possessions.
10 Equipping a vessel with the necessary ropes, chains, stays, etc.
11 I think this is a reference to Ezekiel 23 and the symbolic sisters Oholah and Oholibah, who lost all and were left naked and bare. Is Berridge arguing that in equipping one cause other causes naturally suffer?
12 See May 3, 1773.

To John Thornton[1]

Tabernacle, January 23, 1783

Dear and honoured Sir,

Your kind letter I received, including a ten-pound note on the poor's behalf, for which I thank you heartily, and the Lord will requite you. Blessed are they that sow beside all waters.[2] As you keep abounding in good works, may you also grow rich in faith and abound in sweet humility, feeling yourself nothing, and living as a pauper daily on heavenly alms. The longer I live, the more need I see of the apostle's advice, to pray *always* with *all* prayer,[3] not only the congregational and social, but riding prayer, walking prayer, reading prayer, writing prayer, in short prayer of every posture and exercise. We lose many a good bite and sup for want of asking, and often starve in the midst of plenty.

I have been laid up with a fever and sore throat since Sunday, and was not able to preach at Tabernacle last night. My place was supplied by Mr. Bull,[4] an able minister. The chapel was full, and the congregation seemed at first dissatisfied with his whining prayer (a tone more familiar to our dissenting brethren formerly than now), but his sermon was noble and bold, and the people were so agreeably disappointed, they thought no more of old Everton, but begged he might preach again next Wednesday, which was granted. I should have returned an answer yesterday, but was not able to read or write. Today, through mercy, I am much better. Starvation, and a few grains of James's fever powder,[5]

---

1   This letter was written from the Tabernacle, where Berridge was engaged in his winter preaching. It is taken from *GM* (1838), 71; *WB* (1838), 420–421; and *WB* (1864), 409–410.

2   Isaiah 32:20.

3   Ephesians 6:18.

4   William Bull (1738–1814). See September 17, 1782. This was Bull's first sermon at the Tabernacle. He afterwards often preached there when he was in London and from 1799 undertook to preach for two months of the year at the Tabernacle and Tottenham Court Road Chapels.

5   A popular medicine for treating fever that was prepared by Dr. Robert James (1703–1776). Roy Porter says it was "the Georgian equivalent of aspirin"

through the Lord's blessing, are restoring me. How wonderfully God is bringing his gospel into the establishment, and what sweet humility appears in newly enlightened souls. I am glad Mr. Henry Thornton's[6] election does not make him think it needful to keep a carriage or a town house. I wish him God's election, and a comfortable assurance of it. My hearty respects wait on Mrs. Thornton; the Lord repair her animal frame, and continue her your companion for life. That blessings of every kind may richly descend upon yourself and family, is the prayer of your affectionate and dutiful servant,

John Berridge

P.S. I purpose to wait upon you at Clapham, on some Sunday, at the end of March.

(*Disease, Medicine and Society in England, 1550–1860* [Macmillan, 1987], 29).
6   Henry Thornton (1760–1815), son of John Thornton. He had just been elected MP for Southwark, a position he held until his death. Thornton's humility is an evidence of his enlightenment/conversion according to Berridge. This comment perhaps explains the references to "your Joseph" in November 17, 1784. However, Standish Meacham says: "unlike many of his friends, Henry Thornton underwent no sudden conversion to Evangelicalism" (*Henry Thornton of Clapham, 1760–1815* [Cambridge: Harvard University Press, 1964], 14).

To Stephen Gorham and Co., St. Neots[1]

Everton, September 12, 1783

Dear Sir,

John Clark[2] has now sold most of his Gransden Farm[3] to Mr. King of Waresley,[4] and the money will be paid ten days after Michaelmas.[5] If you will then take my 720 pounds, at 4½ per cent, on a joint bond of yourself and son, and keep it in your hands till my decease you will do me a favour, by taking worldly matters out of my hand.[6] I shall expect to see you on Sunday, that I may know your mind; and may have leisure to look out elsewhere in case my proposal does not suit you. With kind Christian love to your son and daughter and wishing grace and peace I remain your affectionate servant,

John Berridge

John Clark is the bearer of this, and is travelling homewards. Give him a cup of your nappy[7] and a brown crust to quicken his pace.[8]

---

[1] Stephen Gorham (1721–1789) had started the Duck Lane brickworks at St. Neots, and when he died he left a fortune of £30,000 to his only surviving son, George James Gorham (see November 10, 1781). He lived at 22 Market Place, St. Neots. For a history of the Gorhams, see C.F. Tebbutt, *St. Neots: The History of a Huntingdonshire Town* (Phillimore, 1978), 194–195. The manuscript is held in HMC, BER 1/4.

[2] See June 9, 1773.

[3] Great Gransden is about five miles north-east of Everton.

[4] A village three miles north-east of Everton.

[5] September 29 was the Festival of St. Michael and All Angels, and one of the quarter days when rents were paid.

[6] This seems to be part of the family inheritance that had been invested in the Clarks' farm at West Leake, Nottinghamshire.

[7] A kind of strong beer.

[8] This sentence is by the side of the address.

To Benjamin Mills[1]

Everton, October 3, 1783

Dear Sir,

Your kind letter is received with an inclosed note for the poor sufferers at Potton. A haystack, which had long been smoking and neglected, at length threw up large flakes of fire into the air, and these being drove and scattered by the wind, set half the town on fire in twenty minutes. Whatever the fire reached it consumed; and the mischief was done in four hours. If during that time the wind had shifted from north to south-east, the whole town had been fired. The best part of the town, I mean, the best houses are burnt; and the poor have suffered, but not in such numbers as the rich. Professors have fared the best, but not wholly escaped. Much of the market-place is burnt, with the two great inns, and the large street leading from the church into the market. Mr. John Raymond's house, with his woolhouse, barns, stables, and grain, and two thousand pounds worth of wool, just laid in, are all consumed. He computes his loss at five thousand pounds, and says he is still worth twenty thousand, but is so dejected, and his health so impaired by this loss, that his life seems in great danger.[2] Livelong's house, woolhouse, and buildings are also consumed, but

---

1   The letter is from *WB* (1864), 430–431. See November 20, 1784; November 4, 1785; November 1, 1786; October 9, 1788; and November 23, 1790. Mills, a shopkeeper in Moorfields, had sent a gift for those who suffered in the fire that had occurred at Potton on Thursday, August 14. More than a hundred houses were burned down, which may have represented a little under half the town. On August 18, 1783, the *London Chronicle* reported: "On Thursday afternoon a fire broke out in a yard adjoining the house of Mr. Edwards, baker in King Street, Potton, Bedfordshire, occasioned by a small haystack taking fire, which continued burning with unremitting fury till Friday afternoon, the rapidity of the flames being so great that many horses and other cattle perished, though happily, no human lives were lost." Potton History Society produced a report, *The Great Fire of Potton, 1783*, compiled by Peter Ibbett (1983), collecting all the details on the path of the fire, the losses, and the collections and distributions of monies.
2   He died one week after this letter. In the accounts his losses were estimated at more than £5,000. See Ibbett, *Great Fire of Potton*, 7, 39.

part of his stock is insured.[3] John Keeling[4] has escaped. John Miller's house and workshop are consumed.[5] He has suffered more than any of the professors, but is not offensive now to the carnal world, and will be well considered in the general contribution; however, at your desire, I shall send him two guineas. He names himself Elijah, and calls all other ministers Baal's prophets[6]; yet since the fire, has had the vanity to beg of me to recommend him as a preacher to the Tabernacle. He now openly declares that Jesus Christ is no more God, than Paul was, which has this good effect, that it keeps the good people at Potton from hearing him altogether. Indeed he is grown very lofty and censorious, and I wish his late calamity may be sanctified.

The furniture of my curate's[7] house had cost £300, which was all consumed; and no linen saved but what was on their backs, so rapid

---

[3] Mr. John Livelong's reported losses were £1,300 but his name does not appear in the distribution (Ibbett, *Great Fire of Potton*, 33, 35).

[4] One of the early converts in 1759, who is reported in Wesley's *Journal* as one of those who experienced a paroxysm. After Berridge's death he became a founder member of Potton Baptist Church in 1800. See Stan Evers, *Potton's Baptists: The Lord's Faithfulness to a Faithful People* (Potton: 2005).

[5] A John Miller—a carpenter—appears in the accounts as having losses of £74, for which he received £55 11s 6p in the distribution. John Miller, along with seven others, registered the barn of a widow Martha Miller in December 1789, "being desirous of worshipping God according to the rules of his written word, and the dictates of our own Consciences" (Edwin Welch, ed., *Chapels and Meeting Houses: Official Registration, 1672–1901* [Bedford: BHRS, 1996], 75:134).

[6] 1 Kings 18.

[7] Richard Whittingham joined Berridge in April 1782 (see September 24, 1782). Nearly all the banns and marriages are penned with his signature until 1790, when they are shared with John Elard until Berridge's death. In 1807 Whittingham became vicar at nearby Potton until his death. He was born at Minshull Vernon in the parish of Middlewich, Cheshire, the son of Samuel and Hannah Whittingham. He was responsible for *The Works of the Rev. John Berridge* (1838). His estimated losses in the fire were £236 15s 6p, of which he received £50 in the distribution (Ibbett, *Great Fire of Potton*, 38). In the letter of December 30, 1788, Berridge speaks of Whittingham getting a living of his own, and in Whittingham's account of Berridge in *EM* (1793), 19, he refers to himself as "a clergyman who resides near Everton." He does, however, seem to have continued to act as Berridge's curate and continued as curate under the new vicar until his appointment at Potton. In 1799 Thomas Oxenham complained of his having stopped preaching outside the parish church at the request of the new vicar and having stopped praying extemporary prayers in order to please his squire. See *Fruits of the Bedfordshire Union: a letter to the Rev. R. Whittingham curate to the late Rev. John Berridge of Everton, in Bedfordshire*

was the fire. I was forced to take them in, and a mournful sight it was to see them come in the evening, the husband with a cradle, the wife with a young child, and the maid with an infant in her arms.[8] Through mercy a house was provided for them at Gamlingay in a fortnight's time. My feverish complaint is much removed, but my head and breast are but indifferent; however I have been just enabled to preach once a Sunday through the summer.

My kind Christian love to your partner, peace and protection be with you both, and grace with your children. I remain your much indebted and thankful servant,

John Berridge

P.S. Why did you put A.M. on the back of your letter? It makes me seem a coxcomb,[9] got into my dotage.

(1799), 37, 38. His portrait by Richard James Lane is in the National Portrait Gallery (NPG D22520).

[8] Mary Whittingham, née Mary Gaussen (1764–1831), was born to parents of Huguenot origin, and her mother was the sister of the renowned Methodist evangelist Mary Bosanquet-Fletcher (1739–1815). Marianne was the young child (d. June 6, 1862, aged eighty-one) and Samuel was the babe (1783–1874). Two servants are mentioned in the distribution, Ann Careless and Mary Manton.

[9] A cockscomb resembled a jester's cap, and thus a conceited showy person.

To John Thornton[1]

Everton, October 1, 1784

Dear and honoured Sir,

Mr. Astell[2] has just paid us a transient visit, and acquaints me that you are returned from your episcopal visitation of the seaports, and that Lady Balgonie[3] is gone to Scotland. It proved a sad rainy day, I hear, when she set out, not a single dry eye in the family, nor in several of the neighbours'. A comely farewell indeed, discovering the love and esteem she had won. Her marriage is somewhat like Rebecca's,[4] only the groom and not the steward, comes to fetch her from her native soil. May she find an Isaac, a kind and faithful partner in her Lord Balgonie. I suppose you felt a pang at parting, and did not know how much you loved until you took your leave; and though a bustle of business oft diverts your thoughts, your heart will miss your daughter long. But I must sympathize with Mrs. Thornton, who in parting with an amiable daughter, has lost her only female companion, and at a time of life when she may want her converse most. At present you can expect but little of Mrs. Thornton's company, for though abiding at Clapham, she will be taking aerial thoughts to Scotland, and spend many a part of a sweet day there; and her winged imagination will outstrip the balloons in speediness of passage.

Our widow[5] has now got what she long wanted, a governor who will not tamely put the reins into her hand, and suffer her Phaeton-

---

1   This letter is taken from *WB* (1838), 422–424, and *WB* (1864), 411–413.
2   William Thornton Astell. See July 27, 1779.
3   Thornton's daughter Jane (1757–1818) was married on August 11, 1784, to Lord Balgonie, Alexander Leslie-Melville, Seventh Earl of Leven and Sixth Earl of Melville (1749–1820).
4   Abraham sent his servant to acquire a wife for Isaac from his relatives in his own country. Genesis 24.
5   Mrs. Hannah Astell (d.1807) was the widow of Richard Astell (1718–1777), late squire of Everton, whom she married as his second wife in 1770. On August 2, 1784 she married Thomas Pownell (1722–1805), who had been Vice Admiral of Massachusetts and South Carolina and Lieutenant Governor of New Jersey and was now MP for Minehead. Thus the reference to Boston in New England.

like,[6] to set the parish on fire. He seems a sensible good-natured man, and will prove a quiet neighbour, I hope, for I love peace. Gospel doctrines are not offensive to him; he has learnt their chime at Boston, and hitherto attends the whole service of the church patiently when he comes; but madam kicks hard still, and steps out, as usual, before the sermon begins, leaving him alone in the gallery. This occasions some staring, and much speculation; and people whisper, "Hannah is not conquered yet." She left Everton with great reluctance after much procrastination, and is such a knotty piece, I shall not wonder if she does recoil when she gets to Dover.[7] By living in some state at Boston, the governor seems very fond of making a figure; I wish he may not soar too high. They set off with three carriages and four bays; and venison has been so abundant, a small pasty reached the vicarage. Alterations and enlargements of the house are ordered during his absence, which may cost many hundreds. The governor's valet says, his master is worth 3,000 pounds a year. Mr. __ says, 300. The difference is small, only made by the addition of a single cipher, and ciphers are nothings.

Mr. Newton has fallen into the hands of a slaughter-man, I hear, Dr. Mayhew[8] who will certainly cleave him down the chine,[9] if he can. He set Mr. Madan[10] on his head about Aldwinckle,[11] and almost made him crazy. I hope my dear brother will bear the Doctor's operation with Christian patience, and make no reply. Then the matter may rest, and be

---

6   In classical mythology Phaethon was the son of Helios (the sun god) who drove his father's chariot. Because of his anger he nearly set the world on fire.

7   Seaport in Kent for embarkation.

8   The editor of *CM* (1845) says that this is Dr. Mayo. Henry Mayo, DD, LLD (1733–1793) became the pastor of the independent church at Wapping in 1762 after preaching at Castle Hill, Northampton. He played an important role in the attempts to alter the terms of subscription required by the Toleration Act in the 1770s and was appointed as a tutor at the Homerton Academy in 1785. He was known as "the literary anvil." See November 17, 1784.

9   The backbone.

10   Martin Madan. See September 23, 1763.

11   Berridge is referring to a serious dispute over the living at Aldwincle between the patron, John Kimpton and Haweis, who, with Madan's encouragement, had accepted the living and moved in. Arthur Skevington Wood, who gives a sympathetic account of Haweis's difficulties, says that Madan's defence "provoked from Kimpton the first of a series of eleven pamphlets, from various pens, dealing with the pros and cons of the case" (*Haweis*, 133). Henry Mayo had contributed *Aldwinckle: a candid examination of the Rev. Mr. Madan's conduct, as a counsellor and a friend; agreeable to the principles of law and conscience* (1767).

bandied about no further. Controversy usually goes on briskly, but Gospel work goes on heavily, at least amongst us. All decays begin in the closet. No heart thrives without much secret converse with God, and nothing will make amends for the want of it. I can read God's word, or hear a sermon at times, and feel no life; but I never rise from secret prayer without some quickening. Even when I set about it with heaviness or reluctance, the Lord is pleased in mercy to meet me in it; and I find more sweet communion in secret than in social or congregational prayer. Much preaching and hearing is among the Methodists, and plenty of ordinances is a great blessing, but if they do not bring us much upon our knees, they suckle the head without nourishing the heart. We shall never obtain the old Puritan spirit of holiness, till we obtain their spirit of prayer.

The Lord has given you the fat things of the earth in abundance; may he give you a heartful and a houseful of the upper blessings,[12] watering the roots well, and all the branches. With all becoming esteem, I remain your affectionate and dutiful servant,

John Berridge

N.B. If I am called to London in winter, I have thoughts of publishing a hymn-book,[13] which has been often threatened with the fire, and is now designed for the press.

---

[12] Spiritual and heavenly blessings.

[13] Berridge suppressed his first hymn book, *A Collection of Divine Songs*, because of his movement away from the Wesleys to a more Calvinistic understanding of salvation and sanctification. He says: "Many volumes of Hymns have been lately published, some of them a new composition, others a mere collection, and it may seem needless to add one more to the number, especially after having published a collection myself. But ill health, some years past, having kept me from travelling or preaching, I took up the trade of Hymn-making, a handicraft much followed of late, but a business I was not born or bred to, and undertaken chiefly to keep a long sickness from preying on my spirit, and to make tedious nights pass over more smoothly. Some tinkling employment was wanted, which might amuse and not fatigue me. Besides, I was not wholly satisfied with the collection I had published. The bells indeed, had been chiefly cast in a celebrated Foundery, and in ringing were tuneable enough, none more so, but a clear gospel tone was not found in them all. Human wisdom and strength, perfection and merit, give Sion's bells a Levitical twang, and drown the mellow tone to the gospel outright" (*Sion's Songs*, iii–iv). See R. Butterworth, "The Rev. John Berridge and His Hymn-book, 1760 and 1785," *WHS*, 11 (1918), 169–174, and chapter 25, "Berridge: The Hymn-writer," in Pibworth, *Gospel Pedlar*.

To John Thornton[1]

Dear and honoured Sir,

I received your favour of the 8th, conveying a friendly hint to myself, and some friendly relief for the poor. You have my thanks for both. An elbow nudge, seasonably given, is of more use sometimes than a sermon, for preachers often study to say smart things; and letter writers, too, which yield more pleasure than profit: but elbow hints bring close and secret instruction to the heart. Pray, Sir, do not part with your elbows, but reserve them for myself and others on needful occasions.

What a mercy you may daily seek and find Jesus on your knees, when you cannot always trace him, where you might expect him, in a disciple's letter! Yet what is a Christian letter without Christ, but a disciple without his Master? Where Jesus dwells, he will at length become Lord paramount—all in our love, and trust, and hope, uppermost in our preaching and hearing, praying and singing, writing and talking. Grace is best discovered by the value it gives us for Jesus; and where he is duly valued, he will engage our adoration, love, and trust, and these will command a cheerful obedience. As grace groweth, Christ will increase, and we must decrease.[2] He will rise higher in the love, trust, and value of the heart, and self will sink lower, till Christ becomes all, and we become nothing. What a blessed exchange is here of self for Christ, i.e., of folly for wisdom, of weakness for strength, of beggary for riches, and death for life!

Your Joseph[3] showeth, when grace entereth a bosom, Jesus becomes the darling of the heart, the joy and trust of it; and all obedience without this, only nourishes self-righteousness and self-applause, and will end in shame and woeful disappointment. Joseph also showeth, when Christ becomes a sinner's chief joy, self is felt the

---

[1] The letter is found in *GM* (1838), 166–168, and *CM* (1845), 274–275.
[2] John 3:30.
[3] Henry Thornton. See note, January 23, 1783

chief of sinners. But what could the religious sort[4] mean by asking Joseph whether a saving change was wrought in him? We used to say at Cambridge, that the fellows of St. John's College had a receipt of their own for making Latin, it was such crabbed stuff; and it seems this religious sort have a receipt of their own for making Christians, else why did they ask Joseph about his change of heart, when it plainly appeared by his words, looks and whole conduct, that his heart was changed, truly taught to love Jesus, and trust in him alone for salvation. This is regeneration, the new heart that makes a child of God; and without this all convictions of sin and present reformation will come to nothing. This is the true circumcision, mentioned by Moses, when he says, "The Lord will circumcise thine heart to love him with all thine heart and soul, that thou mayst live."[5] And this regeneration, like circumcision, is an instantaneous operation.

It will be well if Mr. Bowman[6] is prevented from publishing a sequel to Mr. Newton; otherwise it may stir up some animosity between the Gospel clergy and dissenting ministers.[7] Dr. Mahew will certainly step forth to the fight again—it seems to be his element; and Mr. Bowman, I fear, has too much pepper, or spleen, to endure chopping with the Doctor's cleaver.

Through mercy I have neither ability nor inclination for controversy,[8] which often proves a Gospel bear-garden,[9] where the combatants are bruising each other, and he that deals hardest blows seems the cleverest fellow. By birth and education I am both a churchman

---

4 *GM* has "silly man."
5 Deuteronomy 30:6.
6 Thomas Bowman (*c*.1728–1792) was one of the clergy connected with Lady Huntingdon. He became vicar of Martham and Cawston in Norfolk in 1758 after graduating from Cambridge in 1750 and gaining full orders in 1752. He was a zealous Calvinist, publishing a vindication of that system in one volume as well as further defences in the *London Magazine*.
7 In March John Newton had published *Apologia. Four letters to a minister of an Independent Church. By a minister of the Church of England, giving his reasons for staying in the establishment* (J. Buckland, 1789). A few months later there appeared a reply, *An Apology, and a Shield for Protestant Dissenters in These Times of Instability and Misrepresentations. Four letters to the Rev. Mr. Newton. By a Dissenting Minister.* Although it was published anonymously, Berridge attributes it to Dr. Mahew (Dr. Mayo). See October 1, 1784.
8 *GM* adds "where the essentials are not concerned."
9 In Tudor and Stuart times bears were kept and baited for public amusement in special gardens, which were famous for noise and disorder.

and a dissenter—I love both, and could be either, and wish real Gospel ministers of every denomination[10] could embrace one another. And though I do think the best Christianity was found before establishments began; and that usually there are more true ministers out of an establishment than in it; and that establishments are commonly of an intolerant spirit, and draw in shoals of hirelings by their loaves and fishes; yet I am very thankful for an establishment which affords me a preaching-house and an eating-house, without clapping a padlock on my lips, or a fetter on my foot. However, I am not indebted to the mercy of church canons or church governors for itinerant liberty, but to the secret overruling providence of Jesus, which rescued me at various times from the claws of a church commissary,[11] an archdeacon,[12] and a bishop,[13] and kept up my heart by a frequent application of these words, "They shall fight against thee, but they shall not prevail against thee, for I am with thee to deliver thee, saith the Lord."[14] Hitherto the Lord has delivered me, and I trust will deliver. No weapon formed against me has prospered.

May this gracious Lord be evermore your mighty protector, and fill your heart and fill your house with his blessings. With becoming respect and gratitude I remain, your affectionate servant,

John Berridge

---

10 *GM* adds "who love the truth."

11 A deputy who supplies a bishop's place in a remote part of a diocese.

12 A chief deacon; next to a bishop in the care of the diocese.

13 For Berridge's early trouble with his bishop, see August 8, 1775.

14 Jeremiah 1:19. On the fly-leaf of Berridge's Bible he wrote against this text: "Often given as fresh troubles came" (*Gospel Gems,* iv).

To Benjamin Mills[1]

Everton, November 20, 1784

Dear Sir,

I thank the Lord, from whom all good desires proceed, for stirring up your heart for a kind remembrance and yearly refreshment of my fellow labourers, who are all poor, some of them very much so, and some of them now sick. I think such a set of men, so poor and illiterate,[2] were never called forth to the ministry since Christ's time, and this in the face of an university, thereby casting a contempt on their boasted wisdom. And I believe more souls have been made alive to God by any one of these preachers during the last twenty years than have been quickened in the university church by the whole body of the clergy during this century.

However, there is a promising prospect at present. Many young students are in a hopeful way. Two Fellows[3] of different colleges preach the gospel *gently,* in two small churches at Cambridge; and one Fellow of Sidney College[4] now preaches Jesus Christ *boldly* in the university church. I believe the Lord Jesus, in half a century, will shut up church-doors, by directing Government to seize on the church-lands, as Harry the Eighth did on the abbey lands; such seizure may lessen

---

[1]   A manuscript of the letter is held in SGC, 0250B. A version in *CM* (1838), 163–164, leaves out the postscript and refines the punctuation. It is addressed to "Mr. Benjamin Mills, No. 15 Middle Moorfields, London." Mills had sent his annual gift and asked questions about the state of the church and divine healing.

[2]   Uneducated.

[3]   Most likely Chistopher Atkinson (1754–1795), fellow of Trinity Hall, vicar of St. Edwards from 1781 until 1785, and Charles Simeon (1759–1836), fellow of Kings, who had been appointed as vicar of Holy Trinity in 1783.

[4]   Henry William Coulthurst (1753–1817) was at Cambridge from 1771, when he started as a student, until 1790, when he moved to Halifax as minister of the parish church. At Cambridge he was minister of the Church of the Holy Sepulchre, better known as the Round Church because of its rotund architecture, from 1782 until 1790. He was a fellow of Sidney Sussex between 1781 and 1791 and was a particular friend of John Venn and Charles Simeon.

the national debt, and a churchman, you know, cannot preach without his tithes[5]; the fleece makes his flock. In the meantime the Lord is sending his ministers into the church to awaken and call out his elect. And wherever a Gospel clergyman comes, and meets with success, at his removal I never see a gospel clergyman succeed him, and of course his flock must become dissenters to get food, for awakened sinners cannot live upon chaff.

If you compare James 5:14,15, with Mark 6:12,13, you will find that the raising up sick people by unction[6] and prayer was a miraculous power bestowed on the apostles and primitive elders, a power not to be exercised whenever they pleased, for they might have kept their flocks continually from dying; yet to be exercised when they found a sudden and strong impression on their minds. Paul says, "I have left Trophimus at Miletum sick."[7] Why did he leave him there sick? Because he had no power to heal him then, any more than to work miracles at all times.

Instead of praying only for the recovery of your child, rather pray for a sweet resignation to God's will. Leave your child with the Lord, in better hands than your own. If the Lord restores her, give him thanks. If he remove her, thank him also for delivering her early from an evil world, and providing her a better mansion than Moorfields can afford her. Give my kind respects to your excellent partner and filial shopman. The Lord bless you with the upper and nether springs, and give you his peace at all times. With due respect, I remain your affectionate servant in the best bonds,

John Berridge

P.S. You are young and may live to see government first nibbling on the Deaneries and Prebends, then on the church livings and Bishopricks. And no outcry will now be raised, so little regard is found for the church, especially since the plunder is to pay off the debt. And will my Jesus give up the church lands, since church ministers eat his bread, and lift up the heel against him.

---

5   The tax of one-tenth used to support the clergy and church.
6   Anointing with oil.
7   2 Timothy 4:20.

To John Thornton[1]

February 22, 1785

Dear and honourable Sir,

I purpose to wait upon you on Sabbath evening, the 13th of March, and beg of Jesus to afford us his presence. If your carriage can be spared, I hope my sinful weight will not crush it down again, and the afternoon service at Tottenham will be over a little before five.

It is a pleasant sight to behold churches and chapels crowded with attentive hearers, and every new opened place quickly filled. And though there will ever be much chaff mingled with the grain, yet surely the Lord is doing great things in the city, and spreading the savour of his name in the country. Oh sir, what a mercy to be found among those who are raised from the dead, and called forth to bear an honourable profession of his name, his grace, and his blood. May his name be growing more savoury to us, his grace become more fruitful in us, and his blood be sprinkled more abundantly upon us. May our hearts be linked more closely to Jesus in faith and love, and, growing up into him, be filled abundantly out of his fullness.

I feel my faculties and senses decay apace; my invention loseth its vigour, and my memory loseth its hold, it grows leaky, and like a sieve, yea a sieve of the worst kind, it lets the grain drop, and retaineth the chaff. My eyes grow dim, my ears dull and my teeth are running away from my mouth, being quite wearied out with long service. However, through the rich mercy of God, I have some comfortable enjoyment of myself, though just on the verge of my seventieth year. I esteem it a kind providence that my faculties and senses decay gradually, that the house cracks before it falls; and I find a blessing attend this gradual decay, it makes me feel my own insignificance, and is gently sinking me into nothing, the very posture I should be in, that Christ may become my all, the whole stay and joy of my heart.

---

[1] This letter is found in PLFELM, GD26/13/739. The manuscript is addressed to "John Thornton, Esq., Lothbury." Thornton had his business at 2 Church Alley, Lothbury Street, which bordered the Bank of England.

340

I am bound to love and honour you, which I do in truth. The Lord himself honour you, and all that are dear to you, with his choicest blessings. As you have the love, so you have the prayers of your much obliged servant,

John Berridge

To Charles Simeon[1]

[Spring 1785?]

...If every parish church were blessed with a Gospel minister, there would be little need of itinerant preaching. But since those ministers are thinly scattered about the country, and neighbouring pulpits are usually locked up against them, it behoves them to take advantage of fields, or barns, or houses, to cast abroad the Gospel seed. But all are not designed to be rural deans. How are we to judge who are? If you are enabled to preach without notes, feel an abiding desire to be useful in spreading the gospel, meet with calls for that purpose, comply with the calls, find the word sealed, and if persecuted and threatened, have a word given for support: where these concur (and these are just my own experience) I have no doubt but such a Minister is designed for a rural dean, or a rambling bishop.

When you open your commission, begin with ripping up the audience, and Moses will lend you a carving knife, which may be often whetted at his grindstone. Lay open the universal sinfulness of nature, the darkness of the mind, the forwardness of the tempers, the earthliness and sensuality of the affections. Speak of the evil of sin in its nature, its rebellion against God as our benefactor, and contempt of his authority and love. Declare the evil of sin in its effects, bringing all our sickness, pains, and sorrows, all the evils we feel, and all the evils we fear. All inundations, fires, famines, pestilences, brawls, quarrels, fighting, wars, with death to close these present sorrows, and Hell to receive all that die in sin.

---

[1] This letter is undated but it was probably written in the spring of 1785 because Berridge is presenting the arguments for itineration, a matter that Simeon was considering at this time. See July 2, 1785. In *WB* (1838), 475–478, and *WB* (1864), 439–441, it is addressed to "the Rev. Mr __." In *AM* (September 1794), 496–498, it identifies Rev. Mr. Simeon as the recipient and in *EM* (May 1794), 198–200, it says, "To the Rev. Mr. __, a gospel clergyman at C__." The letter is also found in *CMR* (1889), 114–115. For Simeon, see September 17, 1782. I have not necessarily assumed as Smyth has (see *Simeon and Church Order*, 276) that the text in *AM* is truer to the original, although it has had the most attention in considering any differences in the text.

Lay open the spirituality of the Law, and its extent, reaching every thought, word and action, and declaring every transgression whether of omission or commission, deserving of death. Declare man's utter helplessness to change his nature, or to make his peace. Pardon and holiness must come from the Saviour. Acquaint them with the searching eye of God, watching us continually, spying out every thought, word, and action, noting them down in the book of his remembrance; bringing every secret work into judgment, whether it be good or evil.

When your hearers have been well harrowed, and the clumps begin to fall (which is seen by their hanging down the head) then bring out your Christ, and bring him out from the heart, through the lips, and tasting of his grace while you publish it. Now lay open the Saviour's almighty power to soften the heart, and give it true repentance, to bring pardon to the broken heart, and the spirit of prayer to the prayerless heart, holiness to the filthy heart, and faith to the unbelieving heart. Let them know that all the treasures of grace are lodged in Jesus Christ, for the use of poor needy sinners, and that he is full of love as well as power, that he turns no beggars away from his gate, but receives all comers kindly, loves to bless them, and bestows all his blessings tithe-free.[2] Farmers, and country people chop at that. Here you must wave the Gospel flag, and magnify the Saviour proudly; speak *"ore rotundo"*[3] that his blood can wash away the foulest stains, and his grace subdue the stoutest corruptions. Exhort the people to seek his grace directly, constantly, and diligently, and acquaint them that all who thus seek shall find the salvation of God.

Never preach in working hours; that would raise a clamour. Where you preach at night, preach also in the morning; but be not longer than an hour in the whole morning service, and conclude before six. Morning preaching will show whether the evening's took effect, by raising them up early to hear.

Expect plain fare, and plain lodging where you preach, yet perhaps, better than your Master had. Suffer no treats to be made for you, but live as your host usually lives, else he may grow weary of entertaining you. "Go not from house to house."[4] If the clergy rail at you where you go, say not one word, good or bad.[5] If you dare be

---

2 We cannot earn our salvation by paying our tithes.
3 With a full mouth.
4 Luke 10:7.
5 Matthew 15:14.

zealous for the Lord of hosts, expect persecution and threats; but heed them not. Bind that word to your heart, Jeremiah 1:19 and 15:20. The promise is doubled for your encouragement. The chief blocks in your way, will be the prudent Peters, who will beg and entreat you to avoid irregularity. Give them the same answer that Christ gave Peter.[6] They savour not the things of God, heed them not. Where you preach at night, go to bed as soon as possible, that the family be not kept up, and that you may rise early. When breakfast and morning family prayer are over, go away directly that the house may be at liberty. Don't dine where you preach, if you can avoid it: it will save expense, and please the people.

If you would do work for the Lord, as you seem designed, you must venture for the Lord. The Christian's motto is "Trust, and go forward," though a sea is before you.[7] Do then as Paul did, give up thyself to the Lord's work, and confer not with flesh and blood.[8] Go, and the Lord be with thee, dear brother. Yours affectionately,

John Berridge

---

[6] Matthew 16:23.
[7] Exodus 14:16.
[8] Galatians 1:16.

To John Thornton[1]

Everton, July 2, 1785

Dear and honoured Sir,

Sin, which has kindled a fire in hell, is kindling fires on earth continually. And when they break out, everyone is asking how they happened. Amos replies, "Shall there be evil in a city, and the Lord hath not done it?"[2] And when desolation is made by fire, Isaiah declares, the Lord hath "consumed us, because of our iniquities."[3] Many years ago my house was oft threatened to be destroyed, but the Lord insured it, by giving the 10th verse of the 91st Psalm[4]; and the Lord's providence is the best insurance.

Potton felt the Lord's fiery ravage some time past[5]; and Biggleswade smarts under it now.[6] One 128 houses, 8 malthouses, and a meeting-house, with barns and stables, are consumed. The wealthy sufferers had insured three-fourths of their substance. This loss, therefore, will not break their backs, nor does it seem to humble their hearts; but the little tradesmen and poor labourers have lost their all, and are herded together in an old malthouse, and barns; among whom are several of the Lord's dear children, begotten under my ministry. I should like to

---

[1] The letter is contained in *GM* (1838), 225–226; *WB* (1838), 424–446 (the letter itself only spans three pages, but twenty page numbers are missing); and *WB* (1864), 413–415. There is a manuscript that is held at the Church Missionary Archive, Venn Manuscripts, ACC81 C71, Cadbury Research Library Special Collections, at Birmingham University. It is simply addressed to "John Thornton Esq., Clapham."

[2] Amos 3:6.

[3] Isaiah 64:7.

[4] "There shall no evil befall thee, neither shall any plague come nigh thy dwelling" (Psalm 91:10).

[5] See November 20, 1784.

[6] The fire at Biggleswade occurred on June 16. A servant-maid at one of the coaching inns deposited live cinders on a rubbish heap near the inn. The fire spread quickly in every direction and made more than 300 people homeless. The meeting-house referred to by Berridge was the Baptist Old Meeting. A new building was opened the following year.

deal out all my mites privately among these, but for the Gospel credit, I must appear a public contributor,[7] which will shorten private relief. A man is taken up on suspicion of firing the town, but alas, sin wants taking up, for sin is the incendiary.

Yelling church is well attended under Mr. Simeon's[8] afternoon ministry. A brave Christian sergeant he is, having the true spirit of an evangelist, but his feet are often put in the stocks by the Archdeacon of Yelling,[9] who is doubtless become a vagabond preacher as well as myself, a right gospel hawker and pedlar, but seems desirous of having the trade to himself. Through mercy he is grown as scandalous as I could wish him, yet he wants to fasten the shackle on Simeon, which he has dropped from himself. Oh, worldly prudence, what a prudish foe thou art to grace!

Some little time before Mr. Venn went to London,[10] he preached at Bluntisham,[11] a large village in the fens, and finding great power and

---

7 Public subscriptions were made town by town. For example, Potton made a subscription on July 7 for those who had suffered as a result of the fire at Biggleswade. There are more than a hundred names, many being the same as suffered in the Potton fire (see October 3, 1783) and £71 was raised. Whittingham, obviously now back in Potton, gave two guineas. See Biggleswade Historical Society, *The Great Fire of Biggleswade, June 16, 1785* (1985), 18.

8 See September 17, 1782.

9 Henry Venn. This is a reference to Venn influencing Simeon against gospel itinerating.

10 To preach for Rowland Hill at Surrey Chapel.

11 Bluntisham is approximately twelve miles north of Yelling, and six miles east of Huntingdon. Cox Feary (1759–1822) had been converted and, finding little help in his local churches, was attending Yelling church at Berridge's suggestion. Throughout the winter of 1784 he had gathered a large group by reading sermons on three evenings of the week. As a result of this, Venn went to preach at Bluntisham, where a Mr. John Kent opened his barn. Feary left an account of his own contact with Berridge: "In the spring of the year 1784, he was called to Huntingdon on business, where, in a bookseller's shop, he providentially met with a Mr. B., a pious clergyman, who preached the gospel at the neighbouring villages of Stukeley and Orford. After some conversation on religious publications, Mr. B. very kindly invited him to take his tea with him. The invitation was gladly accepted, and the interview was truly interesting, as it led him to hear Mr. B. next Lord's day [at Everton], where he found himself at home under the sound of the glorious gospel of the blessed God. After the services of the day he returned home, rejoicing to think he had found a place in the Establishment where the glad tidings of salvation were proclaimed to poor sinners. He now formed the resolution of constantly attending Mr. B.'s preaching, but by the

success, he promised to preach there once a fortnight in some barn at his return. In the meantime I desired Simeon to strike whilst the iron was hot and to visit Bluntisham as well as Yelling. He consented; accordingly after preaching at Cambridge on a Sunday morning, he preached at Yelling in the afternoon, and at Bluntisham in the evening; and finding a very crowded and attentive audience, he preached early on Monday morning, leaving off before six.[12] This he did for three weeks, and then acquaints his principal with what he had done, expecting a letter of congratulation; but lo a funeral answer comes, declaring Mr. Venn is grieved at his conduct, grieved at Simeon for doing what himself had done, and intended to do. This surely is grief of all griefs, too deep even for tragedy. Pray, Sir, lay your cane soundly on the Archdeacon's back, when you see him and brush off his heathen grief else it may spoil a Christian sergeant.

I am growing, as I should, more small and loathsome in my own sight, and Christ is growing more precious and lovely; but I cannot walk in his strength, as I ought, nor feast on his fullness, as I might. Here I am an infant still, but am praying daily for larger stature of faith, faith to remove mole hills at least, if not mountains.[13]

I suppose you are now preparing for an episcopal visitation of the sea coast.[14] The Lord direct your course, and prosper your own, and your chaplain's labours. May the Lord's blessing attend yourself, your partner and children, and make the several families one household of faith. That grace may bring you all to glory is the prayer of your affectionate and dutiful servant,

John Berridge

---

persuasion of that gentleman he was induced to give up his design, and to attend the labours of Mr. Venn, of Yelling, where he could enjoy [as Yelling was nearer] the services both parts of the Lord's day" (R.W. Dixon, *A Century of Village Nonconformity at Bluntisham, Hunts., 1787–1887* [Cambridge: Cambridge University Press, 1887], 173–174).

[12] See Spring 1785.

[13] Matthew 17:20.

[14] Thornton normally took a vacation with several preachers for the spiritual profit of the area. That summer he went to Ireland, taking William Bull from Newport Pagnell. At Thornton's suggestion Bull wrote a tract to be distributed on the journey.

To John Thornton[1]

Everton, July 13, 1785

Dear and honoured Sir,

Your kind letter I have received, which brings comfortable relief to the poor and distressed people at Biggleswade.[2] The Lord has rewards of grace to give, and such you are seeking, being blest with a supernatural ambition of coveting the best things. Most of the wealthy prove bankrupts or beggars at last, spend all, or leave all behind, live rich and die poor, regale their palate here with the choicest wines, and cannot gain a drop of water hereafter to cool their tongue.[3] But God is making you wealthy for both worlds. Providence provides the nether springs for you, and grace is preparing the upper. Oh, Sir, what mercy embraceth you. A rich man, and yet saved—from being high-minded—from loving or trusting Mammon! A rich man in this world, and rich towards God! May your children share in the double blessing!

I am afraid the shop-tax[4] might have lifted Mr. H. Thornton out of the borough,[5] which would have proved shop-lifting indeed, but from Mr. Astell I learn, he has mollified his electors by a prudent piece of conduct. This may be well if he means to keep his seat in the House, but whatever its honour, I had rather be a poor vicar of Everton, than lay under the correction of borough-masters, and be burnt in effigy at pleasure.[6]

---

[1] This letter is found in *GM* (1838), 305–306; *WB* (1838), 446–448; and *WB* (1864), 415–416. *GM* gives the date as March 20, 1785.

[2] See July 2, 1785.

[3] Luke 16:24.

[4] In January 1784 William Pitt the Younger became prime minister as well as chancellor. Due to the disastrous state of the country's finances following the American War of Independence, he went about reforming the tax system. One of the new measures in his second budget of May 9, 1785, was the introduction of a shop tax based on an annual value of the premises. It was considered unfair, causing riots, and was repealed four years later.

[5] Because Henry Thornton was an MP he could have lost his seat because of the unpopularity of the tax.

[6] The paragraph is missed out in *WB*.

I lately preached at Grantchester, one mile from Cambridge, to a very numerous audience, among whom were several gracious young students, and three Masters of Arts. One of the Masters, who had been a zealous Socinian,[7] came to me after preaching, and embracing me with tears, thanked me for the sermons I had preached last summer at Wistow[8] and Harston,[9] in Cambridgeshire, and for the private discourse before and after sermon. From what I saw and heard of him, I hope he is coming home to Jesus.

My church is usually very full in afternoons, and the people are awake and attentive, but the congregation is almost a new one. Many old sheep are housed in the upper fold; and many, who live at a distance, are dropped into neighbouring meetings, and only pay occasional visits to Everton. I shall meet them all by and by and a blessed meeting it will be when sheep and shepherds will give to Jesus all the glory of it. If my dear brother, the Archdeacon of Yelling,[10] comes home uncrippled, quite sound in wind and limb, I conjecture he will pay an annual visit to Surrey chapel.[11] He is now, with all his prudence, advanced very high on the Methodist ladder, is got within one step of Tottenham,[12] which completes the course of Methodism. I find you have thoughts of visiting North Wales; whenever you steer north or south, east or west, my Jesus, the God of the earth go with you, preserve your going out and coming in, and prosper what you undertake for his glory. I am your obedient and affectionate servant,

John Berridge

---

7 Faustus Socinus (1539–1604), an Italian Unitarian. Berridge held similar views himself, rejecting Christ's divinity, in his earlier days at Cambridge.
8 Wistow, near Warboys, is a village about twenty miles north of Cambridge.
9 A village about five miles south of Cambridge.
10 Henry Venn. See July 2, 1785.
11 See February 1782.
12 Berridge is suggesting that Tottenham Court Road Chapel is the top pulpit in Evangelicalism.

To Benjamin Mills[1]

Everton, November 4, 1785

Dear Sir,

Your letter occasioned thankfulness to God, with prayers for blessings on yourself; blessings, according to Scripture, good measure, far exceeding the Winchester,[2] viz., pressed down, shaken together, and running over. I know not what my poor lay-evangelists would do without some assistance received from yourself and your society. They are labouring men, whose paws maintain their jaws, and two of them have seven children, and their wives are kindling every year. They seem the only free grace preachers in the land; for they do preach free grace freely, without money, and without price, having nothing for their preaching but a plain dinner, and sometimes not even that.

I believe Dr. P[eckwell][3] could take leave of the Tabernacle and Tottenham without tears, if he met with church preferment, that is warm and blanketing, such as would lap quite round him, and keep his four wheeled curricles in sprightly order, and support a decent number of liveries.[4] But the Lord seldom loads the back with preferment when the eye has got a squint. Coaching is an evil that creeps among methodist preachers. It brings a high head and a low purse; lifts the preacher above his hearers, and keeps the poor at a distance from him. Gospel seldom runs well on wheels. Our dear Master always rode upon his own legs, except once, when he borrowed a hackney to make a state entry into Jerusalem; and then any disciple might have got up behind if he pleased. No wonder the hearers run into worldly fashions, when preachers lead the way.

I have been ill for two months, much weighed down with coughing and phlegm, sometimes almost strangled with it, which has wasted and weakened my body, and narrowed and bleached my face. I was

---

1   This letter is found in *WB* (1838), 464–465, and *WB* (1864), 432–433.
2   A dry and liquid measure, the original of which was deposited at Winchester.
3   Dr. Peckwell (1746–1787). See March 2, 1776.
4   Servants.

kept out of my pulpit for two Sundays, and my cadaverous countenance made many suspect I was going to take leave of them. Through mercy I am better, but not recovered, and am able to preach once on a Sunday, but am in travail three or four days afterwards. I am naturally fretful in pain, and the Lord sends me coughing and phlegm to puke the fretfulness up, which, along with grace, may do the business. I send my kind respects to your little wife, and being a good wife, there is enough of her, and respects to your brisk shopkeeper, who is a part of you. Much grace and peace be with you, and with your affectionate servant,

John Berridge

To John Newton[1]

Everton, November 12, 1785

My dear Brother,

I thank you for your monument,[2] and can rejoice with yourself and your dear partner, for the gentle dismission and blessed translation of Eliza, no longer your niece, but the Lord's bride, trained up for wedding at your own house and church, and solemnly espoused October 6. Jesus has paid you well for the cares and pains you bestowed in the training, having dropped a recompense into your bosom, with full Gospel measure, far exceeding the Winchester, viz., pressed down, shaken together, and running over. Indeed, our Lord does every kindness royally, and like himself. May his love fill our hearts, and his praise employ our life. I am full of expectation for your *Messiah*,[3] and hope it will not be long before it appears. A glorious subject indeed, and God has engaged your hand to the work.

All ministers should preach about Jesus, but only his secretaries are fit to write about him. I find him growing very precious to my soul, and wrapped more closely round my heart. My daily prayer is to grow up into him and lose myself in him, and find him my all in all. Perhaps

---

[1]   The letter is found in *WB* (1838), 448–449, and *WB* (1864), 416–417.

[2]   After his niece's death on October 6, 1785, John Newton printed a tribute privately for the benefit of his friends: *A Monument to the Praise of the Lord's Goodness, and to the Memory of Dear Eliza Cunningham* (B. Dugdale). On the advice of friends he published his account for the general public on November 17, 1785. Elizabeth Cunningham came as a twelve-year-old to the Newtons in London on March 15, 1783. Her dying mother, Mrs. Newton's sister, who had only recently lost a son, wished the Newtons to care for her. The *Monument* is an account of her two and a half years with the Newtons, her weakness and illness, and the Newtons' great affection for her.

[3]   Newton preached fifty sermons on the texts of the *Messiah* during 1784 and 1785. They were published in two volumes in 1786 as *Messiah: fifty expository discourses, on the series of scriptural passages which form the subject of the celebrated oratorio of Handel* (J. Buckland). The series was inspired by the events commemorating the centenary of Handel's birth, which included elaborate performances in Westminster Abbey and elsewhere.

I may be called upon soon to see him whom my heart loves, and to throw myself at his feet. I have been ill for three months, and for two Sundays kept out of my pulpit. My body is wasted and weakened, and my trumpeter's face is subsided. Through mercy I am somewhat better, and just able to preach only on a Sunday, but am far from well, and not likely to be so, till I get home. What a mercy to have a prospect of a heavenly home, and well founded too, when the earthly cottage is feeble or falling!

My brother Venn came home a cripple from Surrey chapel,[4] and was confined some weeks to his couch. One leg was exceedingly swollen from the ankle to the hip, but the swelling is almost or wholly gone; he can now wear his proper shoes, stockings, and breeches; and is able to ride to Everton and back the same day. A marriage is expected at Yelling, about Christmas, between his eldest daughter and Mr. Elliot.[5]

Mr. Cowper has published more poems,[6] I find; but his poetry, though excellent, is not likely for sale. There is too much Gospel for the world, and too little for most believers. Pray give my kind respects to Mr. Foster,[7] when you see him and to Mr. Romaine,[8] when you catch him. I send my hearty love to you and your dear [wife]. Much grace and peace be with you, and with your affectionate brother,

John Berridge

---

4   See February 1782.
5   Eling Venn (1758–1843) married a silk merchant of Bond Street, Mr. Charles Elliot, a widower with several children. The wedding took place in Yelling on December 20, 1785.
6   *The Task: a poem, in six books* (J. Johnson) was published in 1785.
7   See September 17, 1782.
8   See September 14, 1773.

To John Thornton[1]

Everton, November 15, 1785

Dear and honoured Sir,

On Friday last I had a note from Mr. Venn, which acquaints me with the loss of your partner, who, I find, expired suddenly after a long illness.[2] She had lived to see her daughter married to a peer, and her three sons seated in the House of Commons,[3] and then is quickly removed. What a bubble is human honour, and what a toy is human joy! Happy is he, whose hope the Lord is, and whose heart crieth out for the living God. Creature comforts may fail him, but the God of consolation will be with him; and when human cisterns yield no water, he may drink of the river that waters the throne of God. Your partner's absence will make the house look dreary, and household matters move heavily, for she was a right spring of Economics; but when the rib is gone, you must lean firmer on your staff. Psalm 23.

You may now, perhaps, think of drawing yourself into less compass, [4]a desirable thing for an aged pilgrim, who is going home, and glad to drop encumbrances, having no more house-room, garden, or servants, than are really needful. Youth, without grace, wants every worldly embellishment; but a gracious heart and hoary hairs crieth out for communion with God, and says, nothing on earth I desire in comparison with him.[5] What a mercy, you need not fly to worldly amusements for relief, and run away from yourself to find comfort. Along with plenty of this world's husks, the prodigal's food,[6] God

---

[1] This letter was published in *BM* (1830), 558–559; *GM* (1838), 363–364; *WB* (1838), 421–422; *CM* (1842), 828–829; and *WB* (1864), 410–411. *WB* (1838) has the year as 1783. There is a manuscript copy of the letter in another hand which is held in PLFELM, GD26/13/739.

[2] Lucy Thornton died on November 1, 1785.

[3] Samuel (1754–1838) was MP for Surrey, Robert (1759–1838) represented Colchester, and Henry (1760–1815) was MP for Southwark.

[4] *WB* add "it is."

[5] Psalm 73:25.

[6] Luke 15:16.

has bestowed a pearl on you which createth an appetite for spiritual cheer, and bringeth royal dainties into the bosom. May this season of mourning be sweetened with a sense of the Lord's presence, bringing many tokens of fatherly love, and sanctifying the visitation, by drawing the heart more vigorously unto God, and fixing it on him.

I have been ill for three months, and my body is wasted and weakened pretty much. My disorder seems to be asthmatic, and is attended with a deep cough and much phlegm. For two Sundays I was kept from my pulpit, but through mercy I am now able to preach once a week. My appetite is better, and I sleep better, but am feeble still. Mr. Venn[7] seems wholly restored.[8] May your children, along with this world's tawdry honour, partake of the true honour, by being adopted into God's family, and made the sons and daughters of the Most High. Jesus' grace and peace be with you, and with your affectionate and dutiful servant,

John Berridge

---

7 See November 12, 1785. *WB* (1838) and *WB* (1864) have "Mrs."
8 Sentence missing from *GM* and *CM*.

PART 4

1786–1793

The "old worn–out servant"[1]

1   The phrase comes from an anecdote about Berridge preaching at the Tabernacle in about 1791. After being led up the pulpit stairs to preach, Berridge is reported to have said: "'My dear Tabernacle friends' (the tears trickling down his cheeks) 'I bless my dear Lord that has thus far brought me on my wearisome pilgrimage through the wilderness, and has permitted his old worn-out servant to see your state in the flesh once more, which, in all probability, will be the last time. Satan said to me, as I was coming, "You old fool, how can you think of preaching to that great people, that have neither strength nor memory left?" I said to him, "Well, Satan, I have got a good Master, that has not forsook me these forty years, and in his strength I'll try"; and, blessed be his name, he has thus far helped me; and if you'll pray, I'll try to preach once more in my poor way; and may the Lord make it a blessed opportunity to us all! And I think you'll say amen to it'" (*EM* [1803], 200).

To John Thornton[1]

Tabernacle, February 20, 1786

Dear and honoured Sir,

On Sunday three weeks the 12th of March, I purpose to wait upon you at Clapham, and beg of Christ to give us the meeting. I am to preach at Tottenham[2] in the morning, and the afternoon service will be over before five. May I have leave to expect your carriage to convey an old drone,[3] for such I am now, to Clapham. Indeed I now belong to the family of Dolittles. The Lord make the little I do effectual, and I heartily thank him for giving me a will when I had strength, and for not laying me aside, but continuing a small measure of strength, now I am old.

No Master like Jesus. Every endearment meets in this Master, the Father, the Brother, the Husband and Friend. Every office centres in him, the Prophet, and Priest, and King of his people. He has abundant charms to captivate a heart when the eye is opened to behold him. "Blessed are your eyes, for they see,"[4] Jesus saith to his disciples. And may we not join in thanking God for this blessedness bestowed on us also? The Lord open our eyes more clearly, and keep them open, till we behold this precious Jesus face to face. You are indebted to him for the will and the power to be bountiful; and for continuing the will, notwithstanding the daily trouble and frequent impositions attending your bounty. The praise is his due, give it, I trust you do, give it him all. But chiefly are you indebted to Jesus for giving you a sight of himself, and drawing your heart after him. This is the dawn of eternal blessedness. A view of the Lord of glory, is glory springing up in the soul. And as this view groweth clearer and more abiding, the glory increaseth, till at length it is consummated by an eternal weight of glory. What a

---

[1]   This letter was written from the Tabernacle during Berridge's winter preaching. It is found in Jones, *Memoir of Rowland Hill*, 584–585; *WB* (1838), 449–450; and *WB* (1864), 418–419.

[2]   Tottenham Court Road Chapel.

[3]   Berridge did not think he was much of a worker now.

[4]   Matthew 13:16.

prospect is here opened to the believer, and what a claim to eternal praise from him, who was born a child of wrath, and an heir of hell, but through grace has been snatched like a brand from the burning,[5] adopted into the family above, and made a child, and an heir of God most high. Thus the beggar is lifted up from his dunghill, and exalted among the princes of heaven.

The Lord make all your dear relations partakers of his blessing; and for this purpose may Jesus' grace be with them all, and abound in yourself, and your affectionate servant,

John Berridge

P.S. I send you very early notice of my waiting upon you, lest another appointment should be fixed for that day, and I could not conveniently come at any other time.

---

[5] Amos 4:11.

To Miss L___ [1]

Everton, April 27, 1786

My dear Lissey,

Through the Lord's protection I came safe to Everton on Tuesday, the 11th, at half-past four, and found my servants all well, and everything well about me. Blessed be God for seventy years mercies: may they follow me all my days, and bring me to the land of everlasting praise, where mercy endureth for ever. We lose much of the savoury comfort that springs from providential bounty for want of duly discerning what a mercy it is. The starving beggar, who receives sixpence from a charitable hand feels the value of this mercy, and blesseth his benefactor with a warm heart. And is not every mouthful you eat the same mercy? As much unmerited, and as much a free gift, as a beggar's alms? Why then is not every meal a feast of gratitude? Because we want the beggar's sauce, hunger and poverty, to make us duly thankful for food. One morning last week, as I lay in bed, thinking of a person I could not relish on account of selfishness, these words were dropped

---

[1] The letter is found in *WB* (1838), 450–452, and *WB* (1864), 419–420. See August 2, 1792. Berridge is writing after returning to Everton from his three months' winter preaching in London. Possibly this letter was written to Elizabeth Crabb (d.1807), the housekeeper to John and Mary Newton in London, because of the mention of Betsy and Sally, who were members of the Newton household. The Newtons had just moved house the previous month, and this may form some of the background to the housekeeper's cares, or they may be of a spiritual nature. In his will Newton particularly mentions the way Crabb cared for his wife when she was dying. Newton's attitude to his servants is shown in a later letter: "Phoebe is drooping, and I think will not hold out long; Crabb is very asthmatic; Sally but so-so. Perhaps one young, healthy servant could do as much as all our three; but then we live in love and peace, and bear each other's burdens as much as we can; and for their services, especially in the time of my great trials, from 1788 to 1790, I shall always think myself more obliged to them than they can be to me, and I hope nothing but death shall part us; pray for them, for they all love you and Mrs. Coffin" (Josiah Bull, *The Life of John Newton* [Religious Tract Society, 1868], 341). Bull also mentions that there were still more than a hundred letters addressed by Newton to his servants, chiefly to Crabb, in existence (342).

into my bosom, "Look at what is good in him, overlook the rest." I found the words came from the Lord, by the effect which they had; for they instantly removed the disgust which I had long conceived. Thus when a veil was thrown over selfishness, I could discern good things in him, and think of him with pleasure. This may be of use to my Lissey to remove present disgusts, which are cankers, that prey upon the spirits. Alas, how little do we possess of that love, which beareth, believeth, hopeth, endureth all things.[2] We grow more like Jesus only as we grow up into him in love; and this grace purifies and sweetens the affections, banishing selfishness, so far as it prevails. It is the temper of heaven, and the nature of God; for God is love. And can a God of love suffer his children to want anything needful? Does he feed his birds, and will he starve his babes? Has He given us bodies to be fed and clothed; and will He withhold food and raiment? If you chance to feel anxiety about these matters, remember the sweet, quieting word, which Jesus has dropped to hush the spirit: "Your Father knoweth that you have need of these things"[3]; and again, "Fear not, little flock, it is your Father's good pleasure to give you the kingdom"[4]; and if he give you the kingdom he will bear your charges thither.

I send my love to constant Betsy[5] and Sally[6]; the Lord send his love, and that crowneth all. Grace and peace be with you all, and with your affectionate servant,

John Berridge

---

[2] 1 Corinthians 13:7.

[3] Luke 12:30.

[4] Luke 12:32.

[5] Assuming the letter is indeed to Crabb, this is Elizabeth (Betsy) Catlett (1769–1834), the daughter of Mary Newton's younger brother, was orphaned and then adopted by the Newtons in 1774. She cared for John Newton after the death of his wife in 1790. She suffered a period of mental illness in the early 1800s that led to a stay in Bethlehem Hospital, but she returned, together with her husband, whom she married in 1805, to live with Newton after she had recovered.

[6] Again, assuming the letter is to Crabb, this would be Sally Johnson, one of the Newtons' servants. See September 17, 1782.

To John Newton[1]

Everton, June 14, 1786

My dear Brother,

I have received and read your *Messiah*[2]; and I thank God for the sermons, and for the testimony you have borne against oratorios. They seem a growing evil. The public prints give notice that three oratorios are to be performed in Louth church[3] at the end of this month. The fiddling of Scripture in a theatre seems to me a profanation of God's word, making it a mere carnal amusement; and the matter is made worse by bringing oratorios into God's house, they then become a satanical ordinance; and Mr. Hill's[4] grace before and after the musical treat, was, though not intended, a consecration of it. The bringing an Oratorio band, an army of pipers and fiddlers into God's house, appears to me a worse profanation than bringing doves into the Temple.[5] But the cry is, they were all professors; perhaps so, and they are quickly made by a gallery ticket and a hymn book.

From Sir Richard's[6] avowed vindication of Church oratorios, displayed in two letters to our Trustees,[7] containing twenty quarto

---

1   Besides Jones, *Memoir of Rowland Hill*, 584–585; *WB* (1838), 452–453; and *WB* (1864), 420–422, there is a manuscript of this letter at LPL, MS 3096 ff.112–113. The editing consists mainly of changing numerals into words.
2   See November 12, 1785. Newton felt that the *Messiah* was in danger of being secularized by an audience that missed the spiritual underpinning of the work.
3   Louth was 100 miles north of Everton in the Lincolnshire Wolds.
4   Rowland Hill, minister of Surrey Chapel.
5   John 2:14.
6   Sir Richard Hill (1732–1808), brother of Rowland and MP for Shropshire. Because of Rowland Hill's support for oratorios the trustees had stopped him preaching at Tottenham Court Road Chapel. Richard wrote a long letter to the trustees supporting his brother's position on oratorios, dated April 22, 1786. The trustees replied in a conciliatory manner, saying that the exclusion was only meant to be a temporary silence. Rowland Hill himself decided that oratorios should not continue at Surrey Chapel. It seems obvious that the trustees had asked for Berridge's advice. See Shenton, *Rowland Hill*, 243–251.
7   Trustees of the Tabernacle and Tottenham Court Road Chapels.

pages, it seemed plainly his desire to have annual celebrations in Surrey chapel, and I could not tell how far Mr. Hill might be influenced by his brother and a large band of fiddle-stick professors. Therefore I am not sorry that a stir has been made about this matter, to nip the evil in its bud. But if I had known Mr. Hill's declaration, that no more oratorios should be performed in his chapel, it would have saved me the trouble of writing my letter, which was sent to Mr. Mills[8] of Moorfields, in answer to a letter from him and designed for no one else.

I am sorry to find you all agree in calling oratorios inexpedient things and nothing more. Whereas, if they are lawful exhibitions for God's house, the devil will soon find a way to make them expedient. For what more expedient to ease a chapel of its debt, than a lawful oratorio? And what more expedient to repair a decayed chapel, or to help to support the ministers, than a lawful oratorio? Jesus Christ is Lord of the Sabbath,[9] and Lord of his house, and no one has a right to appoint offices or ordinances but himself. All human inventions are innovations of his authority, neither expedient nor lawful.

I have long laboured to unite Mr. Hill and our Trustees, and thought a union was happily effected before I left London; but breach comes so quickly after breach, and widens the gap so much, that I begin to question whether a solid union can be had. Your letter, for want of a proper direction, paid two visits to your post office, and rambled round Bedfordshire, before it reached Everton.

I bought eight nightcaps[10] of Mr. Marchant, and paid for them before they were made. They are now come, and I find were charged three shillings too little. If you will take your three shillings to Betty King[11] when you pass by the Tabernacle, she will take them to Mr. Marchant, and thus all matters are rectified.

I send my kind Christian respects to Mrs. Newton, and to our common Christian friend, Mr. Good-looks, a Saturday guest, whom I hope to see at Everton. Grace and peace be with you, and with your affectionate brother,

John Berridge

---

8   Benjamin Mills. See September 24, 1782.
9   Matthew 12:8.
10 Presumably for his labourers.
11 She was the housekeeper at the Tabernacle house, where preachers stayed, and thus looked after Berridge during his winter preaching. See April 25, 1778.

To John Thornton[1]

Everton, October 11, 1786

Dear and honoured Sir,

You are now returned, I suppose, from your episcopal visitation, and have made a seaport ring with gospel-tidings.[2] The Lord attend them with his blessing. You do well to change your station every year, and may the cloudy pillar[3] always go before you, and direct you where to fix the gospel standard. What an honour the Lord Jesus puts upon you, in employing you to carry abroad the best news that can be heard, news of salvation; and whilst others travel to behold the vain glitter of earthly glory, you are travelling to show to sinners the unsearchable riches of Christ, and allure them to his arms. The Lord, who employs you, is a good Master, and will remember every labour of love you undertake for his sake. May his presence be ever with you to animate and protect you, and his love to refresh you, and may his own dear self be the growing love and joy of your heart, your strength and confidence, a sweet present portion and your everlasting all.

Infirmities, I find, are growing upon me; but they come at the Lord's bidding, to make him[4] room in the heart; and come with his blessing to make them welcome. My ears are now so dull, they are not fit for converse, and my eyes are so weak, I can read but little, and write less. Old Adam,[5] who is the devil's darling, sometimes whispers in my ears (and he can make me hear with a whisper), what will you do, if you become both deaf and blind? I tell him, I must think the more, and pray the more, yea, and thank the Lord for eyes and ears enjoyed till I was seventy, and for the prospect of a better pair of eyes and ears, when these are gone.

---

[1] The letter is found in *GM* (1838), 419; *WB* (1838), 453–455; and *WB* (1864), 422–423. *GM* has the date as March 15 and contains no postscript.
[2] Thornton had spent a month at Yarmouth with a group of friends, including four preachers.
[3] The cloudy pillar directed the Israelites in the wilderness. Numbers 9:17.
[4] *WB* has "them."
[5] The old man in the Christian.

What a mercy to have a never-failing Jesus, when all things else are failing! O my God, I thank thee for the precious gift of Thy beloved Son, and for sweetly joining my heart unto him. My breast[6] is so weak, I cannot walk ten minutes, yet am enabled to preach once a week, and have more enjoyment of my body, when sitting still, and better rest at nights, than usual. So here is mercy along with judgment, and by and by it will be mercy without judgment. I hear Mr. Robert Thornton[7] is married; may the Lord betroth both the groom and the bride to himself, and plant his faith in the hearts of all your children. Grace and peace be multiplied upon you, dear Sir, and upon your much obliged and affectionate servant,

John Berridge

P.S. Please to accept my thanks for your letter, and two sermons sent by Mr. Astell.[8] The Yelling Archdeacon[9] is well.

---

[6] *GM* has "breath."
[7] Robert Thornton (1759–1826), second son and co-proprietor with his eldest brother Samuel in his father's business after their father withdrew in 1783. He had been elected MP for Bridgwater on July 21, 1785, and later became MP for Colchester. He married Maria Eyre on September 17. He did not share the values of his brothers and seemed to be indifferent to the religious convictions of his father. He died in the United States, having fled to France in 1815 as a bankrupt.
[8] See July 27, 1779.
[9] Henry Venn.

To Benjamin Mills[1]

Everton, November 1, 1786

Dear Sir,

I had bought some very strong good cloth to make two coats and breeches for two very poor but upright preachers, and had sent it a fortnight ago, with a guinea to each to make the clothes up, with some thoughts of your bounty to eke the matter out. But I find you are no friend to eking, for you have made the whole up, with a remnant beside. On opening your letter I gave the Lord hearty thanks for your donation, with a prayer for a blessing on the donor; and may his blessing ever rest on you and yours. Amen.

I had much of my nervous fever[2] in the summer, which kept me at home; and the Lord took away my hearing for three months so that I was not conversable. Then my eyes seemed to be gone apace, and at one time I had an apprehension of being both deaf and blind. At first I prayed daily to the Lord for my hearing, but with submission to his will, and on Sunday fortnight He gave me a better pair of ears (thanks be to his grace), not perfectly restored, yet so as to make me able to converse with comfort; and they seem still to be mending. This has encouraged me to ask for a better pair of eyes. And why should I not? Jesus has eyes to give as well as ears, and he can bear dunning[3]; nay, is never better pleased than with a thousand duns at his door. Well, my eyes are somewhat better (thanks again to my healer), and I keep praying on.

I am glad to hear you write of a visit to Everton; we have always plenty of horse provender at hand, but unless you send me notice beforehand of your coming, you will have a cold and scanty meal, for we roast only twice in the week. Let me have a line, and I will give you the same treat I always gave to Mr. Whitefield[4]—an eighteen

---

[1] The letter is from *WB* (1838), 465–466, and *WB* (1864), 433–434.
[2] See June 3, 1771.
[3] Press repeatedly, especially for money.
[4] See May 22, 1769.

penny barndoor fowl; this will neither burst you, nor ruin me; half you shall have at noon with a pudding, and the rest at night. Much grace and sweet peace be with yourself and partner; and the blessing of a new heart be with your children. With many thanks I remain your affectionate servant,

John Berridge

P.S. Please to present my love to the Trustees, and all the labourers.

To Mr. ___[1]

Everton, November 7, 1786

Dear Sir,

I received your kind letter, along with your present. I thank you for the present, as being a token of your respect, and attended, I find, with your daily prayers for me, which I value more than human presents. The Lord bless you, and lift up the light of his countenance upon you, and give you a sweet enjoyment of his peace. I have hitherto found that Christian people who live in the dark, fearing and doubting, yet waiting on God, have usually a very happy death. They are kept humble, hungering and praying, and the Lord clears up their evidences at length in a last sickness, if not before, and they go off with hallelujahs.

From what I know of you, and from the account you give of yourself, I have no doubt of the safety of your state; yet rest not here, but seek further. Two things should be carefully attended to by all upright people—one is the evidence of the Word, the other is the evidence or witness of the Spirit. The Word says, "all that believe are justified from all things."[2] I ask, then, do you not place your whole dependence on Jesus Christ for salvation? Do you not heartily accept of Jesus Christ in all his offices, and are you not daily seeking to him to teach you and rule you, as well as to pardon you? Then you are certainly a believer, and as such are justified in God's sight from all your sins, according to the plain declaration of God's word. Let this encourage you to seek with confidence for the evidence of the Spirit, to proclaim that justification to your heart. The evidence of the word is given to hold up the heart in a season of doubts and fears, and the evidence of the Spirit comes to scatter those fears. Remember also that salvation does not depend on the *strength* of faith, but the *reality* of it. In the gospels, Jesus often rebukes weak faith, but never

---

1   Berridge is again answering a question on assurance. It is contained in *GS* (1870), 254–255; Ryle, *Christian Leaders*, 251–252; *Gospel Truths, or Old Paths* (1878), 374–375; and *S* (1907), 64.

2   Acts 13:39.

rejects it. Weak faith brings but little comfort, yet is as much entitled to salvation as strong.

I have had much of my nervous fever[3] this summer; never once stirred out of my parish, and never further in it than to my church! Through mercy I am somewhat better; and when alone, with a Bible before me, am composed and comfortable, yet scarce able to bear visits, so weak are my spirits. Give my love, to Mr. G___, and tell him from first to last he has been the friend of my heart. I send my kind respects to your partner. Grace and peace be with you both, and with your affectionate servant,

John Berridge

---

[3] See June 3, 1771.

To John Thornton[1]

Tabernacle, February 20, 1787

Dear and honoured Sir,

My turn is to preach at Tottenham,[2] on Sunday the 11th of March, when there will be no noon sacrament, and on that day I purpose to wait upon you at Clapham, if convenient, and shall be thankful for your conveyance thither. Dr. Peckwell[3] lately hinted to one of our trustees his intention of practising physic; and when the society called the Poor Man's Friend,[4] met at Tottenham on Wednesday last, he proposed himself, as a physician to prescribe for the patients under the care of that society. This looks like an introductory step to the practice of physic, and as a design to make his intentions generally known. A dispensary seems to me a poor exchange for the Bible, and a *Materia Medica*[5] of little value in respect of Christ's Calvary balms. Where Christ is known and felt, his pulpit service is far beyond all medical fees. Happy are they that grow hoary in his service, and find it more and more delightful. A good Master he is, kind to all his servants, his love, like himself, boundless, his wages beyond computation great, and measurable only by eternity, yet wholly undeserved.

When I get a glimpse of Jesus, and we have only glimpses here, he seems so precious, so desirable, so all over glorious, I wonder that my thoughts can be employed on any other object; but mists come on to cloud the spiritual hemisphere, and Christ is hid behind his cloud; yet faith can trust an unseen God, and rear its head when sense and reason fail. Oh, for much of this heaven-born faith, to cheer us on while running the race, and hold up the heart when it is ending! The Lord

---

[1] This letter is found in *GM* (1838), 459; *WB* (1838), 455–456; and *WB* (1864), 423–424. *GM* is dated March 20.
[2] Tottenham Court Road Chapel.
[3] Henry Peckwell (1746–1787). See November 4, 1785.
[4] See March 2, 1776.
[5] A book on drugs. Dioscorides (AD c.40–90) was a Greek physician and botanist who served as a surgeon in the Roman army, and wrote his *Materia Medica*, a pharmacopeia giving the medicinal properties of plants and animal products.

plant this faith in the hearts of all your children and give you the comfort of beholding all its fruits in them. And may the God of peace give you his peace at all times and afford the same to your truly affectionate and much obliged servant,

John Berridge

To Mrs. Wilberforce[1]

Everton, September 22, 1787

Dear Madam,

Mr. Venn informs me, you have been ill, but are now recovering. I dare not say, I am sorry you have been ill, because the Lord Jesus sent the illness, who does all things well; and because affliction is usually a thriving season with his children; but I bless God that you are growing better, and you, I trust, can bless him, that you have been sick. Health, like other temporal blessings, if long continued, is apt to thrust the thought away from our removal, and place the borders of the grave at a distance from us, which weakens the importance of eternal things. Exercised we may be daily in the word of God and prayer, but are we daily looking for the Master's coming? Not only waiting on him in all appointed means, but waiting for him. The best of us, like the wise virgins, are apt to drop into a doze at times,[2] which calls for some alarm to waken us. And when sickness knocketh at the door, it echoes to the heart of the Lord's word. Be ye ready. Trim your Lamp, get your evidences clear, and go ye forth to meet the bridegroom. Nothing helps to solemnize my soul like eternal things, when viewed just at hand. Even comforts at times will make me light and giddy, but the midnight cry, behold the Bridegroom cometh,[3] makes me sink into solemnity. The Lord's word crieth to the sons of men, oh, that they were wise to consider their latter end,[4] to place it daily before their eyes. And the word is directed to saints and sinners, for all need this wisdom. May we be kept standing daily on the brink of Jordan, expecting our passage, and looking to our Jesus to conduct us safely over. How vain all earthly things appear, how light our troubles by the way, when eternity is full before us. Dying people view these

---

[1] Written to Hannah Wilberforce, the letter is found in PLFELM, GD26/13/745. See December 19, 1777.
[2] Matthew 25:5.
[3] Matthew 25:6.
[4] Deuteronomy 32:29.

matters truly. May such dying views live with us daily, and may Jesus rule supremely in our hearts, our everlasting trust and whole desire; to whom be glory now and evermore.

Mrs. Venn[5] is not expected to recover, and Nelly[6] is in a poor way. My own body is very feeble, my eyes are dim, my ears very deaf, and my breast so weak, that writing oversets me; but I look for new eyes, new ears, yea, all things completely and eternally new. Grace and peace be multiplied upon you, dear Madam, and upon your affectionate servant,

John Berridge

---

[5] Catherine (Smith), second wife of Henry Venn. "She was a daughter of the Rev. James Ayscough, vicar of Highworth, Wiltshire, and the widow of a Mr. Smith, and at this time living in Kensington. They were married on July 15, 1771, at Kensington church. For twenty-one years she remained his devoted wife, and acted as a wise and affectionate mother of his children" (John Venn, *Annals*, 96–97).

[6] Henry Venn's eldest daughter, Eling. See November 24, 1781, and August 2, 1792.

To John Thornton[1]

Everton, October 27, 1787

Dear and honoured Sir,

The word of God and prayer has been my employment for a long season, and I had proposed to read no other book but the Bible; but your *Remembrancer*[2] being a small tract and savoury, I read it through, and found it so profitable, that I purpose, if coming again to London, to buy a dozen for my lay-preachers. By duly reading the holy word, and mixing it with prayer, I find my faith and my affection more steadfastly fixed on Jesus, and at times He appears so exceedingly sweet, that I could kiss his feet, were he bodily present, but being absent, I kiss his name in the Bible with reverential love. Oh, dear Sir, if Jesus appears so precious with only a glimpse of his glory, how precious must he appear when beheld in all his glory, and in the full smile of his countenance. What Sheba's Queen said to Solomon, is only verified in our Jesus: "Happy are thy servants who stand continually before thee."[3] I know not of any growth in grace, but what ariseth from growing out of self, carnal, worldly, and righteous self, up into Christ, and finding him become more and more, our love and joy, our strength and confidence, our pleasant meditation, and our all in all.

I do not much prize our Church Catechism. It begins so very ill, calling baptism our new birth, and making us thereby members of Christ, children of God, and heirs of the kingdom of heaven.[4]

---

1 The letter is found in *GM* (1838), 515–516; *WB* (1838), 456–457; and *WB* (1864), 424–425.

2 Ambrose Serle (1742–1812) was Under Secretary of State to the Earl of Dartmouth and then one of the commissioners of the Transport Board. A devotional writer and close friend of Thornton, he had just produced *Christian Remembrancer, or short reflections upon the faith, life, and conduct, of a real Christian* (1786). He gave a long dedication to Thornton, "who, Adorning the doctrine of GOD his Saviour, In an almost unexampled degree, By deeds of piety and benevolence, Various, liberal, and extensive, But without ostentation...."

3 1 Kings 10:8.

4 For Berridge's tensions over infant baptism, see *Christian World*. For a

Mr. Stillingfleet[5] should have spoken more fully and pointedly about this weighty matter; for all carnal churchmen fancy they are new-born, because baptised, and quote the Catechism as a proof of it, and the carnal clergy preach accordingly, and quote the same authority. The acting as sponsors is now become a mere farce, and a gossiping business; and the promising for infants, what they cannot engage for themselves, may suit a covenant of works, but not a covenant of grace.

Mrs. Venn[6] is a little revived, but not likely to recover, somewhat like to Mrs. W___. In my prayers I remember them daily. On Thursday fortnight Mr. Venn dined with me, and came with N[elly][7] in a single-horse chaise. At four he went to Potton, and overturned the chaise. His breast and shoulder were much bruised by the fall. N[elly] was also hurt, but not much. He was blooded[8] at Potton, and went home the next morning in a postchaise.[9] He has not preached since; and remains but indifferent.[10] My health, through mercy, is rather better than in some years past; but my body grows tottering, my eyes dim, my ears deaf, and my faculties feeble. However, I look for new eyes, new ears, and new faculties, when this vile body is ground down in the grave. Thanks be to Jesus for this prospect, the fruit of his purchase and effect of his grace. The Lord give you much of his presence, with a daily waiting for his coming, and bestow the blessings of his spiritual kingdom on all your dear children and relatives. Grace and peace be with you and all of us, and with your affectionate and dutiful servant,

John Berridge

summary, see Pibworth, *Gospel Pedlar,* 218–220.

5   James Stillingfleet (1729–1817), *Explanation of the Church Catechism* (York, 1778).

6   See September 22, 1787.

7   Eling, eldest daughter of Venn. See November 24, 1781.

8   Bled by a doctor.

9   A hired carriage.

10   *GM* misses out the personal details: "Mrs. Venn…but indifferent."

To the Rev. C. Glascott[1]

Tabernacle, January 28, 1788

My dear old Friend,

I am coming to fetch you up to London, and you must not say me, nay. The cause of God requires your attendance here. We are delivered from two high priests, who were grown tyrannical. God removed one by death,[2] and the other removed himself, who laid a trap to catch the Trustees, but it went off the wrong way, and caught himself. Tottenham[3] hearers are somewhat fond of prunello,[4] and there is none for them now, but an old gown of mine, which, like its wearer, is almost worn out. Your preaching is very acceptable to the chapels. The hearers are simple-hearted, none more so; and you can surely make the congregations hear your voice, as easily as old John, who has not a single tooth left in his mouth. The Trustees would be glad to engage you for six or eight weeks every year, or if that cannot be, as often as you can; but your presence will really be needful, when I return to Everton, on the 18th of March, and you will then be at liberty. You will dwell at [the] Tabernacle, in a comfortable chamber, with all needful refreshments, and a coach to convey you to and from Tottenham, and a gratuity for your labours. I beseech you, therefore, my dear brother, for the love of Christ and the good of the chapels, that you will not let any seeming difficulties prevent your coming. Only come, and the Lord will bless your own soul, and make you a blessing. Send me word, you will come, and that will rejoice the hearts of many, as well as your truly affectionate old friend,

John Berridge

---

[1]   The manuscript is held at CBS, DU/10/3. The letter was written from .the Tabernacle, Moorfields, and is addressed "For the Rev. C. Glascot, at Lady Huntingdon's Chapel, Bath." Glascott had helped Berridge during his long illness. See March 23, 1770.

[2]   Possibly Dr. Peckwell, who died on August 18, 1787. See February 20, 1787.

[3]   Tottenham Court Road Chapel.

[4]   A dark, smooth woollen material in the colour of plum that was used to make clerical gowns; hence, the congregation was fond of clergymen.

To John Thornton[1]

Tabernacle, February 21, 1788

Dear and honoured Sir,

I am so tumbled about in preaching, without any regularity, that I know not where I am to preach, till an order comes. However, for once, I will fix my time, viz., the 2nd of March, and wait upon Mrs. Wilberforce[2] afterwards. I begin to be weary of London, gossiping visitors weigh me down. Everton suits me best, where I can be alone, with the Word of God for my companion, and leisure enough for musing and prayer. Never am I well but when at home with Jesus. May he draw me nearer, and keep me closer with him. Yesterday, Dr. Ford[3] was ordained, and it seemed a good season. Captain Scott[4] is here, a truly spiritual man. The Lord give you all you can desire, much grace in your own heart, and much in your children. Jesus' peace be ever with you, and with your dutiful and affectionate servant,

John Berridge

---

[1] The letter is in *GM* (1839), 24; *WB* (1838), 458; and *WB* (1864), 426. *GM* has February 21 and March 2 as one letter and dates it October 26, 1788.

[2] Mrs. Hannah Wilberforce was a half-sister of John Thornton and aunt to William Wilberforce the politician. See December 19, 1777 and [November/ December 1788]. Mrs. Carteret, writing to Lady Huntingdon, records the following on December 19, 1777: "Mrs. Wilberforce much obliged for your kind remembrance of her, she is leaving our neighbourhood, has taken a house near Bedford Row, we met Mr. Berridge with her a few days ago, he seems in good health and spirits has hitherto escaped his London cough" (CCA, F1/0427).

[3] See April 26, 1777.

[4] See November 2, 1773.

To John Thornton[1]

Tabernacle, March 2, 1788

Dear and honoured Sir,

After I left St. James's Place, I spent the afternoon with Mrs. Peckwell,[2] a precious woman, and a living instance of what grace can do. Some little gloom hung upon her countenance, but a cheerfulness appeared in her speech and temper. She did not, so she would not, seem to know of anything amiss in the doctor.[3] She treated with indignation the slander against her husband immediately after his departure, which basely originated from a preacher in connexion with him.[4] She spoke of Dr. Peckwell with great tenderness. The daughter[5] is the very image of the father, and the son[6] pleased me much. At five he came from school, and I asked him whether he had learned to swear. He answered, No. I asked further, has no one tried to make you swear? Yes, he said, many had tried, and once he was offered a guinea to make him swear, but would not. What nurseries of vice are public schools, and the next nursery is a university!

If you can be of any service to Ann Street, you will do an act of kindness to a blind Christian woman. On Tuesday se'nnight I purpose to return to Everton, when I shall be released from gossiping visitors, and have leisure for the word of God and prayer. I am weary of my wretched self, and weary too of prattling visitors. No rest can I find but in God, in musing of him, or in converse with him. All things else are an aching void, promising something, but bringing

---

[1] On this date Berridge was supposed to see Thornton. See February 21, 1788. Presumably the appointment was cancelled. The letter is found in *CM* (1845), 741.

[2] Widow of the late Dr. Peckwell. See November 4, 1785, and February 20, 1787.

[3] Her husband.

[4] Sentence omitted in *WB*.

[5] Selina Mary, named after her godmother, the Countess of Huntingdon.

[6] Robert Henry (1776–1823) was twelve at this time. He later became Chief Justice in Calcutta, where he died.

nothing. The Lord Jesus fill you with his heavenly treasures, and make your seed a holy offspring. Much grace be with you, dear Sir, and with your truly affectionate servant,

John Berridge

To Lady Huntingdon[1]

Everton, September 25, 1788

My Lady,

My ears are so deaf, that I can hear nothing without bawling, as Mr. Dupont[2] knows to his sorrow, which makes a visit very troublesome to others and disagreeable to myself. On this account I thought it more advisable to send you in a letter what has been shouted into my ears by the Trustees, than to wait upon you in person, and the message I have to communicate is this: "When Dr. Ford returns to London, a fortnight hence, the Trustees will consider of the proposal made to them by Mr. Dupont and others."

I was grieved to hear of Mr. Wills's[3] departure; but our wise Jesus can overrule this separation for his glory, as well as that between Paul and Barnabas.[4] I return this week to Everton. May the Lord Jesus abide

---

[1]   This letter is found in CHCA (Letter 29), a copy by Seymour. It is addressed to "The Countess of Huntingdon, Spa Fields Chapel." Both *WB* (1864), 518, and Seymour, *Life of Huntingdon,* 1:216–217, give the date as 1778 but the context is clearly 1788, which is backed up by Seymour's copy of the letter in CHCA. Berridge, who was at the Tabernacle in September, had been commissioned by Lady Huntingdon to propose a plan showing the feasibility of uniting Whitefield's chapels with Lady Huntingdon's group of churches.

[2]   Matthias Peter Dupont, one of the original trustees appointed by Lady Huntingdon for her college and a manager of the Spa Fields Chapel.

[3]   Thomas Wills (1740–1802), a Cornishman converted through the influence of Samuel Walker (1714–1761). He became a clergyman at St. Agnes and married a niece of Lady Huntingdon. He resigned his curacy and became one of Lady Huntingdon's chaplains. In 1780 he left the Church of England and was one of two ex-clergymen who performed the first ordinations in Lady Huntingdon's New Connexion in 1783. Berridge is referring to Wills's dismissal by Lady Huntingdon and his becoming a Dissenting minister at Silver Street Chapel. For an account of Wills's dismissal, see Harding, *Countess of Huntingdon's Connexion,* 193–195.

[4]   Paul and Barnabas disagreed at the beginning of their second missionary journey over whether to take Mark. Paul refused to take him because he had deserted them on their previous journey and Barnabas and Paul separated, travelling to different areas. Acts 15:37–41.

with you and go with me, and give us both a triumphant exit at last. So prayeth your affectionate servant,

John Berridge

To an Unknown Lady[1]

Everton, October 9, 1788

Dear Madam,

When our expectation is too much raised on account of any creature, the Lord Jesus in wisdom disappoints it, that we may seek our whole happiness in him. He expects our whole dependence should be placed on him, and he will have it, and is worthy of it. The human heart would fain be roosting a little on some earthly thing but Jesus will unroost it, and bring it fluttering to himself, like the dove to Noah's ark, where alone it can find rest.[2] Delight thyself in the Lord (in him wholly) and he will give us the desire of our heart.[3] If the heart chance to seek delight elsewhere, it is kindness in the Lord to deny us our desires, and your late disappointment may bring you more profit than a sermon or a visit from myself. Indeed I was so deaf that a visit would have been very troublesome to you. During our warfare, troubles will come by sixes and sevens, a gracious company, and not one too many. If we could live well without them we should not have them, but we cannot, and therefore Jesus in love sends them. You are an afflicted family to be sure, but mercy, much mercy attends you. If three are cast down, one is held up, and though feeble, is supported till some other is raised up. If you see no family so afflicted as yours, can you find any family so blessed. All of one heart and one mind seeking after Jesus. Surely the Lord delights in you, and bestows his blessings on you, a healthy soul, while the world is satisfied with a healthy body. Yet the best need correction, and must have it. Whom the Lord loveth, he does rebuke and chasten.[4] Some foolishness is bound up in the hearts of his children,

---

[1] The letter is from *WB* (1838), 458–459, and *WB* (1864), 426–427. This is probably a friend from London, where Berridge had been in September, and was, perhaps, wondering why she had not received a visit.

[2] Genesis 8:11.

[3] Psalm 37:4.

[4] Proverbs 3:12.

and he will not spoil a child by sparing his rod.[5] Grace and peace be with you all, and with your affectionate servant,

John Berridge

---

5   Proverbs 22:15.

To Benjamin Mills[1]

Everton, October 9, 1788

Dear Sir,

This comes with a thank-offering for your kindness, and a prayer that God may multiply his mercy on yourself, your partner, and your children. Through the Lord's gracious providence I got to Everton safe and well on Saturday afternoon about five, and not quite so much tired as I expected. On Sunday I preached, and felt the effect of Wednesday's sermon. What a poor Dolittle I am, next door to a cumber ground![2] Twenty-one good meals in a week, with a bever[3] besides, and one sermon chiefly. Surely no lazy servant was ever so fed; but I live upon a King's bounty, who exceeds not only all deserts, but all our thanks and praises. He delights to make his servants stand amazed at his bounty and grace, bounty too rich to be exhausted, and grace too deep to be fathomed, except in glory. Let others prattle of their works and one sinner praise another, I will sing of the mercy of the Lord for ever and ever.[4] Thanks be to my God for giving me an appetite for this heavenly manna, and a taste of it. His mercy endureth for ever;[5] how sweet the sound, how rich the food, to a gracious soul! A pleasant thing it is to be thankful; and saints will feel a pleasing, growing debt of gratitude forever, which will fill the heavenly courts with everlasting hallelujahs. May you and I attend and join the choir.

---

1   *Christian Secretary*, 18 (1826), 72; *WB* (1838), 466–467; and *WB* (1864), 434–435. *CS* is highly abbreviated. Mills had sent his annual gift for Berridge's fellow labourers, and we are thankful that he kept the thank-you letters. Berridge had just returned from preaching in London. See October 3, 1783; November 20, 1784; November 4, 1785; November 1, 1786; and November 23, 1790.

2   Useless ground. Luke 13:7 (AV).

3   Drink or a snack.

4   Psalm 89:1.

5   Psalm 107:1.

I was sorry to see Mr. West[6] look so lank and walk so feebly; and as Mr. Keen,[7] though seemingly revived, is old and tottering like myself, I wish another Trustee might be chosen before their removal. It would be bad to have the whole Trust lodged in a single hand, and him a preacher too.[8] I trust the Lord Jesus, who has removed two high priests from the chapels,[9] and has shown a providential care of them hitherto, will direct the Trustees properly.

Solomon's account of old age suits me well.[10] The windows are dark; the daughters of music are low; the grinders cease for all are gone; and the grasshopper is a burden. Well, thanks be to God through Jesus Christ, for the prospect of a better world. Grace and peace be with you and yours, dear Sir, and with your affectionate servant,

John Berridge

---

[6] One of Whitefield's executors and a trustee of his chapels. He was to outlive Berridge and died on September 30, 1796.

[7] The other of Whitefield's executors and a trustee of his chapels. He was to die at the same time as Berridge on January 30, 1793. Berridge thought highly of these men and valued their integrity.

[8] Dr. Ford had been adopted as a third trustee.

[9] See January 28, 1788.

[10] Ecclesiastes 12.

To John Thornton[1]

Everton, October 26, 1788

Dear and honoured Sir,

Mrs. Bewicke[2] tells me that you are now returned from your ecclesiastical circuit, having visited France and Flanders.[3] I believe Great Britain is chiefly designed for your diocese, yet a little gospel seed, scattered in a foreign land, may not be lost; and this kind word follows, wherever you go: "Labour for the Lord shall not be in vain."[4] If others reject the offered blessings, it shall return upon your own head. How much more excellent and kindly are your campaigns than the imperial ones! You are bringing news of life and peace, and they are carrying horror and death, wherever they march, to themselves and others. How mad is worldly ambition, and yet how much admired, if it succeeds, by men of a worldly mind, who call these murderers of the human race, heroes! Little do these heroes think what vengeance they are drawing on themselves by the slaughters they occasion, and how hell will be moved to meet them at their coming down. Isaiah 14:9–15. These heroes are the devil's champions, who go forth to people his dominions, and upon their standards should be written Death and Hell. Blessed be God for engaging us in a better warfare, under the Prince of Peace, who calls us forth to a noble victory, attended with glory, honour, and immortality. All thanks to his grace for enlisting us, and keeping us steadfast to his standard. The praise is all his own, and must be all his own forever. Hallelujah.

Mrs. Berwicke pleases me much. There seems a real heart-work

---

[1] The letter is in *GM* (1838), 560–561; *WB* (1838), 459–460; and *WB* (1864), 427–428.

[2] Jane Bewicke (*c*.1740–1817) was the half-sister of John Thornton through Thornton's father's second wife Jane Newby and had married Calverley Bewicke (d.1774) in 1766. She was living near her brother at Clapham.

[3] In September Thornton, with others, visited Ostend, Ghent, Antwerp, Brussels, Lille and Paris. For Bull's brief account, see *Memorials of Bull* (1844), 175–177.

[4] 1 Corinthians 15:58.

in her, and worldly losses may have brought much gain. Mrs. Astell[5] is some little better, but exceedingly feeble, and not likely to continue very long. I hope there is something good in her, but cannot read her state truly, and fear she has been going backward lately. The Lord revive the work, if begun; or begin it effectually, by sanctifying the visitation, and drawing the heart quite home to Jesus. In neither of the partners can I see anything at present, but decency.

My ears have been stopped for two months, but now are somewhat opened. The Lord does all things well. I am growing infirm, as I must expect; and out of conceit with myself more and more, as I ought; decreasing, that Jesus may increase.[6] A precious Christ, and his precious word, are everything to me. My chief converse is with him, and I find myself best when alone with him. He is instead of all company. The Lord refresh your heart daily with his peace, and bring your children well acquainted with his grace and love. With affectionate and dutiful respects, I remain your much obliged servant,

John Berridge

---

5   This is presumably Mrs. Hannah Astell, now Mrs. Hannah Pownall, widow of Richard Astell. See October 1, 1784.
6   John 3:30.

To Mrs. Wilberforce[1]

[November/December 1788]

...Live as near to Jesus as you possibly can and die, die to self. 'Tis a daily work, 'tis hard work. I find self to be like an insurmountable mountain, or a perpendicular rock, that must be overcome. I have not got over it; nor halfway over. This, this is my greatest trial. Self is like a mountain; Jesus is the sun, that shines on the other side of the mountain, and now and then a sunbeam comes over the top. We get a glimpse, a sort of twilight apprehension of the brightness of the sun, but self must be much more subdued in me before I can bask in the sunbeams of the ever blessed Jesus, or say in everything, Thy will be done....[2]

---

[1] Hannah Wilberforce, sister of John Thornton. The editor of Berridge's *Works* introduces the extract as follows: "The truly pious Mr. Berridge says in a letter written to Mrs. Wilberforce when she was in dying circumstances..." (*WB* [1838], 492). Mrs. Wilberforce died in December 1788. The letter is found in *WB* (1838), 492, and *WB* (1864), 532–533. See December 19, 1777; September 22, 1787; and February 21, 1788.

[2] Matthew 6:10.

To John Thornton[1]

Everton, December 30, 1788

Dear and honoured Sir,

I am favoured with two letters, the former of which brought me ten pounds for the poor. The Lord return it in special blessings on yourself. I am now daily calling on my heavenly Counsellor to provide me a curate: telling him, I am unable to find or to choose one, but He is able to do both, and I am running much to his door on this errand. He will not be offended. Sometimes an anxious thought creeps into my bosom, and weigheth me down, but I send it off to Jesus. He is willing to take, and able to bear all burdens, that are cast upon him. My curate[2] cannot help being glad at having a living of his own, but he is himself in no haste to be gone, and our sorrow will be mutual at parting, whenever it be. There is, I perceive, a horrible fear that he and his partner will be poisoned, but the fear comes too late, for the mischief is done already. Richard's loins are well girt with truth, and his heart upright and stead-fast. His partner also accords well with him. I could wish the purchased living might be at some good distance from Pharisaic friends; however Christian faith must be tried to prove it genuine.

From what you write about Mr. Dyke,[3] he does not seem designed

---

[1] The letter is found in *GM* (1839), 120–121, and *WB* (1864), 429–430. Personal names are removed in *WB*. *GM* has December 26, 1788.

[2] Richard Whittingham. See October 3, 1783. It does not appear that Whittingham actually left, or, if he did, he soon returned.

[3] Thomas Dikes (1761–1847) "spelt his name *Dikes*; but it was a corruption of the family name; and in a memorandum, found among his papers after his death, he directed that it should appear on his coffin with the *y* instead of the *i*" (John King, *Memoir of the Rev. Thomas Dykes, LLB, incumbent of St. John's Church, Hull; with copious extracts from his correspondence* [Seeley, 1849], 26). He was ordained deacon on October 12, 1788, and obtained a curacy at Cottingham in the East Riding of Yorkshire on December 12, 1788 (a short time before Berridge's letter). On March 12, 1789, he married Mary Hey, the daughter of a well-known Evangelical at Leeds. After inheriting a large sum of money from his aunt, he built a new church outside the Hull boundary in the face of considerable opposition. He was the first vicar of this new church and remained

for me. If not settled at Cottingham,[4] his intended wife would scarce like to travel as far as Everton. I am rather sorry, when candidates for the ministry are preparing to get into petticoats, before they get into orders. On Saturday, I wrote to Mr. Venn, acquainting him with my needy want of a curate, and desiring him to inquire among his Cambridge friends about Mr. Dyke, or any other that might seem suitable. But indeed I am not very fond of College youths; they are apt to be lofty and lazy and delicate, and few of them might like to unite with such an offensive character as mine. I should think a young man from the Hull academies[5] might suit better; but my thoughts are not worth a groat, and when they embarrass me, I throw them into the lap of Jesus.

I am glad your dear sister[6] is removed from a frosty world, into a better region, where Jesus, precious Jesus, makes eternal spring and sunshine. Troublous times are coming, I fear, but two things comfort me; the Lord reigneth, and my life is drawing towards its close. The 9th of January is appointed for my journey to London. The Lord accompany me thither and there with his presence, protection, and blessing. May Jesus give you all that you wish for yourself and your children, hearts full of faith and love, and a life adorned with good works. Thus praying, I remain your much obliged and affectionate servant,

John Berridge

---

such until his death. Dykes became a very active and influential Evangelical churchman in Hull.

[4]   Cottingham is north-west of the city of Kingston upon Hull, a distance of 130 miles north of Everton.

[5]   Joseph Milner (1744–1797), a remarkable headmaster of Hull Grammar School, regularly sent pupils to Magdalene and St. John's at Cambridge. Arthur Pollard notes that "There is a veritable roll-call of evangelicals who received their school education from Milner" (Lewis, *Evangelical Biography*, 2:776).

[6]   Thornton's sister, Hannah Wilberforce, had died in December.

To John Thornton[1]

Tabernacle, January 10, 1789

Dear and honoured Sir,

Yesterday I came to Tabernacle safe and well, after some delay and peril in the morning early from a rusty horse. The first five miles he went well, then would only walk, and turn about. At six, when the moon went down, he fell down, and would go no further. We were now eight miles from Stevenage, sitting cold in a chaise. I betook myself lustily to the good old remedy, prayer, and the Lord inclined a wagoner to lend us a horse to Stevenage, and put our rusty one into his team. Is not the Lord wonderful in working? Who would distrust him? After this deliverance, attended with many thanksgivings, I had a fresh occasion for much joy and thankfulness this morning, for your double tens for the poor, who will now be flocking for relief, like sparrows to a barley-stack in winter, and will have the comfort of your silver grains.

I received your account of Mr. Hamilton, which is encouraging, but I commit all to my Master in daily prayer, telling him, the curate is not for me, but for himself, and desiring him to direct my kind friends in their search,[2] and to direct the heart of a youth to Everton, who may profit the people. By means of constant prayer, my heart is quite at ease. Oh the blessing of faith; thanks to my Jesus for a pittance of it! The Lord multiply daily mercies upon you, and bless your children with a heartfelt knowledge of his salvation. I am, dear Sir, your truly affectionate and obliged,

John Berridge

---

[1] The letter is taken from *GM* (1839), 148, and *CM* (1845), 741–742. The letter was written from the Tabernacle just after Berridge had arrived for his winter preaching.
[2] See December 30, 1788.

TO WILLIAM WILBERFORCE[1]

Everton, March 7, 1789

Honoured Sir,

I am going to want a curate and the Rev. Mr. Foster[2] recommends a Mr. Shepherd unto me, and thinks he will suit. He has got a testimonial signed by three regular clergymen in his neighbourhood and I have given him a title, but he fears the bishop of Lincoln[3] may refuse him ordination, because he has not kept terms enough at Oxford for a degree, and being now married, he cannot keep more. If you should please to speak to the bishop of Lincoln on his behalf, it might procure him an easy admission into the church. He is determined to be regular I shall not desire him to be otherwise.[4] Though unknown to your Honour in person, as you are to me, I trust we both belong to the

---

[1] William Wilberforce (1759–1833), the famous philanthropist and opponent of slavery. He had become MP for Hull, his native town, in 1780 and was to become a central figure in the Clapham Sect. He would surely have heard of Berridge during his time at Cambridge (1776–1781). His spiritual interest dates from European tours in 1784 and 1785 with Isaac Milner, with whom he read Doddridge's *The Rise and Progress of Religion in the Soul* and the Greek New Testament. Besides social reform, Wilberforce sought the Christianization of British India and the growth of the Evangelical party within the Church of England. For popular biographies, see J. Pollock, *Wilberforce* (Constable, 1977) or William Hague, *William Wilberforce: The Life of the Great Anti-Slave Trade Campaigner* (Harper Perennial, 2008). The manuscript is held at the Bodleian Library, Oxford, MS Wilberforce d.13 fol.29.

[2] Henry Foster. See April 11, 1775.

[3] George Pretyman Tomline (1750–1827), bishop of Lincoln between 1787 and 1820, was a distinguished academic (senior wrangler at Cambridge in 1772) and theologian. His book refuting Calvinism in 1802 drew a response from Thomas Scott. Tomline tutored William Pitt the Younger at Cambridge and became his close confidant and advisor.

[4] Not preaching outside the parish without permission. How different from Berridge's earlier views! This shows how desperate Berridge must have been for help. In fact, John Elard (*c.*1757–1798) was appointed curate at Everton in September, who later became the vicar of Renhold, Bedfordshire, in 1797, where he died the following year.

family of Jesus, which emboldens me to make this request. May much of the Lord's grace and peace be with you, honoured Sir, and with your unknown, but affectionate servant in the best bonds,

John Berridge

To the Hon. Mrs. Carteret[1]

Everton, November 23, 1789

Dear and honoured Ladies,

Grace, mercy, and peace be multiplied upon you, and upon all that love the Lord Jesus Christ in sincerity. I frequently hear of you from London friends, by which I know you are yet on your pilgrimage, though daily drawing nearer to its period, when sin and sorrow, darkness and dullness, will be done away, and the Lord will become your everlasting light, and the days of your mourning will be ended.

I am now an old pilgrim, crawling up towards eighty, and crawling on towards Jesus, my mental faculties much decayed, and my animal spirits often low. At times I feel, what you may feel, spiritual affections languid, prayers feeble, and faith weak, dropping into the embers, and not fire felt. Formerly, when frames were gone, all seemed to be gone; but the Lord is now teaching me to live by faith upon His precious Word. I tell Him, when my faith is weak, "Lord, I do believe in Thee, for my whole trust is in Thy blood and righteousness; and Thou hast said, whoever believes in Thee hath everlasting life, and shall never come into condemnation." "Pooh, pooh," says Satan, "thou art a dead soul, no life in thee." I won't hearken to his lies, but tell him I have life, though it be feeble, for my heart is daily yearning after Christ, and mourning for an absent Christ is as sure a sign of spiritual life as rejoicing in a felt Christ. What is dead has no mourning. A dead body cannot mourn for the world, nor can a dead soul mourn for Christ. "Nay," says Satan, "you will be slain at last, notwithstanding all your fond hopes." I tell him, though the Lord should seem about to slay me,

---

[1] The letter is taken from *CO* (1868), 708. Although the letter was addressed to Mrs. Carteret, it was to both Mrs. B. Carteret and Mrs. Anne Cavendish. Both ladies had married into wealthy eighteenth-century families and both were converted at the same time through the influence of Lady Huntingdon, whose companions they often were. Seymour speaks of them as being "part of the great harvest collected by Lady Huntingdon's house in London" (*Life of Huntingdon*, 1:461). They shared a house in St. James's Place and both died in 1792. See April 10, 1790.

I will keep on praying and believing, and, like Abraham, against hope believe in hope. By thus holding up the shield of faith, you will quench the fiery darts of the wicked one. The conflict will be over when the body of sin is broken down, and you will enter into peace, and see that Jesus whom your soul loves, and be forever with Him. O blessed world! O precious Jesus, who will then fill our souls with everlasting love and joy, and we shall help to fill His Heaven with everlasting praises. Come then, dear ladies, go forward, run, or walk, or crawl, as you can. Heaven's gates are open to receive you, and crowns of glory ready for you, bought with Jesus' precious blood. Hallelujah!

Give my hearty love to the ladies who assemble at your chamber. The Lord bless you all abundantly, and bless His poor old,

John Berridge

P.S. My eyes are so weak, I can scarce see how I write. If yours are the same, send no answer, for though agreeable to me, it must be troublesome, and perhaps painful, to you—therefore forbear. Poor Lord Huntingdon![2] The Lord support his mother.

---

[2] Francis Hastings (1729–1789), the Tenth Earl of Huntingdon, the eldest son of Lady Huntingdon, had proved a grief to his mother, despite her love and prayers, because of his aggressive unbelief and prodigal lifestyle.

To Lady Huntingdon[1]

Tabernacle, February 25, 1790

Dear and Elect Lady,

Elected of God, and preserved in life for noble purposes. A kingdom is prepared for you. The dear Redeemer's purchase, and you give him all the glory, else I could pay you no honour; religious thieves who labour much to enrich themselves, and steal the Lord's crown, are the worst of villains, and will receive a suitable doom. Plenty of woes are denounced against self-righteous souls, esteemed of men, but abhorred of God. Thanks to my Lord, he makes me grow more poor and blind, and helpless, and guilty, and loathsome in my own eyes; nowhere can I hide my vile head, but at his dear feet, and so rich is his mercy, so sweet his complexion, he cannot thrust a self-condemned wretch away. Indeed, I do love him, for what He has taught me, and can do little else but prattle of him in a pulpit, yet in such feeble accents, as make me loathe myself. Well, I try and try again, but always come away ashamed. Living tongues are dumb at best, we must die to speak of Jesus. When we see him face to face, the heart will be duly warmed, and the tongue enlarged to show forth his praise. Here we view him darkly through the glass of faith, and when he gives a flourish of himself, it is only through a lattice but when we view him, as he is, we shall learn to sing and praise in more becoming strains, but always far beneath his dignity and worth!!!

Grace and peace be with you and with your affectionate servant,

John Berridge

---

1 This letter is found in *GM* (1837), 230–231. The editors include a letter from W. Christmas of Bretford, dated April 19, 1837, explaining that he has the original letter written to Lady Huntingdon. He says: "I have copied it verbatim." Lady Huntingdon died the following year on June 17, 1791. See November 16, 1762.

To the Hon. Mrs. Carteret[1]

Everton, April 10, 1790

Dearly Beloved Friends,

Daughters of Zion and chosen of God from everlasting;[2] grace, mercy, and peace be multiplied upon you; and upon all that love the Lord Jesus Christ in sincerity. You are now bereaved for a while of a sister[3] in Christ; and in her loss, Jesus has shown you how tenderly he treats his drooping saints, when he removes them. O, his compassions are infinite! Love him, and trust him forever. What can he not do, and what will he not do for his ransomed people? Worthless indeed in themselves, yet bought with his blood. His eye is ever with them; his heart ever with them; nor will he cease tending his sheep, till he brings them all safe home to his fold. Jesus calls death the sleep of his saints; but our sister slept out of life in a sleep, and did not awake till she reached the kingdom of glory.

What transports must she feel, to find herself released from sin and sorrow, doubts and fears, for ever; and behold herself encircled with glorified saints, praising God for another inhabitant; yea, Jesus himself, with smiles of love, meeting his daughter to welcome her home. Now she can join with her Baron[4] in singing eternal praise to God and the Lamb, expecting you both very soon to blend your joys and praise with hers, and meet to part no more.

---

[1] The letter is found in the *Episcopal Recorder*, 6 (1843), 24, where it is undated, and also *CO* (1868), 709, where the date is given. In *EpRec* the letter is addressed to "Two Friends." The two friends are Mrs. B. Carteret and Mrs. Anne Cavendish. See November 23, 1789 and April 10, 1790. Personal names are removed in *EpRec*.

[2] "Daughters...everlasting" is omitted in *CO*.

[3] See note 5.

[4] Sir Sidney Stafford Smythe (1705–1778) became Lord Chief Baron in 1772, resigning in 1777 owing to infirmity. Before his death he became a member of the Privy Council. "He is said to have refused the post of Lord Chancellor, and to have been 'the ugliest man of his day.'" (Entry by George Fisher Barker in vol. 53 of L. Stephen and S. Lee, eds., *Dictionary of National Biography*, 66 vols. [Smith, Elder, and Co., 1885–1900].)

Well, then, my dear ladies, lift up your heads and rejoice, for your deliverance is nigh. A little more praying and trusting, a few more conflicts with sin and sorrow, and your wilderness trials are over. Jesus stands at his gate, crying out, "Fear not, only believe; I am with you, and will not forsake you." Disturb not yourself about the manner of dying but leave it to him to sweeten the passage. In Lady Smith[5] he has given you a sample of his tenderness. Therefore, again I say, fear not, only believe, for such as trust in him are never confounded.

If a conflict should assault[6] your faith, hope against hope, and trust him in darkness, as well as in light. When you can see him, and when you cannot. In the meantime, give thanks daily for what he has done, for calling you, and keeping you out of the world, and trust him for what is to come.

And now may the God of my life, and God of my love, and God of hope, conduct you safely through the wilderness, guide you comfortably over Jordan, and bring you triumphantly home to his Canaan. So prayeth your affectionate servant,

John Berridge

---

[5] Lady Sarah Smythe, daughter of Sir Charles Farnaby of Kippington in Kent, had married Sidney Stafford Smythe in 1773. They were both involved in the Evangelical movement. She died on March 18, 1790. Berridge would have learned of her death from Lady Mary Fitzgerald, who attended her in her last illness. She wrote an account to Henry Venn, Lady Smythe being a close friend of Venn, having presented him the living at Yelling. Venn replied on March 22, thanking her for her letter and comments on Lady Smythe's apprehensions concerning her manner of death. See Venn, *Life and Letters of Venn*, 484.

[6] *CO* has "batter."

To Benjamin Mills[1]

Everton, November 23, 1790

Dear Sir,

Our years are rolling away fast, and will quickly roll us into eternity. How needful that admonition: "Prepare to meet thy God!"[2] Without earthly business to mind, my heart will rove in the world, get bemired in it, and stick so fast in a quag, that I am forced to cry, Lord pull my heart out! Thanks to grace, I have been crawling many years on the road to Zion; and sometimes in, and sometimes out, and the Master has somewhat quickened my pace in the summer by a draught of birch wine,[3] as needful at times for a heavy heeled pilgrim, as the wine of the kingdom. Now being almost through the wilderness, very sick of self, and of a draggling world, I am drawing near to Mount Pisgah[4]; and when I stand on its top, the Lord give an open eye of faith, to see all the Promised Land, and rejoice in hope of the glory of God.

The windows of my house grow dimmer, scarce give a straight line, or spell a word right, and dislike a pen much. Yet, thanks to the Lord my health is better, my ears pretty stout, and my legs keep mending, are peaceable in a chair, though fretful in bed. I purpose, with the good leave and help of my Master to set off for Tabernacle on Tuesday, the 28th of December, unless a fall of snow then happen, which would delay me until the roads are tracked. The Lord afford his presence, protection and blessing. Blessed be God for a prospect of peace; much wrangling here about things civil and sacred, but no belligerents above. One heaven holds all, and one temple serves all, and one Jesus feeds all with his own love, joy, and peace. My eyes

---

[1] The letter is found in *WB* (1838), 467–468, and *WB* (1864), 435–436. See September 24, 1782.

[2] Amos 4:12.

[3] Chastisement or purging. Birch sap was fermented into wine, producing a bitter taste; the wine was used as a diuretic.

[4] The mount from which Moses saw the Promised Land. Deuteronomy 34.1.

cry for quarter,[5] so with affectionate respects to your partner, the Trustees, and preachers, I remain your much obliged servant,

John Berridge

---

[5]   His eyes are asking for mercy.

To Miss L___ [1]

Everton, May 6, 1792

Dear Lissey,

Once more I am paying a corresponding visit to you, and others, expecting it to be my last on account of my eyes, which are growing so dim, that I can read but little of what I love dearly, the precious word of God. I now lament the many years I spent at Cambridge in learning useless lumber, that wisdom of the world which is foolishness with God.[2] I see nothing worth knowing but Jesus Christ, and him crucified[3]; for him to know is life eternal.[4] Follow him at all times, and let your heart dance after him, as David danced after the ark.[5] And when he comes into your bosom hold him fast, and turn all other company out. He loves to be alone with his bride. You may find him in the shop, or in the street, if you seek him there; and often whisper in his ear, "Dear Jesus, come and bless me." He sometimes surprises us with his visit, and comes unexpectedly, yet he loves to see the doors open, and the bosom waiting for him. Many kind visits are lost through a gadding heart; therefore keep at home with the Lord and let him hear much of your loving talk, and tell him all your wants, and all your grievances, and cast all your care upon him[6] and hide nothing from him. Lean firmly upon him, and He will cheer your heart in every trying hour, and bring you safe at last to his eternal home, where sin and sorrow never come, but where joy and peace forever dwell. In this world we must expect tribulation; it is the Christian's fare, and comes because it is wanted, and stays no longer than whilst it is wanted.

---

[1] The letter is taken from *WB* (1838), 468–469, and *WB* (1864), 436–437. Berridge seems very conscious that this would be the last letter to this friend because of his failing health. See April 27, 1786, although it may be a different person.
[2] 1 Corinthians 1:20.
[3] 1 Corinthians 2:2.
[4] John 17:3.
[5] 2 Samuel 6:16.
[6] 1 Peter 5:7.

Hereafter He will make us know, if not before, that He hath done all things well.

I am very feeble in body, but as well as I should be, and must suffer my heavenly physician to prescribe for me. My kind respects attend you all and Nathan. Peace be with you, my dear Lissey, with spiritual health and joy in the Lord. The Lord give us a happy meeting above. Farewell,

John Berridge

To John Berridge[1]

Everton, May 24, 1792

Dear Nephew,

I am glad to hear of your success in business, but keep your getting to yourself, lest you tempt others to supplant you. Be thankful for temporal mercies, but remember that money will not save your soul; all earthly things must be parted with at death, and then nothing will stand you in any stead but Jesus Christ. Read his word daily, and pray to him daily to make you wise unto salvation. Remember, you have a soul to be saved, as well as cattle to be fed. Seek to Christ to teach you, and guide your feet in the way of salvation. I am, your affectionate uncle,

John Berridge

---

[1]   Berridge had concern for his nephew as long as he lived. The letter is from S (1893), 30. See November 12, 1773.

To Mrs. E. [Elliott]¹

Everton, August 2, 1792

My dear N[elly],

You ask me how I do? Eyes very dim, ears deaf, head much shattered, and spirits very low, yet much exempt from pain. Here my Jesus shows his tenderness, he knows his old horse can scarce carry his legs, and He will not overload him. I am apt to think the Lord may continue me here a year or two longer, because he has sent me a supply for that time. Having lost my benefactors,² I was thinking what I must do. Go on and trust, was the word. When we are low, Satan will batter us with unbelief. I dare not argue with Satan, but cast myself at Jesus' feet, committing soul and body to him, asking and expecting his assistance, it is not long before it comes with a loving reproof: "O thou of little faith, wherefore didst thou doubt?"³ The last two Sundays⁴ I was led to church and into the pulpit; my voice was feeble but hearable,

---

1   The letter is found in *WB* (1838), 469–470, and *WB* (1864), 437–438. In *WB* the letter is addressed to "Mrs. E___." Loane suggests that the letter was to Venn's eldest daughter, Eling Elliott (1758–1843), who was called Nelly (*Cambridge and the Evangelical Succession*, 115). See November 24, 1781.
2   John Thornton died in 1790 and the Countess of Huntingdon died in 1791.
3   Matthew 14:31.
4   John Warner went to Everton during this summer and notes Berridge's powerful preaching, in spite of his infirmity, as well as his hospitality after the meeting: "I would now run for miles to hear that which was good, but I was in a sad distressed state for five years. At last I had an opportunity of going to Everton to hear Mr. Berridge, who was then very old; and he died shortly afterwards. There was a great crowd, and I stood at the church door. Soon I saw the old gentleman stretch out his hand, and pull himself up into the pulpit. Oh, how I stood ready to devour his word! 'Brethren (he said) no scholarship is required to take you to heaven; Jesus Christ wants broken hearts, true beggars.' My heart was ready to leap out of my body for very joy. I cannot describe my joy—it was a true heaven on earth. Afterwards I was told I might go into his house and refresh myself, where there were many besides; and, oh, how sweet I found it to converse with them on the love of Jesus, and the experience of his blessing in the heart!" ("Diary of the Rev. B. Gilpin," *Beds Mag*, 18, no. 138 [1981], 25).

and Christ was precious. Oh, to see Jesus as he is, and surrounded with his ransomed people, hearts full of love pouring out hallelujahs, and filling heaven with his praise. Thanks to my Jesus for putting me in the way of his kingdom, and for holding me on hitherto. Give me, dear Lord, a safe and honourable passage through the wilderness, and a joyful entrance into Canaan. The Lord bless you, with great and endless blessings, and keep you under his care. Amen.

John Berridge

To George Gorham[1]

Dear Sir,

My brother Thomas Berridge has bought some land at Chatteris with a commonable[2] house. He has 400 towards payment, but wants 200 to make it complete. He applied to me for the money, and how could I refuse a brother? It will not be wanted till Lady-day[3] and I hope it will be ready for my brother at that time, that he may not be disappointed. Grace and peace be with you and with your affectionate servant,

John Berridge

---

[1] The manuscript is held at HMC, BER 1/5. See November 10, 1781.
[2] The house is shared with the land.
[3] March 25. Until 1752, Lady Day was the legal beginning of the year.

PART 5

*Undated or
wrongly dated letters*

To Lady Huntingdon[1]

My Lady,

Your last letter has cast a damp upon my spirit, because I perceive you are reduced very low both in body and spirit. Sharp pains after long weakness are trying things. How unsearchable are the ways of God, and yet how full of grace and love at the bottom. First, he throws you into the water, where billow after billow breaks upon our head: then casts you into the furnace, and heated now a seventh part hotter than usual. Surely Jesus loves you dearly, for he afflicts you deeply; and he will make all his friends pledge him in his own bitter cups. Well, cheer up, my dear Lady, he has said it, who cannot lie, that neither shall the water drown you, nor the fire consume you. He will either keep you from fainting; or, if to show his strength and your weakness, He suffers you to faint for a moment, He will not suffer you to fall, but will catch you in his loving arms. He stands always near you, and his eye is upon you, and his bowels yearn over you, and his arms are underneath you, though you may not always feel their support. And oh, remember, that relief is then at hand, when we are brought to our wits-end. In the mount the Lord will be seen. In the *height* of trouble or danger, Jesus will appear. So Isaac found, when brought to the mount: no voice from heaven, till the knife was lifted up to slay; then the voice comes, at a critical moment indeed, and stops the execution.[2] Think not of pains tomorrow, they may not come; and look through your present pains unto Jesus, whose hands are full of promises. I see two of them, and the Lord help you to read them with comfort, "as your day is, so shall your strength be"[3]; and again, "I will lay no more upon

---

1   The letter is from *ER* (1828), 77–78, where the date June 23, 1763, is clearly a printing mistake—see letter of the same date. This letter's background could be the illness Berridge suffered from the late 1760s. Maybe after Berridge's own long illness and depression ("taught me by a long affliction")—which lasted until 1773–1774—he could empathize with Lady Huntingdon in her troubles.

2   Genesis 22:11–12.

3   Deuteronomy 33:24.

you, than you are able to bear."[4] Who says this? It is Jesus, one who may be trusted, and who has pledged his word that no more shall be laid upon *you* than you are able to bear. Good news and true; the Lord convey it to your heart, and help you to sleep soundly with this ticket in your bosom.

Are you at any time too feeble for prayer? Then lean your heart, my dear Lady, on Jesus; and lift up a languishing eye unto him. He knows the meaning of a look or a sigh, as well as of a prayer; yea, he counteth all your groans. And I hope, when he has clipped both the wings and the comb of his turtle, he will set her a cooing once more in the land of the living. However, at worst, all will soon be over; and heaven will sweeten all, and pay for all. Our life is but a moment, the troubles make that moment seem a long one; but the rest is eternal. Come then, my fellow-traveller and partner in affliction, let us jog on: heaven is before us, and Jesus will bring us safe through. Hosanna to his glorious name. I bear you frequently on my heart before the throne: and indeed my heart is truly united unto you in the bond of Christian affection. I love, esteem and honour you much; and can write with more freedom to you, than to most others. Besides Jesus has taught me by a long affliction, what I knew not well before, now to sympathise. I can now drop a silent tear at a neighbour's groan; and mourn over you, though fifty miles distant from me.

I did not answer your letter immediately; for I was exceedingly heavy in body, before it came; and much grieved in spirit afterwards. I seemed rather in want of a comforter, than in a capacity of being one, so I thought it better to omit the first post, than send a log of wood to a sick lady, a letter more fit to burn than to read. May he who dwelt in the burning bush[5] keep you unhurt whilst lying in the furnace, and preserve you safe to his kingdom and glory. I am your affectionate,

John Berridge

---

[4] 1 Corinthians 10:13
[5] Exodus 3.

To Mr. C__[1]

Dear Sir,

My purpose was to wait upon you when in town, but was disappointed [in] various ways. Here we meet and part, but when we meet above we shall part no more, taking leave of journeying and dying friends will then be over. The Lord will be our everlasting light, and days of mourning will be ended. And should we not live above, while dwelling here below? What is there worth an anxious thought but Jesus Christ, and his salvation, salvation from the lowest depths of misery to the eternal heights of glory? Not only bought and freely offered, but to be tasted and enjoyed in its first fruits, while we journey through this vale of tears. What says Jesus from above to his travelling saints? "Come up thither, and I will show you things, which must be hereafter," (Rev. 4:1) not only prophetic views to be imparted to John, but heavenly views of rich grace to be disclosed to his nether saints,[2] with blessed foretastes of those riches, if they come up hither; but we often lose anticipations of this grace for want of coming up. When the thoughts are hurried or bewildered in the world, the soul is cleaving to the dust, and made unfit for divine refreshments. Many attend duly upon ordinances, a few only are seeking to walk with God; yet the Lord's remnant is among these few; and to these he revealeth his secrets. No little watchfulness and prayer are needful for all who seek to walk with God, but especially for those who have large dealings in the world. To such Jesus says, Take heed your hearts be not overcharged with the care of this life.[3] He knew such a caution was needful, and his children will attend unto it. But if their desires are growing eager after the world, he sends disappointments, or affliction to sicken their pursuit and bring their hearts home to himself. Happy they who are suffered to find no rest but in the Lord. Your affectionate servant,

John Berridge

---

1 The letter is found in *WB* (1838), 470, and *WB* (1864), 438–439.
2 Saints on earth.
3 Luke 21:34.

A Consolatory Letter[1]

Dear Madam,

I have been lately much hurried, or, according to your desire, I should have written before; but, however, agreeable to my promise, I have endeavoured to send you a few lines, which I shall be thankful and rejoice, if they are blessed of God to your support under your present troubles.

I desire to be sensible of my own unworthiness and unfitness for anything of myself that is spiritually good; much more for so hard and difficult a task as the administering effectual consolation to a soul that groans under inward[2] afflictions, and outward troubles; that is tossed upon waves of Satan's temptations and worldly disappointments. Indeed, this is the work of none other than the divine Spirit. It is he alone that can command a calm into a tempestuous soul, and speak peace, rest, and satisfaction in the greatest multitude of perplexities. However, I desire most tenderly to sympathize with you, remembering that also I am, in the body, subject to the same adversities and trials, and would help you all I can to bear your burden with faith, patience, and resignation.

I grant then that your circumstances are very intricate and exercising;

---

[1] This letter was published at the end of Berridge's life as Letter 4 in *Cheerful Piety*. I give them in the order given in *WB* (1838), where the publication *Cheerful Piety* is not mentioned. There is no evidence that Berridge knew or supported its publication. One letter in *Cheerful Piety* (Letter 5) is found in Berridge's other letters, although it is wrongly ascribed to the Countess of Huntingdon. See January 28, 1766. The three letters to Rev. Mr. B. are not typical Berridge, being much more formal and literary in composition. G.C. Gorham (1787–1857), famous for the later Gorham controversy, says in a note in "The Papers of John Berridge," HMC, BER 2/1: "'Cheerful Piety' contains five letters three of them are to Mr. Berridge only two written by him." They may be letters written to himself in his intense period of illness in the early 1770s. This particular letter is found in *WB* (1838), 471–475; *GM* (1849), 475–478; *WB* (1864), 351–355; and *GS* (1872), 505–508. The letter to a lady is entitled "A consolatory letter to a Christian friend under sore trouble." *WB* (1864) has added some of the scriptural references.

[2] *WB* (1838) has "outward."

but let me beg of you not to construe your afflictions as a token of God's displeasure, or a sign of your not belonging to him. That is an old temptation of Satan's, with which he often assaults the afflicted Christian; but take the shield of faith, that you may quench the fiery darts of Satan.[3]

Alas, crosses and afflictions are the common lot of the people of God in this world. Our Lord has told us we shall meet with tribulation.[4] Every saint has his own particular difficulty, temptation, and conflict to grapple with. We have need to be emptied from vessel to vessel. We are too apt to settle on our lees; too apt to be taken with the vanities of this passing world. If we are without afflictions, whereof all are partakers, then we are bastards and not sons.

How many have questioned the truth of their state and relation to God, for want of these exercises and trials. Where are the cause and matter of your fears and despondence? Go search the records of sacred Scripture, and see how it fared with saints in all ages; what Job, David, and Paul, yea, our blessed Lord himself, endured, and passed through in this world. Should that be an argument against your interest in God, which is the common portion of all believers here? We are now chastened, that hereafter we may not be condemned.

Ah, happy afflictions that wean us from this wretched dying world are a means to mortify our corruptions, teach us to live more constantly by faith on Jesus Christ, and to fix all our hopes and expectations on another and a better world; and for that end you should be earnest in your wrestling with God in prayer, that your trials may be all sanctified unto you; that, however, at present, they are not joyous but grievous, yet hereafter they may yield you the peaceable fruits of righteousness, according to God's gracious promise: Hebrews 12:11.

Sanctified afflictions are a thousand times rather to be chosen than unsanctified prosperity; these may consist with, yea, are often the effects of God's special love; he sees we want them, and he knows that they will work for our good. Do then, Lord, what Thou pleasest with me, so I may but die to this world, overcome my corruptions, live more upon Christ, bring more glory to his name, and have more comfortable tastes and pledges of his love, and be often saying, the will of the Lord be done. He is infinitely wise, and knows what is best for me. He is infinitely gracious, and will be tender of the weakest of his children. He is infinitely sovereign, and may do what he pleases with

---

3 Ephesians 6:16.
4 John 16:33.

his own. The heaviest afflictions, on this side of hell, are less, far less, than mine iniquities have deserved.

O boundless grace! The chastening rod of a reconciled father might have been the flaming sword of an avenging judge. I might now have been weeping and wailing with devils and damned spirits in hell. I will bear the indignation of the Lord, because I have sinned against him. It is of mercy alone that I am not consumed; and, O my soul, it is but a little while, and there will be an eternal end of all thy sorrows, fears, trials, and disappointments. Yet a little while, and He that shall come, will come and will not tarry; that heavenly bridegroom, who has, by his Spirit, betrothed thee to himself will, ere long, invite thee into his eternal kingdom, where thou wilt forget the storms and tempests, clouds and darkness, in thy passage through this wilderness world, and all shall be joy and peace, love and praise.

No doubts and fears shall ever assault thee in that happy state; but thou shalt dwell eternally under the immediate shinings of divine love, and shalt sing with the strongest believers, yea, the highest and most glorious Archangel in Heaven, the wondrous mystery of redeeming grace; and the comforts and blessedness of that state of rest will be more brightened, illustrated, and endeared by all thy tears and sighings here below. The remembrance of the gall and wormwood of afflictions will tend to sweeten the taste of heavenly enjoyments.

I pray that God may be with you, support and comfort you, with the divine consolations of his Holy Spirit, and establish you in his own due time. He is a faithful God[5]; a covenant-keeping God, and therefore will not lay upon you more than he will enable you to bear.[6] If you have less of this world, may you have more of his comfortable presence. O blessed exchange, and if he seems to be hiding his reconciled countenance, and suffering Satan to buffet you, may you be supported with his everlasting arms,[7] and have him to sustain and uphold you in every time of need.

Should you want his comfortable presence, if it be ever thus with you, remember it was so with your once dying, but now exalted Redeemer,[8] and is the servant greater than his Lord? Shall we not joyfully tread in his steps, that we may at last be where he is?[9] Can or ought we to repine,

---

5 Deuteronomy 7:9.
6 1 Corinthians 10:13.
7 Deuteronomy 33:27.
8 Mark 15:34.
9 Hebrews 10:32–39.

if God deals with us as he did with his own well beloved Son. The Lord help thee willingly to submit to him; and doubt not, but at the appointed time, when he sees it will be for your good, and his own glory, your heavenly Father will find you out a way to escape[10]; he is never at a loss to bring about his gracious designs, when once his set time is come; and you should rejoice that he is carrying on the great work of your eternal salvation, amidst all your troubles and disappointments, and under all your outward and difficult pressures. O say then with Job: "Though he slay me, yet will I trust in him"[11]; though I am weak in grace, yet I will adore him for the smallest hope; though I am surrounded with terrors, I will bless him that I am out of hell; he that has begun a good work in my soul, will see it perfected. Lord, I desire to submit to thy will; do what thou wilt with me so that I may but bring honour to thy name, and promote my own everlasting welfare.

O that you may find more of this faith and patience; hope and resignation growing and increasing in you every day; and when once you are brought to this humble submission, and resigned temper; to this hoping, believing, waiting, and contented frame, you may be assured deliverance is at hand, even at the very door.[12]

And now, O that you may be embraced in the arms of everlasting love, and enjoy the comforts of your pardoned state; the Lord increase your faith[13]; take from your burdens or add to your strength; and let me beg of you, once more, dear sister, not to suffer the disappointments and crosses of this world, however sore and trying in themselves, to drive from your mind the frequent and joyful forethought of what free, rich, and distinguishing grace has designed for you in a bright and better world; and is fitting and preparing you for every day you live. Let not the hardships of your journey make you forget, but rather long for your home. O, think on that heaven which neither sin, nor death, not hell, shall ever be able to deprive you of; in which you and I, through sovereign grace, I trust, shall spend the endless ages of eternity. I remain, dear Madam, your affectionate,

John Berridge

---

[10] 1 Corinthians 10:13.
[11] Job 13:15.
[12] Mark 13:29.
[13] Luke 17:5.

To the Rev. Mr __ [1]

Dear Sir,

When this comes to hand, I think you owe me two; and you know how the command runs, "Owe no man anything," not even paper and ink, "but love."[2] I believe you have love in your heart but you hide it there, as a miser hoards up money in his chest, unwilling to part with a groat. I suppose your Bible does allow of a peerage, or consanguinity with a peerage, as a reasonable plea for not paying a debt. I talk like a creditor, you see, with a high hand, and if you would not have me saucy, then pay me, friend, what thou owest, and pay all.

I hate compositions; no ten shillings in the pound for me. All my days have been beguiled with composition payments. Either send the whole debt, like a just lawyer, or come to my face and ask forgiveness of the whole, like a good Christian. I think you love conditions, here is a brace for you. I wish you to choose the latter, for I had rather see you once than hear from you twice. A penitential visit would please me more than two sheets of paper well filled; hereby no epistolary debt would be contracted, and I should run no risk of repaying the visit. You could not decently invite a wild goose into Warwickshire, because these birds are mighty apt to chatter in the fields; and wherever they come, always bring hard weather and sharp blasts along with them. The most we can expect from your sweet chirping swallows, who make their nests about the altar,[3] is to call upon the poor geese in any time of their passage. The time is coming when there will be no distinction between goose and swallow; when both shall be arrayed like the peacock, and sing like the nightingale, sing the praises of the dear Emmanuel. Oh, my heart dances at his name; it is music in my ears, and a cordial to my soul. Don't you love him? I know you do, but love too little, like myself. Oh, that glorious God-man, how much has he suffered for us! How little are we doing for him!

---

[1] The letter is found in *WB* (1864), 531–532.
[2] Romans 13:8.
[3] Psalm 84:3.

Raise us up from the dust, O Lord; make us active in thy work, always abounding therein; yet give us to see ourselves in our best estate to be altogether vanity. That the good Shepherd who laid down his life for his sheep may daily guide your steps, and water your flock, is the hearty prayer of your affectionate,

John Berridge

To the Rev. Mr. B__[1]

Everton

Dear Friend,

With a melancholy pleasure, and at the same time self-abasement, I heard your lectures on man's heart as fallen by original apostasy, and the dreadful epidemical disease of sin, which has spread itself over the whole soul.[2] When you dissected and anatomised the heart of man as before and after conversion, you went into the private closet of *my* heart, and the underground vaults, where you have dug up some of the bones of the old man, that have long lain rotting there.

Here is the general exchange for corruption[3]; here the world and the devil often meet together; here they correspond, trade, and traffic; and Satan well knows this is the best place for vending his contraband goods, having so many friends that court the heart, and recommend his wares, viz., vain thoughts, worldly imaginations, evil and impure sensations, earthly affections, inordinate desires, ambitious views, high-mindedness, riches and sinful pleasures, or Pharisaical righteousness, moral confidence, unscriptural hopes, formal sanctity, uncovenanted mercy, &c., &c.

Satan takes a turn round these walks, and pays his compliments (if I may so say) to the inmates of my soul, who are his good friends every day, aye, every hour. He tries all ways to find out the consti-tutional sin, or what the Apostle calls, my most easy besetting sin.[4] He has baits for all sorts of corruptions, and he endeavours to time his assaults. Sometimes he bids good-morrow to one lust or corruption, sometimes to another, and so makes his cruel visits from one place of the soul to another all day long, and never bids good night; for even

---

1   The letter is found in *WB* (1838), 478–482, and *WB* (1864), 341–344. This was the first letter in *Cheerful Piety*. *WB* (1838) uses some italics.
2   Isaiah 1:5,6.
3   Mark 7:21.
4   Hebrews 12:1.

when I go to bed he lays down with me, and sometimes in my sleep he haunts and awakes me.

If I go into my closet, in order to lock myself up from the busy world, this impertinent intruder, the devil, will break in there too, without asking me leave; and so in the family, and even in the sanctuary, the house of God, I am dogged by this roaring lion.[5] Sometimes he snatches the preached word from me in a way of forgetfulness; sometimes presents other objects to my view, and sometimes would have me make an ill use of it, by misapplying it. Sometimes I pray as if I was praying to a wooden god, without a proper sense of his divinity and omniscience, and so only *word* it with God. By the way, I would not charge the devil with more than is his just due, for I know my own corrupt heart sometimes invites Satan to come in, and has often entertained and bid him welcome.

Oh, how I ought to be humbled, that I have so often fetched a chair for Satan the tempter to sit down in, while he has entertained himself upon the lusts and affections of my soul; and has he not had the insolence sometimes to tempt me to sin from the aboundings of grace? O horrid injection! And sometimes such cogitations have worked upon the imagination and the heart in and under ordinances. What power Satan's temptations have had, and how often the seeds of sin have sprung up, and blossomed, and budded, and brought forth fruit, to my sorrow as well as shame, I cannot express; but I would open the matter with soul-abasement to the eye of him who looks down into my heart, and sees all the workings of iniquity within me.

Respecting what you are now upon, it is pleasing to find experience answers experience, as face to face in a glass.[6] There is a prodigious alliance formed by the empire of hell, the god of this world, and by unbelief, with all its train of sins, in the heart of every natural man, and the unrenewed part in every true believer. This is the threefold cord that is not easily broken; this is the grand alliance, Sir. Thus the case stands, and on these accounts my soul has often bled; afraid of myself, afraid of the devil, afraid of everyone, and sometimes afraid even of my God.[7] I have sometimes had hopes that grace had enthroned itself in my heart, and I have had, as it were,

---

[5] 1 Peter 5:8.
[6] Proverbs 27:19.
[7] Job 23:15,16.

a cessation from corruption; at least in some branches. The war has seemed to be at an end almost, and I have often sung a funeral song of victory over (as I thought) a *dead* corruption; but Satan has called up all his forces, and fired again, and with his fire balls has set the whole city of my soul into flame, and there has been a resurrection of the monster sin again.

Oh, pity me, all you combatants in the field of battle, that know the force of temptation, and are haunted, as I am, with these ghosts continually. The devil sometimes gets me down and buffets me with the sin that most easily besets me, and then turns accuser, and brings railing accusations against me; and if he cannot keep me from a throne of grace,[8] he makes me go limping and halting there, afraid to open my mouth; and sometimes I can only hold up my hand at the bar and cry, guilty! guilty!

And now, Sir, let me ask you, is this balm in Gilead[9] for an old stinking sore, as well as for a constant running one? A sore that I thought had been healed long ago, but breaks out again and again with its bloody issue. Is there a physician? What, for such a nauseous, defiled, stinking, as well as weak and sin-sick soul as mine? I truly need a physician within as well as without; Christ and his blood and righteousness to justify and acquit, and the blessed Spirit to sanctify and cure the inward diseases of my soul; for what would it avail a condemned malefactor, to be pardoned and acquitted of his crimes, if he had the jail distemper upon him, and was to die by it?

Indeed God never justifies but he sanctifies. Election is God's mark to know his own children by. Calling and sanctification are our marks, by which we come to know that we ourselves are his elected children. Oh, then set forth the work of the Spirit in a rebellious will, a blind understanding, a hard heart, a stupid conscience, and vile affections; renewing and sanctifying all these powers, and so proving it to be truly the work of God and not of man. This Gospel sanctification I need and earnestly desire; and if you could help me in the present prospect, of the eye of Christ scanning the hidden parts of man, it would be doing a good piece of service, not only to me, but perhaps to many others who may be in the same case.

Dear Sir, may you be helped to lay open the inward powers of the soul and the deceitful arts of the body, for the alarming and arousing

---

8   Hebrews 4:16.
9   Jeremiah 8:22.

[of] the stupid and careless, and for the search and enquiry of every real Christian, both with regard to the principle, growth, and activity of grace, or the decays and witherings of it; what interest God has in the heart, and how much sin and Satan have; what advances heaven-ward, or what loitering, backslidings, or falls there are found too often in the way to glory. I am, dear friend, your &c.,

John Berridge

To the Rev. Mr. B___[1]

Everton

Dear Friend,

I perceive, by some hints in a late discourse, the rough draught of the portrait of my soul has reached your hands; the lines perhaps were strong in many parts, but yet imperfect. This I call its fellow; but alas were I to write whole volumes upon the subjects, they would still be but small sketches.

To anatomise my own soul, and point out the irregular turnings and windings of a deceitful heart, is beyond my skill. Satan is always beating and hunting the powers of my soul; watching what will start next, whether *pride, sensuality, covetousness, worldly pleasures*, &c. and whatever sins they are he will be sure to strike in and follow. How often has the soul gone hand in hand with Satan in chase for pleasures, till it has been even tried, and then what fruit has it produced but sorrow and shame?

But, Sir, in order to my deciphering the combined forces of sin, hell, and the world, against me, you have justly opposed the threefold grand alliance that is for every believer, viz., *Father, Son*, and *Spirit.* True; but the query still remains, can such a one as you be in alliance with the King of Heaven, or bear the image and stamp of the Lord Jesus? Where is the consistency? I want to know the worst of myself. I own a spark of real grace shall be kept alive, let the wind of temptation blow ever so high and strong, or the waves of temptation beat ever so hard, true grace shall be victorious. This is a matter of comfort, to find a smoking ember under a load of ashes.

There may be, indeed, two men in one person, the old and the new man, flesh and spirit.[2] So upon a medal there may be on one side the image of the devil, rebellion, slavery, lust, and tyranny; and on the

---

[1]   The letter is taken from *WB* (1838), 482–485, and *WB* (1864), 344–348. See note on previous letter. This was Letter 2 in *Cheerful Piety.* It was also printed in *GS* (1884), 29–31. *WB* (1838) has some italics as well as *GS.*
[2]   Romans 7:15,21–23.

other side, the effigy of a good prince, loyal subjects, peace and plenty, and the enemies' hearts trampled upon as conquered. This I think a lively representation of the case, and it would be a happy turn, could I make it out so to my own soul.

I want to see the divine image carved more legibly on my heart. I am sure I see the picture of the devil strong enough there. I do not so much fear the allied army of the prince of the world, and the world itself, under the command of its captain-general, the devil, as I fear the rebellion in my own bowels, the restless monster sin within me. Civil wars are the most shocking and the most fatal; besides, my soul is the seat of wars and conflicts, and you know, Sir, what havoc is made usually in such places.

I know all the powers of the enemies (let the devil call them invincible if he will) cannot harm me, were it not for inbred foes. It is the corruptions within me, not the contagion of commerce without me, which I fear, or the bloody armies around me. It is that unruly rebellious regiment of banditti within my heart, my lusts, appetites, and passions that I fear will destroy me. It is I that infect myself, and therefore it is my daily prayer, Lord, deliver me from myself. This is always a part of my litany, and sometimes the first voice of my retired ejaculations.

Indeed, Sir, this is an unnatural rebellion, to be in arms and in conjunction with one's inveterate foes, who are aiming at my heart's blood. What, fight against myself? Yes, so it is; flesh against spirit; the unrenewed against the renewed; sin against grace. Indeed I have proclaimed war in the name of the King of Heaven, against the States-General of hell (so far as it is in league with Satan) and against the potentate of sin; but to tell you the times, how often I have been foiled and beat, or raised the siege, or been wounded, or had a limb shot off, or been trepanned or taken prisoner, I know not; but I can never sign a truce, and I am determined through grace, if I die, to die sword in hand.

I must own I have sent out a hue and cry many times after the traitors, and have sometimes hoped I had secured some of them. I have had them in prison and in fetters perhaps for weeks and months together, and they have been brought out to several courts of judicature, particularly the court of conscience, but that is partial. There have been bribes at times, and not sufficient chastisement; but at other times there have been very severe rebukes, and conscience has condemned the vassals to run the gauntlet with horror, doubt, and despair. The charges of the court of conscience have been read aloud;

terrible peals have been rung, and the chains of hell have rattled on the ear. Though sometimes conscience has given the verdict on the side of grace, at other times there has been an arrest of judgment, and a citation before the Lord Chief Justice of the King's Bench of Heaven; and though the wretch deserves no hearing, as being outlawed, yet, to the honour of the grace and mercy of the sovereign, the criminal is brought to the bar; and though there is no room to say anything but Guilty! yet every plea that can be made in his favour is heard; how they were drawn in by some of the clans of hell, perhaps forced, as it were, against the settled judgment of the soul, and perhaps, through weakness and infirmity, would not get out of the way, or from ignorance of the crime, or from extenuation of the guilt, or from being hurried away into the service of the invader without so much as giving time for a cool thought. And sometimes the poor soul has been like a galley slave, wishing for deliverance from the bondage of corruption, and crying out of the load and fetters of sin, and saying with him of old, Bring my soul out of prison, that I may praise thy name.[3]

The high court of judicature hears particularly the relenting groan; and the Attorney General of Heaven has compassion enough to put in a petitionary plea for the guilty wretch whose hand is still upon the bar. But the death warrant is come down from heaven for the execution of sin, and all the heads of the clans of hell. Mortify therefore your members which are on the earth, fornication, etc.,[4] so if an eye or hand offend thee, cut it off.[5]

A reprieve at last has been issued out for the soul; and the repenting rebel has gone again in pursuit of those invaders of the peace and court of grace, and the soul has laid hold of some of them, and cried out afresh for justice and revenge against these traitors in his own breast, and has laid the sacrificing knife to the throat of these brats of hell. But how often have they raised up their seemingly dying heads when on the very block, and asked for pity, and during the very execution have done much mischief, and made me bleed and groan afresh.

I hope at times they are crucifying; but crucifixion is a lingering death, and I find they have still life, which with the help of Satan

---

3   Psalm 142:7.
4   Colossians 3:5.
5   Matthew 5:30.

their grand ally, they too often discover, and break out again; and all I can do, is to cry out Murder! Murder! to the Lord Jesus. I may truly call them murderers, for they often destroy my peace and comfort; I long to see them dead, dead, dead! I desire your prayers for the poor wounded but your affectionate humble servant,

John Berridge

To the Rev. Mr. B__ [1]

Dear Sir,

After having been so free already as to disclose to you the secrets of my heart, you will not think it strange if I subjoin a *third* letter. There is one point more that deserves animadverting upon, and that is *speculative* sins, which I believe are too often overlooked by many professors, or at least very superficially regarded. If it does not amount to an outward act, it is too often passed over with silence; but truly I think there may be a committing adultery in the *heart*.[2] So the statute law of heaven runs: it is out of the *heart* proceeds all evil[3]; the seeds of it are sown there, and it takes root and grows, blossoms, buds, and brings forth fruit in the soul, and no eye but Omniscience sees it.

How often have speculative evils been acted in the heart. The heart has been both the adulterer and adulteress. Sin has been begotten, nursed, and bred up, and acted its part upon the theatre of the heart. How often have sinful objects been represented to the fancy by speculation? The heart can bring forth, dress up, and act the part of anything; and there has been not only an interview, but an intercourse and sinful familiarity.

There has been many a mortal blow given by revenge in the *heart*. This is *speculative* murder; and there has been coveting a neighbour's estate, etc., and what is this but speculative robbery? So spiritual pride shows itself in many branches. When I have been enlarged in prayer, how has pride and the devil clapped me on the back and said, Well done; you have been very great today. How abominable is this, to attribute an enlarged frame, in any respect, to self? How often have I been pleased with flowery words and fluency in prayer more than spirituality? Again, how often have worldly objects and creature comforts been set up in the heart; and have not the affections too frequently

---

[1]   The letter is from *WB* (1838), 485–489, and *WB* (1864), 348–351. This is Letter 3 in *Cheerful Piety*. Again *WB* (1838) has some italics.
[2]   Matthew 5:28.
[3]   Mark 7:21.

bowed down to them? Or when a near relation, or a beloved prattling child it may be, have been called away by the superior owner, how often has the heart whispered, and the tongue been ready to blab out, You have taken away my gods, and what have I more? What is this but speculative idolatry!

How have pride and covetousness worked themselves up sometimes into a coach and six; aye, into a palace! Really, Sir, I am ashamed of these inward masquerades. The heart will turn into any shape. Well may it be said to be *deceitful above all things, and desperately wicked*.[4] This is still a black picture; but in a distant prospect. I sometimes hope at the closing hour, when I shall exchange worlds, Jesus will help me to lay hold of every sinful serpent that has long twisted round my soul, and keeps me company all my pilgrimage; and enable me, by the hand of faith, to hold them up, crying out, Behold the heads of traitors, which shall never come to life again! Oh, what a joyful shout shall I give when I shall feel these vermin drop off!

At times I am ready to hope the gloomy territories of the grave are almost ready for me, that I may lay down this body of sin upon the block for everlasting execution. Oh, when shall these clogs and fetters be knocked off, and the dark and gloomy walks of this vale of tears turned into bright and peaceful realms?

Dear Sir, these have been black letters for your aspiring soul to read; though I do not question but you have found something of these combats yourself, and therefore can pity and sympathize with a poor, weak, wounded, shall I call myself, *brother* soldier. You have your enemies, I doubt not, and can trample upon them. I congratulate you on your victory, though not yet a *complete* conquest, through the Captain of your salvation. I would fain bear a part in shouting salvation and honour, glory, and power, to the conquering Saviour.[5] He rode triumphantly to glory, after he had obtained a complete conquest over sin, death, and hell, and dragged the monsters at his chariot wheels; he then gave Satan such a blow that he has not recovered since, nor ever will.

From hence I fetch all my hope. If ever I am saved, it will be, I am well assured, by mere grace and almighty all-conquering power.[6]

---

4 Jeremiah 17:9.
5 Revelation 5:13.
6 Ephesians 2:8.

Alas, what has such a depraved, polluted, and corrupted miscreant as I to reckon upon, why mercy and grace should be exerted in my salvation, but free, rich, sovereign grace? This will be the topic of the eternal songs of redeemed souls. And what, Sir, if such a poor weak, weather-beaten, tossed, tempted, and almost shipwrecked vessel as I, should, at last, land safely on the shore of everlasting rest? Sure you would strike up a new song to see me harbour in the heavenly port, if you are there before me. And what, if such a poor, weak stripling as I should come off a conqueror, and more than so, over an armada of enemies, from sin, death, and hell? And what, if you should meet me in the peaceful realms above, with my robes washed in the blood of the Lamb, and a palm of victory in my hand? Perhaps you may know me by my scars; but even every one of these will be a set off to the freeness, sovereignty, and unchangeableness of the love of God; the worth and efficacy of the dear Redeemer's merits; and the power and prevalency of the almighty and ever blessed Spirit. The burden of my song will be *Grace! Grace!* if ever I reach the heights of Zion.

I bless the Lord, since the first essay I wrote to you, I have found some new recruits from the inexhaustible magazine. The brave general has got the field, and is keeping off the enemy, and I trust has given a renewed blow to all the confederate troops that are in league against me; and I firmly believe that I shall be an overcomer through the blood of the Lamb. As I have experienced some special advantage from the study of the old man and all his cursed artillery, with the powers of the infernal kingdom, and this world, with all its bewitching sweets, I would earnestly recommend soul study, devil study, and the snares of the world study, to every Christian friend. Commune with your own heart daily[7]; beware of Satan's devices; and be ever on the watch, lest you enter into temptation; for though the spirit may be willing, the flesh is weak.[8]

But it may be, dear Sir, while I have been giving you some of the living sorrows of my heart, I have ript it open, in order to examine the entrails of the soul with more freedom than you have met with before; but either I have a worse heart than another, or there are many counterparts in the experience of others. Indeed, I sometimes think I am by myself; and if ever I get to heaven, I shall be truly a *wonder*

---

[7] Psalm 4:4.
[8] Matthew 26:41.

there. I shall be as an eternal monument set up to the honour of divine grace, and the inscription upon me will be this; A black hellish brand plucked out of the burning, now made, through rich mercy, a pillar to stand for ever in the temple of God. Wishing you the prosperous gales of the Divine Spirit, and all success in your sacred work, I am dear Sir, sincerely and repeatedly yours, etc.,

John Berridge

To Joshua Symonds[1]

...I have lost my reputation for thirty years, ever since I went to preach out of doors, and have neither hope nor wish to retrieve it.... Opinions of me are various; some call me an Independent, some a Baptist, some an Arminian. Indeed, sir, I am nothing, and Jesus, precious Jesus, is my all....

---

[1] This valuable little extract comes from H.G. Tibbutt, "Joshua Symonds, an Eighteenth-Century Bedfordshire Minister" in *Worthington George Smith and Other Studies* (Bedford: BHRS, 1978), 57:65. The date given—1792—is obviously wrong as Symonds had been dead for four years by then! The "thirty years" would date this extract in about 1788, the year of Symonds's death (November 1788). Symonds (1739–1788), the minister of the Old Meeting at Bedford, was a friend of Berridge. In his diary for September 20, 1776, he records: "I paid a Visit this day to my dear and good Friend the Revd. Mr. Berridge and a profitable one I hope it was. I opened my mind very freely to him as I often do to my dear and good friend the Revd. Mr. Newton. They both converse in the same strain—are both very evangelical and experimental, their conversation useful and delightful. Mr. Berridge's very such so today" (63). He records "13th November 1776. Heard Mr. Berridge preach a sweet Sermon at Cople from Micah 6,8.... I cannot recollect the many excellent striking expressions he delivered" (64). On August 3: "Wednesday last I visited that chosen Vessel Mr. Berridge of Everton" (64).

Sources

Aug. 25, 1755	John Jones	Manuscript, DWL, Jones, 39.B.24. f.3
[April?] 1758	Mr. Daw	*AM* (1797), 612–613; *EM* (1797), 460–462
July 3, 1758	Notts. clergyman [Dr. Poynton]	*Fragment* (1760); *WB* (1838), 349–364; *WB* (1864), 345–357
[July–Aug 1758]	Notts. clergyman	*Fragment* (1760), 24–25
Nov. 28, 1758	Mr. Pilkington	Manuscript, LPL, MS 2595 ff.83–90
[May ?] 1759	Unknown	Ex., *WW* (1992), 21:199–200; *WB* (1838), 50–51; *WB* (1864), xv
July 9, 1759	James Berridge	*S* (1893), 28–29
July 16, 1759	John Wesley	*AM* (1780), 611
Nov. 22, 1760	John Wesley	*AM* (1797), 305–306
April 22, 1761	Alexander Coats	*MissM* (1801), 162–163; *WB* (1838), 364–366; *WB* (1864), 361–362
July 16, 1762	John Walsh	Manuscript, MARC, EMV-134, 5–6
Nov. 16, 1762	Lady Huntingdon	CHCA (Letter 1); Seymour, 1:323–324; *WB* (1864), 445; *FCEM* (1867), 248–249
May 18, 1763	Lady Huntingdon	CHCA (Letter 2); *FCEM* (1867), 291–292
June 23, 1763	Lady Huntingdon	CHCA (Letter 3); *ER* (1828), 14–15; Seymour, 1:356–357; *WB* (1864), 446–447; *FCEM* (1867), 292–293
June 27, 1763	Lady Huntingdon	CHCA (Letter 4); Seymour, 1:357–358; *WB* (1864), 447; *FCEM* (1867), 308–309
July 3, 1763	Lady Huntingdon	CHCA (Letter 5); Seymour, 1:358; *WB* (1864), 448; *FCEM* (1867), 309–311
July 9, 1763	Lady Huntingdon	CHCA (Letter 6); exs. Seymour, 1:358; *WB* (1864), 448; *FCEM* (1867), 346–347
July 16, 1763	Lady Huntingdon	CHCA (Letter 7); *FCEM* (1867), 347
July 20, [1763]	Lady Huntingdon	CHCA (Letter 28)
Sept. 2, 1763	Lady Huntingdon	CHCA (Letter 8); *FCEM* (1868), 25–27
Sept. 23, 1763	Mr. Reynolds	Manuscript, MARC, PLP 8 43.2
Sept. 27, 1763	Lady Huntingdon	CHCA (Letter 9)
Dec. 18, 1764	Rowland Hill	Sidney, 21; *WB* (1864), 449
[Jan.?] 1765	Walter Shirley	*WB* (1838), 491; *WB* (1864), 533–534
Aug. 21, 1765	Mr. Adams	Housman, lix–lx; *WB* (1864), 526–527
Jan. 28, 1766	Lady Margaret Ingham	*CP*(1792);*GS*(1842),165–166;*CMus*(copy); *WB* (1838), 366–369; *GM* (1848), 1; *WB* (1864), 355–358
March 6, 1766	Lady Huntingdon	CHCA (Letter 10); ex., Seymour, 1:366

July 28, 1766	Lady Huntingdon	CHCA (Letter 11)
Sept. 7, 1767	William Lee	GM (1827), 363–364; GH (1835), 278–279; GS (1843), 179–180; WB (1864), 450–452; S (1893), 262–263
[Winter?] 1767	Cornelius Winter	Exs., Jay, 84–6; WB (1838), 489–490; WB (1864), 442–443; S (1892), 262–263
Dec. 26, 1767	Lady Huntingdon	CHCA (Letter 12); Seymour, 2:92; WB (1864), 502–503
Jan. 1, 1768	John Wesley	AM (1783), 616
Dec. 30, 1768	Lady Huntingdon	CHCA (Letter 17); ER (1824), 74; Seymour, 2:94–96; GS (1842), 165–166; WB (1864), 504–505
May 22, 1769	George Whitefield	WB (1864), 443–444; ST (1879), 476
Summer 1769	Lady Huntingdon	Ex., Seymour, 2:28
Jan. 9, 1770	Lady Huntingdon	Ex., Seymour, 1:386–387; WB (1864), 506–507
March 23, 1770	Lady Huntingdon	Seymour, 1:388–390; WB (1864), 507–510
April 20, 1770	Friend in London	Manuscript, MARC, PLP 8 43.3
June 9, 1770	James Berridge	S (1893), 29
Oct. 31, 1770	Rowland Hill	Manuscript, JWFP MARBL, Box 1 Folder 70; MNCM (1817), 300–301; CM (1841), 601; GS (1852), 147–148
Jan. 19, 177[1]	Rowland Hill	Manuscript, JWFP MARBL, Box 1 Folder 69; CM (1841), 600–601; Sidney, 50–53
Feb. 12, 1771	Cornelius Winter	WHSLMB 70–71
March 13, 1771	John Newton	Manuscript, LPL, MS 3972 f.13; WB (1838), 369–371; WB (1864), 362–364
March 20, 1771	Miss Orton	Manuscript, FBC, Box CO10
May 8, 1771	Rowland Hill	Sidney, 57–58; Seymour, 2:50–51; CM (1841), 601–602; WB (1864), 510–511
May 8, 1771	Lady Huntingdon	Seymour, 2:49, 255
June 3, 1771	Mr. Adams	Housman, lxi–lxii; WB (1864), 527–528
June 8, 1771	Lady Huntingdon	Seymour, 2:51–2; WB (1864), 511–513
June 10, 1771	John Newton	Manuscript, LPL, MS 3972 ff.15–16; WB (1838), 373–374; WB (1864), 366–367
Oct. 18, 1771	John Newton	Jones, 144–145; WB (1838), 374–376; WB (1864), 367–368
Oct. 20, 1771	Rowland Hill	Manuscript, JWFP MARBL, Box 1 Folder 24; CM (1841), 868; GS (1856), 57
Nov. 26, 1771	David Edwards	MissM (1801), 113–114; NYMM (1801), 454–456; MNCM (1802), 355; EM (1812), 128–129; EMMC (1814), 504–505; WB (1838), 371–373; WB (1864), 364–365; Ryle, 250–251; S (1892), 96–97
Feb. 27, 1772	Rowland Hill	WHSLMB, 71–73; CM (1841), 869
Sept. 29, 1772	John Thornton	GM (1837), 125–126; CM (1842), 218
April 3, 1773	John Thornton	GM (1837), 126–127; WB (1838), 376–378; CM (1842), 218–220; WB (1864), 368–370
April 20, 1773	Mr. Woodgate	Manuscript, SGC, c.12 b.2
May 3, 1773	John Thornton	GM (1837), 168–170; CM (1842), 220–221

June 9, 1773	Mr. Adams	Housman, lxii–lxiii; *WB* (1864), 528–529
Aug. 18, 1773	John Thornton	*GM* (1837), 170–172; *WB* (1838), 378–382; *CM* (1842), 821–823; *GS* (1848), 78–80; *WB* (1864), 370–374
Aug. 31, 1773	John Thornton	*GM* (1837), 214–215; *WB* (1838), 383–385; *WB* (1864), 374–376
Sept. 3, 1773	Rowland Hill	WHSLMB (copy), 69–70; Sidney, 91–92; *CM* (1841), 870; *WB* (1864), 513
Sept. 14, 1773	Unknown	*GS* (1869), 364–365; Ryle, 251; *GTOP* (1878), 200–201; *S* (1907), 63
Sept. 20, 1773	John Newton	*WB* (1838), 385–386; *WB* (1864), 376–377
Sept. 25, 1773	John Thornton	Manuscript, LPL, MS 3096 ff.114–115; *GM* (1837), 215–216; *WB* (1838), 386–388; *WB* (1864), 377–379
Nov. 2, 1773	John Newton	Manuscript, LPL, MS 3972 ff.17–18; *WB* (1838), 389–390; *WB* (1864), 379–381; *GB* (1885), 359–360
Nov. 10, 1773	John Thornton	*GM* (1837), 217–218; *WB* (1838), 390–392; *WB* (1864), 381–383
Nov. 12, 1773	John Berridge	*S* (1893), 29–30
Jan. 14, 1774	John Thornton	*GM* (1837), 254–255; *CM* (1845), 27–28; *GS* (1849), 116–118
Jan. 15, 1774	Mr. N__	*GS* (1852), 148–149; Gadsby, 34–35
April 8, 1774	Samuel Wilks	*WB* (1838), 392–393; *WB* (1864), 383–384
April 14, 1774	Fellow Preacher	*GS* (1851), 168; *CCM* (1851), 308–309; *GS* (1871), 287–288
Aug. 10, 1774	John Thornton	*GM* (1837), 310–312; *WB* (1838), 394–396; *WB* (1864), 384–386
Aug. 16, 1774	Samuel Wilks	*WB* (1838), 396–397; *WB* (1864), 386–387
Aug. 30, 1774	Messrs. Dilly	*CMR* (1890), 210
April 11, 1775	Samuel Wilks	*WB* (1838), 397–398; *WB* (1864), 388–389
April 11, 1775	John Thornton	*GM* (1837), 354–355; *WB* (1838), 399–400; *WB* (1864), 389–390
April 21, 1775	Richard Woodgate	Manuscript, MARC, PLP 8 43.6
Aug. 8, 1775	David Simpson	Simpson, xxiii–xxv; *CO* (1841), 721; *WB* (1864), 529–530
Sept. 21, 1775	John Thornton	*MNCM* (1812), 168–170; *GM* (1862), 231–232; *WB* (1864), 518–521
Oct. 22, 1775	John Thornton	*MNCM* (1818), 255–257; Seymour, 1:373–374; *CM* (1845), 28–29; *WB* (1864), 524–526
March 2, 1776	Miss Orton	Manuscript, FBC, Box C010
April 26, 1776	Friend	*MNCM* (1818), 254–255; *GS* (1852), 214
June 7, 1776	Rowland Hill	Manuscript, JWFP MARBL, Box 1 Folder 84; CUL (copy), add 8781/51; *CM* (1841), 870–871; *GS* (1856), 120–121
Sept. 20, 1776	J.S.	*CM* (1845), 271–273
April 16, 1777	Fellow Preacher	*GS* (1851), 304
April 26, 1777	Lady Huntingdon	Seymour, 2:422–424; *WB* (1864), 514–517
Dec. 19, 1777	Mrs. Wilberforce	Manuscript, BLSC, ALS 11/2:115
April 10, 1778	Mrs. Hillier	Manuscript, MARC, PLP 8 43.7

April 11, 1778	Mrs. King	Manuscript, FBC, Box C010
April 25, 1778	Robert Heath	*TM* (10/1797), 20; *CW* (1833), 22:1; *BM* (1861), 198
June 12, 1778	John Thornton	*GM* (1837), 450–451; *WB* (1838), 401–402; *WB* (1864), 391–392
Oct. 24, 1778	John Thornton	*GM* (1837), 492–493; *WB* (1838), 402–404; *WB* (1864), 392–394
Feb. 11, 1779	John Thornton	*GM* (1837), 536; *WB* (1838), 404–405; *WB* (1864), 394–395
March 12, 1779	John Thornton	*GM* (1837), 536–537; *CM* (1845), 29–30
April 28, 1779	Rev. Mr. Woodgate	*BR*, 14 (1823): 54; *In* (1823), 75–76; *WB* (1838), 405–407; *WB* (1864), 395–396; *S* (1885), 15
July 27, 1779	John Thornton	*GM* (1838), 30–31; *WB* (1838), 405–407; *WB* (1864), 395–396
Sept. 28, 1779	Rev. Mr. Collins	*WHS*, 9.2 (1913/14): 30
Oct. 23, 1779	Samuel Lucas	*EM* (1812), 385–386; *ZC* (1835), 103–104; *WB* (1838), 407–408; *GS* (1840), 193–194; *ZT* (1847), 228–229; Gadsby, 34; *GS* (1857), 311; *GM* (1861), 482; *WB* (1864), 396–398; *GB* (1885), 331–332; *CMR* (1889), 327
March 31, 1780	Elizabeth H__	*WB* (1838), 408–410; *WB* (1864), 398–399
May 30, 1780	John Berridge	*WB* (1838), 411–412; *WB* (1864), 401
Oct. 20, 1780	John Thornton	*GM* (1838), 113–114; *WB* (1864), 399–400
Dec. 12, 1780	John Newton	Manuscript, LPL, MS 3972 ff.19–20; *WB* (1838), 412–413; *WB* (1864), 401–402
Jan. 1781	Rev. Mr. Mayor	Manuscript, HEC, AM.0614 40
June 29, 1781	Mrs. Hillier	Manuscript, MARC, PLP 8 43.8
July 21, 1781	John Berridge	*WB* (1838), 413–414; *WB* (1864), 403
Nov 10, 1781	George Gorham	Manuscript, HMC, BER 1/1
Nov 21, 1781	George Gorham	Manuscript HMC, BER 1/2
Nov. 24, 1781	John Thornton	*WB* (1838), 414–416; *WB* (1864), 403–405
Nov. 24, 1781	Mrs Thornton	Manuscript, PLFELM, GD26/13/710
Dec 17, 1781	George Gorham	Manuscript, HMC, BER 1/3
Feb. 1782	Lady Huntingdon	Seymour, 2:320
April 13, 1782	John Newton	Manuscript, LPL, MS 3972 ff.21–22; *WB* (1838), 416–417; *WB* (1864), 405–406
Sept. 17, 1782	John Newton	Manuscript, LPL, MS 3972 ff.23–24; *WB* (1838), 418–419; *WB* (1864), 407–408
Sept. 24, 1782	Benjamin Mills	*CM* (1845), 273
Jan. 23, 1783	John Thornton	*GM* (1838), 71; *WB* (1838), 420–421; *WB* (1864), 409–410
Sept. 12, 1783	Stephen Gorham & Co.	Manuscript, HMC, BER 1/4
Oct. 3, 1783	Benjamin Mills	*WB* (1864), 430–431
Oct. 1, 1784	John Thornton	*WB* (1838), 422–424; *WB* (1864), 411–413
Nov. 17, 1784	John Thornton	*GM* (1839), 166–168; *CM* (1845), 274–275
Nov. 20, 1784	Benjamin Mills	Manuscript, SGC, 0250B; *CM* (1838), 163–164
Feb. 22, 1785	John Thornton	Manuscript, PLFELM, GD26/13/739

[Spring 1785?]	Charles Simeon	*EM* (1794), 198–200; *AM* (1794), 496–498; *WB* (1838), 475–478; *WB* (1864), 439–441; *CMR* (1889), 114–115
July 2, 1785	John Thornton	Manuscript, VM, ACC81 C71; *WB* (1838), 424–426 [426]; *GM* (1838), 225–226; *WB* (1864), 413–415
July 13, 1785	John Thornton	*GM* (1838), 305–306; *WB* (1838), 446–448; *WB* (1864), 415–416
Nov. 4, 1785	Benjamin Mills	*WB* (1838), 464–465; *WB* (1864), 432–433
Nov. 12, 1785	John Newton	*WB* (1838), 448–449; *WB* (1864), 416–417
Nov. 15, 1785	John Thornton	Manuscript, PLFELM, GD26/13/739 (copy); *BM* (1830), 558–559; *GM* (1838), 363–364; *WB* (1838), 421–422; *CM* (1842), 828–829; *WB* (1864), 410–411
Feb. 20, 1786	John Thornton	Jones, 584–5; *WB* (1838), 449–450; *WB* (1864), 418–419
April 27, 1786	Miss L__	*WB* (1838), 450–452; *WB* (1864), 419–420
June 14, 1786	John Newton	Manuscript, LPL, MS 3096 ff.112–113; Jones, 584–585; *WB* (1838), 452–453; *WB* (1864), 420–422
Oct. 11, 1786	John Thornton	*GM* (1838), 419; *WB* (1838), 453–455; *WB* (1864), 422–423
Nov. 1, 1786	Benjamin Mills	*WB* (1838), 465–466; *WB* (1864), 433–434
Nov. 7, 1786	Mr. __	*GS* (1870), 254–255; Ryle, 251–252; *GTOP* (1878), 374–375; *S* (1907), 64
Feb. 20, 1787	John Thornton	*GM* (1838), 459; *WB* (1838), 455–456; *WB* (1864), 423–424
Sept. 22, 1787	Mrs. Wilberforce	Manuscript, PLFELM, GD26/13/745
Oct. 27, 1787	John Thornton	*GM* (1838), 515–416; *WB* (1838), 456–457; *WB* (1864), 424–425
Jan. 28, 1788	Rev. C. Glascott	Manuscript, CBS, DU/10/3
Feb. 21, 1788	John Thornton	*WB* (1838), 458; *GM* (1839), 24; *WB* (1864), 426
March 2, 1788	John Thornton	*CM* (1845), 741
Sept. 25, 1788	Lady Huntingdon	CHCA (Letter 29); Seymour, 1:216–217; *WB* (1864), 518
Oct. 9, 1788	Unknown Lady	*WB* (1838), 458–9; *WB* (1864), 426–427
Oct. 9, 1788	Benjamin Mills	*CS*, 18 (1826): 72; *WB* (1838), 466–467; *WB* (1864), 434–435
Oct. 26, 1788	John Thornton	*GM* (1838), 560–561; *WB* (1838), 459–460; *WB* (1864), 427–428
[Nov./Dec. 1788]	Mrs. Wilberforce	*WB* (1838), 492; *WB* (1864), 532–533
Dec. 30, 1788	John Thornton	*GM* (1839), 120–121; *WB* (1864), 429–430
Jan. 10, 1789	John Thornton	*GM* (1839), 148; *CM* (1845), 741–742
March 7, 1789	William Wilberforce	Manuscript, BL, MS Wilberforce d.13 fol.29
Nov. 23, 1789	Mrs. Carteret	*CO* (1868), 708
Feb. 25, 1790	Lady Huntingdon	*GM* (1837), 230–231
April 10, 1790	Mrs. Carteret	*EpRec*, 6 (1843): 24; *CO* (1868), 709
Nov. 23, 1790	Benjamin Mills	*WB* (1838), 467–468; *WB* (1864), 435–436
May 6, 1792	Miss L__	*WB* (1838), 468–469; *WB* (1864), 436–437

May 24, 1792	John Berridge	S (1893), 30
Aug. 2, 1792	Mrs E. [Elliott]	WB (1838), 469–470; WB (1864), 437–438
Aug. 17, 1792	George Gorham	Manuscript, HMC, BER1/5
Undated		

	Lady Huntingdon	ER (1828), 77–78
	Mr. C__	WB (1838), 470; WB (1864), 438–439
	Consolatory Letter	WB (1838), 471–475; GM (1849), 475–478; WB (1864), CP, 351–355; GS (1872), 505–508
	Rev. Mr. __	WB (1864), 531–532
	Rev. Mr. B__	WB (1838), 478–482; WB (1864), CP, 341–344
	Rev. Mr. B__	WB (1838), 482–485; WB (1864), CP, 344–348; GS (1884), 29–31
	Rev. Mr. B__	WB (1838), 485–489; WB (1864), CP, 348–351
	Joshua Symonds	BHRS (1978), 57:65

Additional abbreviations for the sources (see also pp.xiii–xv):

CP	John Berridge, *Cheerful Piety: or religion without gloom: exemplified in selected letters on the most important truths of Christianity* (J. S. Jordan, J. Matthews, H. Trapp, and G. Terry, 1792)
Fragment	*Fragment of True Religion being the substance of Two Letters from a Methodist Preacher in Cambridgeshire to a Clergyman in Nottinghamshire* (1760)
Gadsby	*Memoirs of the Principal Hymn Writers and Compilers of the 17th and 18th Centuries* (Gadsby, 1855)
Housman	Robert F. Housman, *The Life and Remains of the Rev. Robert Housman* (1841)
Jay	W. Jay, *Memoirs of the Life and Character of the Late Reverend Cornelius Winter* (1808)
Jones	W. Jones, *Memoir of the Rev. Rowland Hill* (1837)
Notts.	Nottinghamshire
Seymour	A.C.H. Seymour, *Life and Times of Selina Countess of Huntingdon*, vols. 1 and 2 (1839)
Sidney	Edwin Sidney, *The Life of the Rev. Rowland Hill* (1834)
Simpson	David Simpson, *A Plea for Religion and the Sacred Writings* (1837)
Ryle	J.C. Ryle, *The Christian Leaders of the Last Century* (1876)

Bibliography

— *An Apology, and a Shield for Protestant Dissenters in These Times of Instability and Misrepresentations. Four letters to the Rev. Mr. Newton. By a Dissenting minister*

— *Oxford Dictionary of National Biography* (Oxford: Oxford University Press, 2004; online ed.)

Abbey, Charles and John Overton. *The English Church in the Eighteenth Century*, 2 vols. Longmans, Green, and Co., 1878.

Aitken, James, ed. *English Letters of the XVIII Century*. Pelican, 1946.

Aitken, Jonathan. *John Newton: From Disgrace to Amazing Grace*. Continuum, 2007.

Alleine, Joseph. *An Admonition to the Unconverted or An Alarm to the Unconverted and A Sure Guide to Heaven*. 1671.

Anderson, Howard, Philip B. Daghlian and Irvin Ehrenpreis, eds. *The Familiar Letter in the Eighteenth Century*. Kansas: University Press of Kansas, 1996.

Anderson, Joan M. *Early Methodism in Bedford*. Rush and Warwick, 1953.

Archer, Mary. *Rupert Brooke and the Old Vicarage, Grantchester*. Cambridge: Silent Books, 1989.

Atmore, Charles. *Methodist Memorial, being an impartial sketch of the lives and characters of the preachers who have departed this life since the commencement of the work of God among the people called Methodists*. Bristol: Edwards, 1801.

Baker, Frank. *William Grimshaw, 1708–1763*. Epworth Press, 1963.

Baker, Margaret. *Discovering English Fairs*. Tring: Shire, n.d..

Baker, Thomas. *History of the College of St. John the Evangelist*, ed. John E. Mayor, 2 vols. Cambridge: Cambridge University Press, 1869.

Balleine, G.R. *A History of the Evangelical Party in the Church of England*. Longman, Green, and Co., 1908.

Bebbington, David. *Victorian Religious Revivals: Culture and Piety in Local and Global Contexts*. Oxford: Oxford University Press, 2012.

Berridge, John. *Cheerful Piety: or religion without gloom: exemplified in selected letters on the most important truths of Christianity.* J.S. Jordan, J. Matthews, H. Trapp, and G. Terry, 1792.

— *The Christian World Unmasked: pray come and peep.* Edward and Charles Dilly, 1773.

— *The Christian World Unmasked.* 3rd ed., revised and corrected. Edward and Charles Dilly, 1774.

— *The Christian World Unmasked.* Edinburgh: Adam and Charles Black, 1853.

— *A Collection of Divine Songs: designed chiefly for the religious societies of Churchmen, in the neighbourhood of Everton, Bedfordshire.* 1760.

— *A Fragment of the True Religion, being the substance of two letters from a Methodist-Preacher in Cambridgeshire, to a clergyman in Nottinghamshire.* J. Williams, 1760.

— *Gospel Gems: a collection of notes from the margins of the Bible of John Berridge, Vicar of Everton, 1755–1793,* ed. W. Wileman. Wileman, 1882.

— *Justification by Faith Alone: being the substance of a letter from the Rev. Mr. Berridge in Cambridge to a clergyman in Nottinghamshire, giving an account of a great work of God wrought in his own heart.* 1760.

— *The Last Farewell Sermon, preached at the Tabernacle, near Moorfields April 1, 1792. By the Rev. John Berridge, MA, late vicar of Everton, Bedfordshire. Taken in short hand, at the time it was delivered and faithfully transcribed. To which is added a short account of Mr. Berridge's death, in a letter from a friend, who was with him the day he died. Also a narrative of the respect shewed to him by his friends in London.* J. Chalmers, 1793.

— *Sion's Songs, or Hymns: composed for the use of them that love and follow the Lord Jesus Christ in sincerity.* Vallance and Conder, 1785.

— *The Works of the Rev. John Berridge, AM, late Fellow of Clare Hall, Cambridge, Vicar of Everton, Bedfordshire, and Chaplain to the Right Honourable Earl of Buchan, with an enlarged memoir of his life, numerous letters, anecdotes, outlines of sermons, and observations on passages of Scripture and his original Sion's Songs,* ed. Richard Whittingham. Simpkin, Marshall, and Co., 1838.

— *The Works of the Rev. John Berridge, AM, late Fellow of Clare Hall, Cambridge, Vicar of Everton, Bedfordshire, and Chaplain to the Earl of Buchan, with an memoir of his life, by the Rev. Richard Whittingham, late vicar of Potton, Bedfordshire, and previously curate to the author at Everton.* 2nd ed. with additions. Ebenezer Palmer, 1864.

Best, G.F.A. *Temporal Pillars: Queen Anne's Bounty, the Ecclesiastical Commissioners, and the Church of England*. Cambridge: Cambridge University Press, 1964.

Biggleswade Historical Society. *The Great Fire of Biggleswade, June 16, 1785*. 1985.

Bogatzky, Carl Heinrich Von. *Bogatzky's Golden Treasury: a reprint of Mr. John Thornton's edition of 1775 together with critical notes hitherto unpublished, by John Berridge, vicar of Everton, and important corrections by the same hand*. ed. Charles P. Phinn. Elliot Stock, 1891.

Boswell, James. *The Life of Johnson*, ed. G.B. Hill. 6 vols. Oxford: Clarendon Press, 1934–1964.

Brewer, E. Cobham. *Brewer's Dictionary of Phrase and Fable*. Revised by Ivor Evans. Book Club, 1977.

Brooks, Peter, ed. *Christian Spirituality: Essays in Honour of Gordon Rupp*. Student Christian Movement, 1975.

Brown, Abner William. *Recollections of the Conversation Parties of the Rev. Charles Simeon, MA: Senior Fellow of King's College, and Perpetual Curate of Trinity Church, Cambridge*. Hamilton, Adams, and Co., 1863.

Brown, Ford K. *Fathers of the Victorians: The Age of Wilberforce*. Cambridge: Cambridge University Press, 1961.

Bull, Josiah. *The Life of John Newton*. Religious Tract Society, 1868.

Bull, William. *Memorials of the Rev. William Bull*. Nisbet, 1864.

Bullock, F.W.B. *Evangelical Conversion in Great Britain, 1696–1834*. St. Leonards-on-Sea: Budd and Gillatt, 1959.

Carus, William. *Memoirs of the Life of the Rev. Charles Simeon, MA*. Hatchard, 1848.

Cashin, Edward J. *Beloved Bethesda: A History of George Whitefield's Home for Boys, 1740–2000*. Macon: Mercer University Press, 2001.

Cecil, Richard, *The Life of John Newton*. Updated by Marylynn Rousse. Fearn: Christian Focus, 2000.

Cheyne, George. *The English Malady, or a treatise of nervous diseases of all kinds, as spleen, vapours, lowness of spirits, hypochondriacal, and hysterical distempers, &c*. Routledge, 1991.

Clark, John A. *Gathered Fragments*. Philadelphia: Marshall, 1836.

Cohen, Sheldon S. *British Supporters of the American Revolution, 1775–1783: The Role of the "Middling Level" Activists*. Woodbridge: Boydell Press, 2004.

Compston, H.F.B. *The Magdalen Hospital: The Story of a Great Charity*. SPCK, 1917.

Cook, Faith. *Selina, Countess of Huntingdon: Her Pivotal Role in the Eighteenth-Century Evangelical Awakening*. Edinburgh: Banner of Truth, 2001.

Cooper, Reginald Denness. *The History of the "Old Meeting House," St. Neots, 1691–1890*. Thomson, 1890.

Coughlan, Laurence. *An Account of the Work of God in Newfoundland, North America*. W. Gilbert, 1776.

Cowper, William. *The Task: a poem, in six books*. J. Johnson, 1785.

— *The Unpublished and Uncollected Letters of William Cowper*, ed. Thomas Wright. Farncombe, 1925.

Dallimore, Arnold. *George Whitefield*, 2 vols. Edinburgh: Banner of Truth, 1970, 1980.

Davies, Gaius. *Genius and Grace*. London: Hodder and Stoughton, 1992.

Deacon, Malcom. *Philip Doddridge of Northampton, 1702–1751*. Northampton: Northamptonshire Library, 1980.

Defoe, Daniel. *A Tour Through England*. 1724–1727.

Ditchfield, G.M. *The Evangelical Revival*. UCL, 1998.

Dixon, R.W. *A Century of Village Nonconformity at Bluntisham, Hunts., 1787–1887*. Cambridge: Cambridge University Press, 1887.

Doddridge, Philip. *The Rise and Progress of Religion in the Soul*. J. Brackstone and J. Waugh, 1745.

Dunan-Page, Anne, ed. *The Cambridge Companion to Bunyan*. Cambridge: Cambridge University Press, 2010.

Dyer, George. *Memoirs of the Life and Writings of Robert Robinson*. G.G. and J. Robinson, 1796.

Edwards, David. *Sermons to the Condemned*. J. Hawes, 1775.

Ella, George M. *William Cowper: Poet of Paradise*. Darlington: Evangelical Press, 1993.

Elliott-Binns, L.E. *The Early Evangelicals: A Religious and Social Study*. Lutterworth, 1853.

Escott, Harry. *Isaac Watts, Hymnographer*. Independent Press, 1962.

Evers, Stan. *Potton's Baptists: The Lord's Faithfulness to a Faithful People*. Potton: 2005.

Fletcher, John. *Logica Genevensis Continued, or the first part of the Fifth Check to Antinomianism*. R. Hawes, 1773.

— *Logica Genevensis Continued, or the second part of the Fifth Check to Antinomianism*. Bristol: W. Pine, 1774.

— *The Works of the Reverend John Fletcher, late vicar of Madeley*. 7 vols. John Kershaw, 1826.

Forbes, Mansfield D., ed. *Clare College, 1326–1926*, 2 vols. Cambridge: Cambridge University Press, 1928, 1930.

Foster, William. *A Guide to the India Office Records, 1600–1858*. India Office, 1919.

Gadsby, John. *Memoirs of the Principal Hymn Writers and Compilers of the 17th and 18th Centuries.* Gadsby, 1855.

Gadsby, William. *A Selection of Hymns for Public Worship.* Manchester: 1838; repr., Gospel Standard Societies, 1977.

Gascoigne, John. *Cambridge in the Age of the Enlightenment.* Cambridge: Cambridge University Press, 1989.

Gibbons, Roy. *The Tale of a Village Chapel: A Brief History of Gamlingay Baptist Church, 1652–2009.* Roy Gibbons, 2009.

Gillies, John. *Memoirs of the Rev. George Whitefield.* Middletown: Hunt and Noyes, 1841.

Gosse, Edmund. *A History of Eighteenth Century Literature, 1660–1780.* Macmillan, 1891.

Green, John. *An Appeal to the Oracles of God: or reasons of disagreement from the doctrine of the Rev. Mr. Wesley.* Hart, 1746.

— *The Principles and Practices of the Methodists Considered: in some letters to the leaders of that sect. The first addressed to the Reverend Mr. Berridge. Wherein are some remarks in his two letters to a clergyman in Nottinghamshire, lately published.* London: W. Bristow, 1760.

Hague, William. *William Wilberforce: The Life of the Great Anti-Slave Trade Campaigner.* Harper Perennial, 2008.

Hallifax, Samuel. *Saint Paul's Doctrine of Justification by Faith, explained in three discourses, preached before the University of Cambridge, in the year 1760.* 2nd ed., corrected and enlarged. Cambridge: 1762.

Harding, Alan. *The Countess of Huntingdon's Connexion: A Sect in Action in Eighteenth-Century England.* Oxford: Oxford University Press, 2003.

Heitzenrater, Richard. *The Elusive Mr. Wesley.* Nashville: Abingdon, 2003.

Hennell, Michael. *John Venn and the Clapham Sect.* Lutterworth, 1958.

Hicks, Samuel. *Six Discourses on the Following Subjects: The Use of the Law—The Insufficiency of the Creature—The All-Sufficiency of Christ—The Effect of the Grace of God upon the Hearts and Lives of Professors—The Parable of the Sower.* J. and W. Oliver, 1766.

Hindmarsh, D. Bruce. *The Evangelical Conversion Narrative: Spiritual Autobiography in Early Modern England.* Oxford: Oxford University Press, 2005.

— *John Newton and the English Evangelical Tradition.* Oxford: Clarendon Press, 1996.

Hopkins, Kenneth. *The Poets Laureate.* Bodley Head, 1954.

Horner, Barry E. *Pilgrim's Progress: Themes and Issues.* Darlington: Evangelical Press, 2003.

Housman, Robert F. *The Life and Remains of the Rev. Robert Housman.* Simpkin, Marshall, and Co., 1841.

Howse, Ernest Marshall. *Saints in Politics: The "Clapham Sect" and the Growth of Freedom*. Allen and Unwin, 1953.

Hutchinson, Mark and John A. Wolffe. *A Short History of Global Evangelicalism*. Cambridge: Cambridge University Press, 2012.

Hutton, J. *A History of the Moravian Church*. Moravian Publication Office, 1909.

Hylson-Smith, Kenneth. *Evangelicals in the Church of England, 1734–1984*. Edinburgh: T. and T. Clark, 1988.

Ibbett, Peter. *The Great Fire of Potton, 1783*. Potton Historical Society, 1983.

Jackson, Thomas. *The Lives of Early Methodist Preachers, chiefly written by themselves*. Wesleyan Conference Office, 1871.

Jay, William. *Memoirs of the Life and Character of the late Reverend Cornelius Winter*. Bath: M. Gye, 1808.

Jones, John. *Free and Candid Disquisitions Relating to the Church of England, and the Means of Advancing Religion Therein*. London: A. Millar, 1749.

Jones, T.S. *The Life of the Right Honourable Willielma Viscountess Glenorchy, containing extracts from her diary and correspondence*. Edinburgh: White, 1824.

Jones, William. *Memoir of the Rev. Rowland Hill*. Fisher, 1837.

Kelly, John. *The Life and Work of Charles Von Bogatzky, author of "The Golden Treasury": a chapter from the religious life of the eighteenth century*. Religious Tract Society, 1889.

Ken, Thomas. *A Manual of Prayers for the Use of the Scholars of Winchester College*. 1674.

Kent, John. *Wesley and the Wesleyans: Religion in Eighteenth-Century Britain*. Cambridge: Cambridge University Press, 2002.

King, James. *William Cowper: A Biography*. Durham: Duke University Press, 1986.

King, John. *Memoir of the Rev. Thomas Dykes, LLB, incumbent of St. John's Church, Hull; with copious extracts from his correspondence*. Seeley, 1849.

Klein, Milton M. *"An Amazing Grace": John Thornton and the Clapham Sect*. New Orleans: University Press of the South, 2004.

Knight, Helen C. *Lady Huntingdon and Her Friends*. New York: American Tract Society, 1853.

Knox, Ronald. *Enthusiasm: A Chapter in the History of Religion*. Oxford: Clarendon Press, 1950.

Law, William. *The Works of the Reverend William Law, AM*. 9 vols. Richardson, 1762; repr., Canterbury: Morton, 1893.

Lawton, George. *Within the Rock of Ages: The Life and Work of Augustus Montague Toplady*. Cambridge: James Clarke, 1983.

Lecky, William. *A History of England in the Eighteenth Century*. 6 vols. New York: Appleton, 1888.

Lewis, Donald M., ed. *Blackwell Dictionary of Evangelical Biography, 1730–1860*. 2 vols. Oxford: Blackwell, 1995.

Lloyd, Gareth. *Charles Wesley and the Struggle for Methodist Identity*. Oxford: Oxford University Press, 2007.

Loane, Marcus L. *Cambridge and the Evangelical Succession*. Lutterworth, 1952.

Madan, Falconer. *The Madan Family, and Maddens in Ireland and England*. Oxford: Oxford University Press, 1933.

Madan, Martin. *Thelyphthora; or, a treatise on female ruin, in its causes, effects, consequenes, prevention, and remedy; considered on the basis of the divine law*. 2 vols. Dodsley, 1780.

Maddox, Randy L. and Jason E. Vickers. *The Cambridge Companion to John Wesley*. Cambridge: Cambridge University Press, 2010.

Mason, J.C.S. *The Moravian Church and the Missionary Awakening in England, 1760–1800*. Woodbridge: Boydell, and Brewer, 2001.

Maxfield, Thomas. *A Vindication of the Rev. Mr. Maxfield's Conduct*. 1767.

Mayo, Henry. *Aldwinckle: a candid examination of the Rev. Mr. Madan's conduct, as a counsellor and a friend; agreeable to the principles of law and conscience*. 1767.

Meacham, Standish. *Henry Thornton of Clapham, 1760–1815*. Cambridge: Harvard University Press, 1964.

Mursell, Gordon. *English Spirituality: From 1700 to the Present Day*. Louisville: Westminster John Knox Press, 2001.

Newey, Vincent. *Cowper's Poetry: A Critical Study and Reassessment*. Liverpool: Liverpool University Press, 1982.

Newman, John Henry. *Essays Critical and Historical*. 2 vols. Longmans, Green, and Co., 1914.

Newport, Kenneth G.C. and Ted A. Campbell, eds. *Charles Wesley: Life, Literature and Legacy*. Peterborough: Epworth Press, 2007.

Newton, John. *Apologia. Four letters to a minister of an Independent Church. By a minister of the Church of England, giving his reasons for staying in the establishment*. J. Buckland, 1789.

— *Cardiphonia, or, The utterance of the heart: in the course of a real correspondence*. Edinburgh: Waugh and Innes, 1824.

— *Messiah: fifty expository discourses, on the series of scriptural passages which form the subject of the celebrated oratorio of Handel*. 2 vols. J. Buckland, 1786.

— *A Monument to the Praise of the Lord's Goodness, and to the Memory of Dear Eliza Cunningham*. B. Dugdale, 1787.

— *A Plan of Academical Preparation for the Ministry, in a Letter to a Friend.* 1784.

— *A Review of Ecclesiastical History, so far as it concerns the progress, declensions and revivals of Evangelical doctrine and practice with a brief account of the spirit and methods by which vital and experimental religion have been opposed in all ages of the church.* Edward and Charles Dilly, 1769.

— *Sermons Preached in the Parish Church of Olney in Buckinghamshire.* 1767.

— *Six Discourses (or Sermons), as Intended for the Pulpit.* Liverpool: 1760.

Newton, John and William Cowper. *Olney Hymns.* W. Oliver, 1779.

Noll, Mark A. *The Rise of Evangelicalism: The Age of Edwards, Whitefield and the Wesleys.* Leicester: InterVarsity Press, 2004.

Nuttall, Geoffrey F., ed. *Philip Doddridge, 1702–51: His Contribution to English Religion.* Independent Press, 1951.

— *The Significance of Trevecca College, 1768–1791.* Epworth Press, 1968.

O'Connor, Bernard. *The History of St. Mary's Church, Everton-cum-Tetworth.* O'Connor, 2002.

— *Rev. John Berridge, Vicar of Everton, Bedfordshire, 1716–1793.* 2001.

Omicron. *Twenty Six Letters on Religious Subjects: to which are added hymns etc.* Oliver, 1774.

Osborn, George, ed. *The Poetical Works of John and Charles Wesley.* 13 vols. 1868–1872.

Overton, John H. and Frederic Relton. *History of the English Church, 1714–1800.* Macmillan, 1906.

Oxenham, Thomas. *Fruits of the Bedfordshire Union: a letter to the Rev. R. Whittingham, curate to the late Rev. John Berridge of Everton, in Bedfordshire.* 1799.

Palmer, Thomas Fyshe. *Narrative of the Sufferings of T.F. Palmer and W. Skirving, during a voyage to New South Wales, 1794, on board the Surprise Transport.* Cambridge: B. Flower, 1797.

Peers, John Witherington. *Eight Sermons in Defence of the Divinity of Our Lord.* 1816.

Pibworth, Nigel. *The Gospel Pedlar: The Story of John Berridge and the Eighteenth-Century Revival.* Welwyn: Evangelical Press, 1987.

Pickford, Chris. *Bedfordshire Churches in the Nineteenth Century.* Bedford: BHRS, 2001.

Pickles, H.M. *Benjamin Ingham: Preacher Amongst the Dales of Yorkshire, the Forests of Lancashire and the Fells of Cumbria.* Coventry: Pickles, 1995.

Pilkington, Matthew. *The Evangelical History and Harmony.* Bowyer, 1747.

— *A Rational Concordance, or an Index to the Bible.* Ayscough, 1749.

Podmore, Colin. *The Moravian Church in England, 1728–1760*. Oxford: Oxford University Press, 1998.

Pollard, Arthur and Michael Hennell, eds. *Charles Simeon (1759–1836)*. SPCK, 1959.

Pollock, J. *Wilberforce*. Constable, 1977.

Porter, Roy. *Disease, Medicine and Society in England, 1550–1860*. Macmillan, 1987.

Rack, Henry D. *Reasonable Enthusiast: John Wesley and the Rise of Methodism*. Epworth Press, 1989.

Rawlin, Richard. *Christ the Righteousness of His People, or the doctrine of justification by faith in him, represented by several sermons at Pinner Hall*. 1741.

Ridout, Honor. *Cambridge and Stourbridge Fair*. Cambridge: Blue Ocean Publishing, 2011.

Rodell, Jonathan. *The Rise of Methodism: A Study of Bedfordshire, 1736–1851*. BHRS, 2014.

Romaine, William. *The Life, Walk and Triumph of Faith*. Cambridge: James Clarke, 1970.

— *The Whole Works of the Late Reverend William Romaine, AM*. Tegg, 1837.

Rupp, Gordon. *Religion in England, 1688–1791*. Oxford: Clarendon Press, 1986.

Rutherford, Thomas. *Four Charges to the Clergy of the Archdeaconry of Essex*. 8 vols. Cambridge: 1763.

Ryle, J.C. *The Christian Leaders of the Last Century*. Thomas Nelson, 1876.

Sargant, William. *Battle for the Mind: A Physiology of Conversion and Brain-Washing*. Heinemann, 1957.

Scott, Thomas. *The Force of Truth: an authentic narrative*. Seeley, 1836.

Seeley, M. *The Later Evangelical Fathers*. Thynne and Jarvis, 1913.

Serle, Ambrose. *Christian Remembrancer, or short reflections upon the faith, life, and conduct, of a real Christian*. 1786.

Seymour, A.C.H. *The Life and Times of Selina, Countess of Huntingdon*. 2 vols. William Painter, 1839–1840.

Sheils, W.J. and D. Wood, eds. *Voluntary Religion*. Studies in Church History 23. Oxford: Blackwell, 1986.

Shenton, Tim. *Forgotten Heroes of Revival: Great Men of the 18th Century Evangelical Awakening*. Leominster: Day One, 2004.

— *"An Iron Pillar": The Life and Times of William Romaine*. Darlington: Evangelical Press, 2004.

— *The Life of Rowland Hill: "The Second Whitefield."* Darlington: Evangelical Press, 2008.

Shrubsole, William. *Christian Memoirs: or, a review of the present state of religion in England ; in the form of a new pilgrimage to the heavenly Jerusalem.* Rochester: Fisher, 1776.

Sidney, Edwin. *The Life and Ministry of the Rev. Samuel Walker, BA, formerly of Truro.* Seeley, 1838.

— *The Life of Sir Richard Hill.* Seeley, 1839.

— *The Life of the Rev. Rowland Hill.* Baldwin and Cradock, 1834.

Smith, Brian W. *A History of Kingston-on-Soar up to the 19th Century.* Nottingham: Brickyard Publishing, 1988.

Smyth, Charles. *Simeon and Church Order: A Study of the Origins of the Evangelical Revival in Cambridge in the Eighteenth Century.* Cambridge: Cambridge University Press, 1940.

Southey, Robert. *The Life of Wesley, and the Rise and Progress of Methodism.* 2nd ed. 2 vols. Longman, 1820.

Spurgeon, C.H. *Eccentric Preachers.* London: Passmore and Alabaster, 1879.

Stephen, Leslie. *History of English Thought in the Eighteenth Century.* 2 vols. Smith, Elder, and Co., 1876; repr., New York: Peter Smith, 1949.

Stephen, L. and S. Lee, eds. *Dictionary of National Biography.* 66 vols. Smith, Elder, and Co., 1855–1900.

Stillingfleet, James. *Explanation of the Church Catechism.* York: 1778.

Stout, Harry S. *The Divine Dramatist.* Grand Rapids: Eerdmans, 1991.

Streiff, Patrick. *Reluctant Saint? A Theological Biography of Fletcher of Madeley.* Peterborough: Epworth Press, 2001.

Tebbutt, C.F. *St. Neots: The History of a Huntingdonshire Town.* Phillimore, 1978.

Thomson, D.P. *Lady Glenorchy and Her Churches—The Story of 200 Years.* Crieff: Barnoak, 1967.

Tibbutt, H.G. *Bunyan Meeting Bedford, 1650–1950.* Bedford: Trustees of Bunyan Meeting, 1950.

Toplady, Augustus. *The Church of England Vindicated from the Charge of Arminianism.* Joseph Gurney, 1769.

— *Historic Proof of the Doctrinal Calvinism of the Church of England.* 2 vols. Keith, 1774.

— *The Works of Augustus Toplady, BA, Late Vicar of Broad Hembury, Devon. A new edition, complete in one volume printed verbatim from the first edition of his works.* Chidley, 1794.

Trevelyan, G.M. *Illustrated English Social History.* 4 vols. Longmans, 1951.

Trueman, Carl R. *The Claims of Truth: John Owen's Trinitarian Theology.* Carlisle: Paternoster, 1998.

Tydeman, Garwood S. *A Brief History of Gamlingay Old Meeting Baptist Church.* 1981.

Tyerman, Luke. *The Oxford Methodists: memoirs of the Rev. Messrs. Clayton, Ingham, Gambold, Hervey and Broughton, with biographical notices of others*. Hodder and Stoughton, 1873.

Tyson, John R. *Charles Wesley: A Reader*. Oxford: Oxford University Press, 1989.

Tytler, Sarah. *The Countess of Huntingdon and Her Circle*. Pitman, 1907.

Venn, Henry. *The Complete Duty of Man: or, a system of doctrinal and practical Christianity; with prayers for families and individuals*. Glasgow: Collins, 1829.

— *The Life and a Selection from the Letters of the Late Rev. Henry Venn, MA... with a memoir by John Venn*. Hatchard, 1836.

Venn, John. *Annals of a Clerical Family*. Macmillan, 1902.

Vila, Anne C. *Enlightenment and Pathology*. John Hopkins University Press, 1998.

Vulliamy, C.E. *John Wesley*. Geoffrey Bles, 1933.

Walsh, John, Colin Haydon, and Stephen Taylor, eds. *The Church of England c.1689–c.1833: From Toleration to Tractarianism*. Cambridge: Cambridge University Press, 1993.

Watts, Isaac. *Divine and Moral Songs for the Use of Children*. 1715.

— *Hymns and Spiritual Songs*. 1707–1709.

Webster, Robert. *Methodism and the Miraculous: John Wesley's Idea of the Supernatural and the Identification of Methodists in the Eighteenth Century*. Lexington: Emeth Press, 2014.

Welch, Edwin, ed. *Chapels and Meeting Houses: Official Registration, 1672–1901*. Bedford: BHRS, 1996.

— *Two Calvinistic Methodist Chapels, 1743–1811: The London Tabernacle and Spa Fields Chapel*. London Record Society, 1975.

— *Cheshunt College—The Early Years: A Selection of Records edited with an introduction by Edwin Welch*. HRS, 1990.

— *Spiritual Pilgrim: A Reassessment of the Life of the Countess of Huntingdon*. Cardiff: University of Wales Press, 1995.

— *The Bedford Moravian Church in the Eighteenth Century*. Bedford: BHRS, 1989.

Wesley, John. *The Letters of the Rev. John Wesley, AM*. ed. John Telford. 8 vols. Epworth Press, 1931.

— *The Works of John Wesley*. ed. W. Reginald Ward and Richard P. Heitzenrater. 24 vols. Nashville: Abingdon Press, 1984–2003.

Whelan, Timothy D. *Baptist Autographs in the John Rylands University Library, 1741–1845, transcribed and edited by Timothy D. Whelan*. Mercer: Mercer University Press, 2009.

Whitefield, George. *An Expostulatory Letter, Addressed to Nicholas Lewis, Count Zinzendorf.* G. Keith, 1753.

— *A Select Collection of Letters of the Late Reverend George Whitefield.* 3 vols. Dilly, 1772.

Whitehead, William. *Plays and Poems.* 2 vols. Dodsley, 1774.

Williams, E.N. *Life in Georgian England.* Batsford, 1962.

Winstanley, D.A. *Unreformed Cambridge: A Study of Certain Aspects of the University in the Eighteenth Century.* Cambridge: Cambridge University Press, 1935.

Wood, A. Skevington. *Thomas Haweis, 1734–1820.* SPCK, 1957.

Wright, Thomas. *Augustus M. Toplady and Contemporary Hymn-Writers.* Farncombe, 1911.

— *The Correspondence of William Cowper.* 4 vols. Hodder and Stoughton, 2004.

— *Joseph Hart.* Farncombe, 1910.

Young, Arthur. *English Tours.* 1768–1771.

Index of Scriptures

451

Index of people

Index of subjects and biblical and place names

127, 228; doctrinal 191, exhaustion 162, 320, 351; extempore 302: frequency 68, 91, 125, 194, 225, 248; in houses 21, 25, 65, 70, 120, 133, 156, 183, 302, 337, 342; limitations 102, 189, 285, 313, 334; live as hosts 343–344; irregularity 22n, 230, 244; itinerancy 8n, 25, 27, 33, 118, 126, 243–244, 248, 259, 302, 306, 342; in London 12, 14, 25, 28, 35, 54n, 79n, 88, 95, 101, 102, 103, 137, 175n, 197, 226, 230, 233, 235, 237, 241, 243, 258, 261, 267–8, 285, 292, 302, 304n, 315, 334, 361, 364, 371, 378, 379, 391, 392, 400; in open air 53, 65–7, 69, 70n, 107, 193; manner 15, 16, 66, 89, 302, 342, 432; mere Sunday preacher 26, 155, 162, 197, 206, 261, 331, 351, 353, 385; message 41, 51, 95–96, 103, 172, 298; offer 47, 387, 413; preparation 128, 166, 189, 205, 221, 225, 229, 295; stations (shops) 2n, 25, 26, 91, 104n, 111, 127, 349; success 2, 3, 4, 14, 15, 22, 23, 41, 56, 89, 111, 281, 289, 338, 349; times 247, 304, 343; before university 23, 24
– reading 160, 166, 173, 184
– relationship with Wesley 59n, 69n, 72, 81; see Wesley (and Berridge)
– reputation 13, 104, 152, 213, 231, 302, 321, 432
– self-evaluation: abhor myself 217; ashamed of sorry services 128, 232; ass 87, 117, 154, 195, 224; awkward old bachelor 216; blind 81, 224; blundering fool 94; booby 138; broken vessel 169; churlish 138, 282; conceited ass 87; conceited dunce 117; corrupt heart 74, 75, 159; crazy 162, 163, 322; Dolittle 359, 385; dubious judgement 128; fool 17, 82, 89, 92, 218, 219, 250; growing more poor and blind 397; heart quintessence of

folly and madness 216; ignoramus 111; inconsistent 18; infant still 347; lazy servant 385; limping traveller 223; little faith 102, 405; little heavenly mindedness 277; loving the Lord so little 299; madman 302; mere nothing 232; poverty of spirit 115, 185; proud 111, 155, 176, 184, 245, 246, 260, 289; saucy will 184; scarce know the Master 115; self-condemned 18; sick of 82–83, 87, 102, 400; slovenly walk 314; small and loathsome 347; strange blunt fellow 94; stupid ass 87; thief and villain 81; vile 162, 185, 196, 224; wavering and whirling 118–119; wayward ass 117; weariness of self 82, 136, 138, 277, 379; wild ass in wilderness 129; worthless 248; wretched 50, 217, 379
– seeking a wife 145
– sermon notes 15
– support 110n, 193, 202, 211, 221, 231, 247, 281, 291, 311, 324, 326, 335, 350, 367, 405
– thankfulness 296, 299, 302, 313, 350, 359, 361, 365, 385, 390, 392
– views on controversy 192, 205, 212; cast away 263–4; detrimental 285, 334, 336; drop 202; enemy to 212; keep out of 178; not trust heart 203; persecution would stop 213; source 213; weariness of 133
– *Works* 2–3, 12, 31
Bethel 127
Bethesda 167n, 168n
Bethleham Hospital 13, 244, 362n
Bible, *see* Scriptures; *see* Berridge (Bible)
Bibles distributed 202, 211
Biggleswade 305, 345, 346n, 348
Biggleswade Old Baptist Meeting 345
Blackfriars 93n 207, 235n, 239n
Blessing: God 26, 42, 72n, 75, 82, 84, 106, 115, 121, 149, 152, 155, 183, 187, 265, 269, 361, 387, 400;

95, 107, 108, 111, 112, 113, 115, 117, 119, 120, 124, 127, 128, 133, 135, 138, 144, 151, 152, 157, 163, 165, 177, 183, 184, 185, 190, 197, 203, 209, 210n, 213, 215, 219, 230, 238, 250, 261, 265, 272, 273, 285, 335, 343, 350, 358, 359, 365, 371, 373, 392, 400; merits 53, 55, 430; never-failing 366; offices 359; paramount 335; physician 102, 135, 177, 241, 296, 403, 422; portion 128, 133, 308, 365; precious 162, 163, 248, 347, 352, 359, 371, 375, 388, 391, 395, 406, 432; presence 29, 66, 70, 95, 115, 189, 275, 340, 355, 365, 376, 391, 400, 416; priest 359; promises 411; prophet 359; righteousness 47, 55, 63, 81, 111, 128n, 175, 197, 222, 223, 265, 395, 422; Saviour 49, 53, 54, 75, 115, 159, 162, 193, 198, 199, 213, 343, 429; school 117, 138; second Adam 76; shield 133; sun 133, 389; surety 215, 217, 222–223; union with 226; visits of 138, 402; wisdom 63, 76, 222, 223, 224, 383; word 147, 172, 197, 256, 262, 297, 299, 300, 362, 404, 412; work 30, 71, 281, 417, 419

Christian('s): affection 412; afflicted 415; aged 277; ambition 155, 348; birch-wine 261; cheer 188; dangers 188; discipline 295; experience 321; faith 102, 390; friends 176, 196, 261, 414, 430; generosity 209; grace 246; growing drowsy 233; improvements 174, 324; letter 335; laziness 191, 242; kings and priests 84, 180; letter 335; love 328, 331; mariners 147; minister 249n; money 324; motto 344; orator 189; patience 333; people 369; perfection 74n, 76, 99n, 200n; pilgrim 152; poor 193, 194, 202, 221, 283; profession 291; professor 26, 145, 146, 177, 191, 198, 200, 230, 287, 324, 330, 329, 363, 364, 428; race 314;

real 423; salutation 210, 216; seniors 242; sergeant 175, 346, 347; simplicity 231; soldier 121, 175, 259; traffic 227; triumphant 148; understanding 188; walk 233; world 212

Christian Remembrancer 375
Christian World Unmasked, The 2–3, 10n, 13n, 17n, 21n, 25n, 26, 196n, 218n, 200, 221, 225, 279n, 375n
Christianity 9, 61, 69, 224, 337
Christmas 41, 46, 56, 89, 92, 104n, 167, 223, 353
Church 51, 53, 269; decline 141, 269; Fathers 55; Jewish 141, 145; Moravian 58; Roman 53, 55, 56, 286, 300; vineyard 210
Church of England: archbishop 43, 61, 99; articles 20n, 53, 55, 56, 153, 155; bishops 10, 19, 20, 22, 23, 39n, 42n, 55, 59, 61, 70, 83, 100, 106, 116, 126, 145, 150n, 153n, 155, 173, 205, 231, 243, 244, 261, 271, 286, 304, 312, 321, 337, 393; catechism 375–376; clergy 4, 7, 8, 9, 10, 14, 21, 22, 23, 25, 42, 44, 52, 53, 55, 56, 58, 79n, 93, 126, 158, 159, 196, 243, 268, 269, 271, 286, 312, 336, 338, 339, 342, 343, 376, 377, 381, 393; confirmations 83; decay 10, 269, 321; doctrines 53, 55, 269, 272; establishments 9, 286, 327, 337; Evangelical succession 10, 100n, 250–251, 269–270; Evangelicalism 8, 9, 11, 93, 321, 327; gospel clergy 8, 126, 342, 366; homilies 20n, 55, 56, 72; irregularities 2, 7, 8, 9, 244, 321n, 337; liturgy 20n, 153n, 155, 269; orders 52, 151, 155n, 158, 205, 206, 292n, 293, 312, 321, 336, 391; ordination 123, 150n, 153, 163, 189, 214, 238, 271, 292, 393; Prayer Book 10, 155n; visitation 332, 347, 365
Church of the Holy Sepulchre 338
Cincinnatus 127n
Clapham 184n, 282, 286, 313, 327,

465

243, 400, 411, 412, 417, 429; husbandman 282; Judge 4, 68, 416; judgements, *see* Judgement; law, *see* law; living 113, 311, 354; love of 48, 54, 65, 223, 430; means 71, 150, 258, 280, 373; mercy 56, 57, 118, 137, 147, 159, 174, 182, 183, 184; of Jeshurun 187; peace of 42, 80, 96; peace with 46, 54, 62, 84, 191; potter 86, 238

Godmanchester 230

Godstone 173

Golden Treasury, see Bogatzky's Golden Treasury: a reprint

Gordon Riots 286n

gospel 8, 20, 23, 45, 72, 200, 202, 221, 247; ass 154; bear garden 336; blessings 47; brokenness 162, 170, 174, 189, 196, 217; of Christ 169, 181; clergy 7, 336, 339; curate 322; departure 263, 271; deception 240; divines 154; doctrines 271, 333; flag 343; glorious 5; hindrances 350; limner 249; joy 240, 295; junketing 239; message 53, 55, 68, 143n, 231, 279; minister 13, 41n, 260, 261, 269, 337, 342; mixed, *see* faith and works; need 10; net 69; offer 47, 413; pedlar 111, 261, 346; preached 22, 52, 55, 65n, 71n, 192, 193, 269, 338; proclamation 140, 166, 316, 365, 387; real 41; reception 51, 69, 147, 159, 162, 327, 353; sanctifies 422; school 138; simplicity 55, 107; soup 305; spring 147; standard 365; wife 163; work 94, 334

Gospel Gems 3, 22, 145, 230, 337

Gospel Standard Strict Baptists 1n

gourd 259

government 31, 70n 193n, 269, 291n, 299, 300n, 338–339, 387

grace 185, 187, 203, 211, 217, 218, 271, 274, 282, 285, 291, 299, 303, 313, 335, 340, 343, 360, 362, 367, 379, 387, 400, 413, 416, 421, 424, 425, 426, 430

Gransden Farm 328

Grantchester 67, 70, 104n, 349

Grantchester Mill 105

Grantham 40, 44n

Great Britain 94, 387

Great Gransden 195n

Great Paxton 310

Green Street Independent Meeting House 156n

grief/sorrow 84, 92, 93, 94, 268, 273, 275, 320, 342, 347, 381, 390, 395, 399, 402, 421, 430

Grubb Street 235

Hagar 151

Hardwick 258

Harkstone 155

Harston 349

Hatherleigh 140n

Hawkshone 104n, 153n, 155, 182

hay 40, 83, 329

heart 17, 20, 22, 30, 34, 46, 51, 115, 120, 124, 141, 191, 199, 202, 206, 208, 228, 250, 275, 276, 291, 371, 390, 430; assured 62; believing 62, 187, 266, 372; bleeding 143; broken 63, 138, 162, 170, 174, 180, 185, 189, 196, 215, 218, 263, 288, 343, 355, 405; changed 336, and Christ 47, 48, 54, 189, 213, 219, 226, 352, 365, 366, 374, 388, 395; circumcised 336; convicted 66, 112; corruptions 74, 76, 197, 207, 295, 420, 421, 424, 428; cries out 113, 354; dangers 220, 240, 244, 259, 322, 400, 413; delighting in 183, 285, 383; deceived 260; devoted 222, 308, 340, 431, 353; divided 85, 103, 128, 425; enlarged 81, 165, 194, 203, 211, 268, 313, 402, 406; evil 45, 84, 89, 159, 203, 213, 217, 223, 282, 314, 343, 429; feeble 172; felt 28, 35; frets 26, 109; given to Christ 256; hard 422; humbled 138, 142, 145n, 156, 163, 223, 249, 345; hypocrisy of 82, 87, 111; legal 217; love in 418; new 247, 368; plague 18, 84, 176; proud 159, 160, 166, 177, 184,

187, 246, 289; purified 75, 93, 165; refreshed 205, 255, 388; rest 42, 392; roaming 80; sanctified 198; smitten 50; sore 92, 163, 273, 286; spiritual 153, 344; unbelieving 71, 280; warm 361, 397; willing 299; work 387

heaven(ly) 12, 23, 45, 46, 48, 62, 84–5, 135, 136, 138, 139, 143, 148, 154, 163, 165, 166, 174, 177, 180, 187, 199, 207, 227, 232, 238, 240, 241, 262, 273, 277, 288, 306, 307, 308, 311, 353, 360, 362, 371, 375, 385, 390, 396, 398, 400, 403, 405n, 406, 411, 412, 413, 416, 417, 424, 425, 426, 428, 430

Helicon 322

hell 10n, 119, 138, 148, 174, 207, 217, 230, 289, 342, 345, 360, 387, 416, 417, 421, 424, 426, 429, 430

Helmsley 100n, 250

Henfield 39

Hertfordshire 16, 20n, 67, 193, 302n

Hezekiah 186, 187

Highworth 374

Hitchin 302

Holy Club 52n, 86n

Holy Spirit 21, 106, 181, 424, 430, 431; adoption 66, 262; anointing 52; baptism 160, 189; comfort 188, 248; communicating 54, 62, 306; convincing 55; divine 52, 414; enabling 48, 62, 313, 416, 422; enlightening 21, 47, 63, 265; fruits 198, 199, 200, 295; guiding 147, 298; leading 57, 273; poured out 70, 143, 311; sanctifying 46, 48; quickening 172, 185, 238; witness 48, 54, 369

Holy Trinity, Cambridge 321n, 338n

Homerton academy 333

Homilies 20, 55, 56, 72

horn-book 117

horse block 216

hospital chaplains 89, 94

hospitality, see Berridge (hospitality)

housekeeper, see Berridge (household)

House of Commons 354

Hoxton Square 158n

Huddersfield 269n

Hudibras 15

Hull 193n, 390n, 393n

Hull academies 391

humour, see Berridge (humour); laughter 240

humours 170, 241

Huntingdon 42n, 230

Huntingdon jail 244

Huntingdon Street, St. Neots 309

Huntingdonshire 16, 20, 45n

hymn-books 1, 3, 26, 59, 186, 192, 211, 231, 238, 281, 290, 334, 363

hymns 3, 26, 72, 73, 136, 192, 212, 225, 290, 304, 305, 317

Ickleford 302

Iliad 62

ill-health, see Berridge (illness and health)

Ipswich 179n, 268n, 294

Ireland 72, 83n, 85, 97n, 106n, 143n, 238, 256, 347

irregularity, see Berridge (preaching)

Isaac 120, 128, 151, 332, 411

Isaiah 146, 345

Ishmael 120

Israel 80, 115, 145, 147n, 154n, 168n, 169, 171, 213, 249, 365

Jacob 128, 240

James (disciple) 135n

James 209

Jehu 128

Jericho 205

Jewin Street congregation 189, 241, 288

Jezebel 144

Job 121, 162, 217, 325, 415

John 135n, 207

John the Baptist 279

Jonah 26n, 135

Joseph 123, 135, 150

Joshua 145

joy 5, 29, 48, 54, 62, 70, 103, 108, 115, 142, 156, 170, 181, 198, 211, 240, 241, 261, 273, 275, 314, 335, 341, 354, 365, 366, 375, 392, 396,

martyrs 288; Marian 213n, 286
Mary 128
Mary Magdalene 162, 207, 288
Materia Medica 371
medical practice 135, 143, 241, 296, 376
Meldreth 65, 66
Merton College 105n
Messiah, Newton 352, 363
metaphors and figures 16, 32, 126n; ant 83; ballast 139; base hedgehog 175; beehive 258; beggar's sauce 361; bellows 118; bespattered for Jesus 152; brewers for Christ 191; candles 159; *Canterbury Tales* man 239; chirping of a chicken 45; Christian mariners 147; Christian sergeant 175; cocks 258; cottage cracking 237; croaking from a raven 250; crutch 75; Devil's cradle 142; Devil's quagmire 142; doctrinal throat 140; drone 82; dung hill covered with snow 159; eagle 137; ecclesiastical lions 244; faith to remove mole hills 347; ferrets 144; flea in the wilderness 150; fool's cap 218, 250; foolish gnat 143; fried like a cake 174; frogship 74, 224, 237; furnace 74, 156, 159, 160, 174, 185, 195n, 196n, 197, 203, 216, 238, 249, 250, 258, 259, 294, 295, 321, 411, 412; gospel ass 154; gospel bear garden 336; gospel hawker and pedlar 261, 346; gospel pipe 140; gospel soup 305; harlequin 82; heathen chaff 269; hot bread from the oven 225; house dog spaniel 151; King's Cassock regiment 171; Lady Mistrust 275; Lamb's wife 128; lark 198; leeches 155; legal crusts 269; livery 111; Lord Wilbewill 280; magpie 136; mezzotint print 93; more heads than the Nile 246; Moses' chair 80; muckworm 82; officers 126; owl 137, 198; petticoat snares 143, 167; piper 125n;

polecat 225; Pope 80, 178; pottery 86–7; prattle a little for him 171; prudent Peters 344; recruiting sergeant 244; regiment 126, 171; rod 92, 112, 126, 138, 170, 174, 185, 197, 215, 233, 238, 214, 416; school 128, 138, 296; scorpion letters 125; slaughter-man 333; snaffle 126; snakes 89; sparrow 137; stump of a Methodist parson 225; tenterhook 144; toads 170, 265; treacle pot 114, 138, 221; twitch 175; useless lumber 402; Vatican Bull 80; vineyards 188; wares 111; whipping post 184;
Methodism 1, 9, 24, 26, 42n, 54n, 70n, 71n, 99n, 349
Methodists 19, 21, 23, 24, 52, 113n, 174n, 193, 225, 270, 334, 349
Michael 121
Michaelmas 40n, 83, 328
Miletum 339
millennium 213
minister 4, 7, 9, 12, 13, 26n, 41n, 68, 93, 99, 123n, 124, 134, 269, 321, 322, 326, 336, 339, 352, 364; Baptist 68n, 155n, 281; gospel, *see* gospel (minister)
Minories, Aldgate 264
Minshull Vernon 330
Mnemosyne 322n
money 47, 59n, 79n, 83n, 93n, 109, 110, 111, 149, 152, 165, 184n, 193, 194, 203, 231n, 281, 284, 285, 309, 322, 325, 328, 342, 350, 390n, 404, 407, 418
monody 153n, 157
Monument to the Praise…, A, Newton 352
Moorfields 329n, 338n, 339, 364; *see* Tabernacle (Moorfields)
Moravians 58–9, 113n
Moses 103, 265, 295, 336, 400; chair 80; church wall 103; coupled with Christ 141; law 63, 135, 342; school 81
motto 175, 203, 205, 344

472

Portsmouth 324
Portugal 300
post office 364
postal service 31
Potton 41, 42n, 329, 330, 376;
Baptist church 330n; carrier 236;
cathedral 305; fire 329–331, 345;
vicars 21, 22, 70, 145
Poultry, London 235
"Praise God from whom" 304
prayer 89, 122, 123–4, 166, 171, 188;
all prayer 240, 326; answered 25n,
46, 92; for blessings 327, 350; constant 123, 124, 220, 326, 365, 392;
conversion whilst in 65, 66; daily
224, 298, 352, 369, 376, 392, 404,
425; dangers 136, 147, 274, 428;
disciples 103n, 117; for enlightenment 21, 51, 347; everywhere
188, 192, 285, 326; and faith 76,
78, 136; family 106, 304, 344; and
fasting 199; fervent 116, 282, 301,
419; for guidance 124; for healing
339, 367; mark of true conversion
50; need 188, 240, 166, 190, 211,
217, 240, 250, 280, 314, 427; poor
83, 395, 421; for others 74, 181,
251, 255, 367, 376, 385, 416; for
patience 138, 258, 263; reviving
296–297; and preaching 154, 189,
225, 229; private 19, 192, 242, 295,
334, 334, 378; public 70, 218n,
225n, 249n, 326, 334; short 326,
412; spirit of 311, 334, 334, 343;
struggle 148, 171, 415; thankfulness 232, 284; volley 316; and
watchfulness 44, 147, 213, 227,
278, 285; and word of God 52,
127, 220, 264, 373, 375, 379
Prayer Book, see Church of England
preacher, see Berridge (preaching);
Berridge (pulpit)
predestination, see Calvinism
presumption 52, 56, 247n, 262, 265
pride 30, 72, 78, 111, 153, 155, 156,
159, 160, 166, 175, 176, 177, 184,
185, 187, 192, 202, 203, 216, 219,
245, 246, 247, 260, 279, 280, 288,

318, 219n, 424, 428, 429
Princes Street, Westminster 256n
*Principles and Practices of
Methodists..., The* 23, 44n
prison 123, 150, 171, 212n, 221n,
256n, 261, 279n, 299, 425, 426
proprietary chapel 79n
Proverbs 133
providence 9, 14, 153, 166, 298, 300,
337, 340, 345, 348, 385
pulpit 5, 12, 60, 89, 91n, 97, 98, 124,
126, 171, 189, 191, 209, 216, 219,
225, 239, 246, 249, 258, 261, 265,
289, 302, 304, 312, 342, 349n, 351,
353, 355, 358, 371, 395, 397, 405
Puritan 213n, 285, 295, 334
Queen Anne's bounty 158n
razor 309, 310
reason 13, 23, 52, 117, 133, 149, 151,
196n, 200, 299
Rebecca 145, 332
Reformation 43n, 55, 160, 186, 286
regeneration 30, 45–46, 336, 375
relatives 68n
Remembrancer, Serle 338, 375
Renhold 393n
resurrection 141, 181, 213, 422
Revelation 142, 213
Review of Ecclesiastical History 160
revival (Revival) 1, 283n; doctrine
26, 141–142; Eighteenth-Century
2, 10, 11, 42n, 58n, 79n, 108, 137,
184; Everton and district 2, 5,
6, 20n, 21, 22, 41–42n, 65–66,
69–70, 78n, 79, 156n, 200; expla-
nations 22n; music 65; physical
manifestations 5, 6, 22, 69–70;
retrospective view 143, 147; revivalism 42n
reviving 125, 315, 334
righteousness 55, 64, 197, 222, 298;
Christ's 47, 63, 81, 110n, 112, 128,
172, 175, 222, 223, 265, 395, 422;
fruits 48, 188, 415; God's 48, 49,
55, 220; pharisaical 217, 420; self-
47, 48, 49, 50, 335
Roborough 279n
Royal George 324

Royston 322
rural deans 342
sacraments, *see* ordinances
St. Agnes 381
St. Alkmund 143n
St. Ann's Blackfriars 93n, 207n,
    235n, 239n
St. Christopher, West Indies 162n
St. Dunstans, Fleet Street 89, 93n
St. Edmund Hall 134n
St. Edwards, Cambridge 338n
St. George's, Southwark 88n
St. Giles, Camberwell 214n
St. James Place 273, 379, 395
St. John's College, Cambridge 336
St. Mary Woolnoth 303n
St. Neots 20, 179n, 309n, 310, 328
St. Paul's 194
salt of amber 163
salvation 49, 68, 365, 392; by faith
    41n, 370; not by good works 46,
    49, 51, 207; hindrances to 51, 53,
    56, 63, 197, 230; only in Christ 30,
    41n, 46, 55, 112, 307, 336, 369,
    413; by the power of God 73n, 97,
    271, 334n, 417, 430; results 207,
    291; seek 343, 369, 404; wait for
    76, 223
Samson 215n
sanctification 222; and affliction
    170, 299, 330, 355, 388, 415; and
    Christ 76, 81n, 99n, 222, 223;
    false view 44–46, 50, 63; holiness
    45, 48, 50, 149, 170, 197, 198, 232,
    422; and justification 113, 199,
    422; priority of the cross 198–199,
    207; and Wesley 69n, 74n, 217,
    288, 334
Sandemanianism 110n, 113n, 199
Sandy 215
Satan, *see* Devil/Satan
schools 81, 89n, 116n, 127, 128, 138,
    154, 168, 178n, 195, 296, 321, 379,
    391
Scotch thistle 303
Scotland 125n, 150n, 332
Scriptures 16, 24, 220, 221; in evan-
    gelism 202, 211, 220, 239, 281,

371; in special guidance 145–146;
    and study 72, 166, 375; word of
    God 43, 51, 62, 166, 211, 220,
    246, 264, 275, 298, 373, 375, 378,
    379, 402
schismatics 53
scout 151
seasons: spring 27, 147, 155, 160,
    213, 215, 282, 342, 346n; summer
    23, 27, 29, 34, 40, 59, 70n, 118,
    124, 135, 140, 152, 154, 156, 158,
    169, 171, 174, 178, 183n, 196, 259,
    294, 320, 321, 349, 367, 370, 400,
    405n; autumn 28, 80n, 209; win-
    ter 16, 25, 35, 56n, 118, 135, 137,
    143, 149, 153, 155, 169, 182, 183,
    195, 215, 239, 265n, 285n, 292n,
    294, 299, 304, 316, 326, 334, 346n,
    359n, 361n, 364n, 392
sea-bathing 7, 9n
sermon 2, 3, 15n, 25n, 41, 53, 55n,
    66, 86n, 99, 103, 150; assize 300;
    Berridge, *see* Berridge (preach-
    ing – manner) *and* Berridge
    (preaching – message); Bull 326;
    charity 324; Coughlan 239;
    Edward 179n; Hallifax 24; Hicks
    65n; Newton 160, 173, 174, 352;
    Peckwell 256n; Peers 302; Rawlin
    56n; Rutherford 25n; Tillotson
    99; university 23, 24; Venn 300;
    Wesley 86n; wet 98, 289
servants 40, 106n, 151n, 193, 305,
    312, 331n, 345n, 350, 354, 361,
    362, 416; spiritual 30, 112, 115,
    121, 123, 127, 133, 153, 210, 268,
    284, 371, 375
Shaphall 20
Shawbury 304n
Sheba, Queen 375
Sheerness 123n
Shelford 66
shop-tax 348
Shovel 140n
Shrewsbury 304n
Shropshire 100n, 104n, 175n, 200n,
    216n, 363n
Shrove Tuesday 258

Other titles available from Joshua Press…

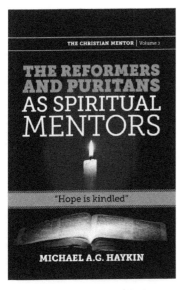

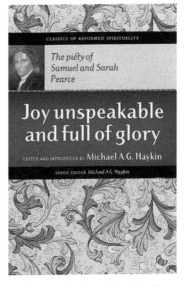

The Christian Mentor | *Volume 2*	*Classics of Reformed spirituality*

The reformers and Puritans as spiritual mentors

"Hope is kindled"

By Michael A. G. Haykin

REFORMERS SUCH as Tyndale, Cranmer and Calvin, and Puritans Richard Greenham, John Owen, etc. are examined to see how their display of the light of the gospel provides us with models of Christian conviction and living.

ISBN 978–1-894400–39–8

Joy unspeakable and full of glory

The piety of
Samuel and Sarah Pearce

By Michael A. G. Haykin

SAMUEL PEARCE played a key role in the formation and early days of the Baptist Missionary Society in eighteenth-century England. Through Samuel and Sarah's letters we are given a window into their rich spiritual life and living piety.

ISBN 978–1-894400–48–0

Other titles available from Joshua Press...

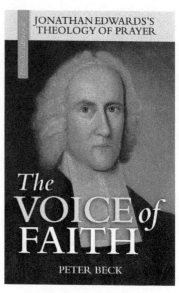

Great themes in Puritan preaching
Compiled and edited
By Mariano Di Gangi

DRAWING FROM a gold mine of Puritan writings, this book provides a taste of the riches of Puritan theology and its application to life. This title will whet your appetite and stir your faith to greater views of Christ, his Person and his work.

ISBN 978–1-894400-26–8 (HC)
ISBN 978-1-894400-24–4 (PB)

The voice of faith
Jonathan Edwards's theology of prayer
By Peter Beck

EXPLORING THE sermons and writings of Jonathan Edwards, Dr. Beck draws a comprehensive picture of his theology of prayer and why Edwards believed God would hear the prayers of his people. Interspersed are three external biographies that set the historical and theological scene.

ISBN 978–1-894400-33–6 (HC)
ISBN 978-1-894400-32–9 (PB)

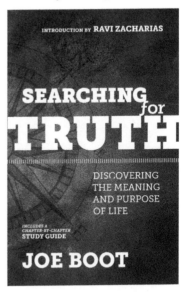

The grace of godliness

An introduction to doctrine and piety in the Canons of Dort

By Matthew Barrett

BARRETT opens a window on the synod's deliberations with the Remonstrants and examines the main emphases of the canons, with special attention on their relationship to biblical piety and spirituality.

ISBN 978-1-894400-52–7 (PB)

Searching for truth

Discovering the meaning and purpose of life

By Joe Boot

BEGINNING WITH a basic understanding of the world, Joe Boot explains the biblical worldview, giving special attention to the life and claims of Jesus Christ. He wrestles with questions about suffering, truth, morality and guilt.

ISBN 978–1-894400–40–4

Deo Optimo et Maximo Gloria
To God, best and greatest, be glory

www.joshuapress.com